OECD/G20 Base Erosion and Profit Shifting Project

Harmful Tax Practices – 2022 Peer Review Reports on the Exchange of Information on Tax Rulings

INCLUSIVE FRAMEWORK ON BEPS: ACTION 5

OECD

BETTER POLICIES FOR BETTER LIVES

This document, as well as any data and map included herein, are without prejudice to the status of or sovereignty over any territory, to the delimitation of international frontiers and boundaries and to the name of any territory, city or area.

The statistical data for Israel are supplied by and under the responsibility of the relevant Israeli authorities. The use of such data by the OECD is without prejudice to the status of the Golan Heights, East Jerusalem and Israeli settlements in the West Bank under the terms of international law.

Note by the Republic of Türkiye
The information in this document with reference to "Cyprus" relates to the southern part of the Island. There is no single authority representing both Turkish and Greek Cypriot people on the Island. Türkiye recognises the Turkish Republic of Northern Cyprus (TRNC). Until a lasting and equitable solution is found within the context of the United Nations, Türkiye shall preserve its position concerning the "Cyprus issue".

Note by all the European Union Member States of the OECD and the European Union
The Republic of Cyprus is recognised by all members of the United Nations with the exception of Türkiye. The information in this document relates to the area under the effective control of the Government of the Republic of Cyprus.

Please cite this publication as:
OECD (2023), *Harmful Tax Practices – 2022 Peer Review Reports on the Exchange of Information on Tax Rulings: Inclusive Framework on BEPS: Action 5*, OECD/G20 Base Erosion and Profit Shifting Project, OECD Publishing, Paris, https://doi.org/10.1787/22bbeacc-en.

ISBN 978-92-64-42865-2 (print)
ISBN 978-92-64-60104-8 (pdf)
ISBN 978-92-64-93271-5 (HTML)
ISBN 978-92-64-93495-5 (epub)

OECD/G20 Base Erosion and Profit Shifting Project
ISSN 2313-2604 (print)
ISSN 2313-2612 (online)

Photo credits: Cover © ninog-Fotolia.com.

Corrigenda to OECD publications may be found on line at: www.oecd.org/about/publishing/corrigenda.htm.

Foreword

The integration of national economies and markets has increased substantially in recent years, putting a strain on the international tax rules, which were designed more than a century ago. Weaknesses in the current rules create opportunities for base erosion and profit shifting (BEPS), requiring bold moves by policy makers to restore confidence in the system and ensure that profits are taxed where economic activities take place and value is created.

Following the release of the report Addressing Base Erosion and Profit Shifting in February 2013, OECD and G20 countries adopted a 15-point Action Plan to address BEPS in September 2013. The Action Plan identified 15 actions along three key pillars: introducing coherence in the domestic rules that affect cross-border activities, reinforcing substance requirements in the existing international standards, and improving transparency as well as certainty.

After two years of work, measures in response to the 15 actions were delivered to G20 Leaders in Antalya in November 2015. All the different outputs, including those delivered in an interim form in 2014, were consolidated into a comprehensive package. The BEPS package of measures represents the first substantial renovation of the international tax rules in almost a century. Once the new measures become applicable, it is expected that profits will be reported where the economic activities that generate them are carried out and where value is created. BEPS planning strategies that rely on outdated rules or on poorly co-ordinated domestic measures will be rendered ineffective.

Implementation is now the focus of this work. The BEPS package is designed to be implemented via changes in domestic law and practices, and in tax treaties. With the negotiation of a multilateral instrument (MLI) having been finalised in 2016 to facilitate the implementation of the treaty related BEPS measures, 100 jurisdictions are covered by the MLI. The entry into force of the MLI on 1 July 2018 paves the way for swift implementation of the treaty related measures. OECD and G20 countries also agreed to continue to work together to ensure a consistent and co-ordinated implementation of the BEPS recommendations and to make the project more inclusive. Globalisation requires that global solutions and a global dialogue be established which go beyond OECD and G20 countries.

A better understanding of how the BEPS recommendations are implemented in practice could reduce misunderstandings and disputes between governments. Greater focus on implementation and tax administration should therefore be mutually beneficial to governments and business. Proposed improvements to data and analysis will help support ongoing evaluation of the quantitative impact of BEPS, as well as evaluating the impact of the countermeasures developed under the BEPS Project.

As a result, the OECD established the OECD/G20 Inclusive Framework on BEPS (Inclusive Framework), bringing all interested and committed countries and jurisdictions on an equal footing in the Committee on Fiscal Affairs and all its subsidiary bodies. The Inclusive Framework, which already has more than 140 members, is monitoring and peer reviewing the implementation of the minimum standards as well as completing the work on standard setting to address BEPS issues. In addition to BEPS members, other international organisations and regional tax bodies are involved in the work of the Inclusive Framework, which also consults business and the civil society on its different work streams.

This report was approved by the Inclusive Framework on 28 November 2023 and prepared for publication by the OECD Secretariat.

Table of contents

TABLES

Abbreviations and acronyms

AGT	Angolian Revenue Administration
APA	Advance pricing arrangement
ATAF	African Tax Administration Forum
ATR	Advance tax ruling
BEPS	Base Erosion and Profit Shifting
CTS	Common Transmission System
EOI	Exchange of Information?
EU	European Union
FHTP	Forum on Harmful Tax Practices
GDT	General Directorate of Taxation (Albania)
IP	Intellectual Property
ISTD	Income and Sales Tax Department (Jordan)
OECD	Organization for Economic Co-operation and Development
PE	Permanent Establishment
R&D	Research and Development
SAARC	South Asian Association for Regional Cooperation
SEOI	Spontaneous Exchange of Information
TAKS	Faroe Islands Tax Administration
TIEA	Tax Information Exchange Agreements
ToR	Terms of reference
XML	Extensible Mark-Up Language

Executive summary

Context for the exchange of information on tax rulings (the "transparency framework")

The BEPS Action 5 minimum standard on the compulsory spontaneous exchange of information on tax rulings (the "transparency framework") provides tax administrations with timely information on rulings that have been granted to a foreign related party of their resident taxpayer or a permanent establishment, which can be used in conducting risk assessments and which, in the absence of exchange, could give rise to BEPS concerns.

The transparency framework requires spontaneous exchange of information on five categories of taxpayer-specific rulings: (i) rulings related to certain preferential regimes, (ii) unilateral advance pricing arrangements (APAs) or other cross-border unilateral rulings in respect of transfer pricing, (iii) rulings providing for a downward adjustment of taxable profits, (iv) permanent establishment (PE) rulings; and (v) related party conduit rulings.[1] The requirement to exchange information on the rulings in the above categories includes certain past rulings as well as future rulings, pursuant to pre-defined periods which are outlined in each jurisdiction's report and that varies according to the time when a certain jurisdiction has joined the Inclusive Framework or has been identified as a Jurisdiction of Relevance. The exchanges occur pursuant to international exchange of information agreements, which provide the legal conditions under which exchanges take place, including the need to ensure taxpayer confidentiality.

The inclusion of the above categories of rulings in the scope of the transparency framework is not intended to suggest that the issuance of such rulings constitutes a preferential regime or a harmful tax practice. In practice, tax rulings can be an effective way to provide certainty to taxpayers and reduce the risk of disputes. Rather, the need for transparency on rulings is that a tax administration's lack of knowledge or information on the tax treatment of a taxpayer in another jurisdiction can impact the treatment of transactions or arrangements undertaken with a related taxpayer resident in their own jurisdiction and thus lead to BEPS concerns. The availability of timely and targeted information about such rulings, as agreed in the template in Annex C of the Action 5 Report, Countering Harmful Tax Practices More Effectively, Taking Into Account Transparency and Substance (OECD, 2015[1]), is intended to better equip tax authorities to quickly identify risk areas.

This framework was designed with a view to finding a balance between ensuring that the information exchanged is relevant to other tax administrations and that it does not impose an unnecessary administrative burden on either the country exchanging the information or the country receiving it.

Scope of this review

This is the seventh annual peer review of the transparency framework, and covers 131 Inclusive Framework member jurisdictions and Jurisdictions of Relevance. This comprises all Inclusive Framework members that joined prior to 30 June 2022 and Jurisdictions of Relevance identified by the Inclusive

Framework prior to 30 June 2022.[2] Of these 131 jurisdictions, there were 27 jurisdictions which are not able to legally, or in practice, issue rulings in scope of the transparency framework, and therefore no separate peer review report is included for these jurisdictions.[3]

Eight other members of the Inclusive Framework have not been assessed under the transparency framework, namely Anguilla, the Bahamas, Bahrain, Bermuda, the British Virgin Islands, the Cayman Islands, the Turks and Caicos Islands and the United Arab Emirates. These jurisdictions do not impose any corporate income tax, during the year in review, and therefore cannot legally issue rulings within scope of the transparency framework and nor do Inclusive Framework members exchange information on rulings with them. Therefore, these jurisdictions are considered to be outside the scope of the transparency framework.

The reviews contained in this annual report cover the steps jurisdictions have taken to implement the transparency framework during the calendar year 2022. The reviews have been prepared using information from each reviewed jurisdiction, input from peers who received exchanges of information under the transparency framework, and input from the delegates of the Forum on Harmful Tax Practices ("FHTP").

Key findings

Key findings from this sixth annual peer review include:

- As at 31 December 2022, over 24,000 tax rulings in scope of the transparency framework had been issued by the jurisdictions being reviewed. This is the cumulative figure, including certain past rulings issued since 2010. Over 1,800 tax rulings in scope of the transparency framework were issued in 2022 by the 131 jurisdictions reviewed.
- Over 54,000 exchanges of information took place by 31 December 2022, with approximately 5,000 exchanges undertaken in 2022, 5,000 exchanges undertaken in 2021, 5,000 exchanges undertaken during 2020, 7,000 exchanges undertaken during 2019, 9,000 exchanges undertaken during 2018, 14,000 exchanges undertaken during 2017 and 6,000 exchanges during 2016.
- 100 jurisdictions did not receive any recommendations, as they have met all the terms of reference. A further seven jurisdictions received only one recommendation.
- 58 recommendations for improvement have been made for the year in review.
- 115 peer input questionnaires were submitted providing feedback on the conduct of the exchanges by Inclusive Framework members. Peer input is not mandatory, but in cases where it was provided it has in a number of cases allowed jurisdictions to revise their processes and improve the clarity and quality of information exchanged.
- In a number of cases, the peer review process has assisted jurisdictions in identifying areas where improvement is required, and jurisdictions have been able to take action to implement changes over 2023 while the peer review was ongoing. Where these changes were implemented in 2023, they are generally not taken into account in the recommendations for the year 2022. However, these changes would be reviewed in a subsequent peer review.

Table 1. Compilation of recommendations

Aspect of the implementation of the transparency framework that should be improved	Recommendation for improvement
Albania	
Albania does not yet have the necessary information gathering process in place.	Albania is recommended to put in place an effective information gathering process to identify all potential exchange jurisdictions for future rulings on preferential regimes and to implement a review and supervision mechanism, as soon as possible.
Albania does not yet have a process to complete the templates on relevant rulings, to make them available to the Competent Authority for exchange of information, and to exchange them with relevant jurisdictions.	Albania is recommended to continue to develop a process to complete the templates for all relevant rulings and to ensure that the exchanges of information on rulings occur in accordance with the form and timelines under the transparency framework.
Andorra	
Andorra still experiences difficulties in identifying all potential exchange jurisdictions for future rulings.	Andorra is recommended to continue its efforts to ensure that all potential exchange jurisdictions are identified swiftly for all future rulings. This recommendation remains unchanged since the 2017, 2018, 2019, 2020 and 2021 peer review reports.
Andorra has been developing a process to ensure that the information is completed in the required form and exchanges are performed in accordance with the timelines. Andorra noted that modifications to the tax law have been approved by the Andorran parliament in 2023 and will enter into force in 2024. As these issues have not yet been resolved and the modification to the tax law has not been approved in the year of review, this will be taken into account during next years' peer review.	Andorra is recommended to continue its efforts to put in place the necessary process to complete the information in the form of Annex C of the Action 5 Report, to ensure that information is submitted to the Competent Authority without undue delay and exchanges are performed in accordance with the timelines. These recommendations remain unchanged since the 2017, 2018, 2019, 2020 and 2021 peer review reports but since the 2019 peer review report they are targeted to specific aspects of the ToR that still need to be put in place.
Angola	
Angola has not yet finalised the steps to have in place its necessary information and gathering process.	Angola is recommended to finalise its information gathering process for identifying future rulings and all potential exchange jurisdictions as soon as possible. During the year in review, Angola built an internal database that keeps track of all issued rulings and confirmed there were no past rulings issued. In addition, Angola implemented a review and supervision mechanism for future rulings. This recommendation has been partly addressed but remains in place for the other part since the 2017, 2018, 2019, 2020 and 2021 peer review reports.
Angola has not yet finalised the steps to have effective compulsory spontaneous exchange of information on the tax rulings within the scope of the transparency framework	Angola is recommended to continue to put in place a domestic legal framework allowing spontaneous exchange of information on rulings and to continue its efforts to complete the templates for all relevant rulings and to ensure that the exchanges of information on rulings occur as soon as possible. This recommendation remains unchanged since the 2017, 2018, 2019, 2020 and 2021 peer review reports.
Antigua and Barbuda	
	No recommendations are made.
Argentina	
	No recommendation are made.
Armenia	
Armenia is in the process to finalise the information gathering process and to put in place a system for the identification and registration of issued tax rulings.	Armenia is recommended to continue its efforts to finalise and have in place the necessary information gathering process for identifying all relevant rulings and potential exchange jurisdictions, as soon as possible. This recommendation remains unchanged since the 2019, 2020 and 2021 peer review reports.
Armenia does not have a process to complete the templates on relevant rulings, to make them available to the Competent Authority for exchange of information, and to exchange them with relevant jurisdictions.	Armenia is recommended to continue its efforts to develop a process to complete the templates for all relevant rulings and to ensure that the exchanges of information on rulings occur in accordance with the form and timelines under the transparency framework as soon as possible. This recommendation remains unchanged since the 2019, 2020 and 2021 peer review reports.
Aruba	
	No recommendations are made.
Australia	

<table>
<tr><td></td><td>No recommendations are made.</td></tr>
<tr><th colspan="2">Austria</th></tr>
<tr><td></td><td>No recommendations are made.</td></tr>
<tr><th colspan="2">Barbados</th></tr>
<tr><td></td><td>No recommendations are made.</td></tr>
<tr><th colspan="2">Belgium</th></tr>
<tr><td></td><td>No recommendations are made.</td></tr>
<tr><th colspan="2">Belize</th></tr>
<tr><td></td><td>No recommendations are made.</td></tr>
<tr><th colspan="2">Benin</th></tr>
<tr><td>Benin has not finalised the steps to have in place its necessary information gathering process, with a review and supervision mechanism.</td><td>Benin is recommended to finalise its information gathering process for identifying all relevant rulings and all potential exchange jurisdictions, with a review and supervision mechanism, as soon as possible. This recommendation remains unchanged since the 2018, 2019, 2020 and 2021 peer review reports.</td></tr>
<tr><td>Benin has not yet finalised the steps to have effective compulsory spontaneous exchange of information on the tax rulings within the scope of the transparency framework.</td><td>Benin is recommended to continue to put in place a domestic legal framework allowing spontaneous exchange of information on rulings and to continue its efforts to complete the templates for all relevant rulings and to ensure that the exchanges of information on rulings occur as soon as possible. This recommendation remains unchanged since the 2018, 2019, 2020 and 2021 peer review reports.</td></tr>
<tr><th colspan="2">Bosnia and Herzegovina</th></tr>
<tr><td>Bosnia and Herzegovina does not have specific mechanisms in place for identifying relevant rulings and potential exchange jurisdictions within the scope of the transparency framework as well as for reviewing and supervising that all relevant information is captured adequately.</td><td>Bosnia and Herzegovina is recommended to put in place its information gathering process for identifying all past and future rulings and all potential exchange jurisdictions, with a review and supervision mechanism, as soon as possible. This recommendation remains unchanged since the 2020 and 2021 peer review report.</td></tr>
<tr><td>Bosnia and Herzegovina does not yet have the necessary domestic legal basis to exchange information spontaneously and a process for completing the templates in a timely way.</td><td>Bosnia and Herzegovina is recommended to put in place a domestic legal framework allowing spontaneous exchange of information on rulings and to ensure the timely exchange of information on rulings in the form required by the transparency framework, as soon as possible. This recommendation remains unchanged since the 2020 and 2021 peer review report.</td></tr>
<tr><th colspan="2">Botswana</th></tr>
<tr><td>Botswana does not have a review and supervision mechanism in place.</td><td>Botswana is recommended to put in place a review and supervision mechanism, as soon as possible. This recommendation remains unchanged since the 2018, 2019, 2020 and 2021 peer review reports.</td></tr>
<tr><td>Botswana does not yet have the necessary legal framework in place for exchanging information on rulings and a process in place to ensure the timely exchange of information on rulings in the form required by the transparency framework.</td><td>Botswana is recommended to continue its efforts to put in place a domestic legal framework allowing spontaneous exchange of information on rulings and to complete the templates for all relevant rulings and to ensure that the exchanges of information on rulings occur as soon as possible. This recommendation remains unchanged since the 2018, 2019, 2020 and 2021 peer review reports.</td></tr>
<tr><th colspan="2">Brazil</th></tr>
<tr><td></td><td>No recommendations are made.</td></tr>
<tr><th colspan="2">Brunei Darussalam</th></tr>
<tr><td></td><td>No recommendations are made.</td></tr>
<tr><th colspan="2">Bulgaria</th></tr>
<tr><td></td><td>No recommendations are made.</td></tr>
<tr><th colspan="2">Burkina Faso</th></tr>
<tr><td>Burkina Faso has not taken all measures to put in place the required information gathering process.</td><td>Burkina Faso is recommended to finalise its information gathering process and implement a review and supervision mechanism as soon as possible. This recommendation remains unchanged since the 2020 and 2021 peer review reports.</td></tr>
<tr><td>Burkina Faso has not yet put in place the process to develop templates on relevant rulings, to make them available to the Competent Authority for exchange of information, and to exchange them with relevant jurisdictions.</td><td>Burkina Faso is recommended to establish a process to develop templates on relevant rulings and ensure that information on these rulings is exchanged in a timely manner and in the format required by the transparency framework. This recommendation remains unchanged since the 2020 and 2021 peer review reports.</td></tr>
</table>

Cabo Verde	
Cabo Verde does not have a process to complete the templates on relevant rulings and to make them available to the Competent Authority for exchange of information.	Cabo Verde is recommended to continue its efforts to develop a process to complete the templates for all relevant rulings and to ensure that the exchanges of information on rulings occur in accordance with the form and timelines under the transparency framework as soon as possible. This recommendation remains unchanged since the 2019, 2020 and 2021 peer review reports.
Cameroon	
	No recommendations are made.
Canada	
	No recommendations are made.
Chile	
	No recommendations are made.
China (People's Republic of)	
	No recommendations are made.
Colombia	
	No recommendations are made.
Congo	
It is not known whether Congo has finalised the steps to have in place its necessary information and gathering process.	Congo is recommended to finalise its information gathering process, with a review and supervision mechanism, as soon as possible. This recommendation remains unchanged since the 2017, 2018, 2019, 2020 and 2021 peer review reports.
It is not known whether Congo has finalised the steps to have effective compulsory spontaneous exchange of information on the tax rulings within the scope of the transparency framework.	Congo is recommended to continue to put in place a domestic legal framework allowing spontaneous exchange of information on rulings and to continue its efforts to complete the templates for all relevant rulings and to ensure that the exchanges of information on rulings occur as soon as possible. This recommendation remains unchanged since the 2017, 2018, 2019, 2020 and 2021 peer review reports.
Cook Islands	
	No recommendations are made.
Costa Rica	
	No recommendations are made.
Côte d'Ivoire	
	No recommendations are made.
Croatia	
	No recommendations are made.
Curaçao	
The information gathering process is still underway in Curaçao with respect to past and future rulings within the scope of the transparency framework and the classification of these rulings under each category.	Curaçao is recommended to finalise its information gathering process for identifying all past and future rulings within the scope of the transparency framework as soon as possible. This recommendation remains unchanged since the 2017, 2018, 2019, 2020 and 2021 peer review reports.
Curaçao experienced delays in exchanging information on past and future rulings.	Curaçao is recommended to continue its efforts to ensure that all information on past and future rulings is exchanged as soon as possible. This recommendation remains unchanged since the 2017, 2018, 2019, 2020 and 2021 peer review reports.
Czechia	
	No recommendations are made.
Democratic Republic of the Congo	
It is not known whether the Democratic Republic of the Congo has put in place the necessary information and gathering process.	The Democratic Republic of the Congo is recommended to finalise its information gathering process, with a review and supervision mechanism, as soon as possible. This recommendation remains unchanged since the 2020 and 2021 peer review reports.
It is not known whether the Democratic Republic of the Congo has put in place an effective compulsory spontaneous exchange of information on the tax rulings within the scope of the transparency framework.	The Democratic Republic of the Congo is recommended to continue to put in place a domestic legal framework allowing spontaneous exchange of information on rulings and to continue its efforts to complete the templates for all relevant rulings and to ensure that the exchanges of information on rulings occur as soon as possible. This recommendation remains unchanged since the 2020 and 2021 peer review reports.

Denmark	
	No recommendations are made.
Djibouti	
	No recommendations are made.
Dominica	
	No recommendations are made.
Dominican Republic	
	No recommendations are made.
Egypt	
Egypt has not yet identified all potential exchange jurisdictions for both past and future rulings and does not have a review and supervision mechanism in place to ensure that all relevant information on the identification of rulings and potential exchange jurisdictions is captured adequately.	Egypt is recommended to continue its efforts to identify all potential exchange jurisdictions for both past and future rulings and to implement a review and supervision mechanism, as soon as possible. This recommendation remains unchanged since the 2018, 2019, 2020 and 2021 review reports.
Egypt does not have in place a process to ensure the timely exchange of information on rulings in the form required by the transparency framework.	Egypt is recommended to swiftly implement its process to complete the templates on relevant rulings and to ensure that the exchanges of information on rulings occur as soon as possible. This recommendation remains unchanged since the 2018, 2019, 2020 and 2021 peer review reports.
Estonia	
	No recommendations are made.
Eswatini	
Eswatini is currently taking steps to ensure the identification of all relevant rulings and all potential exchange jurisdictions as well as to have a review and supervision mechanism under the transparency framework.	Eswatini is recommended to put in place its information gathering process for identifying all relevant rulings and all potential exchange jurisdictions, with a review and supervision mechanism, as soon as possible. This recommendation remains unchanged since the 2020 and 2021 peer review reports.
Eswatini is currently taking steps to put a process in place for the completion and exchange of information on rulings in accordance with the form and timelines required by the transparency framework.	Eswatini is recommended to develop a process to complete the templates on relevant rulings and to ensure that the exchanges of information on rulings occur in accordance with the form and timelines under the transparency framework. This recommendation remains unchanged since the 2020 and 2021 peer review reports.
Faroe Islands	
The Faroe Islands does not yet have a process in place to identify all potential exchange jurisdictions for permanent establishment rulings.	The Faroe Islands is recommended to put in place a process to identify all potential exchange jurisdictions for permanent establishment rulings. This recommendation remains unchanged since the 2019, 2020 and 2021 peer review reports, but is now targeted to the specific ToR that still needs to be put in place.
The Faroe Islands does not have a process for the timely exchange of information on rulings with relevant jurisdictions.	The Faroe Islands is recommended to put in place a process to ensure that the exchanges of information on rulings occur in accordance with the form and timelines under the transparency framework going forward This recommendation remains unchanged since the 2019, 2020 and 2021 peer review reports, but is now targeted to the specific ToR that still needs to be put in place.
Finland	
	No recommendations are made.
France	
	No recommendations are made.
Gabon	
Gabon has not finalised the steps to have in place its necessary information gathering process, with a review and supervision mechanism.	Gabon is recommended to finalise its information gathering process for identifying all relevant rulings and all potential exchange jurisdictions, with a review and supervision mechanism, as soon as possible. This recommendation remains unchanged since the 2018, 2019, 2020 and 2021 peer review reports.
Gabon has not finalised the steps to put in place a process to complete the templates for all relevant rulings and to ensure that the exchanges of information on rulings occur as soon as possible.	Gabon is recommended to continue its efforts to put in place a process to complete the templates for all relevant rulings and to ensure that the exchanges of information on rulings occur as soon as possible. This recommendation remains unchanged since the 2018, 2019, 2020 and 2021 peer review reports.
Georgia	

	No recommendations are made.
Germany	
	No recommendations are made.
Gibraltar	
	No recommendations are made.
Greece	
	No recommendations are made.
Greenland	
	No recommendations are made.
Grenada	
Grenada has not put in place the necessary information gathering process.	Grenada is recommended to finalise its information gathering process for identifying all future rulings and potential exchange jurisdictions, with a review and supervision mechanism, as soon as possible. This recommendation remains unchanged since the 2019, 2020 and 2021 peer review reports.
Grenada does not have a process to complete the templates on relevant rulings, to make them available to the Competent Authority for exchange of information, and to exchange them with relevant jurisdictions.	Grenada is recommended to develop a process to complete the templates on relevant rulings and to ensure that the exchanges of information on rulings occur in accordance with the form and timelines under the transparency framework. This recommendation remains unchanged since the 2019, 2020 and 2021 peer review reports.
Guernsey	
	No recommendations are made.
Haiti	
	No recommendations are made.
Honduras	
	No recommendations are made..
Hong Kong (China)	
	No recommendations are made.
Hungary	
Hungary did not yet apply the "best efforts approach" to identify potential exchange jurisdictions for all past rulings.	Hungary is recommended to continue to apply the "best efforts approach" to identify potential exchange jurisdictions for all past rulings. This recommendation remains unchanged since the 2016, 2017, 2018, 2019, 2020 and 2021 peer review reports
Iceland	
	No recommendations are made.
India	
India experienced delays in the exchange of information on future APAs.	India is recommended to continue its efforts to ensure that all information on future APAs is exchanged as soon as possible. This recommendation remains unchanged since the 2017, 2018, 2019, 2020 and 2021 peer review reports.
Indonesia	
	No recommendations are made.
Ireland	
	No recommendations are made.
Isle of Man	
	No recommendations are made.
Israel	
	No recommendations are made.
Italy	
	No recommendations are made.
Jamaica	
	No recommendations are made.
Japan	
	No recommendations are made.
Jersey	
	No recommendations are made.

Jordan	
Jordan does not have specific mechanisms in place for identifying relevant rulings and potential exchange jurisdictions within the scope of the transparency framework as well as for reviewing and supervising that all relevant information is captured adequately.	Jordan is recommended to ensure that it has put in place an effective information gathering process to identify all relevant rulings and potential exchange jurisdictions, with a review and supervision mechanism, as soon as possible. This recommendation remains unchanged since the 2019, 2020 and 2021 peer review reports.
Jordan does not yet have the necessary domestic legal basis to exchange information spontaneously and a process to exchange information on rulings in the required format and timelines.	Jordan is recommended to put in place a domestic legal framework allowing spontaneous exchange of information on the relevant tax rulings and to ensure the timely exchange of information on rulings in the form required by the transparency framework, as soon as possible. This recommendation remains unchanged since the 2019, 2020 and 2021 peer review reports.
Jordan has not identified information on new entrants to the Development zone IP regime during the relevant period and has not exchanged information on these taxpayers.	Jordan is recommended to identify information and to put in place a domestic legal framework allowing spontaneous exchange of information on all new entrants to the IP regime, as soon as possible. This recommendation remains unchanged since the prior year's peer review report. This recommendation remains unchanged since the 2019, 2020 and 2021 peer review reports.
Kazakhstan	
Kazakhstan has not yet finalised the steps to have in place its necessary information and gathering process.	Kazakhstan is recommended to finalise its information gathering process, with a review and supervision mechanism, as soon as possible. This recommendation remains unchanged since the 2018, 2019, 2020 and 2021 peer review reports.
Kazakhstan has not yet finalised the steps to have effective compulsory spontaneous exchange of information on the tax rulings within the scope of the transparency framework.	Kazakhstan is recommended to continue to put in place a domestic legal framework allowing spontaneous exchange of information on rulings and to continue its efforts to complete the templates for all relevant rulings and to ensure that the exchanges of information on rulings occur as soon as possible. This recommendation remains unchanged since the 2018, 2019, 2020 and 2021 peer review reports
Kenya	
	No recommendations are made.
Korea	
	No recommendations are made.
Latvia	
	No recommendations are made.
Liberia	
Liberia does not yet have the necessary information gathering process in place.	Liberia is recommended to ensure that it has put in place an effective information gathering process to identify all relevant past and future rulings and all potential exchange jurisdictions and to implement a review and supervision mechanism, as soon as possible.
Liberia does not yet have a process to complete the templates on relevant rulings, to make them available to the Competent Authority for exchange of information, and to exchange them with relevant jurisdictions.	Liberia is recommended to develop a process to complete the templates for all relevant rulings and to ensure that the exchanges of information on rulings occur in accordance with the form and timelines under the transparency framework going forward.
Liechtenstein	
	No recommendations are made.
Lithuania	
	No recommendations are made.
Luxembourg	
	No recommendations are made.
Macau (China)	
	No recommendations are made.
Malaysia	
Malaysia experienced difficulties in identifying all potential exchange jurisdictions for future rulings.	Malaysia is recommended to continue its efforts to ensure that all potential exchange jurisdictions are identified swiftly for all future rulings. This recommendation remains unchanged since the 2019, 2020 and 2021 year peer review reports.
Malaysia experienced delays in the provision of rulings to the Competent Authority and did not undertake spontaneous exchange of information on all future tax rulings within the scope of the transparency framework	Malaysia is recommended to continue its efforts to reduce the timeliness for providing the information on rulings to the Competent Authority and to complete the templates for all relevant future rulings and to ensure that

during the year in review. Malaysia is in process of identifying future rulings that need to be exchanged and is estimating that the rulings will be exchanged via OECD XML Schema in 2023.	the exchanges of information on future rulings occur as soon as possible. This recommendation remains unchanged since the 2017, 2018, 2019, 2020 and 2021 peer review reports.
Maldives	
	No recommendations are made.
Malta	
	No recommendations are made.
Mauritius	
	No recommendations are made.
Mexico	
	No recommendations are made.
Monaco	
	No recommendations are made.
Mongolia	
	No recommendations are made.
Montenegro	
	No recommendations are made.
Montserrat	
	No recommendations are made.
Morocco	
	No recommendations are made.
Namibia	
Namibia does not yet have the necessary information gathering process in place.	Namibia is recommended to ensure that it has put in place an effective information gathering process to identify all relevant past and future rulings and all potential exchange jurisdictions and to implement a review and supervision mechanism, as soon as possible. This recommendation remains unchanged since the 2020 and 2021 peer reviews.
Namibia does not yet have a process to complete the templates on relevant rulings, to make them available to the Competent Authority for exchange of information, and to exchange them with relevant jurisdictions.	Namibia is recommended to develop a process to complete the templates for all relevant rulings and to ensure that the exchanges of information on rulings occur in accordance with the form and timelines under the transparency framework going forward. This recommendation remains unchanged since the 2020 and 2021 peer reviews.
Netherlands	
	No recommendations are made.
New Zealand	
	No recommendations are made.
Nigeria	
Nigeria does not yet have the necessary information gathering process in place. Nigeria is currently in the process of putting in place the administrative framework which would enable identifying and keeping track on the relevant future rulings as well as ensuring efficient review and supervision mechanism. As the process has not yet been completed, the recommendation remains in place.	Nigeria is recommended to ensure that it has put in place an effective information gathering process to identify all relevant past and future rulings and all potential exchange jurisdictions and to implement a review and supervision mechanism, as soon as possible. This recommendation remains unchanged since the 2021 peer review report.
Nigeria does not yet have a process to complete the templates on relevant rulings, to make them available to the Competent Authority for exchange of information, and to exchange them with relevant jurisdictions. Nigeria is currently in the process of putting in place the administrative framework which ensures a process for making the information on rulings available to the competent authority. As the process has not yet been completed, the recommendation remains in place.	Nigeria is recommended to develop a process to complete the templates for all relevant rulings and to ensure that the exchanges of information on rulings occur in accordance with the form and timelines under the transparency framework going forward. This recommendation remains unchanged since the 2021 peer review report.
North Macedonia	
	No recommendations are made.
Norway	
	No recommendations are made.
Oman	
	No recommendations are made.
Pakistan	

Pakistan is taking steps to put the necessary information gathering process in place.	Pakistan is recommended to ensure that it has put in place an effective information gathering process to identify all relevant past and future rulings and all potential exchange jurisdictions and to implement a review and supervision mechanism, as soon as possible. This recommendation remains unchanged since the prior year's peer review report.
Pakistan is taking steps to put a process in place to complete the templates on relevant rulings, to make them available to the Competent Authority for exchange of information, and to exchange them with relevant jurisdictions.	Pakistan is recommended to develop a process to complete the templates for all relevant rulings and to ensure that the exchanges of information on rulings occur in accordance with the form and timelines under the transparency framework going forward. This recommendation remains unchanged since the prior year's peer review report.
Panama	
	No recommendations are made.
Papua New Guinea	
	No recommendations are made.
Paraguay	
	No recommendations are made.
Peru	
	No recommendations are made.
Philippines	
The Philippines does not yet have a process in place to ensure the timely exchange of information on rulings in the form required by the transparency framework. The Philippines has made efforts on this during the year 2023, which will be taken into account in next year's peer review report.	The Philippines is recommended to continue its efforts to put in place a process to complete the templates for all relevant rulings and to ensure that the exchanges of information on rulings occur as soon as possible. This recommendation remains unchanged since the 2017, 2018, 2019, 2020 and 2021 peer review reports.
Poland	
	No recommendations are made.
Portugal	
	No recommendations are made.
Qatar	
	No recommendations are made.
Romania	
	No recommendations are made.
Saint Kitts and Nevis	
	No recommendations are made.
Saint Lucia	
Saint Lucia does not require taxpayers to provide all necessary information to identify all potential exchange jurisdictions for future rulings.	Saint Lucia is recommended to ensure that all potential exchange jurisdictions are identified swiftly for all future rulings. This recommendation remains unchanged since the 2018, 2019, 2020 and 2021 peer review reports.
Saint Vincent and the Grenadines	
Saint Vincent and the Grenadines does not yet have an effective information gathering process in place to identify all relevant future rulings and all potential exchange jurisdictions.	Saint Vincent and the Grenadines is recommended to continue its work on its information gathering process for identifying all past and future rulings within the scope of the transparency framework as soon as possible.
Saint Vincent and the Grenadines does not yet have a process to complete the templates on all relevant rulings, to make them available to the Competent Authority for exchange of information, and to exchange them with relevant jurisdictions	Saint Vincent and the Grenadines is recommended to develop a process to complete the templates for all relevant rulings and to ensure that the exchanges of information on rulings occur in accordance with the form and timelines under the transparency framework going forward.
Samoa	
	No recommendations are made.
San Marino	
	No recommendations are made.
Saudi Arabia	
	No recommendations are made.
Senegal	
	No recommendations are made.
Serbia	

<table>
<tr><td></td><td>No recommendations are made.</td></tr>
<tr><td colspan="2">Seychelles</td></tr>
<tr><td></td><td>No recommendations are made.</td></tr>
<tr><td colspan="2">Sierra Leone</td></tr>
<tr><td></td><td>No recommendations are made.</td></tr>
<tr><td colspan="2">Singapore</td></tr>
<tr><td></td><td>No recommendations are made.</td></tr>
<tr><td colspan="2">Sint Maarten</td></tr>
<tr><td></td><td>No recommendations are made.</td></tr>
<tr><td colspan="2">Slovak Republic</td></tr>
<tr><td></td><td>No recommendations are made.</td></tr>
<tr><td colspan="2">Slovenia</td></tr>
<tr><td></td><td>No recommendations are made.</td></tr>
<tr><td colspan="2">South Africa</td></tr>
<tr><td></td><td>No recommendations are made.</td></tr>
<tr><td colspan="2">Spain</td></tr>
<tr><td></td><td>No recommendations are made.</td></tr>
<tr><td colspan="2">Sri Lanka</td></tr>
<tr><td></td><td>No recommendations are made.</td></tr>
<tr><td colspan="2">Sweden</td></tr>
<tr><td></td><td>No recommendations are made.</td></tr>
<tr><td colspan="2">Switzerland</td></tr>
<tr><td>Switzerland experienced delays in the exchange of information on past and future rulings.</td><td>Switzerland is recommended to continue to ensure that all information on past and future rulings is exchanged as soon as possible. This recommendation remains unchanged since the 2019, 2020 and 2021 peer review reports.</td></tr>
<tr><td colspan="2">Thailand</td></tr>
<tr><td>Thailand implemented a legal provision which has taken effect in 2022 and now has the necessary legal framework to exchange information on rulings spontaneously. Thailand has commenced exchanges of information on past and future rulings. However, Thailand still experienced delays on exchanges of information on future rulings during the year in review.</td><td>Thailand is recommended to exchange information on the remaining future rulings as soon as possible.</td></tr>
<tr><td colspan="2">Trinidad & Tobago</td></tr>
<tr><td></td><td>No recommendations are made.</td></tr>
<tr><td colspan="2">Tunisia</td></tr>
<tr><td></td><td>No recommendations are made.</td></tr>
<tr><td colspan="2">Türkiye</td></tr>
<tr><td></td><td>No recommendations are made.</td></tr>
<tr><td colspan="2">Ukraine</td></tr>
<tr><td></td><td>No recommendations are made.</td></tr>
<tr><td colspan="2">United Kingdom</td></tr>
<tr><td></td><td>No recommendations are made.</td></tr>
<tr><td colspan="2">United States</td></tr>
<tr><td></td><td>No recommendations are made.</td></tr>
<tr><td colspan="2">Uruguay</td></tr>
<tr><td></td><td>No recommendations are made.</td></tr>
<tr><td colspan="2">Viet Nam</td></tr>
<tr><td>Viet Nam is still developing a process for completion of templates and exchange of information on rulings.</td><td>Viet Nam is recommended to develop a process to complete the templates on relevant rulings and to ensure that the exchanges of information on rulings occur in accordance with the form and timelines under the transparency framework. This recommendation remains unchanged since the 2017, 2018, 2019, 2020 and 2021 peer review reports.</td></tr>
<tr><td colspan="2">Zambia</td></tr>
<tr><td></td><td>No recommendations are made.</td></tr>
</table>

References

OECD (2015), *Countering Harmful Tax Practices More Effectively, Taking into Account Transparency and Substance, Action 5 - 2015 Final Report*, OECD/G20 Base Erosion and Profit Shifting Project, OECD Publishing, Paris, https://doi.org/10.1787/9789264241190-en. [1]

Notes

[1] The Action 5 Report, *Countering Harmful Tax Practices More Effectively, Taking Into Account Transparency and Substance* (OECD, 2015) also provides that additional types of rulings could be added to the scope of the transparency framework in the future, where the FHTP and the Inclusive Framework agree that such a ruling could lead to BEPS concerns in the absence of spontaneous information exchange.

[2] In next year's peer review (taking into account the year in review 2023), the following jurisdictions will be reviewed for the first time: Azerbeijan, Mauritania, Togo, United Arab Emirates and Uzbekistan.

[3] The relevant jurisdictions that do not issue rulings within the scope of the transparency framework are: Belize, Bulgaria, Cameroon, Cook Islands, Côte d'Ivoire, Djibouti, Dominica, Greenland, Haiti, Honduras, Macau (China), Maldives, Monaco, Mongolia, Montenegro, Montserrat, North Macedonia, Oman, Panama, Papua New Guinea, Paraguay, Saudi Arabia, Serbia, Sierra Leone, Trinidad & Tobago, Tunisia, and Zambia.

1 Introduction

Overview of the peer review on the exchange of information on tax rulings

The Action 5 Report (OECD, 2015[1]) is one of the four BEPS minimum standards. It involves two distinct aspects: a review of certain preferential tax regimes and substantial activities in no or only nominal tax jurisdictions to ensure they are not harmful, and the transparency framework. Each of the four BEPS minimum standards is subject to peer review in order to ensure timely and accurate implementation and thus safeguard the level playing field. All members of the Inclusive Framework on BEPS commit to implementing the Action 5 minimum standard and to participating in the peer review, on an equal footing. The peer review of the Action 5 minimum standard is undertaken by the FHTP and approved by the Inclusive Framework on BEPS. It covers all Inclusive Framework members as well as Jurisdictions of relevance, i.e. jurisdictions that have not become members of the Inclusive Framework, but whose adherence to the standards is necessary to ensure a level playing field is achieved.

The purpose of a peer review is to ensure the effective and consistent implementation of an agreed standard and to recognise progress made by jurisdictions in this regard. The peer review evaluates the implementation of the standard against an agreed set of criteria. These criteria are set out in terms of reference, which include each of the elements that a jurisdiction needs to demonstrate it has fulfilled in order to show effective implementation of the standard.[1]

The peer review has been conducted in accordance with the agreed methodology. The methodology sets out the process for undertaking the peer review, including the process for collecting the relevant data, the preparation and approval of annual reports, the outputs of the review and the follow up process.

The terms of reference and agreed methodology do not alter the Action 5 minimum standard. Any terms used in the terms of reference or methodology take their meaning from the language and context of the Action 5 Report (OECD, 2015[1])and the references therein. Any terms in this report which are not included in the glossary take their meaning from the language and context of the Action 5 Report (OECD, 2015[1]).

Outline of the key aspects assessed in the annual report

This annual report contains the findings of the seventh annual peer review of jurisdictions' compliance with the transparency framework. It assesses the implementation of the transparency framework for the period 1 January 2022 - 31 December 2022.

The reports on each reviewed jurisdiction cover each of the aspects of the terms of reference. These capture the key elements of the transparency framework which are briefly described below. Where recommendations from prior years' peer review reports were not addressed, the report specifically notes this. Jurisdictions are urged to address these recommendations that have remained in place for more than one review.

A. The information gathering process

This involves assessing the processes in place in each of the jurisdictions for identifying past and future rulings that fall within the scope of the transparency framework, and for each of these rulings, identifying the jurisdictions with which the information should be exchanged. The review of the information gathering process also covers any supervision mechanism that the jurisdiction has in place to ensure that all relevant information is captured adequately.

B. The exchange of information

The exchange of information requires the legal and administrative framework to be in place to allow spontaneous exchange of information on the relevant tax rulings and subsequent exchange of the relevant rulings where a valid exchange of information request is received. Information on past rulings was to be spontaneously exchanged pursuant to the relevant deadline outlined in each jurisdiction's report.[2] Information on future rulings is to be spontaneously exchanged as soon as possible and no later than three months after the date on which the ruling becomes available to the Competent Authority for exchange of information. The exchange of information should occur in the agreed standardised form, either using the template contained in Annex C of the Action 5 Report (OECD, 2015[1]) or the OECD XML Schema. Adequate completion of the summary section in the Annex C template or the OECD XML Schema should be ensured through adherence to the instruction sheet to the summary section or the internal FHTP suggested guidance, or an alternate process that allows the summary section to contain sufficient detail for the receiving jurisdiction's tax administration to appropriately assess the potential base erosion and profit shifting risks posed by the ruling where applicable.

The peer review includes reviewing (i) that there is a sufficient domestic and international legal framework for the exchange information related to rulings; (ii) that the summary templates for information on rulings being exchanged are complete and in the appropriate form; and (iii) that the systems are in place to ensure that information on rulings is transmitted to the jurisdiction's Competent Authority for exchange of information without undue delay and exchanged with relevant jurisdictions in accordance with the appropriate timelines.

With respect to the international exchange of information, the terms of reference required jurisdictions to exchange information with Inclusive Framework members being reviewed for the same year, to the extent that an exchange of information agreement was in force for such exchanges and subject to the recipient jurisdiction demonstrating that it would keep the information received confidential.[3]

C. Statistics

Each jurisdiction is required to report statistics on the exchange of information under the transparency framework including (i) the total number of spontaneous exchanges sent, (ii) the number of spontaneous exchanges under each category of ruling and (iii) a list of jurisdictions with which the information was exchanged for each type of ruling.

D. Exchange of information on IP regimes

The review of the transparency framework also includes a review of the spontaneous exchanges of information which are required to occur in respect of certain features of IP regimes, as set out in the Action 5 "nexus approach." This includes, irrespective of whether a tax ruling is provided, identifying and exchanging information on taxpayers which benefit from the third category of IP assets (as defined in paragraph 37 of the Action 5 Report (OECD, 2015[1])), and taxpayers making use of the option to treat the nexus ratio as a rebuttable presumption (as defined in paragraphs 67- 69 of the Action 5 Report (OECD,

2015[1])). This aspect of the review is only relevant for those jurisdictions which offer IP regimes, and the minimum standard does not require any jurisdiction to introduce such a regime.

Spontaneous exchange of information is also required with respect to new entrants benefiting from grandfathered IP regimes (regardless of whether a ruling is provided). This applies with respect to IP regimes that were not compliant with the nexus approach, and where jurisdictions have taken steps to abolish the regime, or amend it, as part of the FHTP's regime review process. In some cases, when introducing those legislative changes, jurisdictions have chosen to provide grandfathering to existing taxpayers to provide time to transition to the new rules. Additional spontaneous exchange of information on the taxpayers benefiting from this grandfathering is required where taxpayers or new IP assets were transferred into a non-nexus IP regime in the period between the announcement of forthcoming changes and those changes taking place. The timelines for which enhanced transparency applies vary according to the time at which the FHTP reviewed the regime, and are set out in Annex A of the 2017 Progress Report on Preferential Regimes (OECD, 2017[2]).

Response to the report

In addition, jurisdictions had the option to include a response to the report and update on recent developments which occurred after the 2022 year in review. Where included, this reflects the individual jurisdiction's views, and not those of the FHTP or the OECD Secretariat.

References

OECD (2017), *Harmful Tax Practices - 2017 Progress Report on Preferential Regimes: Inclusive Framework on BEPS: Action 5*, OECD/G20 Base Erosion and Profit Shifting Project, OECD Publishing, Paris, https://doi.org/10.1787/9789264283954-en. [2]

OECD (2015), *Countering Harmful Tax Practices More Effectively, Taking into Account Transparency and Substance, Action 5 - 2015 Final Report*, OECD/G20 Base Erosion and Profit Shifting Project, OECD Publishing, Paris, https://doi.org/10.1787/9789264241190-en. [1]

Notes

[1] Terms of Reference and Methodology for the review available at www.oecd.org/tax/beps/beps-action-5-harmful-tax-practices-peer-review-transparency-framework.pdf (OECD, 2021).

[2] The Action 5 Report (OECD, 2015) acknowledged that some jurisdictions may need to put in place the domestic or international legal framework in order to comply with the obligations under Action 5. In such cases the timelines for exchange of information on rulings are subject to a jurisdiction's legal framework.

[3] Where a ruling related only to tax years which were not covered by the relevant exchange of information agreement, no exchange of information would be required to occur in respect of that ruling. No negative inference is drawn in the peer review where an exchange was not permitted to occur because of the absence of, or the tax years covered by, an exchange of information agreement, although Inclusive Framework members are encouraged to expand their exchange of information agreements where relevant.

2 Country profiles

Albania

Albania has met all aspects of the terms of reference (OECD, 2021[1]) (ToR) for the calendar year 2022 (year in review) except for having the necessary information gathering process in place (ToR I.A) and exchanging information on the tax rulings in accordance with the form and timelines under the transparency framework (ToR II.B). Albania receives two recommendations on these points for the year in review.

In the prior year report, Albania had received the same two recommendations. As they have not been addressed, the recommendations remain in place.

Albania can legally issue two types of rulings within the scope of the transparency framework.

In practice, Albania issued no rulings within the scope of the transparency framework.

As no exchanges took place, no peer input was received in respect of the exchanges of information on rulings received from Albania.

Information gathering process (ToR I.A)

1. Albania can legally issue the following two types of rulings within the scope of the transparency framework: (i) preferential regimes;[1] (ii) cross-border unilateral APAs and any other cross-border unilateral tax rulings (such as an advance tax ruling) covering transfer pricing or the application of transfer pricing principles.

Past rulings (ToR I.A.1.1, I.A.1.2, I.A.2.1, I.A.2.2)

2. For Albania, past rulings are any tax rulings issued prior to 1 March 2020. However, there is no obligation for Albania to conduct spontaneous exchange information on past rulings.

Future rulings (ToR I.A.1.1, I.A.1.2, I.A.2.1)

3. For Albania, future rulings are any tax rulings within scope that are issued on or after 1 March 2020.

4. No future rulings were issued by Albania during the year in review.

5. In the prior year's peer review report, it was determined that Albania issues rulings based on legal provisions and that the General Directorate of Taxation (GDT) identifies these rulings and has all relevant information in relation to APAs, including information on relevant exchange jurisdictions. Albania confirmed that taxpayers are required to provide information on related parties, as well immediate and ultimate parent companies at the time the request for a ruling is submitted to the tax administration as well as additional information at the request of the tax administration. Regarding rulings on preferential regimes, it was determined that there were no processes yet in place to ensure the identification of all relevant exchange jurisdictions and thus to ensure the implementation of the obligations relating to the transparency framework.

6. During the year in review, Albania did not provide additional information and was in the process of taking appropriate steps to implement the transparency framework and action the recommendations of the prior year's peer review report.

Review and supervision (ToR I.A.3)

7. In the prior year's peer review report, it was determined that Albania did not yet have a review and supervision mechanism under the transparency framework. During the year in review, Albania did not implement such a review and supervision mechanism, and therefore the recommendation remains in place.

Conclusion on section A

8. Albania is recommended to put in place an effective information gathering process to identify all potential exchange jurisdictions for future rulings on preferential regimes and to implement a review and supervision mechanism, as soon as possible (ToR I.A).

Exchange of information (ToR II.B)

9. Albania has the necessary domestic legal basis to exchange information spontaneously. Albania notes that there are no legal or practical impediments that prevent the spontaneous exchange of information on rulings as contemplated in the Action 5 minimum standard.

10. Albania has international agreements permitting spontaneous exchange of information, including: (i) the *Multilateral Convention on Mutual Administrative Assistance in Tax Matters: Amended by the 2010*

Protocol (OECD/Council of Europe, 2011[2]) ("the Convention") and (ii) bilateral agreements in force with 43 jurisdictions.[2]

Completion and exchange of templates (ToR II.B.3, II.B.4, II.B.5, II.B.6, II.B.7)

11. In the prior year's peer review report, it was determined that Albania did not yet have a process to complete the templates on all relevant rulings, to make them available to the Competent Authority for exchange of information, and to exchange them with relevant jurisdictions. Therefore, Albania was recommended to develop a process for the completion and exchange of information as soon as possible. During the year in review, Albania notes that it is currently in the process of taking appropriate steps.

12. During the year in review, no exchanges were required to take place and no data on the timeliness of exchanges is reported.

Conclusion on section B

13. Albania is recommended to continue to develop a process to complete the templates for all relevant rulings and to ensure that the exchanges of information on rulings occur in accordance with the form and timelines under the transparency framework going forward (ToR II.B).

Statistics (ToR IV.D)

14. As no rulings were issued, no statistics can be reported.

Matters related to intellectual property regimes (ToR I.A.1.3)

15. Albania does not offer an intellectual property regime for which transparency requirements under the Action 5 Report (OECD, 2015[3]) were imposed.

Summary of recommendations on implementation of the transparency framework

Aspect of implementation of the transparency framework that should be improved	Recommendation for improvement
Albania does not yet have the necessary information gathering process in place.	Albania is recommended to put in place an effective information gathering process to identify all potential exchange jurisdictions for future rulings on preferential regimes and to implement a review and supervision mechanism, as soon as possible.
Albania does not yet have a process to complete the templates on relevant rulings, to make them available to the Competent Authority for exchange of information, and to exchange them with relevant jurisdictions.	Albania is recommended to continue to develop a process to complete the templates for all relevant rulings and to ensure that the exchanges of information on rulings occur in accordance with the form and timelines under the transparency framework.

References

OECD (2021), *BEPS Action 5 on Harmful Tax Practices - Terms of Reference and Methodology for the Conduct of the Peer Reviews of the Action 5 Transparency Framework*, OECD Publishing, Paris, https://www.oecd.org/tax/beps/beps-action-5-harmful-tax-practices-peer-review-transparency-framework.pdf. [1]

OECD (2015), *Countering Harmful Tax Practices More Effectively, Taking into Account Transparency and Substance, Action 5 - 2015 Final Report*, OECD/G20 Base Erosion and Profit Shifting Project, OECD Publishing, Paris, https://doi.org/10.1787/9789264241190-en. [3]

OECD/Council of Europe (2011), *The Multilateral Convention on Mutual Administrative Assistance in Tax Matters: Amended by the 2010 Protocol*, OECD Publishing, Paris, https://doi.org/10.1787/9789264115606-en. [2]

Notes

[1] Industry Incentive Regime.

[2] Participating jurisdictions to the Convention are available here: www.oecd.org/tax/exchange-of-tax-information/convention-on-mutual-administrative-assistance-in-tax-matters.htm. Albania also has bilateral agreements with Austria, Belgium, Bosnia and Herzegovina, Bulgaria, China (People's Republic of), Croatia, Czechia, Egypt, Estonia, France, Germany, Greece, Hungary, Iceland, India, Ireland, Israel, Italy, Korea, Kosovo, Kuwait, Latvia, Malaysia, Malta, Moldova, Montenegro, Netherlands, North Macedonia, Norway, Poland, Qatar, Romania, Russia, Saudi Arabia, Serbia, Singapore, Slovenia, Spain, Sweden, Switzerland, Türkiye, United Arab Emirates, United Kingdom.

Andorra

Andorra has met all aspects of the terms of reference (OECD, 2021[1]) (ToR) for the calendar year 2022 (year in review), except for identifying all potential exchange jurisdictions for future rulings (ToR I.A.2.1) and for ensuring that the information is completed in the required form (II.B.4) and exchanges are performed in accordance with the timelines (ToR II.B.5 and II.B.6). Andorra receives two recommendations on these points for the year in review.

In the prior year report, as well as in the 2017-2020 peer reviews, Andorra had received the same two recommendations. As they have not been addressed, the recommendations remain in place.

Andorra can legally issue five types of rulings within the scope of the transparency framework.

In practice, Andorra issued no rulings within the scope of the transparency framework.[1]

As no exchanges were required to take place, no peer input was received in respect of the exchanges of information on rulings received from Andorra.

Information gathering process (ToR I.A)

16. Andorra can legally issue the following five types of rulings within the scope of the transparency framework: (i) preferential regimes;[2] (ii) cross-border unilateral APAs and any other cross-border unilateral tax rulings (such as an advance tax ruling) covering transfer pricing or the application of transfer pricing principles; (iii) rulings providing for unilateral downward adjustments; (iv) permanent establishment rulings; and (v) related party conduit rulings.

Past rulings (ToR I.A.1.1, I.A.1.2, I.A.2.1, I.A.2.2)

17. For Andorra, past rulings are any tax rulings within scope that are issued either (i) on or after 1 January 2015 but before 1 April 2017; and (ii) on or after 1 January 2012 but before 1 January 2015, provided they were still in effect as at 1 January 2015.

18. In the prior years' peer review reports, it was determined that Andorra's undertakings to identify past rulings and all potential exchange jurisdictions were sufficient to meet the minimum standard. Andorra's implementation in this regard remains unchanged, and therefore continues to meet the minimum standard.

Future rulings (ToR I.A.1.1, I.A.1.2, I.A.2.1)

19. For Andorra, future rulings are any tax rulings within scope that are issued on or after 1 April 2017.

20. In the prior years' peer review reports, it was determined future rulings were able to be identified, but that the information on potential exchange jurisdictions was not always being collected, and instead this was being performed by the application of the "best efforts approach." The prior years' reports noted that Andorra intended to amend the application process to require the taxpayer to identify all relevant jurisdictions when requesting the ruling.

21. Andorra adopted this amendment in the beginning of 2023, and this will be taken into account in the next year's peer review report. Since the amendment did not take place during the year in review, Andorra is recommended to continue its efforts to ensure that all potential exchange jurisdictions are identified swiftly for all future rulings.

Review and supervision (ToR I.A.3)

22. In the prior years' peer review reports, it was determined that Andorra's review and supervision mechanism was sufficient to meet the minimum standard. Andorra's implementation in this regard remains unchanged, and therefore continues to meet the minimum standard.

Conclusion on section A

23. Andorra has met all of the ToR for the information gathering process except for identifying all potential exchange jurisdictions for future rulings (ToR I.A.2.1). Andorra is recommended to ensure that all potential exchange jurisdictions are identified swiftly for all future rulings.

Exchange of information (ToR II.B)

Legal basis for spontaneous exchange of information (ToR II.B.1, II.B.2)

24. Andorra has the necessary domestic legal basis to exchange information spontaneously. Andorra notes that there are no legal or practical impediments that prevent the spontaneous exchange of information on rulings as contemplated in the Action 5 minimum standard.

25. Andorra has international agreements permitting spontaneous exchange of information, including: (i) the *Multilateral Convention on Mutual Administrative Assistance in Tax Matters: Amended by the 2010*

Protocol (OECD/Council of Europe, 2011[2]) ("the Convention") and (ii) bilateral agreements in force with 28 jurisdictions.[3]

Completion and exchange of templates (ToR II.B.3, II.B.4, II.B.5, II.B.6, II.B.7)

26. In the prior years' peer review reports, it was determined that Andorra's process for the completion and exchange of templates met all the ToR, except for undertaking spontaneous exchange of information on tax rulings within the scope of the transparency framework (ToR II.B). Therefore, Andorra was recommended to complete the templates for all relevant rulings and to ensure that the exchanges of information on rulings occur as soon as possible.

27. In the prior years' peer review reports, it was determined that Andorra's previously issued rulings related to preferential regimes were related to wholly domestic taxpayers without any related parties in a foreign jurisdiction, and therefore, no exchange of information needed to take place. However, in the event that a relevant ruling is issued in future, Andorra will need to have the processes in place to complete the templates and conduct the exchanges in accordance with the transparency framework.

28. In the prior years' peer review reports, it was noted that Andorra intends to require taxpayers to provide all relevant information needed to complete the template contained in Annex C of the Action 5 Report (OECD, 2015[3]). Andorra is in the process of including such an obligation in future tax reforms. Andorra notes that modifications to the tax law have been approved by the Andorran parliament in 2023 and will enter into force in 2024.

29. As these issues have not yet been resolved and the modification to the tax law has not been approved in the year of review, the recommendation remains in place. In particular, Andorra is recommended to ensure that the information on future rulings is completed in the form of the template contained in Annex C of the Action 5 Report (OECD, 2015[3]) (ToR II.B.4), to put in place appropriate systems to ensure that information on rulings is transmitted to the competent authority responsible for international exchange of information without undue delay (ToR II.B.5) and to ensure that the information to be exchanged is transmitted to the relevant jurisdictions in accordance with the agreed timelines (ToR II.B.6).

30. As there were no exchanges for the year in review, no data on the timeliness of exchanges can be reported.

Conclusion on section B

31. Andorra has met all of the ToR for the exchange of information process except for ensuring that the information is completed in the required form (II.B.4) and having a process in place to ensure any exchanges will be performed in accordance with the timelines (ToR II.B.5 and II.B.6). Andorra is recommended to continue its efforts to put in place the necessary process to complete the information in the form of Annex C of the Action 5 Report (OECD, 2015[3]), to ensure that information is submitted to the Competent Authority without undue delay and exchanges are performed in accordance with the timelines.

Statistics (ToR IV.D)

32. As no rulings were issued, no statistics can be reported.

Matters related to intellectual property regimes (ToR I.A.1.3)

33. In the prior years' peer review reports, it was determined that Andorra's information gathering and exchange of information processes for matters related to intellectual property regimes[4] were sufficient to

meet the minimum standard. Andorra's implementation in this regard remains unchanged and therefore continues to meet the minimum standard.

Summary of recommendations on implementation of the transparency framework

Aspect of implementation of the transparency framework that should be improved	Recommendation for improvement
Andorra still experiences difficulties in identifying all potential exchange jurisdictions for future rulings.	Andorra is recommended to continue its efforts to ensure that all potential exchange jurisdictions are identified swiftly for all future rulings. This recommendation remains unchanged since the 2017, 2018, 2019, 2020 and 2021 peer review reports.
Andorra has been developing a process to ensure that the information is completed in the required form and exchanges are performed in accordance with the timelines. Andorra noted that modifications to the tax law have been approved by the Andorran parliament in 2023 and will enter into force in 2024. As these issues have not yet been resolved and the modification to the tax law has not been approved in the year of review, this will be taken into account during next years' peer review.	Andorra is recommended to continue its efforts to put in place the necessary process to complete the information in the form of Annex C of the Action 5 Report, to ensure that information is submitted to the Competent Authority without undue delay and exchanges are performed in accordance with the timelines. These recommendations remain unchanged since the 2017, 2018, 2019, 2020 and 2021 peer review reports but since the 2019 peer review report they are targeted to specific aspects of the ToR that still need to be put in place.

References

OECD (2021), *BEPS Action 5 on Harmful Tax Practices - Terms of Reference and Methodology for the Conduct of the Peer Reviews of the Action 5 Transparency Framework*, OECD Publishing, Paris, https://www.oecd.org/tax/beps/beps-action-5-harmful-tax-practices-peer-review-transparency-framework.pdf. [1]

OECD (2015), *Countering Harmful Tax Practices More Effectively, Taking into Account Transparency and Substance, Action 5 - 2015 Final Report*, OECD/G20 Base Erosion and Profit Shifting Project, OECD Publishing, Paris, https://doi.org/10.1787/9789264241190-en. [3]

OECD/Council of Europe (2011), *The Multilateral Convention on Mutual Administrative Assistance in Tax Matters: Amended by the 2010 Protocol*, OECD Publishing, Paris, https://doi.org/10.1787/9789264115606-en. [2]

Notes

[1] Andorra has issued 169 past rulings and 96 future rulings. All these rulings were related to preferential regimes, but all taxpayers were domestic taxpayers (not part of a multinational group) and therefore no exchanges on these rulings were required for the Action 5 transparency framework.

[2] 1) Holding company regime and 2) Special regime for exploitation of certain intangibles.

[3] Participating jurisdictions to the Convention are available here: www.oecd.org/tax/exchange-of-tax-information/convention-on-mutual-administrative-assistance-in-tax-matters.htm. Andorra also has bilateral agreements with Argentina, Australia, Austria, Belgium, Cyprus, Denmark, Faroe Islands, Finland, France, Germany, Greenland, Iceland, Italy, Korea, Liechtenstein, Luxembourg, Malta, Monaco, Netherlands, Norway, Poland, Portugal, San Marino, Spain, Sweden, Switzerland and United Arab Emirates.

[4] Special regime for exploitation of certain intangibles.

Angola

Angola has met all aspects of the terms of reference (OECD, 2021[1]) (ToR) for the calendar year 2022 (year in review), except for identifying future rulings and all potential exchange jurisdictions (ToR I.A and for exchanging information on the tax rulings in a timely manner (ToR II.B). Angola receives two recommendations on these points for the year in review.

In the prior year report, as well as in the 2017-2020 peer reviews, Angola had received the same two recommendations. One recommendation has been partially addressed but remains in place for the other part and the other recommendation has not been addressed and remains in place.

Angola can legally issue five types of rulings within the scope of the transparency framework.

In practice, Angola issued rulings within the scope of the transparency framework as follows:

Type of ruling	Number of rulings
Past rulings	0
Future rulings in the period 1 April 2016 – 31 December 2016	1
Future rulings in the calendar year 2017	0
Future rulings in the calendar year 2018	0
Future rulings in the calendar year 2019	0
Future rulings in the calendar year 2020	0
Future rulings in the calendar year 2021	0
Future rulings in the year in review	2

No peer input was received in respect of the exchanges of information on rulings received from Angola.

Information gathering process (ToR I.A)

34. Angola can legally issue the following five types of rulings within the scope of the transparency framework: (i) preferential regimes;[1] (ii) cross-border unilateral APAs and any other cross-border unilateral tax rulings (such as an advance tax ruling) covering transfer pricing or the application of transfer pricing principles; (iii) rulings providing for unilateral downward adjustments; (iv) permanent establishment rulings; and (v) related party conduit rulings.

Past rulings (ToR I.A.1.1, I.A.1.2, I.A.2.1, I.A.2.2)

35. For Angola, past rulings are any tax rulings within scope that are issued either (i) on or after 1 January 2015 but before 1 April 2017; and (ii) on or after 1 January 2012 but before 1 January 2015, provided they were still in effect as at 1 January 2015.

36. In the prior years' peer review reports, it was determined that Angola had not yet identified all past rulings and potential exchange jurisdictions. During the year in review, Angola built an internal database that keeps track of all issued rulings. Angola confirms that there were no past rulings issued and therefore, no potential exchange jurisdictions needed to be identified. The previous years' recommendation is now removed.

Future rulings (ToR I.A.1.1, I.A.1.2, I.A.2.1)

37. For Angola, future rulings are any tax rulings within scope that are issued on or after 1 April 2017.

38. In the prior years' peer review reports, it was determined that Angola was following guidelines covering which rulings would fall within the scope of the transparency framework and what information should be kept in order to meet the level of detail required by the transparency framework.

39. In the prior year's peer review report, it was noted Angola started to identify all rulings that have been issued by the Angola Revenue Administration (AGT). During the year in review, Angola developed an internal database where all issued rulings are recorded. In accordance with internal procedures, the different departments within AGT send the identified rulings to the International Cooperation Department. This department is responsible for analysing whether the rulings fall within the scope of the transparency framework, and saves the rulings in the database. When issuing a ruling, the AGT requests the taxpayer for information, but not in all cases on the immediate parent, ultimate parent and related parties with which the taxpayer entered into a transaction with. Therefore, Angola is recommended to put in place a process of identifying potential exchange jurisdictions.

Review and supervision (ToR I.A.3)

40. In the prior years' peer review reports, it was determined that Angola did not yet have a review and supervision mechanism for past rulings under the transparency framework. During the year in review, Angola implemented a review and supervision mechanism for future rulings by requiring that the information on tax rulings be recorded in hard copy and electronically in spreadsheets with the name, date and topic of the information requested or issue being complained or appealed. The previous years' recommendation is now removed.

Conclusion on section A

41. Angola is recommended to finalise its information gathering process for identifying future rulings and all potential exchange jurisdictions as soon as possible (ToR I.A).

Exchange of information (ToR II.B)

Legal basis for spontaneous exchange of information (ToR II.B.1, II.B.2)

42. In the prior years' peer review reports, it was determined that Angola did not have the necessary domestic legal basis to exchange information spontaneously. Angola is still in the process of putting in place the necessary domestic legal basis to exchange information spontaneously.

43. Angola has international agreements permitting spontaneous exchange of information, including bilateral agreements in force with two jurisdictions.[2] Angola is not a party to the *Multilateral Convention on Mutual Administrative Assistance in Tax Matters: Amended by the 2010 Protocol* (OECD/Council of Europe, 2011[2]) ("the Convention"). Angola is encouraged to continue its efforts to expand its international exchange of information instruments to be able to exchange information on rulings. It is noted, however, that jurisdictions are assessed on their compliance with the transparency framework in respect of the exchange of information network in effect for the year of the particular annual review.

Completion and exchange of templates (ToR II.B.3, II.B.4, II.B.5, II.B.6, II.B.7)

44. In the prior years' peer review reports, it was determined that Angola is still developing a process to complete the templates on relevant rulings, to make them available to the Competent Authority for exchange of information and to exchange them with relevant jurisdictions.

45. An information exchange unit was created to assume the role of the Competent Authority and Angola's tax offices are henceforth required to send reports to this unit. Angola notes that during the year in review, a process was put in place to require that the list of issued rulings is send on a monthly basis to the Competent Authority. The Competent Authority is responsible for completing the template in Annex C of the BEPS Action 5 report (OECD, 2015[3]). The summary section will be competed in line with the FHTP internal guidance. The information is sent to jurisdictions within three months after the Competent Authority received the list of issued rulings.

46. Angola is still in the process negotiating to obtain an electronic tool for the exchange of information. Angola confirms that until then, information is sent either hard copy or via an official encrypted channel agreed between the parties.

47. As Angola did not have the necessary legal basis to conduct exchanges, no data on the timeliness of exchanges can be reported.

Conclusion on section B

48. Angola is recommended to continue its efforts to put in place a domestic legal framework allowing spontaneous exchange of information on rulings and to complete the templates for all relevant rulings and to ensure that the exchanges of information on rulings occur as soon as possible (ToR II.B).

Statistics (ToR IV.D)

49. The statistics for the year in review are as follows:

Category of ruling	Number of exchanges	Jurisdictions exchanged with
Ruling related to a preferential regime	0	N/A
Cross-border unilateral APAs and any other cross-border unilateral tax rulings (such as an advance tax ruling) covering transfer pricing or the application of transfer pricing principles	0	N/A
Cross-border rulings providing for a unilateral downward adjustment to the taxpayer's taxable profits that is not directly reflected in the taxpayer's financial / commercial accounts	0	N/A
Permanent establishment rulings	0	N/A
Related party conduit rulings	*De minimis rule* applies	N/A
De minimis rule	2	N/A
Total	2	

Matters related to intellectual property regimes (ToR I.A.1.3)

50. Angola does not offer an intellectual property regime for which transparency requirements under the Action 5 Report (OECD, 2015[3]) were imposed.

Summary of recommendations on implementation of the transparency framework

Aspect of implementation of the transparency framework that should be improved	Recommendation for improvement
Angola has not yet finalised the steps to have in place its necessary information and gathering process.	Angola is recommended to finalise its information gathering process for identifying future rulings and all potential exchange jurisdictions as soon as possible. During the year in review, Angola built an internal database that keeps track of all issued rulings and confirmed there were no past rulings issued. In addition, Angola implemented a review and supervision mechanism for future rulings. This recommendation has been partly addressed but remains in place for the other part since the 2017, 2018, 2019, 2020 and 2021 peer review reports.
Angola has not yet finalised the steps to have effective compulsory spontaneous exchange of information on the tax rulings within the scope of the transparency framework	Angola is recommended to continue to put in place a domestic legal framework allowing spontaneous exchange of information on rulings and to continue its efforts to complete the templates for all relevant rulings and to ensure that the exchanges of information on rulings occur as soon as possible. This recommendation remains unchanged since the 2017, 2018, 2019, 2020 and 2021 peer review reports.

References

OECD (2021), *BEPS Action 5 on Harmful Tax Practices - Terms of Reference and Methodology for the Conduct of the Peer Reviews of the Action 5 Transparency Framework*, OECD Publishing, Paris, https://www.oecd.org/tax/beps/beps-action-5-harmful-tax-practices-peer-review-transparency-framework.pdf. [1]

OECD (2015), *Countering Harmful Tax Practices More Effectively, Taking into Account Transparency and Substance, Action 5 - 2015 Final Report*, OECD/G20 Base Erosion and Profit Shifting Project, OECD Publishing, Paris, https://doi.org/10.1787/9789264241190-en. [3]

OECD/Council of Europe (2011), *The Multilateral Convention on Mutual Administrative Assistance in Tax Matters: Amended by the 2010 Protocol*, OECD Publishing, Paris, https://doi.org/10.1787/9789264115606-en. [2]

Notes

[1] A special tax regime for oil and gas.

[2] Angola has bilateral agreements with China (People's Republic of), Portugal and the United Arab Emirates.

Antigua and Barbuda

Antigua and Barbuda has met all aspects of the terms of reference (OECD, 2021[1]) (ToR) for the calendar year 2022 (year in review), and no recommendations are made.

Antigua and Barbuda can legally issue four types of rulings within the scope of the transparency framework.

In practice, Antigua and Barbuda issued no rulings within the scope of the transparency framework.

As no exchanges were required to take place, no peer input was received in respect of the exchanges of information on rulings received from Antigua and Barbuda.

Information gathering process (ToR I.A)

51. Antigua and Barbuda can legally issue the following four types of rulings within the scope of the transparency framework: (i) (cross-border unilateral APAs and any other cross-border unilateral tax rulings (such as an advance tax ruling) covering transfer pricing or the application of transfer pricing principles; (ii) rulings providing for unilateral downward adjustments; (iii) permanent establishment rulings; and (iv) related party conduit rulings.

52. For Antigua and Barbuda, past rulings are any tax rulings issued prior to 1 March 2019. Future rulings are any tax rulings within scope that are issued on or after 1 March 2019.

53. In the prior year's peer review reports, it was determined that Antigua and Barbuda's undertakings to identify past and future rulings and all potential exchange jurisdictions were sufficient to meet the minimum standard. In addition, it was determined that Antigua and Barbuda's review and supervision mechanism was sufficient to meet the minimum standard. Antigua and Barbuda's implementation remains unchanged, and therefore continues to meet the minimum standard.

54. Antigua and Barbuda has met all of the ToR for the information gathering and no recommendations are made.

Exchange of information (ToR II.B)

55. Antigua and Barbuda has the necessary domestic legal basis to exchange information spontaneously. Antigua and Barbuda notes that there are no legal or practical impediments that prevent the spontaneous exchange of information on rulings as contemplated in the Action 5 minimum standard.

56. Antigua and Barbuda has international agreements permitting spontaneous exchange of information, including: (i) the *Multilateral Convention on Mutual Administrative Assistance in Tax Matters: Amended by the 2010 Protocol* (OECD/Council of Europe, 2011[2]) ("the Convention"), (ii) bilateral agreements in force with 11 jurisdictions and (iii) tax information exchange agreements in force with 11 jurisdictions.[1]

57. During the year in review, no exchanges were required to take place and no data on the timeliness of exchanges is reported.

58. In the prior year's peer review report, it was determined that Antigua and Barbuda's process for the completion and exchange of templates were sufficient to meet the minimum standard. With respect to past rulings, no further action was required. Antigua and Barbuda's implementation in this regard remains unchanged and therefore continues to meet the minimum standard.

59. Antigua and Barbuda has the necessary legal basis for spontaneous exchange of information. Antigua and Barbuda has met all of the ToR for the exchange of information process and no recommendations are made

Statistics (ToR IV.D)

60. As no rulings were issued, no statistics can be reported.

Matters related to intellectual property regimes (ToR I.A.1.3)

61. Antigua and Barbuda does not offer an intellectual property regime for which transparency requirements under the Action 5 Report (OECD, 2015[3]) were imposed.

Summary of recommendations on implementation of the transparency framework

Aspect of implementation of the transparency framework that should be improved	Recommendation for improvement
	No recommendations are made.

References

OECD (2021), *BEPS Action 5 on Harmful Tax Practices - Terms of Reference and Methodology for the Conduct of the Peer Reviews of the Action 5 Transparency Framework*, OECD Publishing, Paris, https://www.oecd.org/tax/beps/beps-action-5-harmful-tax-practices-peer-review-transparency-framework.pdf. [1]

OECD (2015), *Countering Harmful Tax Practices More Effectively, Taking into Account Transparency and Substance, Action 5 - 2015 Final Report*, OECD/G20 Base Erosion and Profit Shifting Project, OECD Publishing, Paris, https://doi.org/10.1787/9789264241190-en. [3]

OECD/Council of Europe (2011), *The Multilateral Convention on Mutual Administrative Assistance in Tax Matters: Amended by the 2010 Protocol*, OECD Publishing, Paris, https://doi.org/10.1787/9789264115606-en. [2]

Note

[1] Participating jurisdictions to the Convention are available here: www.oecd.org/tax/exchange-of-tax-information/convention-on-mutual-administrative-assistance-in-tax-matters.htm. Antigua and Barbuda also has bilateral agreements with Switzerland and jurisdictions party to the CARICOM agreement. Tax information exchange agreements with Aruba, Australia, Denmark, Finland, France, Germany, Ireland, Netherlands, Norway, United Kingdom and United States also permit for the spontaneous exchange of information.

Argentina

Argentina has met all aspects of the terms of reference (OECD, 2021[1]) (ToR) for the calendar year 2022 (year in review), and no recommendations are made.

Argentina can legally issue five types of rulings within the scope of the transparency framework.

In practice, Argentina issued rulings within the scope of the transparency framework as follows:

Type of ruling	Number of rulings
Past rulings	2
Future rulings in the period 1 April 2016 – 31 December 2016	0
Future rulings in the calendar year 2017	1
Future rulings in the calendar year 2018	0
Future rulings in the calendar year 2019	1
Future rulings in the calendar year 2020	0
Future rulings in the calendar year 2021	0
Future rulings in the year in review	0

As no exchanges were required to take place, no peer input was received in respect of the exchanges of information on rulings received from Argentina.

Information gathering process (ToR I.A)

62. Argentina can legally issue the following five types of rulings within the scope of the transparency framework: (i) preferential regimes;[1] (ii) cross-border unilateral APAs and any other cross-border unilateral tax rulings (such as an advance tax ruling) covering transfer pricing or the application of transfer pricing principles; (iii) rulings providing for unilateral downward adjustments; (iv) permanent establishment rulings; and (v) related party conduit rulings.

63. For Argentina, past rulings are any tax rulings within scope that are issued either: (i) on or after 1 January 2014 but before 1 April 2016; or (ii) on or after 1 January 2010 but before 1 January 2014, provided they were still in effect as at 1 January 2014. Future rulings are any tax rulings within scope that are issued on or after 1 April 2016.

64. In the prior years' peer review reports, it was determined that Argentina's undertakings to identify past and future rulings and all potential exchange jurisdictions were sufficient to meet the minimum standard. In addition, it was determined that Argentina's review and supervision mechanism was sufficient to meet the minimum standard. Argentina's implementation remains unchanged, and therefore continues to meet the minimum standard.

65. Argentina has met all of the ToR for the information gathering process and no recommendations are made.

Exchange of information (ToR II.B)

66. Argentina has the necessary domestic legal basis to exchange information spontaneously. Argentina notes that there are no legal or practical impediments that prevent the spontaneous exchange of information on rulings as contemplated in the Action 5 minimum standard.

67. Argentina has international agreements permitting spontaneous exchange of information, including: (i) the *Multilateral Convention on Mutual Administrative Assistance in Tax Matters: Amended by the 2010 Protocol* (OECD/Council of Europe, 2011[2]) ("the Convention") and (ii) bilateral agreements in force with 24 jurisdictions.[2]

68. During the year in review, no exchanges were required to take place and no data on the timeliness of exchanges is reported.

69. In the prior years' peer review reports, it was determined that Argentina's process for the completion and exchange of templates were sufficient to meet the minimum standard. With respect to past rulings, no further action was required. Argentina's implementation in this regard remains unchanged and therefore continues to meet the minimum standard.

70. Argentina has the necessary legal basis for spontaneous exchange of information, a process for completing the templates in a timely way and has completed all exchanges. Argentina has met all of the ToR for the exchange of information process and no recommendations are made.

Statistics (ToR IV.D)

71. As no rulings were issued, no statistics can be reported.

Matters related to intellectual property regimes (ToR I.A.1.3)

72. Argentina does not offer an intellectual property regime for which transparency requirements under the Action 5 Report (OECD, 2015[3]) were imposed.

Summary of recommendations on implementation of the transparency framework

Aspect of implementation of the transparency framework that should be improved	Recommendation for improvement
	No recommendations are made.

References

OECD (2021), *BEPS Action 5 on Harmful Tax Practices - Terms of Reference and Methodology for the Conduct of the Peer Reviews of the Action 5 Transparency Framework*, OECD Publishing, Paris, https://www.oecd.org/tax/beps/beps-action-5-harmful-tax-practices-peer-review-transparency-framework.pdf. [1]

OECD (2015), *Countering Harmful Tax Practices More Effectively, Taking into Account Transparency and Substance, Action 5 - 2015 Final Report*, OECD/G20 Base Erosion and Profit Shifting Project, OECD Publishing, Paris, https://doi.org/10.1787/9789264241190-en. [3]

OECD/Council of Europe (2011), *The Multilateral Convention on Mutual Administrative Assistance in Tax Matters: Amended by the 2010 Protocol*, OECD Publishing, Paris, https://doi.org/10.1787/9789264115606-en. [2]

Notes

[1] Promotional regime for software industry.

[2] Participating jurisdictions to the Convention are available here: www.oecd.org/tax/exchange-of-tax-information/convention-on-mutual-administrative-assistance-in-tax-matters.htm. Argentina also has bilateral agreements with Aruba, Australia, Azerbaijan, Belgium, Bolivia, Brazil, Canada, Chile, Denmark, Ecuador, Finland, France, Italy, Mexico, Netherlands, Norway, Qatar, Russia, Spain, Sweden, United Arab Emirates, United States, United Kingdom and Venezuela.

Armenia

Armenia is continuing to take steps to implement the aspects of the terms of reference (OECD, 2021[1]) (ToR) for the transparency framework and to commence administrative preparations to ensure that the necessary information gathering process for relevant rulings is finalised and in place (ToR I.A) and that information on rulings is exchanged in accordance with the form and timelines under the transparency framework (ToR II.B). Armenia receives two recommendations on these points for the calendar year 2022 (year in review).

In the prior year report, as well as in the 2019 and 2020 peer review reports, Armenia had received the same recommendations. As they have not been addressed, the recommendations remain in place.

Armenia can legally issue two types of rulings within the scope of the transparency framework.

In practice, Armenia issued no rulings within the scope of the transparency framework.

As no exchanges were required to take place, no peer input was received in respect of the exchanges of information on rulings received from Armenia.

Information gathering process (ToR I.A)

73. Armenia can legally issue the following two types of rulings within the scope of the transparency framework: (i) preferential regimes;[1] and (ii) permanent establishment rulings.[2]

Past rulings (ToR I.A.1.1, I.A.1.2, I.A.2.1, I.A.2.2)

74. For Armenia, past rulings are any tax rulings issued prior to 1 September 2019. However, there is no obligation for Armenia to conduct spontaneous exchange information on past rulings.

Future rulings (ToR I.A.1.1, I.A.1.2, I.A.2.1)

75. For Armenia, future rulings are any tax rulings within scope that are issued on or after 1 September 2019.

76. In the prior years' peer review reports, it was determined that processes to ensure the implementation of the obligations relating to the transparency framework with regard to the information gathering process were not yet in place (ToR I.A). Therefore, Armenia was recommended to finalise its information gathering process for identifying all future rulings and potential exchange jurisdictions, as soon as possible.

77. During the year in review, Armenia indicates that a system is in the process of being finalised for the identification and registration of issued tax rulings. Armenia already developed this system, but it still needs to be implemented. As this process is still ongoing, the previous years' recommendation remains in place.

Review and supervision (ToR I.A.3)

78. In the prior years' peer review reports, it was determined that Armenia's review and supervision mechanism was sufficient to meet the minimum standard. Armenia's implementation in this regard remains unchanged, and therefore continues to meet the minimum standard.

Conclusion on section A

79. Armenia is recommended to continue its efforts to finalise and have in place the necessary information gathering process for identifying all relevant rulings and potential exchange jurisdictions, as soon as possible (ToR I.A).

Exchange of information (ToR II.B)

Legal basis for spontaneous exchange of information (ToR II.B.1, II.B.2)

80. Armenia has the necessary domestic legal basis to exchange information spontaneously. Armenia notes that there are no legal or practical impediments that prevent the spontaneous exchange of information on rulings as contemplated in the Action 5 minimum standard.

81. Armenia has international agreements permitting spontaneous exchange of information, including: (i) the *Multilateral Convention on Mutual Administrative Assistance in Tax Matters: Amended by the 2010 Protocol* (OECD/Council of Europe, 2011[2]) ("the Convention") and (ii) bilateral agreements in force with 51 jurisdictions.[3]

Completion and exchange of templates (ToR II.B.3, II.B.4, II.B.5, II.B.6, II.B.7)

82. In the prior years' peer review reports, it was determined that Armenia's process for the completion and exchange of templates was not yet in place. Therefore, Armenia was recommended to develop a process to complete the templates on relevant rulings and to ensure that the exchanges of information on

rulings occur in accordance with the form and timelines under the transparency framework. With respect to past rulings, no action was required.

83. During the year in review, Armenia indicates that a system is in the process of being finalised for the completion and exchange of templates on relevant rulings according to the FHTP framework and timelines. As this process is still ongoing, the previous years' recommendation remains in place.

84. During the year in review, no exchanges were required to take place and no data on the timeliness of exchanges is reported.

Conclusion on section B

85. Armenia has the necessary legal basis for spontaneous exchange of information. Armenia is recommended to continue its efforts to develop a process to complete the templates for all relevant rulings and to ensure that the exchanges of information on rulings occur in accordance with the form and timelines under the transparency framework as soon as possible (ToR II.B).

Statistics (ToR IV.D)

86. As no rulings were issued, no statistics can be reported.

Matters related to intellectual property regimes (ToR I.A.1.3)

87. Armenia does not offer an intellectual property regime for which transparency requirements under the Action 5 Report (OECD, 2015[3]) were imposed.

Summary of recommendations on implementation of the transparency framework

Aspect of implementation of the transparency framework that should be improved	Recommendation for improvement
Armenia is in the process to finalise the information gathering process and to put in place a system for the identification and registration of issued tax rulings.	Armenia is recommended to continue its efforts to finalise and have in place the necessary information gathering process for identifying all relevant rulings and potential exchange jurisdictions, as soon as possible. This recommendation remains unchanged since the 2019, 2020 and 2021 peer review reports.
Armenia does not have a process to complete the templates on relevant rulings, to make them available to the Competent Authority for exchange of information, and to exchange them with relevant jurisdictions.	Armenia is recommended to continue its efforts to develop a process to complete the templates for all relevant rulings and to ensure that the exchanges of information on rulings occur in accordance with the form and timelines under the transparency framework as soon as possible. This recommendation remains unchanged since the 2019, 2020 and 2021 peer review reports.

References

OECD (2021), *BEPS Action 5 on Harmful Tax Practices - Terms of Reference and Methodology for the Conduct of the Peer Reviews of the Action 5 Transparency Framework*, OECD Publishing, Paris, https://www.oecd.org/tax/beps/beps-action-5-harmful-tax-practices-peer-review-transparency-framework.pdf. [1]

OECD (2015), *Countering Harmful Tax Practices More Effectively, Taking into Account Transparency and Substance, Action 5 - 2015 Final Report*, OECD/G20 Base Erosion and Profit Shifting Project, OECD Publishing, Paris, https://doi.org/10.1787/9789264241190-en. [3]

OECD/Council of Europe (2011), *The Multilateral Convention on Mutual Administrative Assistance in Tax Matters: Amended by the 2010 Protocol*, OECD Publishing, Paris, https://doi.org/10.1787/9789264115606-en. [2]

Notes

[1] 1) Free economic zones and 2) Information technology projects.

[2] As of 1 January 2024, Armenia will be able to issue cross-border unilateral APAs and any other cross-border unilateral tax rulings (such as an advance tax ruling) covering transfer pricing or the application of transfer pricing principles.

[3] Participating jurisdictions to the Convention are available here: www.oecd.org/tax/exchange-of-tax-information/convention-on-mutual-administrative-assistance-in-tax-matters.htm. Armenia also has bilateral agreements with Austria, Belarus, Belgium, Bulgaria, Canada, China (People's Republic of), Croatia, Cyprus, Czechia, Denmark, Estonia, Finland, France, Georgia, Germany, Greece, Hungary, India, Indonesia, Iran, Ireland, Israel, Italy, Kazakhstan, Kuwait, Kyrgyzstan, Latvia, Lebanon, Lithuania, Luxembourg, Malta, Moldova, Netherlands, Poland, Qatar, Romania, Russia, Serbia, Singapore, Slovak Republic, Slovenia, Spain, Sweden, Switzerland, Syrian Arab Republic, Thailand, Tajikistan, Turkmenistan, Ukraine, United Arab Emirates and United Kingdom.

Aruba

Aruba has met all aspects of the terms of reference (OECD, 2021[1]) (ToR) for the calendar year 2022 (year in review), and no recommendations are made.

In the prior year report, Aruba did not receive any recommendations.

Aruba can legally issue five types of rulings within the scope of the transparency framework.

In practice, Aruba issued no rulings within the scope of the transparency framework.

As no exchanges were required to take place, no peer input was received in respect of the exchanges of information on rulings received from Aruba.

Information gathering process (ToR I.A)

88. Aruba can legally issue the following five types of rulings within the scope of the transparency framework: (i) preferential regimes;[1] (ii) cross-border unilateral APAs and any other cross-border unilateral tax rulings (such as an advance tax ruling) covering transfer pricing or the application of transfer pricing principles; (iii) rulings providing for unilateral downward adjustments; (iv) permanent establishment rulings; and (v) related party conduit rulings.

89. For Aruba, past rulings are any tax rulings issued prior to 1 September 2018. However, there is no obligation for Aruba to conduct spontaneous exchange information on past rulings. Future rulings are any tax rulings within scope that are issued on or after 1 September 2018.

90. In the prior year's peer review report, it was determined that Aruba's undertakings to identify future rulings and all potential exchange jurisdictions were sufficient to meet the minimum standard. In addition, it was determined that Aruba's review and supervision mechanism was sufficient to meet the minimum standard. Aruba's implementation remains unchanged, and therefore continues to meet the minimum standard.

91. Aruba has met all of the ToR for the information gathering process and no recommendations are made.

Exchange of information (ToR II.B)

92. Aruba has the necessary domestic legal basis to exchange information spontaneously. Aruba notes that there are no legal or practical impediments that prevent the spontaneous exchange of information on rulings as contemplated in the Action 5 minimum standard.

93. Aruba has international agreements permitting spontaneous exchange of information, including being a jurisdiction participating in (i) the *Multilateral Convention on Mutual Administrative Assistance in Tax Matters: Amended by the 2010 Protocol* (OECD/Council of Europe, 2011[2]) ("the Convention") and (ii) bilateral agreements in force with 25 jurisdictions.[2]

94. In the prior years' peer review reports, it was determined that Aruba's process for the completion and exchange of templates were sufficient to meet the minimum standard. Aruba's implementation in this regard remains unchanged and therefore continues to meet the minimum standard.

95. During the year in review, no exchanges were required to take place and no data on the timeliness of exchanges is reported.

96. Aruba has the necessary legal basis for spontaneous exchange of information, a process for completing the templates in a timely way and has completed all exchanges. Aruba has met all of the ToR for the exchange of information process and no recommendations are made.

Statistics (ToR IV.D)

97. As no rulings were issued, no statistics can be reported.

Matters related to intellectual property regimes (ToR I.A.1.3)

98. In the prior years' peer review reports, it was determined that Aruba's information gathering and exchange of information processes for matters related to intellectual property regimes[3] were sufficient to

meet the minimum standard. Aruba's implementation in this regard remains unchanged and therefore continues to meet the minimum standard.

Summary of recommendations on implementation of the transparency framework

Aspect of implementation of the transparency framework that should be improved	Recommendation for improvement
	No recommendations are made.

References

OECD (2021), *BEPS Action 5 on Harmful Tax Practices - Terms of Reference and Methodology for the Conduct of the Peer Reviews of the Action 5 Transparency Framework*, OECD Publishing, Paris, https://www.oecd.org/tax/beps/beps-action-5-harmful-tax-practices-peer-review-transparency-framework.pdf. [1]

OECD (2015), *Countering Harmful Tax Practices More Effectively, Taking into Account Transparency and Substance, Action 5 - 2015 Final Report*, OECD/G20 Base Erosion and Profit Shifting Project, OECD Publishing, Paris, https://doi.org/10.1787/9789264241190-en. [3]

OECD/Council of Europe (2011), *The Multilateral Convention on Mutual Administrative Assistance in Tax Matters: Amended by the 2010 Protocol*, OECD Publishing, Paris, https://doi.org/10.1787/9789264115606-en. [2]

Notes

[1] Exempt companies, 2) Investment promotion, 3) Free zone, 4) Transparency regime and 5) Shipping regime.

[2] Participating jurisdictions to the Convention are available here: www.oecd.org/tax/exchange-of-tax-information/convention-on-mutual-administrative-assistance-in-tax-matters.htm. Aruba also has bilateral agreements with Antigua and Barbuda, Argentina, Australia, Bahamas, Bermuda, British Virgin Islands, Canada, Cayman Islands, Czechia, Denmark, Faroe Islands, Finland, France, Greenland, Iceland, Mexico, Netherlands, Norway, Saint Kitts and Nevis, Saint Lucia, Saint Vincent and the Grenadines, Spain, Sweden, United Kingdom and United States.

[3] Exempt companies regime.

Australia

Australia has met all aspects of the terms of reference (OECD, 2021[1]) (ToR) for the calendar year 2022 (year in review), and no recommendations are made.

Australia can legally issue five types of rulings within the scope of the transparency framework.

In practice, Australia issued rulings within the scope of the transparency framework as follows:

Type of ruling	Number of rulings
Past rulings	202
Future rulings in the period 1 April 2016 – 31 December 2016	15
Future rulings in the calendar year 2017	13
Future rulings in the calendar year 2018	10
Future rulings in the calendar year 2019	15
Future rulings in the calendar year 2020	17
Future rulings in the calendar year 2021	3
Future rulings in the year in review	9

Peer input was received from one jurisdiction in respect of the exchanges of information on rulings received from Australia. The input was positive, noting that information was complete, in a correct format and received in a timely manner.

Information gathering process (ToR I.A)

99. Australia can legally the following five types of rulings within the scope of the transparency framework: (i) preferential regimes;[1] (ii) cross-border unilateral APAs and any other cross-border unilateral tax rulings (such as an advance tax ruling) covering transfer pricing or the application of transfer pricing principles; (iii) rulings providing for unilateral downward adjustments; (iv) permanent establishment rulings; and (v) related party conduit rulings.

100. For Australia, past rulings are any tax rulings within scope that are issued either: (i) on or after 1 January 2014 but before 1 April 2016; or (ii) on or after 1 January 2010 but before 1 January 2014, provided they were still in effect as at 1 January 2014. Future rulings are any tax rulings within scope that are issued on or after 1 April 2016.

101. In the prior years' peer review reports, it was determined that Australia's undertakings to identify past and future rulings and all potential exchange jurisdictions were sufficient to meet the minimum standard. In addition, it was determined that Australia's review and supervision mechanism was sufficient to meet the minimum standard. Australia's implementation remains unchanged, and therefore continues to meet the minimum standard.

102. Australia has met all of the ToR for the information gathering process and no recommendations are made.

Exchange of information (ToR II.B)

103. Australia has the necessary domestic legal basis to exchange information spontaneously. Australia notes that there are no legal or practical impediments that prevent the spontaneous exchange of information on rulings as contemplated in the Action 5 minimum standard.

104. Australia has international agreements permitting spontaneous exchange of information, including: (i) the *Multilateral Convention on Mutual Administrative Assistance in Tax Matters: Amended by the 2010 Protocol* (OECD/Council of Europe, 2011[2]) ("the Convention") and (ii) bilateral agreements in force with 45 jurisdictions.[2]

105. For the year in review, the timeliness of exchanges is as follows:

Future rulings within the scope of the transparency framework	Number of exchanges transmitted within three months of the information becoming available to the competent authority or immediately after legal impediments have been lifted	Delayed exchanges		
		Number of exchanges transmitted later than three months of the information on rulings becoming available to the competent authority	Reasons for the delays	Any other comments
	25	0	N/A	N/A

Follow-up requests received for exchange of the ruling	Number	Average time to provide response	Number of requests not answered
	0	N/A	N/A

106. In the prior years' peer review reports, it was determined that Australia's process for the completion and exchange of templates were sufficient to meet the minimum standard. With respect to past rulings, no further action was required. Australia's implementation in this regard remains unchanged and therefore continues to meet the minimum standard.

107. Australia has the necessary legal basis for spontaneous exchange of information, a process for completing the templates in a timely way and has completed all exchanges. Australia has met all of the ToR for the exchange of information process and no recommendations are made.

Statistics (ToR IV.D)

108. The statistics for the year in review are as follows:

Category of ruling	Number of exchanges	Jurisdictions exchanged with
Ruling related to a preferential regime	1	*De minims rule* applies
Cross-border unilateral APAs and any other cross-border unilateral tax rulings (such as an advance tax ruling) covering transfer pricing or the application of transfer pricing principles	14	Curaçao, Netherlands, Singapore, Switzerland, United Kingdom, United States
Cross-border rulings providing for a unilateral downward adjustment to the taxpayer's taxable profits that is not directly reflected in the taxpayer's financial / commercial accounts	4	*De minimis rule* applies
Permanent establishment rulings	6	Hong Kong (China), New Zealand, United States
Related party conduit rulings	0	N/A
Total	25	

Matters related to intellectual property regimes (ToR I.A.1.3)

109. Australia does not offer an intellectual property regime for which transparency requirements under the Action 5 Report (OECD, 2015[3]) were imposed.

Summary of recommendations on implementation of the transparency framework

Aspect of implementation of the transparency framework that should be improved	Recommendation for improvement
	No recommendations are made.

References

OECD (2021), *BEPS Action 5 on Harmful Tax Practices - Terms of Reference and Methodology for the Conduct of the Peer Reviews of the Action 5 Transparency Framework*, OECD Publishing, Paris, https://www.oecd.org/tax/beps/beps-action-5-harmful-tax-practices-peer-review-transparency-framework.pdf. [1]

OECD (2015), *Countering Harmful Tax Practices More Effectively, Taking into Account Transparency and Substance, Action 5 - 2015 Final Report*, OECD/G20 Base Erosion and Profit Shifting Project, OECD Publishing, Paris, https://doi.org/10.1787/9789264241190-en. [3]

OECD/Council of Europe (2011), *The Multilateral Convention on Mutual Administrative Assistance in Tax Matters: Amended by the 2010 Protocol*, OECD Publishing, Paris, https://doi.org/10.1787/9789264115606-en. [2]

Notes

[1] Tonnage tax.

[2] Participating jurisdictions to the Convention are available here: www.oecd.org/tax/exchange-of-tax-information/convention-on-mutual-administrative-assistance-in-tax-matters.htm. Australia also has bilateral agreements with Argentina, Austria, Belgium, Canada, Chile, China (People's Republic of), Czechia, Denmark, Fiji, Finland, France, Germany, Hungary, India, Indonesia, Ireland, Israel, Italy, Japan, Kiribati, Korea, Malaysia, Malta, Mexico, Netherlands, New Zealand, Norway, Papua New Guinea, Philippines, Poland, Romania, Russia, Singapore, Slovak Republic, South Africa, Spain, Sri Lanka, Sweden, Switzerland, Chinese Taipei, Thailand, Türkiye, United Kingdom, United States and Viet Nam.

Austria

Austria has met all aspects of the terms of reference (OECD, 2021[1]) (ToR) for the calendar year 2022 (year in review), and no recommendations are made.

Austria can legally issue three types of rulings within the scope of the transparency framework.

In practice, Austria issued rulings within the scope of the transparency framework as follows:

Type of ruling	Number of rulings
Past rulings	59
Future rulings in the period 1 April 2016 – 31 December 2016	13
Future rulings in the calendar year 2017	10
Future rulings in the calendar year 2018	9
Future rulings in the calendar year 2019	14
Future rulings in the calendar year 2020	23
Future rulings in the calendar year 2021	18
Future rulings in the year in review	24

Peer input was received from one jurisdiction in respect of the exchanges of information on rulings received from Austria. The input was positive, noting that overall information was complete, in a correct format and almost all received in a timely manner.

Information gathering process (ToR I.A)

110. Austria can legally issue the following three types of rulings within the scope of the transparency framework: (i) cross-border unilateral APAs and any other cross-border unilateral tax rulings (such as an advance tax ruling) covering transfer pricing or the application of transfer pricing principles; (ii) permanent establishment rulings; and (iii) related party conduit rulings.

111. For Austria, past rulings are any tax rulings within scope that are issued either: (i) on or after 1 January 2014 but before 1 April 2016; or (ii) on or after 1 January 2010 but before 1 January 2014, provided they were still in effect as at 1 January 2014. Future rulings are any tax rulings within scope that are issued on or after 1 April 2016.

112. In the prior years' peer review reports, it was determined that Austria's undertakings to identify past and future rulings and all potential exchange jurisdictions were sufficient to meet the minimum standard. In addition, it was determined that Austria's review and supervision mechanism was sufficient to meet the minimum standard. Austria's implementation remains unchanged, and therefore continues to meet the minimum standard.

113. Austria has met all of the ToR for the information gathering process and no recommendations are made.

Exchange of information (ToR II.B)

114. Austria has the necessary domestic legal basis to exchange information spontaneously. Austria notes that there are no legal or practical impediments that prevent the spontaneous exchange of information on rulings as contemplated in the Action 5 minimum standard.

115. Austria has international agreements permitting spontaneous exchange of information, including: (i) the *Multilateral Convention on Mutual Administrative Assistance in Tax Matters: Amended by the 2010 Protocol* (OECD/Council of Europe, 2011[2]) ("the Convention"), (ii) the Directive 2011/16/EU with all other European Union Member States and (iii) bilateral agreements in force with 83 jurisdictions.[1]

116. For the year in review, the timeliness of exchanges is as follows:

Future rulings within the scope of the transparency framework	Number of exchanges transmitted within three months of the information becoming available to the competent authority or immediately after legal impediments have been lifted	Delayed exchanges		
		Number of exchanges transmitted later than three months of the information on rulings becoming available to the competent authority	Reasons for the delays	Any other comments
	46	0	N/A	N/A

Follow-up requests received for exchange of the ruling	Number	Average time to provide response	Number of requests not answered
	0	N/A	N/A

117. In the prior years' peer review reports, it was determined that Austria's process for the completion and exchange of templates were sufficient to meet the minimum standard. With respect to past rulings, no further action was required. Austria's implementation in this regard remains unchanged and therefore continues to meet the minimum standard.

118. Austria has the necessary legal basis for spontaneous exchange of information, a process for completing the templates in a timely way and has completed all exchanges. Austria has met all of the ToR for the exchange of information process and no recommendations are made.

Statistics (ToR IV.D)

119. The statistics for the year in review are as follows:

Category of ruling	Number of exchanges	Jurisdictions exchanged with
Cross-border unilateral APAs and any other cross-border unilateral tax rulings (such as an advance tax ruling) covering transfer pricing or the application of transfer pricing principles	46	Australia, Belgium, Bosnia and Herzegovina, Brazil, Bulgaria, China (People's Republic of), Croatia, Cyprus, Czechia, Denmark, Estonia, Finland, France, Germany, Greece, Hong Kong (China), Hungary, Ireland, Italy, Latvia, Lithuania, Luxembourg, Malta, Moldova, Montenegro, Netherlands, North Macedonia, Poland, Portugal, Romania, Slovak Republic, Slovenia, Spain, Sweden, Switzerland, Serbia, United Kingdom, United States
Permanent establishment rulings	0	N/A
Related party conduit rulings	0	N/A
Total	46	

Matters related to intellectual property regimes (ToR I.A.1.3)

120. Austria does not offer an intellectual property regime for which transparency requirements under the Action 5 Report (OECD, 2015[3]) were imposed.

Summary of recommendations on implementation of the transparency framework

Aspect of implementation of the transparency framework that should be improved	Recommendation for improvement
	No recommendations are made.

References

OECD (2021), *BEPS Action 5 on Harmful Tax Practices - Terms of Reference and Methodology for the Conduct of the Peer Reviews of the Action 5 Transparency Framework*, OECD Publishing, Paris, https://www.oecd.org/tax/beps/beps-action-5-harmful-tax-practices-peer-review-transparency-framework.pdf. [1]

OECD (2015), *Countering Harmful Tax Practices More Effectively, Taking into Account Transparency and Substance, Action 5 - 2015 Final Report*, OECD/G20 Base Erosion and Profit Shifting Project, OECD Publishing, Paris, https://doi.org/10.1787/9789264241190-en. [3]

OECD/Council of Europe (2011), *The Multilateral Convention on Mutual Administrative Assistance in Tax Matters: Amended by the 2010 Protocol*, OECD Publishing, Paris, https://doi.org/10.1787/9789264115606-en. [2]

Note

[1] Participating jurisdictions to the Convention are available here: www.oecd.org/tax/exchange-of-tax-information/convention-on-mutual-administrative-assistance-in-tax-matters.htm. Austria also has bilateral agreements with Albania, Algeria, Armenia, Australia, Azerbaijan, Bahrain, Barbados, Belarus, Belgium, Belize, Bosnia and Herzegovina, Brazil, Bulgaria, Canada, Chile, China (People's Republic of), Croatia, Cyprus, Czechia, Denmark, Egypt, Estonia, Finland, France, Georgia, Germany, Greece, Hong Kong (China), Hungary, Iceland, India, Indonesia, Ireland, Israel, Italy, Japan, Kazakhstan, Korea, Kosovo, Kuwait, Latvia, Liechtenstein, Lithuania, Luxembourg, Malaysia, Malta, Mexico, Moldova, Montenegro, Morocco, Netherlands, New Zealand, North Macedonia, Norway, Pakistan, Philippines, Poland, Portugal, Qatar, Romania, Russia, San Marino, Saudi Arabia, Serbia, Singapore, Slovak Republic, Slovenia, South Africa, Spain, Sweden, Switzerland, Chinese Taipei, Tajikistan, Thailand, Tunisia, Türkiye, Turkmenistan, Ukraine, United Arab Emirates, United Kingdom, United States, Venezuela and Viet Nam.

Barbados

Barbados has met all aspects of the terms of reference (OECD, 2021[1]) (ToR) for the calendar year 2022 (year in review), and no recommendations are made.

Barbados can legally issue five types of rulings within the scope of the transparency framework.

In practice, Barbados issued rulings within the scope of the transparency framework as follows:

Type of ruling	Number of rulings
Past rulings	2
Future rulings in the period 1 September 2017 – 31 December 2017	0
Future rulings in the calendar year 2018	1
Future rulings in the calendar year 2019	0
Future rulings in the calendar year 2020	1
Future rulings in the calendar year 2021	1
Future rulings in the year in review	1

No peer input was received in respect of the exchanges of information on rulings received from Barbados.

Information gathering process (ToR I.A)

121. Barbados can legally issue the following five types of rulings within the scope of the transparency framework: (i) preferential regimes;[1] (ii) cross-border unilateral APAs and any other cross-border unilateral tax rulings (such as an advance tax ruling) covering transfer pricing or the application of transfer pricing principles; (iii) rulings providing for unilateral downward adjustments; (iv) permanent establishment rulings; and (v) related party conduit rulings.

122. For Barbados, past rulings are any tax rulings within scope that are issued either: (i) on or after 1 January 2015 but before 1 September 2017; or (ii) on or after 1 January 2012 but before 1 January 2015, provided they were still in effect as at 1 January 2015. Future rulings are any tax rulings within scope that are issued on or after 1 September 2017.

123. In the prior years' peer review reports, it was determined that Barbados's undertakings to identify past and future rulings and all potential exchange jurisdictions were sufficient to meet the minimum standard. In addition, it was determined that Barbados's review and supervision mechanism was sufficient to meet the minimum standard. Barbados's implementation remains unchanged, and therefore continues to meet the minimum standard.

124. Barbados has met all of the ToR for the information gathering process and no recommendations are made.

Exchange of information (ToR II.B)

125. Barbados has international agreements permitting spontaneous exchange of information, including: (i) the *Multilateral Convention on Mutual Administrative Assistance in Tax Matters: Amended by the 2010 Protocol* (OECD/Council of Europe, 2011[2]) ("the Convention") and (ii) bilateral agreements in force with 40 jurisdictions.[2]

126. For the year in review, the timeliness of exchanges is as follows:

Future rulings within the scope of the transparency framework	Number of exchanges transmitted within three months of the information becoming available to the competent authority or immediately after legal impediments have been lifted	Delayed exchanges		
		Number of exchanges transmitted later than three months of the information on rulings becoming available to the competent authority	Reasons for the delays	Any other comments
	3	0	N/A	N/A

Follow-up requests received for exchange of the ruling	Number	Average time to provide response	Number of requests not answered
	0	N/A	N/A

127. In the prior year's peer review report, it was determined that Barbados's process for the completion and exchange of templates were sufficient to meet the minimum standard. With respect to past rulings, no further action was required. Barbados's implementation in this regard remains unchanged and therefore continues to meet the minimum standard.

128. Barbados has the necessary legal basis for spontaneous exchange of information, a process for completing the templates in a timely way and has completed all exchanges. Barbados has met all of the ToR for the exchange of information process and no recommendations are made.

Statistics (ToR IV.D)

129. The statistics for the year in review are as follows:

Category of ruling	Number of exchanges	Jurisdictions exchanged with
Ruling related to a preferential regime	0	N/A
Cross-border unilateral APAs and any other cross-border unilateral tax rulings (such as an advance tax ruling) covering transfer pricing or the application of transfer pricing principles	0	N/A
Cross-border rulings providing for a unilateral downward adjustment to the taxpayer's taxable profits that is not directly reflected in the taxpayer's financial / commercial accounts	0	N/A
Permanent establishment rulings	*De minimis* rule applies	N/A
Related party conduit rulings	0	N/A
De minimis rule	3	N/A
Total	3	

Matters related to intellectual property regimes (ToR I.A.1.3)

130. Barbados does not offer an intellectual property regime for which transparency requirements under the Action 5 Report (OECD, 2015[3]) were imposed.

Summary of recommendations on implementation of the transparency framework

Aspect of implementation of the transparency framework that should be improved	Recommendation for improvement
	No recommendations are made.

References

OECD (2021), *BEPS Action 5 on Harmful Tax Practices - Terms of Reference and Methodology for the Conduct of the Peer Reviews of the Action 5 Transparency Framework*, OECD Publishing, Paris, https://www.oecd.org/tax/beps/beps-action-5-harmful-tax-practices-peer-review-transparency-framework.pdf. [1]

OECD (2015), *Countering Harmful Tax Practices More Effectively, Taking into Account Transparency and Substance, Action 5 - 2015 Final Report*, OECD/G20 Base Erosion and Profit Shifting Project, OECD Publishing, Paris, https://doi.org/10.1787/9789264241190-en. [3]

OECD/Council of Europe (2011), *The Multilateral Convention on Mutual Administrative Assistance in Tax Matters: Amended by the 2010 Protocol*, OECD Publishing, Paris, https://doi.org/10.1787/9789264115606-en. [2]

Notes

[1] Credit for foreign currency earnings.

[2] Participating jurisdictions to the Convention are available here: www.oecd.org/tax/exchange-of-tax-information/convention-on-mutual-administrative-assistance-in-tax-matters.htm. Barbados also has bilateral agreements with Antigua and Barbuda, Austria, Bahrain, Belize, Botswana, Canada, China (People's Republic of), Cyprus, Cuba, Czechia, Dominica, Finland, Grenada, Guyana, Iceland, Italy, Jamaica, Luxembourg, Malta, Mauritius, Mexico, Netherlands, Norway, Panama, Portugal, Saint Kitts and Nevis, Saint Lucia, Saint Vincent and the Grenadines, San Marino, Seychelles, Singapore, Spain, Sweden, Switzerland, Trinidad & Tobago, Qatar, United Arab Emirates, United Kingdom, United States and Venezuela.

Belgium

Belgium has met all aspects of the terms of reference (OECD, 2021[1]) (ToR) for the calendar year 2022 (year in review), and no recommendations are made.

Belgium can legally issue four types of rulings within the scope of the transparency framework.

In practice, Belgium issued rulings within the scope of the transparency framework as follows:

Type of ruling	Number of rulings
Past rulings	586
Future rulings in the period 1 April 2016 – 31 December 2016	57
Future rulings in the calendar year 2017	107
Future rulings in the calendar year 2018	103
Future rulings in the calendar year 2019	73
Future rulings in the calendar year 2020	74
Future rulings in the calendar year 2021	67
Future rulings in the year in review	85

Peer input was received from six jurisdictions in respect of the exchanges of information on rulings received from Belgium. The input was generally positive, noting that overall information was complete, in a correct format and received in a timely manner.

Information gathering process (ToR I.A)

131. Belgium can legally issue the following four types of rulings within the scope of the transparency framework: (i) preferential regimes;[1] (ii) cross-border unilateral APAs and any other cross-border unilateral tax rulings (such as an advance tax ruling) covering transfer pricing or the application of transfer pricing principles; (iii) rulings providing for unilateral downward adjustments; and (iv) permanent establishment rulings.

132. For Belgium, past rulings are any tax rulings within scope that are issued either: (i) on or after 1 January 2014 but before 1 April 2016; or (ii) on or after 1 January 2010 but before 1 January 2014, provided they were still in effect as at 1 January 2014. Future rulings are any tax rulings within scope that are issued on or after 1 April 2016.

133. In the prior years' peer review reports, it was determined that Belgium's undertakings to identify past and future rulings and all potential exchange jurisdictions were sufficient to meet the minimum standard. In addition, it was determined that Belgium's review and supervision mechanism was sufficient to meet the minimum standard. Belgium's implementation remains unchanged, and therefore continues to meet the minimum standard.

134. Belgium has met all of the ToR for the information gathering process and no recommendations are made.

Exchange of information (ToR II.B)

135. Belgium has the necessary domestic legal basis to exchange information spontaneously. Belgium notes that there are no legal or practical impediments that prevent the spontaneous exchange of information on rulings as contemplated in the Action 5 minimum standard.

136. Belgium has international agreements permitting spontaneous exchange of information, including: (i) the *Multilateral Convention on Mutual Administrative Assistance in Tax Matters: Amended by the 2010 Protocol* (OECD/Council of Europe, 2011[2]) ("the Convention"), (ii) the Directive 2011/16/EU with all other European Union Member States and (iii) bilateral agreements in force with 72 jurisdictions.[2]

137. For the year in review, the timeliness of exchanges is as follows:

Future rulings within the scope of the transparency framework	Number of exchanges transmitted within three months of the information becoming available to the competent authority or immediately after legal impediments have been lifted	Delayed exchanges		
		Number of exchanges transmitted later than three months of the information on rulings becoming available to the competent authority	Reasons for the delays	Any other comments
	391	0	N/A	N/A

Follow-up requests received for exchange of the ruling	Number	Average time to provide response	Number of requests not answered
	1	55 days	0

138. In the prior years' peer review reports, it was determined that Belgium's process for the completion and exchange of templates were sufficient to meet the minimum standard. With respect to past rulings, no further action was required. Belgium's implementation in this regard remains unchanged and therefore continues to meet the minimum standard.

139. Belgium has the necessary legal basis for spontaneous exchange of information, a process for completing the templates in a timely way and has completed all exchanges. Belgium has met all of the ToR for the exchange of information process and no recommendations are made.

Statistics (ToR IV.D)

140. The statistics for the year in review are as follows:

Category of ruling	Number of exchanges	Jurisdictions exchanged with
Ruling related to a preferential regime	0	N/A
Cross-border unilateral APAs and any other cross-border unilateral tax rulings (such as an advance tax ruling) covering transfer pricing or the application of transfer pricing principles	370	Albania, Antigua and Barbuda, Argentina, Australia, Austria, Barbados, Brazil, Bulgaria, Canada, Chile, China (People's Republic of), Colombia, Croatia, Curaçao, Czechia, Denmark, Estonia, Finland, France, Germany, Greece, Grenada, Guernsey, Hong Kong (China), Hungary, India, Indonesia, Ireland, Israel, Italy, Jamaica, Kenya, Korea, Latvia, Lithuania, Luxembourg, Malaysia, Mexico, Monaco, Netherlands, New Zealand, Nigeria, Norway, Panama, Peru, Poland, Portugal, Romania, Saint Kitts and Nevis, Saint Lucia, Saudi Arabia, Singapore, Slovak Republic, South Africa, Spain, Sweden, Switzerland, Türkiye, United Kingdom, United States
Cross-border rulings providing for a unilateral downward adjustment to the taxpayer's taxable profits that is not directly reflected in the taxpayer's financial / commercial accounts	0	N/A
Permanent establishment rulings	29	Austria, Bulgaria, Canada, Chile, France, Germany, Greece, Netherlands, Panama, Romania, Spain, Sweden, United Kingdom, United States
IP regimes: total exchanges on taxpayers benefitting from the third category of IP assets, new entrants benefitting from grandfathered IP regimes; and taxpayers making use of the option to treat the nexus ratio as a rebuttable presumption	0	N/A
Total	399[3]	

Matters related to intellectual property regimes (ToR I.A.1.3)

141. In the prior years' peer review reports, it was determined that Belgium's information gathering and exchange of information processes for matters related to intellectual property regimes[4] were sufficient to meet the minimum standard. Belgium's implementation in this regard remains unchanged and therefore continues to meet the minimum standard.

Summary of recommendations on implementation of the transparency framework

Aspect of implementation of the transparency framework that should be improved	Recommendation for improvement
	No recommendations are made.

References

OECD (2021), *BEPS Action 5 on Harmful Tax Practices - Terms of Reference and Methodology for the Conduct of the Peer Reviews of the Action 5 Transparency Framework*, OECD Publishing, Paris, https://www.oecd.org/tax/beps/beps-action-5-harmful-tax-practices-peer-review-transparency-framework.pdf. [1]

OECD (2015), *Countering Harmful Tax Practices More Effectively, Taking into Account Transparency and Substance, Action 5 - 2015 Final Report*, OECD/G20 Base Erosion and Profit Shifting Project, OECD Publishing, Paris, https://doi.org/10.1787/9789264241190-en. [3]

OECD/Council of Europe (2011), *The Multilateral Convention on Mutual Administrative Assistance in Tax Matters: Amended by the 2010 Protocol*, OECD Publishing, Paris, https://doi.org/10.1787/9789264115606-en. [2]

Notes

[1] 1) Patent income deduction, 2) tax shelter regime for maritime exploitation and 3) excess profits.

[2] Participating jurisdictions to the Convention are available here: www.oecd.org/tax/exchange-of-tax-information/convention-on-mutual-administrative-assistance-in-tax-matters.htm. Belgium also has bilateral agreements with Albania, Algeria, Andorra, Antigua and Barbuda, Argentina, Armenia, Australia, Azerbaijan, Bahrain, Bangladesh, Belarus, Brazil, Belize, Bosnia and Herzegovina, Canada, Chile, China (People's Republic of), Côte d'Ivoire, Democratic Republic of the Congo, Ecuador, Egypt, Gabon, Georgia, Ghana, Hong Kong (China), Iceland, India, Indonesia, Israel, Japan, Kazakhstan, Korea, Kosovo, Kyrgyzstan, Kuwait, Malaysia, Mauritius, Mexico, Moldova, Mongolia, Montenegro, Morocco, New Zealand, Nigeria, North Macedonia, Norway, Pakistan, Philippines, Russia, Rwanda, San Marino, Senegal, Serbia, Seychelles, Singapore, South Africa, Sri Lanka, Switzerland, Tajikistan, Chinese Taipei, Thailand, Tunisia, Türkiye, Turkmenistan, Ukraine, United Arab Emirates, United Kingdom, United States, Uruguay, Uzbekistan, Venezuela and Viet Nam.

[3] There were 391 unique exchanges. The total number of exchanges given in this table, 399, is higher due to the fact that 8 exchanges fall under two ruling categories.

[4] Innovation income deduction.

Benin

Benin is taking steps to implement the legal basis for the transparency framework and to commence administrative preparations (in accordance with the terms of reference (OECD, 2021[1]) (ToR) to ensure that it establishes an information gathering process (ToR I.A) and that information on rulings will be identified and exchanged in a timely manner (ToR II.B). Benin receives two recommendations on these points for the calendar year 2022 (year in review).

In the prior year report, as well as in the 2018-2020 peer reviews, Benin had received the same two recommendations. As they have not been addressed, the recommendations remain in place.

Benin can legally issue one type of rulings within the scope of the transparency framework.

In practice, Benin issued no rulings within the scope of the transparency framework.

As no exchanges were required to take place, no peer input was received in respect of the exchanges of information on rulings received from Benin.

Information gathering process (ToR I.A)

142. Benin can legally issue the following one type of rulings within the scope of the transparency framework: permanent establishment rulings.

Past rulings (ToR I.A.1.1, I.A.1.2, I.A.2.1, I.A.2.2)

143. For Benin, past rulings are any tax rulings within scope that are issued either (i) on or after 1 January 2015 but before 1 April 2017; and (ii) on or after 1 January 2012 but before 1 January 2015, provided they were still in effect as at 1 January 2015. Benin issued no past rulings within the scope of the transparency framework. As such, there was no need to identify potential exchange jurisdictions.

Future rulings (ToR I.A.1.1, I.A.1.2, I.A.2.1)

144. For Benin, future rulings are any tax rulings within scope that are issued on or after 1 April 2017.

145. In the prior years' peer review reports, Benin indicated that there were no processes in place for the record keeping of rulings for the purposes of the transparency framework. It was also noted that Benin intended to implement guidelines to ensure the necessary information to meet the requirements of the transparency framework is required in all cases. Therefore, Benin was recommended to finalise its information gathering process for identifying all relevant rulings and potential exchange jurisdictions, as soon as possible.

146. During the year in review, no additional steps to finalise its information gathering process were taken, and therefore the prior years' recommendation remains in place.

Review and supervision (ToR I.A.3)

147. In the prior years' peer review reports, it was determined that Benin did not yet have a review and supervision mechanism under the transparency framework. Therefore, Benin was recommended to put in place a review and supervision mechanism as soon as possible. Benin was in the process of considering the implementation of a review and supervision mechanism for ensuring implementation of the transparency framework. During the year in review, no additional steps were taken, and therefore the prior year recommendation remains.

Conclusion on section A

148. Benin is recommended to finalise its information gathering process for identifying all relevant rulings and all potential exchange jurisdictions, with a review and supervision mechanism, as soon as possible (ToR I.A).

Exchange of information (ToR II.B)

Legal basis for spontaneous exchange of information (ToR II.B.1, II.B.2)

149. Benin is still in the process of putting in place the necessary domestic legal basis to exchange information spontaneously.

150. Benin has international agreements permitting spontaneous exchange of information, including: (i) the *Multilateral Convention on Mutual Administrative Assistance in Tax Matters: Amended by the 2010 Protocol* (OECD/Council of Europe, 2011[2]) ("the Convention") and (ii) bilateral agreements in force with 9 jurisdictions[1]. Benin signed the Convention in 27 November 2019 and deposited its instrument of ratification on 24 January 2023. The Convention entered into force on 1 May 2023 and will have effect for administrative assistance related to taxable periods beginning on or after 1 January 2024.

Completion and exchange of templates (ToR II.B.3, II.B.4, II.B.5, II.B.6, II.B.7)

151. In the prior years' peer review reports, it was determined that Benin was developing a process to complete the templates on relevant rulings, to make them available to the Competent Authority for exchange of information, and to exchange them with relevant jurisdictions.

152. During the year in review, no additional steps were taken, and therefore the prior year recommendation remains.

153. As no exchanges were required to take place for the year in review, no data on the timeliness of exchanges can be reported.

Conclusion on section B

154. Benin is recommended to put in place a domestic legal framework allowing spontaneous exchange of information on rulings and to continue its efforts to complete the templates for all relevant rulings and to ensure that the exchanges of information on rulings occur as soon as possible (ToR II.B).

Statistics (ToR IV.D)

155. As no rulings were issued, no statistics can be reported.

Matters related to intellectual property regimes (ToR I.A.1.3)

156. Benin does not offer an intellectual property regime for which transparency requirements under the Action 5 Report (OECD, 2015[3]) were imposed.

Summary of recommendations on implementation of the transparency framework

Aspect of implementation of the transparency framework that should be improved	Recommendation for improvement
Benin has not finalised the steps to have in place its necessary information gathering process, with a review and supervision mechanism.	Benin is recommended to finalise its information gathering process for identifying all relevant rulings and all potential exchange jurisdictions, with a review and supervision mechanism, as soon as possible. This recommendation remains unchanged since the 2018, 2019, 2020 and 2021 peer review reports.
Benin has not yet finalised the steps to have effective compulsory spontaneous exchange of information on the tax rulings within the scope of the transparency framework.	Benin is recommended to continue to put in place a domestic legal framework allowing spontaneous exchange of information on rulings and to continue its efforts to complete the templates for all relevant rulings and to ensure that the exchanges of information on rulings occur as soon as possible. This recommendation remains unchanged since the 2018, 2019, 2020 and 2021 peer review reports.

References

OECD (2021), *BEPS Action 5 on Harmful Tax Practices - Terms of Reference and Methodology for the Conduct of the Peer Reviews of the Action 5 Transparency Framework*, OECD Publishing, Paris, https://www.oecd.org/tax/beps/beps-action-5-harmful-tax-practices-peer-review-transparency-framework.pdf. [1]

OECD (2015), *Countering Harmful Tax Practices More Effectively, Taking into Account Transparency and Substance, Action 5 - 2015 Final Report*, OECD/G20 Base Erosion and Profit Shifting Project, OECD Publishing, Paris, https://doi.org/10.1787/9789264241190-en. [3]

OECD/Council of Europe (2011), *The Multilateral Convention on Mutual Administrative Assistance in Tax Matters: Amended by the 2010 Protocol*, OECD Publishing, Paris, https://doi.org/10.1787/9789264115606-en. [2]

Note

[1] Participating jurisdictions to the Convention are available here: www.oecd.org/tax/exchange-of-tax-information/convention-on-mutual-administrative-assistance-in-tax-matters.htm. Benin also has bilateral agreement with France and Norway and multilateral agreements with Burkina Faso, Cabo Verde, Cote d'Ivoire, Gambia, Ghana, Guinea-Bissau, Mali, Niger, Nigeria, Senegal and Togo within WAEMU and ECOWAS.

Bosnia and Herzegovina

Bosnia and Herzegovina is taking steps to implement the aspects of the terms of reference (OECD, 2021[1]) (ToR) for the transparency framework, including the legal basis, and to commence administrative preparations to ensure that the necessary information gathering process for relevant rulings is in place (ToR I.A) and that information on rulings is exchanged in accordance with the form and timelines under the transparency framework (ToR II.B). Bosnia and Herzegovina receives two recommendations on these points for the calendar year 2022 (year in review).

In the prior year report, Bosnia and Herzegovina had received the same two recommendations. As they have not been addressed, the recommendations remain in place.

Bosnia and Herzegovina can legally issue four types of rulings within the scope of the transparency framework.

In practice, Bosnia and Herzegovina issued no rulings within the scope of the transparency framework.

As no exchanges were required to take place, no peer input was received in respect of the exchanges of information on rulings received from Bosnia and Herzegovina.

Information gathering process (ToR I.A)

157. Bosnia and Herzegovina can legally issue the following four types of rulings within the scope of the transparency framework: (i) cross-border unilateral APAs and any other cross-border unilateral tax rulings (such as an advance tax ruling) covering transfer pricing or the application of transfer pricing principles; (ii) rulings providing for unilateral downward adjustments; (iii) permanent establishment rulings; and (iv) related party conduit rulings. It is noted that the Tax Administration in the Bosnia and Herzegovina entity of Republic of Srpska is the only authority issuing rulings in scope of the FHTP work.

Past rulings (ToR I.A.1.1, I.A.1.2, I.A.2.1, I.A.2.2)

158. For Bosnia and Herzegovina, past rulings are any tax rulings issued prior to 1 March 2020. However, there is no obligation for Bosnia and Herzegovina to conduct spontaneous exchange information on past rulings.

Future rulings (ToR I.A.1.1, I.A.1.2, I.A.2.1)

159. For Bosnia and Herzegovina, future rulings are any tax rulings within scope that are issued on or after 1 March 2020. No rulings were issued by Bosnia and Herzegovina during the year in review.

160. In the prior year's peer review report, it was determined that Bosnia and Herzegovina did not yet have specific mechanisms in place for identifying future rulings and potential exchange jurisdictions within the scope of the transparency framework. Therefore, Bosnia and Herzegovina was recommended to put in place an effective information gathering process to identify all relevant future rulings and all potential exchange jurisdictions, as soon as possible. During the year in review, Bosnia and Herzegovina did not implement such mechanisms. As this process is still under development, the previous year's recommendation remains in place.

Review and supervision (ToR I.A.3)

161. In the prior year's peer review report, it was determined that Bosnia and Herzegovina did not yet have a review and supervision mechanism under the transparency framework. Therefore, Bosnia and Herzegovina was recommended to implement a review and supervision mechanism as soon as possible. During the year in review, Bosnia and Herzegovina did not implement such a review and supervision mechanism. As this process is still under development, the previous year recommendation remains in place.

Conclusion on section A

162. Bosnia and Herzegovina does not have specific mechanisms in place for identifying relevant rulings and potential exchange jurisdictions within the scope of the transparency framework as well as for reviewing and supervising that all relevant information is captured adequately. Bosnia and Herzegovina is recommended to put in place its information gathering process for identifying all past and future rulings and all potential exchange jurisdictions, with a review and supervision mechanism, as soon as possible (ToR I.A).

Exchange of information (ToR II.B)

Legal basis for spontaneous exchange of information (ToR II.B.1, II.B.2)

163. In the prior year's peer review report, it was determined that Bosnia and Herzegovina did not yet have the necessary domestic legal basis to exchange information spontaneously. Bosnia and Herzegovina can only exchange information on request. Therefore, Bosnia and Herzegovina was recommended to put in place the necessary domestic legal basis allowing spontaneous exchange of information on rulings.

During the year in review, Bosnia and Herzegovina did not introduce such a domestic legal framework. As this process is still under development, the previous year recommendation remains in place.

164. Bosnia and Herzegovina has international agreements permitting spontaneous exchange of information, including: (i) the *Multilateral Convention on Mutual Administrative Assistance in Tax Matters: Amended by the 2010 Protocol* (OECD/Council of Europe, 2011[2]) ("the Convention") and (ii) bilateral agreements in force with 38 jurisdictions.[1]

Completion and exchange of templates (ToR II.B.3, II.B.4, II.B.5, II.B.6, II.B.7)

165. In the prior year's peer review report, it was determined that Bosnia and Herzegovina did not yet have a process to exchange information on rulings in accordance with the form and timelines required by the transparency framework. Therefore, Bosnia and Herzegovina was recommended to develop a process for the completion and exchange of information on relevant rulings going forward. With respect to past rulings, no action was required. During the year in review, Bosnia and Herzegovina did not introduce such a process. As this process is still under development, the previous year recommendation remains in place.

166. During the year in review, no exchanges were required to take place and no data on the timeliness of exchanges is reported.

Conclusion on section B

167. Bosnia and Herzegovina does not yet have the necessary domestic legal basis to exchange information spontaneously and a process for completing the templates in a timely way. Bosnia and Herzegovina is recommended to put in place a domestic legal framework allowing spontaneous exchange of information on rulings and to ensure the timely exchange of information on rulings in the form required by the transparency framework, as soon as possible (ToR II.B).

Statistics (ToR IV.D)

168. As no rulings were issued, no statistics can be reported.

Matters related to intellectual property regimes (ToR I.A.1.3)

169. Bosnia and Herzegovina does not offer an intellectual property regime for which transparency requirements under the Action 5 Report (OECD, 2015[3]) were imposed.

Summary of recommendations on implementation of the transparency framework

Aspect of implementation of the transparency framework that should be improved	Recommendation for improvement
Bosnia and Herzegovina does not have specific mechanisms in place for identifying relevant rulings and potential exchange jurisdictions within the scope of the transparency framework as well as for reviewing and supervising that all relevant information is captured adequately.	Bosnia and Herzegovina is recommended to put in place its information gathering process for identifying all past and future rulings and all potential exchange jurisdictions, with a review and supervision mechanism, as soon as possible. This recommendation remains unchanged since the 2020 and 2021 peer review report.
Bosnia and Herzegovina does not yet have the necessary domestic legal basis to exchange information spontaneously and a process for completing the templates in a timely way.	Bosnia and Herzegovina is recommended to put in place a domestic legal framework allowing spontaneous exchange of information on rulings and to ensure the timely exchange of information on rulings in the form required by the transparency framework, as soon as possible. This recommendation remains unchanged since the 2020 and 2021 peer review report.

References

OECD (2021), *BEPS Action 5 on Harmful Tax Practices - Terms of Reference and Methodology for the Conduct of the Peer Reviews of the Action 5 Transparency Framework*, OECD Publishing, Paris, https://www.oecd.org/tax/beps/beps-action-5-harmful-tax-practices-peer-review-transparency-framework.pdf. [1]

OECD (2015), *Countering Harmful Tax Practices More Effectively, Taking into Account Transparency and Substance, Action 5 - 2015 Final Report*, OECD/G20 Base Erosion and Profit Shifting Project, OECD Publishing, Paris, https://doi.org/10.1787/9789264241190-en. [3]

OECD/Council of Europe (2011), *The Multilateral Convention on Mutual Administrative Assistance in Tax Matters: Amended by the 2010 Protocol*, OECD Publishing, Paris, https://doi.org/10.1787/9789264115606-en. [2]

Note

[1] Participating jurisdictions to the Convention are available here: www.oecd.org/tax/exchange-of-tax-information/convention-on-mutual-administrative-assistance-in-tax-matters.htm. Bosnia and Herzegovina also has bilateral agreements with Albania, Algeria, Austria, Azerbaijan, Belgium, Czechia, Finland, France, Germany, Greece, Croatia, Iran, Ireland, Italy, Jordan, Kuwait, Qatar, China (People's Republic of), Cyprus, Hungary, Malaysia, Montenegro, Moldova, Netherlands, North Macedonia, Norway, Pakistan, Poland, Romania, Slovak Republic, Slovenia, Serbia, Spain, Sweden, Sri Lanka, Türkiye, United Arab Emirates and United Kingdom.

Botswana

Botswana has met all aspects of the terms of reference (OECD, 2021[1]) (ToR) for the calendar year 2022 (year in review) except for having in place a review and supervision mechanism (ToR I.A.3) and having a domestic legal basis for spontaneous exchange of information and exchanging information on the tax rulings in accordance with the form and timelines under the transparency framework (ToR II.B). Botswana receives two recommendations on these points for the year in review.

In the prior year report, as well as in the 2018-2020 peer reviews, Botswana had received the same two recommendations. As they have not been addressed, the recommendations remain in place.

Botswana can legally issue three types of rulings within the scope of the transparency framework.

In practice, Botswana issued rulings within the scope of the transparency framework as follows:

Type of ruling	Number of rulings
Past rulings	10
Future rulings in the period 1 April 2018 – 31 December 2018	1
Future rulings in the calendar year 2019	3
Future rulings in the calendar year 2020	2
Future rulings in the calendar year 2021	0
Future rulings in the year in review	0

As no exchanges took place, no peer input was received in respect of the exchanges of information on rulings received from Botswana.

Information gathering process (ToR I.A)

170. Botswana can legally issue the following three types of rulings within the scope of the transparency framework: (i) preferential regimes;[1] (ii) cross-border unilateral APAs and any other cross-border unilateral tax rulings (such as an advance tax ruling) covering transfer pricing or the application of transfer pricing principles, and (iii) permanent establishment rulings.

Past rulings (ToR I.A.1.1, I.A.1.2, I.A.2.1, I.A.2.2)

171. For Botswana, past rulings are any tax rulings within scope that are issued either (i) on or after 1 January 2016 but before 1 April 2018; and (ii) on or after 1 January 2014 but before 1 January 2016, provided still in effect as at 1 January 2016.

172. In the prior years' peer review report, it was determined that Botswana's undertakings to identify past rulings and all potential exchange jurisdictions were sufficient to meet the minimum standard. Botswana's implementation in this regard remains unchanged, and therefore continues to meet the minimum standard.

Future rulings (ToR I.A.1.1, I.A.1.2, I.A.2.1)

173. For Botswana, future rulings are any tax rulings within scope that are issued on or after 1 April 2018.

174. In the prior years' peer review reports, it was determined that Botswana's implementation of a new system to identify future rulings and all potential exchange jurisdictions was sufficient to meet the minimum standard. Botswana's implementation in this regard remains unchanged, and therefore continues to meet the minimum standard.

Review and supervision (ToR I.A.3)

175. In the prior years' peer review reports, it was determined that Botswana did not yet have a review and supervision mechanism for past and future rulings under the transparency framework. Therefore, Botswana was recommended to put in place a review and supervision mechanism as soon as possible.

176. During the year in review, no additional work was undertaken and therefore, the prior years' recommendation remains.

Conclusion on section A

177. Botswana has met all of the ToR for the information gathering process except for having in place a review and supervision mechanism. Botswana is recommended to put in place a review and supervision mechanism, as soon as possible (ToR I.A.3).

Exchange of information (ToR II.B)

Legal basis for spontaneous exchange of information (ToR II.B.1, II.B.2)

178. In the prior years' peer review reports, it was determined that Botswana did not have the necessary domestic legal basis to exchange information spontaneously. Botswana can only exchange information on request. Botswana is undergoing a comprehensive reform of its tax laws. Botswana notes that it has commenced a review of the exchange of information legislative framework with the support of the African Tax Administration Forum (ATAF) with a view to correcting identified shortcomings in this area. Botswana notes that this review has been delayed.

179. Botswana has international agreements permitting spontaneous exchange of information, including: (i) the *Multilateral Convention on Mutual Administrative Assistance in Tax Matters: Amended by the 2010 Protocol* (OECD/Council of Europe, 2011[2]) ("the Convention") and (ii) bilateral agreements in

force with 28 jurisdictions.[2] Botswana signed the Convention on 29 September 2020 and deposited its instrument of ratification on 15 June 2021. The Convention entered into force on 1 October 2021 and will have effect for administrative assistance related to taxable periods beginning on or after 1 January 2022. No exchanges could occur under the Convention for the year in review.

Completion and exchange of templates (ToR II.B.3, II.B.4, II.B.5, II.B.6, II.B.7)

180. In the prior years' peer review reports, it was determined that Botswana is currently developing a process to complete the templates on relevant rulings, to make them available to the Competent Authority for exchange of information, and to exchange them with relevant jurisdictions.

181. During the year in review, no exchanges took place and no data on the timeliness of exchanges is reported.

Conclusion on section B

182. Botswana is recommended to continue its efforts to put in place a domestic legal framework allowing spontaneous exchange of information on rulings and to complete the templates for all relevant rulings and to ensure that the exchanges of information on rulings occur as soon as possible (ToR II.B).

Statistics (ToR IV.D)

183. As there was no information on rulings exchanged by Botswana for the year in review, no statistics can be reported.

Matters related to intellectual property regimes (ToR I.A.1.3)

184. In the prior years' peer review reports, it was determined that Botswana's information gathering and exchange of information processes for matters related to intellectual property regimes[3] were sufficient to meet the minimum standard. Botswana's implementation in this regard remains unchanged and therefore continues to meet the minimum standard.

Summary of recommendations on implementation of the transparency framework

Aspect of implementation of the transparency framework that should be improved	Recommendation for improvement
Botswana does not have a review and supervision mechanism in place.	Botswana is recommended to put in place a review and supervision mechanism, as soon as possible. This recommendation remains unchanged since the 2018, 2019, 2020 and 2021 peer review reports.
Botswana does not yet have the necessary legal framework in place for exchanging information on rulings and a process in place to ensure the timely exchange of information on rulings in the form required by the transparency framework.	Botswana is recommended to continue its efforts to put in place a domestic legal framework allowing spontaneous exchange of information on rulings and to complete the templates for all relevant rulings and to ensure that the exchanges of information on rulings occur as soon as possible. This recommendation remains unchanged since the 2018, 2019, 2020 and 2021 peer review reports.

References

OECD (2021), *BEPS Action 5 on Harmful Tax Practices - Terms of Reference and Methodology for the Conduct of the Peer Reviews of the Action 5 Transparency Framework*, OECD Publishing, Paris, https://www.oecd.org/tax/beps/beps-action-5-harmful-tax-practices-peer-review-transparency-framework.pdf. [1]

OECD (2015), *Countering Harmful Tax Practices More Effectively, Taking into Account Transparency and Substance, Action 5 - 2015 Final Report*, OECD/G20 Base Erosion and Profit Shifting Project, OECD Publishing, Paris, https://doi.org/10.1787/9789264241190-en. [3]

OECD/Council of Europe (2011), *The Multilateral Convention on Mutual Administrative Assistance in Tax Matters: Amended by the 2010 Protocol*, OECD Publishing, Paris, https://doi.org/10.1787/9789264115606-en. [2]

Notes

[1] International financial services company.

[2] Participating jurisdictions to the Convention are available here: www.oecd.org/tax/exchange-of-tax-information/convention-on-mutual-administrative-assistance-in-tax-matters.htm. Botswana also has bilateral agreements with Barbados, China (People's Republic of), Czechia, Denmark, Eswatini, Faroe Islands, Finland, France, Greenland, Iceland, India, Ireland, Isle of Man, Lesotho, Luxembourg, Malta, Mauritius, Mozambique, Namibia, Norway, Russia, Seychelles, South Africa, Sweden, United Arab Emirates, United Kingdom, Zambia and Zimbabwe.

[3] International financial services company.

Brazil

Brazil has met all aspects of the terms of reference (OECD, 2021[1]) (ToR) for the calendar year 2022 (year in review), and no recommendations are made.

Brazil can legally issue two types of rulings within the scope of the transparency framework.

In practice, Brazil issued rulings within the scope of the transparency framework as follows:

Type of ruling	Number of rulings
Past rulings	10
Future rulings in the period 1 April 2016 – 31 December 2016	1
Future rulings in the calendar year 2017	2
Future rulings in the calendar year 2018	5
Future rulings in the calendar year 2019	0
Future rulings in the calendar year 2020	0
Future rulings in the calendar year 2021	0
Future rulings in the year in review	0

No peer input was received in respect of the exchanges of information on rulings received from Brazil.

Information gathering process (ToR I.A)

185. Brazil can legally issue the following two types of rulings within the scope of the transparency framework: (i) preferential regimes[1] and (ii) cross-border unilateral APAs and any other cross-border unilateral tax rulings (such as an advance tax ruling) covering transfer pricing or the application of transfer pricing principles.

186. For Brazil, past rulings are any tax rulings within scope that are issued either: (i) on or after 1 January 2014 but before 1 April 2016; or (ii) on or after 1 January 2010 but before 1 January 2014, provided they were still in effect as at 1 January 2014. Future rulings are any tax rulings within scope that are issued on or after 1 April 2016.

187. In the prior years' peer review reports, it was determined that Brazil's undertakings to identify past and future rulings and all potential exchange jurisdictions were sufficient to meet the minimum standard. In addition, it was determined that Brazil's review and supervision mechanism was sufficient to meet the minimum standard. Brazil's implementation remains unchanged, and therefore continues to meet the minimum standard.

188. Brazil has met all of the ToR for the information gathering process and no recommendations are made.

Exchange of information (ToR II.B)

189. Brazil has the necessary domestic legal basis to exchange information spontaneously. Brazil notes that there are no legal or practical impediments that prevent the spontaneous exchange of information on rulings as contemplated in the Action 5 minimum standard.

190. Brazil has international agreements permitting spontaneous exchange of information, including: (i) the *Multilateral Convention on Mutual Administrative Assistance in Tax Matters: Amended by the 2010 Protocol* (OECD/Council of Europe, 2011[2]) ("the Convention"), (ii) bilateral agreements in force with 36 jurisdictions and (iii) tax information exchange agreements in force with two jurisdictions.[2]

191. During the year in review, no exchanges were required to take place and no data on the timeliness of exchanges is reported.

192. In the prior years' peer review reports, it was determined that Brazil's process for the completion and exchange of templates were sufficient to meet the minimum standard. With respect to past rulings, no further action was required. Brazil's implementation in this regard remains unchanged and therefore continues to meet the minimum standard.

193. Brazil has the necessary legal basis for spontaneous exchange of information, a process for completing the templates in a timely way and has completed all exchanges. Brazil has met all of the ToR for the exchange of information process and no recommendations are made.

Statistics (ToR IV.D)

194. As no rulings were issued, no statistics can be reported.

Matters related to intellectual property regimes (ToR I.A.1.3)

195. Brazil does not offer an intellectual property regime for which transparency requirements under the Action 5 Report (OECD, 2015[3]) were imposed.

Summary of recommendations on implementation of the transparency framework

Aspect of implementation of the transparency framework that should be improved	Recommendation for improvement
	No recommendations are made.

References

OECD (2021), *BEPS Action 5 on Harmful Tax Practices - Terms of Reference and Methodology for the Conduct of the Peer Reviews of the Action 5 Transparency Framework*, OECD Publishing, Paris, https://www.oecd.org/tax/beps/beps-action-5-harmful-tax-practices-peer-review-transparency-framework.pdf. [1]

OECD (2015), *Countering Harmful Tax Practices More Effectively, Taking into Account Transparency and Substance, Action 5 - 2015 Final Report*, OECD/G20 Base Erosion and Profit Shifting Project, OECD Publishing, Paris, https://doi.org/10.1787/9789264241190-en. [3]

OECD/Council of Europe (2011), *The Multilateral Convention on Mutual Administrative Assistance in Tax Matters: Amended by the 2010 Protocol*, OECD Publishing, Paris, https://doi.org/10.1787/9789264115606-en. [2]

Notes

[1] PADIS – Semiconductors Industry.

[2] Participating jurisdictions to the Convention are available here: www.oecd.org/tax/exchange-of-tax-information/convention-on-mutual-administrative-assistance-in-tax-matters.htm. Brazil also has bilateral agreements with Argentina, Austria, Belgium, Canada, Chile, China (People's Republic of), Czechia, Denmark, Equator, Finland, France, Hungary, India, Israel, Italy, Japan, Korea, Luxembourg, Mexico, Norway, Netherlands, Peru, Portugal, Philippines, Slovak Republic, Russia, Singapore, South Africa, Spain, Sweden, Switzerland, Trinidad and Tobago, Türkiye, Ukraine, United Arab Emirates and Venezuela. The TIEAs with Jersey and the United Kingdom also permit for the spontaneous exchange of information.

Brunei Darussalam

Brunei Darussalam has met all aspects of the terms of reference (OECD, 2021[1]) (ToR) for the calendar year 2022 (year in review), and no recommendations are made.

Brunei Darussalam can legally issue five types of rulings within the scope of the transparency framework.

Brunei Darussalam issued no rulings within the scope of the transparency framework.

As no exchanges were required to take place, no peer input was received in respect of the exchanges of information on rulings received from Brunei Darussalam.

Information gathering process (ToR I.A)

196. Brunei Darussalam can legally issue the following five types of rulings within the scope of the transparency framework: (i) preferential regimes;[1] (ii) cross-border unilateral APAs and any other cross-border unilateral tax rulings (such as an advance tax ruling) covering transfer pricing or the application of transfer pricing principles; (iii) rulings providing for unilateral downward adjustments; (iv) permanent establishment rulings; and (v) related party conduit rulings.

197. For Brunei Darussalam, past rulings are any tax rulings within scope that are issued either: (i) on or after 1 January 2015 but before 1 April 2017; or (ii) on or after 1 January 2012 but before 1 January 2015, provided they were still in effect as at 1 January 2015. Future rulings are any tax rulings within scope that are issued on or after 1 April 2017.

198. In the prior years' peer review reports, it was determined that Brunei Darussalam's undertakings to identify past and future rulings and all potential exchange jurisdictions were sufficient to meet the minimum standard. In addition, it was determined that Brunei Darussalam's review and supervision mechanism was sufficient to meet the minimum standard. Brunei Darussalam's implementation remains unchanged, and therefore continues to meet the minimum standard.

199. Brunei Darussalam has met all of the ToR for the information gathering process and no recommendations are made.

Exchange of information (ToR II.B)

200. Brunei Darussalam has the necessary domestic legal basis to exchange information spontaneously. Brunei Darussalam notes that there are no legal or practical impediments that prevent the spontaneous exchange of information on rulings as contemplated in the Action 5 minimum standard.

201. Brunei Darussalam has international agreements permitting spontaneous exchange of information, including: (i) the *Multilateral Convention on Mutual Administrative Assistance in Tax Matters: Amended by the 2010 Protocol* (OECD/Council of Europe, 2011[2]) ("the Convention") and (ii) bilateral agreements in force with 18 jurisdictions.[2]

202. During the year in review, no exchanges were required to take place and no data on the timeliness of exchanges is reported.

203. In the prior years' peer review reports, it was determined that Brunei Darussalam's process for the completion and exchange of templates were sufficient to meet the minimum standard. With respect to past rulings, no further action was required. Brunei Darussalam's implementation in this regard remains unchanged and therefore continues to meet the minimum standard.

204. Brunei Darussalam has the necessary legal basis for spontaneous exchange of information, a process for completing the templates in a timely way and has completed all exchanges. Brunei Darussalam has met all of the ToR for the exchange of information process and no recommendations are made.

Statistics (ToR IV.D)

205. As no rulings were issued, no statistics can be reported.

Matters related to intellectual property regimes (ToR I.A.1.3)

206. Brunei Darussalam does not offer an intellectual property regime for which transparency requirements under the Action 5 Report (OECD, 2015[3]) were imposed.

Summary of recommendations on implementation of the transparency framework

Aspect of implementation of the transparency framework that should be improved	Recommendation for improvement
	No recommendations are made.

References

OECD (2021), *BEPS Action 5 on Harmful Tax Practices - Terms of Reference and Methodology for the Conduct of the Peer Reviews of the Action 5 Transparency Framework*, OECD Publishing, Paris, https://www.oecd.org/tax/beps/beps-action-5-harmful-tax-practices-peer-review-transparency-framework.pdf. [1]

OECD (2015), *Countering Harmful Tax Practices More Effectively, Taking into Account Transparency and Substance, Action 5 - 2015 Final Report*, OECD/G20 Base Erosion and Profit Shifting Project, OECD Publishing, Paris, https://doi.org/10.1787/9789264241190-en. [3]

OECD/Council of Europe (2011), *The Multilateral Convention on Mutual Administrative Assistance in Tax Matters: Amended by the 2010 Protocol*, OECD Publishing, Paris, https://doi.org/10.1787/9789264115606-en. [2]

Notes

[1] Investment incentive order.

[2] Participating jurisdictions to the Convention are available here: www.oecd.org/tax/exchange-of-tax-information/convention-on-mutual-administrative-assistance-in-tax-matters.htm. Brunei Darussalam also has bilateral agreements with Bahrain, Cambodia, China (People's Republic of), Hong Kong (China), Indonesia, Japan, Korea, Kuwait, Lao People's Democratic Republic, Luxembourg, Malaysia, Oman, Pakistan, Qatar, Singapore, United Arab Emirates, United Kingdom and Viet Nam.

Burkina Faso

Burkina Faso has met all aspects of the terms of reference (OECD, 2021[1]) (ToR) for the transparency framework and to commence administrative preparations to ensure that it establishes an information gathering process (ToR I.A) and that information on rulings will be identified and exchanged in a timely manner (ToR II.B). Burkina Faso receives two recommendations on these points for the year in review.

In the 2017-2019 peer reviews, it was determined that Burkina Faso could not issue advance rulings under the transparency framework due to the lack of an administrative process to make such rulings binding within the tax administration. The administrative process was put in place in 2020.

In the prior year's report, as well as the 2020 report, Burkina Faso had received two recommendations. As they have not been addressed, the recommendations remain in place.

Burkina Faso can legally issue four types of rulings within the scope of the transparency framework.

In practice, Burkina Faso has not issued rulings within the scope of the transparency framework.

No peer input was received in respect of the exchanges of information on rulings received from Burkina Faso.

Information gathering process (ToR I.A)

207. Burkina Faso can legally issue the following four types of rulings within the scope of the transparency framework: (i) preferential regimes; (ii) rulings providing for unilateral downward adjustments; (iii) permanent establishment rulings; and (iv) related party conduit rulings.

Past rulings (ToR I.A.1.1, I.A.1.2, I.A.2.1, I.A.2.2)

208. For Burkina Faso, past rulings are any tax rulings within scope that are issued either: (i) on or after 1 January 2015 but before 1 April 2017; or (ii) on or after 1 January 2012 but before 1 January 2015, provided they were still in effect as at 1 January 2015.

209. In the prior years' peer review reports, it was determined that Burkina Faso could not issue rulings under the transparency framework before 2020, therefore this section is not evaluated.

Future rulings (ToR I.A.1.1, I.A.1.2, I.A.2.1)

210. For Burkina Faso, future rulings are any tax rulings within scope that are issued on or after 1 April 2017.

211. Based on the responses to the questionnaire for the year 2021, Burkina Faso indicates that it has issued a decision on preferential regimes, but it is unclear what specific regime the decision was issued on and whether it is a regime allowing preference to income from geographically mobile activities (such as financial and other services) or the provision of intangibles, which would therefore fall under Action 5. Furthermore, during the year in review, Burkina Faso has not yet put in place a process to report rulings for the purposes of the transparency framework.

Review and supervision (ToR I.A.3)

212. During the year in review, it was determined that Burkina Faso did not yet have a review and supervision mechanism for past rulings under the transparency framework.

Conclusion on section A

213. Burkina Faso is recommended to put in place its information gathering process for identifying all past and future rulings and all potential exchange jurisdictions, with a review and supervision mechanism, as soon as possible (ToR I.A).

Exchange of information (ToR II.B)

214. Burkina Faso has the necessary domestic legal basis to exchange information spontaneously. Burkina Faso notes that there are no legal or practical impediments that prevent the spontaneous exchange of information on rulings as contemplated in the Action 5 minimum standard.

215. Burkina Faso signed the *Multilateral Convention on Mutual Administrative Assistance in Tax Matters: Amended by the 2010 Protocol* (OECD/Council of Europe, 2011[2]) ("the Convention") in August 2016, deposited the instrument of ratification in December 2022 and became a party to the Convention in April 2023. Burkina Faso has international agreements permitting spontaneous exchange of information, including bilateral agreements in force with two jurisdictions.[1]

Completion and exchange of templates (ToR II.B.3, II.B.4, II.B.5, II.B.6, II.B.7)

216. During the year in review, Burkina Faso has not made exchanges of information nor put in place a process to develop templates on relevant rulings, to make them available to the Competent Authority for exchange of information, and to exchange them with relevant jurisdictions.

Conclusion on section B

217. Burkina Faso is recommended to put in place a domestic legal framework allowing spontaneous exchange of information on rulings and to complete the templates for all relevant rulings and to ensure that the exchanges of information on rulings occur as soon as possible (ToR II.B).

Statistics (ToR IV.D)

218. As there was no rulings exchanged by Burkina Faso for the year in review, no statistics can be reported.

Matters related to intellectual property regimes (ToR I.A.1.3)

219. Burkina Faso does not offer an intellectual property regime for which transparency requirements under the Action 5 Report (OECD, 2015[3]) were imposed.

Summary of recommendations on implementation of the transparency framework

Aspect of implementation of the transparency framework that should be improved	Recommendation for improvement
Burkina Faso has not taken all measures to put in place the required information gathering process.	Burkina Faso is recommended to finalise its information gathering process and implement a review and supervision mechanism as soon as possible. This recommendation remains unchanged since the 2020 and 2021 peer review reports.
Burkina Faso has not yet put in place the process to develop templates on relevant rulings, to make them available to the Competent Authority for exchange of information, and to exchange them with relevant jurisdictions.	Burkina Faso is recommended to establish a process to develop templates on relevant rulings and ensure that information on these rulings is exchanged in a timely manner and in the format required by the transparency framework. This recommendation remains unchanged since the 2020 and 2021 peer review reports.

References

OECD (2021), *BEPS Action 5 on Harmful Tax Practices - Terms of Reference and Methodology for the Conduct of the Peer Reviews of the Action 5 Transparency Framework*, OECD Publishing, Paris, https://www.oecd.org/tax/beps/beps-action-5-harmful-tax-practices-peer-review-transparency-framework.pdf. [1]

OECD (2015), *Countering Harmful Tax Practices More Effectively, Taking into Account Transparency and Substance, Action 5 - 2015 Final Report*, OECD/G20 Base Erosion and Profit Shifting Project, OECD Publishing, Paris, https://doi.org/10.1787/9789264241190-en. [3]

OECD/Council of Europe (2011), *The Multilateral Convention on Mutual Administrative Assistance in Tax Matters: Amended by the 2010 Protocol*, OECD Publishing, Paris, https://doi.org/10.1787/9789264115606-en. [2]

Note

[1] Participating jurisdictions to the Convention are available here: www.oecd.org/tax/exchange-of-tax-information/convention-on-mutual-administrative-assistance-in-tax-matters.htm. Burkina Faso also has bilateral agreements with France and Tunisia within WAEMU and ECOWAS.

Cabo Verde

Cabo Verde has met all aspects of the terms of reference (OECD, 2021[1]) (ToR) for the calendar year 2022 (year in review), except for exchanging information on the tax rulings in accordance with the form and timelines under the transparency framework (ToR II.B). Cabo Verde receives one recommendation on this point for the year in review.

In the prior year report, as well as in the 2019 and 2020 peer review reports, Cabo Verde had received the same recommendation. As it has not been addressed, the recommendation remains in place.

Cabo Verde can legally issue three types of rulings within the scope of the transparency framework.

In practice, Cabo Verde issued no rulings within the scope of the transparency framework.

As no exchanges were required to take place, no peer input was received in respect of the exchanges of information on rulings received from Cabo Verde.

Information gathering process (ToR I.A)

220. Cabo Verde can legally issue the following three types of rulings within the scope of the transparency framework: (i) preferential regimes;[1] (ii) cross-border unilateral APAs and any other cross-border unilateral tax rulings (such as an advance tax ruling) covering transfer pricing or the application of transfer pricing principles; and (iii) permanent establishment rulings.

221. For Cabo Verde, past rulings are any tax rulings issued prior to 1 March 2019. However, there is no obligation for Cabo Verde to conduct spontaneous exchange of information on past rulings. Future rulings are any tax rulings within scope that are issued on or after 1 March 2019.

222. In the prior years' peer review reports, it was determined that Cabo Verde's undertakings to identify past and future rulings and all potential exchange jurisdictions were sufficient to meet the minimum standard. In addition, it was determined that Cabo Verde's review and supervision mechanism was sufficient to meet the minimum standard. Cabo Verde's implementation remains unchanged, and therefore continues to meet the minimum standard.

223. Cabo Verde has met all of the ToR for the information gathering process and no recommendations are made.

Exchange of information (ToR II.B)

Legal basis for spontaneous exchange of information (ToR II.B.1, II.B.2)

224. Cabo Verde has the necessary domestic legal basis to exchange information spontaneously. Cabo Verde notes that there are no legal or practical impediments that prevent the spontaneous exchange of information on rulings as contemplated in the Action 5 minimum standard.

225. Cabo Verde has international agreements permitting spontaneous exchange of information, including: (i) the *Multilateral Convention on Mutual Administrative Assistance in Tax Matters: Amended by the 2010 Protocol* (OECD/Council of Europe, 2011[2]) ("the Convention") and (ii) bilateral agreements in force with two jurisdictions.[2]

Completion and exchange of templates (ToR II.B.3, II.B.4, II.B.5, II.B.6, II.B.7)

226. In the prior years' peer review reports, it was determined that Cabo Verde did not have a process in place to complete the templates on relevant rulings in the agreed form, to make them available to the Competent Authority for exchange of information without undue delay, and to exchange them with relevant jurisdictions in accordance with the agreed timelines. Therefore, Cabo Verde was recommended to develop a process to complete the templates on relevant rulings and to ensure that the exchanges of information on rulings occur in accordance with the form and timelines under the transparency framework going forward. With respect to past rulings, no action was required. During the year in review, Cabo Verde indicated that this process is not yet in place and internal guidance is in the process of being developed to address this issue. Therefore, the prior year recommendation remains.

227. During the year in review, no exchanges were required to take place and no data on the timeliness of exchanges is reported.

Conclusion on section B

228. Cabo Verde has the necessary legal basis for spontaneous exchange of information. Cabo Verde does not have a process to complete the templates on relevant rulings and to make them available to the Competent Authority for exchange of information.

229. Cabo Verde is recommended to continue its efforts to develop a process to complete the templates for all relevant rulings and to ensure that the exchanges of information on rulings occur in accordance with the form and timelines under the transparency framework as soon as possible (ToR II.B).

Statistics (ToR IV)

230. As no rulings were issued, no statistics can be reported.

Matters related to intellectual property regimes (ToR I.A.1.3)

231. Cabo Verde does not offer an intellectual property regime for which transparency requirements under the Action 5 Report (OECD, 2015[3]) were imposed.

Summary of recommendations on implementation of the transparency framework

Aspect of implementation of the transparency framework that should be improved	Recommendation for improvement
Cabo Verde does not have a process to complete the templates on relevant rulings and to make them available to the Competent Authority for exchange of information.	Cabo Verde is recommended to continue its efforts to develop a process to complete the templates for all relevant rulings and to ensure that the exchanges of information on rulings occur in accordance with the form and timelines under the transparency framework as soon as possible. This recommendation remains unchanged since the 2019, 2020 and 2021 peer review reports.

References

OECD (2021), *BEPS Action 5 on Harmful Tax Practices - Terms of Reference and Methodology for the Conduct of the Peer Reviews of the Action 5 Transparency Framework*, OECD Publishing, Paris, https://www.oecd.org/tax/beps/beps-action-5-harmful-tax-practices-peer-review-transparency-framework.pdf. [1]

OECD (2015), *Countering Harmful Tax Practices More Effectively, Taking into Account Transparency and Substance, Action 5 - 2015 Final Report*, OECD/G20 Base Erosion and Profit Shifting Project, OECD Publishing, Paris, https://doi.org/10.1787/9789264241190-en. [3]

OECD/Council of Europe (2011), *The Multilateral Convention on Mutual Administrative Assistance in Tax Matters: Amended by the 2010 Protocol*, OECD Publishing, Paris, https://doi.org/10.1787/9789264115606-en. [2]

Notes

[1] Maio Special Economic Zone.

[2] Participating jurisdictions to the Convention are available here: www.oecd.org/tax/exchange-of-tax-information/convention-on-mutual-administrative-assistance-in-tax-matters.htm Cabo Verde also has bilateral agreements with Portugal and Spain.

Canada

Canada has met all aspects of the terms of reference (OECD, 2021[1]) (ToR) for the calendar year 2022 (year in review), and no recommendations are made.

Canada can legally issue four types of rulings within the scope of the transparency framework.

In practice, Canada issued rulings within the scope of the transparency framework as follows:

Type of ruling	Number of rulings
Past rulings	12
Future rulings in the period 1 April 2016 – 31 December 2016	2
Future rulings in the calendar year 2017	2
Future rulings in the calendar year 2018	1
Future rulings in the calendar year 2019	1
Future rulings in the calendar year 2020	1
Future rulings in the calendar year 2021	1
Future rulings in the year in review	3

Peer input was received from one jurisdiction in respect of the exchanges of information on rulings received from Canada. The input was positive, noting that information was complete, in a correct format and received in a timely manner.

Information gathering process (ToR I.A)

232. Canada can legally issue the following four types of rulings within the scope of the transparency framework: (i) preferential regimes;[1] (ii) cross-border unilateral APAs and any other cross-border unilateral tax rulings (such as an advance tax ruling) covering transfer pricing or the application of transfer pricing principles; (iii) permanent establishment rulings; and (iv) related party conduit rulings.

233. For Canada, past rulings are any tax rulings within scope that are issued either: (i) on or after 1 January 2014 but before 1 April 2016; or (ii) on or after 1 January 2010 but before 1 January 2014, provided they were still in effect as at 1 January 2014. Future rulings are any tax rulings within scope that are issued on or after 1 April 2016.

234. In the prior years' peer review reports, it was determined that Canada's undertakings to identify past and future rulings and all potential exchange jurisdictions were sufficient to meet the minimum standard. In addition, it was determined that Canada's review and supervision mechanism was sufficient to meet the minimum standard. Canada's implementation remains unchanged, and therefore continues to meet the minimum standard.

235. Canada has met all of the ToR for the information gathering process and no recommendations are made.

Exchange of information (ToR II.B)

236. Canada has the necessary domestic legal basis to exchange information spontaneously. Canada notes that there are no legal or practical impediments that prevent the spontaneous exchange of information on rulings as contemplated in the Action 5 minimum standard.

237. Canada has international agreements permitting spontaneous exchange of information, including: (i) the *Multilateral Convention on Mutual Administrative Assistance in Tax Matters: Amended by the 2010 Protocol* (OECD/Council of Europe, 2011[2]) ("the Convention") and (ii) bilateral agreements in force with 94 jurisdictions.[2]

238. For the year in review, the timeliness of exchanges is as follows:

Future rulings within the scope of the transparency framework	Number of exchanges transmitted within three months of the information becoming available to the competent authority or immediately after legal impediments have been lifted	Delayed exchanges		
		Number of exchanges transmitted later than three months of the information on rulings becoming available to the competent authority	Reasons for the delays	Any other comments
	3	0	N/A	N/A

Follow-up requests received for exchange of the ruling	Number	Average time to provide response	Number of requests not answered
	0	N/A	N/A

239. Canada notes that the exchanges relate to a ruling issued in 2021, which, as noted in the prior year review report, was submitted to its competent authority in late December 2021 and exchanged in January 2022. Three other rulings were issued in December 2022 and will be exchanged in 2023. This will be reflected in next year's report.

240. In the prior years' peer review reports, it was determined that Canada's process for the completion and exchange of templates were sufficient to meet the minimum standard. With respect to past rulings, no further action was required. Canada's implementation in this regard remains unchanged and therefore continues to meet the minimum standard.

241. Canada has the necessary legal basis for spontaneous exchange of information, a process for completing the templates in a timely way and has completed all exchanges. Canada has met all of the ToR for the exchange of information process and no recommendations are made.

Statistics (ToR IV.D)

242. The statistics for the year in review are as follows:

Category of ruling	Number of exchanges	Jurisdictions exchanged with
Ruling related to a preferential regime	0	N/A
Cross-border unilateral APAs and any other cross-border unilateral tax rulings (such as an advance tax ruling) covering transfer pricing or the application of transfer pricing principles	*De minimis* rule applies	N/A
Permanent establishment rulings	0	N/A
Related party conduit rulings	0	N/A
De minimis rule	3	N/A
Total	3	

Matters related to intellectual property regimes (ToR I.A.1.3)

243. Canada does not offer an intellectual property regime for which transparency requirements under the Action 5 Report (OECD, 2015[3]) were imposed.

Summary of recommendations on implementation of the transparency framework

Aspect of implementation of the transparency framework that should be improved	Recommendation for improvement
	No recommendations are made.

References

OECD (2021), *BEPS Action 5 on Harmful Tax Practices - Terms of Reference and Methodology for the Conduct of the Peer Reviews of the Action 5 Transparency Framework*, OECD Publishing, Paris, https://www.oecd.org/tax/beps/beps-action-5-harmful-tax-practices-peer-review-transparency-framework.pdf. [1]

OECD (2015), *Countering Harmful Tax Practices More Effectively, Taking into Account Transparency and Substance, Action 5 - 2015 Final Report*, OECD/G20 Base Erosion and Profit Shifting Project, OECD Publishing, Paris, https://doi.org/10.1787/9789264241190-en. [3]

OECD/Council of Europe (2011), *The Multilateral Convention on Mutual Administrative Assistance in Tax Matters: Amended by the 2010 Protocol*, OECD Publishing, Paris, https://doi.org/10.1787/9789264115606-en. [2]

Notes

[1] 1) Life insurance business and 2) International shipping.

[2] Participating jurisdictions to the Convention are available here: www.oecd.org/tax/exchange-of-tax-information/convention-on-mutual-administrative-assistance-in-tax-matters.htm. Canada also has bilateral agreements with Algeria, Argentina, Armenia, Australia, Austria, Azerbaijan, Bangladesh, Barbados, Belgium, Brazil, Bulgaria, Cameroon, Chile, China (People's Republic of), Colombia, Cote d'Ivoire, Croatia, Cyprus, Czechia, Denmark, Dominican Republic, Ecuador, Egypt, Estonia, Finland, France, Gabon, Germany, Greece, Guyana, Hong Kong (China), Hungary, Iceland, India, Indonesia, Ireland, Israel, Italy, Jamaica, Japan, Jordan, Kazakhstan, Kenya, Korea, Kuwait, Kyrgyzstan, Latvia, Lithuania, Luxembourg, Madagascar, Malaysia, Malta, Mexico, Moldova, Mongolia, Morocco, Netherlands, New Zealand, Nigeria, Norway, Oman, Pakistan, Papua New Guinea, Peru, Philippines, Poland, Portugal, Romania, Russia, Senegal, Serbia, Singapore, Slovak Republic, Slovenia, South Africa, Spain, Sri Lanka, Sweden, Switzerland, Chinese Taipei, Tanzania, Thailand, Trinidad & Tobago, Tunisia, Türkiye, Ukraine, United Arab Emirates, United Kingdom, United States, Uzbekistan, Venezuela, Viet Nam, Zambia and Zimbabwe. The Tax Information Exchange Agreement with Aruba also permits spontaneous exchange of information.

Chile

Chile has met all aspects of the terms of reference (OECD, 2021[1]) (ToR) for the calendar year 2022 (year in review), and no recommendations are made.

Chile can legally issue two types of rulings within the scope of the transparency framework.

In practice, Chile issued rulings within the scope of the transparency framework as follows:

Type of ruling	Number of rulings
Past rulings	0
Future rulings in the period 1 April 2016 – 31 December 2016	0
Future rulings in the calendar year 2017	0
Future rulings in the calendar year 2018	0
Future rulings in the calendar year 2019	2
Future rulings in the calendar year 2020	0
Future rulings in the calendar year 2021	3
Future rulings in the year in review	1

No peer input was received in respect of the exchanges of information on rulings received from Chile.

Information gathering process (ToR I.A)

244. Chile can legally issue the following two types of rulings within the scope of the transparency framework: (i) cross-border unilateral APAs and any other cross-border unilateral tax rulings (such as an advance tax ruling) covering transfer pricing or the application of transfer pricing principles; and (ii) related party conduit rulings.

245. For Chile, past rulings are any tax rulings within scope that are issued either: (i) on or after 1 January 2014 but before 1 April 2016; or (ii) on or after 1 January 2010 but before 1 January 2014, provided they were still in effect as at 1 January 2014. Future rulings are any tax rulings within scope that are issued on or after 1 April 2016.

246. In the prior years' peer review reports, it was determined that Chile's undertakings to identify past and future rulings and all potential exchange jurisdictions were sufficient to meet the minimum standard. In addition, it was determined that Chile's review and supervision mechanism was sufficient to meet the minimum standard. Chile's implementation remains unchanged, and therefore continues to meet the minimum standard.

247. Chile has met all of the ToR for the information gathering process and no recommendations are made.

Exchange of information (ToR II.B)

248. Chile has the necessary domestic legal basis to exchange information spontaneously. Chile notes that there are no legal or practical impediments that prevent the spontaneous exchange of information on rulings as contemplated in the Action 5 minimum standard.

249. Chile has international agreements permitting spontaneous exchange of information, including: (i) the *Multilateral Convention on Mutual Administrative Assistance in Tax Matters: Amended by the 2010 Protocol* (OECD/Council of Europe, 2011[2]) ("the Convention") and (ii) bilateral agreements in force with 33 jurisdictions.[1]

250. For the year in review, the timeliness of exchanges is as follows:

Future rulings within the scope of the transparency framework	Number of exchanges transmitted within three months of the information becoming available to the competent authority or immediately after legal impediments have been lifted	Delayed exchanges		
		Number of exchanges transmitted later than three months of the information on rulings becoming available to the competent authority	Reasons for the delays	Any other comments
	1	N/A	N/A	N/A

Follow-up requests received for exchange of the ruling	Number	Average time to provide response	Number of requests not answered
	0	N/A	N/A

251. In the prior years' peer review reports, it was determined that Chile's process for the completion and exchange of templates were sufficient to meet the minimum standard. With respect to past rulings, no further action was required. Chile's implementation in this regard remains unchanged and therefore continues to meet the minimum standard.

252. Chile has the necessary legal basis for spontaneous exchange of information, a process for completing the templates in a timely way and has completed all exchanges. Chile has met all of the ToR for the exchange of information process and no recommendations are made.

Statistics (ToR IV.D)

253. The statistics for the year in review are as follows:

Category of ruling	Number of exchanges	Jurisdictions exchanged with
Cross-border unilateral APAs and any other cross-border unilateral tax rulings (such as an advance tax ruling) covering transfer pricing or the application of transfer pricing principles	*De minimis* rule applies	N/A
Related party conduit rulings	0	N/A
De minimis rule	1	N/A
Total	1	

Matters related to intellectual property regimes (ToR I.A.1.3)

254. Chile does not offer an intellectual property regime for which transparency requirements under the Action 5 Report (OECD, 2015[3]) were imposed.

Summary of recommendations on implementation of the transparency framework

Aspect of implementation of the transparency framework that should be improved	Recommendation for improvement
	No recommendations are made.

References

OECD (2021), *BEPS Action 5 on Harmful Tax Practices - Terms of Reference and Methodology for the Conduct of the Peer Reviews of the Action 5 Transparency Framework*, OECD Publishing, Paris, https://www.oecd.org/tax/beps/beps-action-5-harmful-tax-practices-peer-review-transparency-framework.pdf. [1]

OECD (2015), *Countering Harmful Tax Practices More Effectively, Taking into Account Transparency and Substance, Action 5 - 2015 Final Report*, OECD/G20 Base Erosion and Profit Shifting Project, OECD Publishing, Paris, https://doi.org/10.1787/9789264241190-en. [3]

OECD/Council of Europe (2011), *The Multilateral Convention on Mutual Administrative Assistance in Tax Matters: Amended by the 2010 Protocol*, OECD Publishing, Paris, https://doi.org/10.1787/9789264115606-en. [2]

Note

[1] Participating jurisdictions to the Convention are available here: www.oecd.org/tax/exchange-of-tax-information/convention-on-mutual-administrative-assistance-in-tax-matters.htm. Chile also has bilateral agreements with Argentina, Australia, Austria, Belgium, Brazil, Canada, China (People's Republic of), Colombia, Croatia, Czechia, Denmark, Ecuador, France, India, Ireland, Italy, Japan, Korea, Malaysia, Mexico, Netherlands, Norway, New Zealand, Paraguay, Peru, Poland, Portugal, Russia, Spain, South Africa, Sweden, Switzerland, Thailand, United Arab Emirates, United Kingdom and Uruguay.

China (People's Republic of)

China has met all aspects of the terms of reference (OECD, 2021[1]) (ToR) for the calendar year 2022 (year in review), and no recommendations are made.

China can legally issue one type of rulings within the scope of the transparency framework.

In practice, China issued rulings within the scope of the transparency framework as follows:

Type of ruling	Number of rulings
Past rulings	11
Future rulings in the period 1 April 2016 – 31 December 2016	6
Future rulings in the calendar year 2017	3
Future rulings in the calendar year 2018	2
Future rulings in the calendar year 2019	4
Future rulings in the calendar year 2020	15
Future rulings in the calendar year 2021	4
Future rulings in the year in review	19

No peer input was received in respect of the exchanges of information on rulings received from China.

Information gathering process (ToR I.A)

255. China can legally issue one type of ruling within the scope of the transparency framework: cross-border unilateral APAs and any other cross-border unilateral tax rulings (such as an advance tax ruling) covering transfer pricing or the application of transfer pricing principles.

256. There was previously a legal barrier to the exchange of information on rulings in China, which did not allow the exchange of past rulings. The legal framework in China was subsequently amended to allow exchanges on future rulings. Future rulings are any tax rulings within scope that are issued on or after 1 April 2016.

257. In the prior years' peer review reports, it was determined that China's undertakings to identify past and future rulings and all potential exchange jurisdictions were sufficient to meet the minimum standard. In addition, it was determined that China's review and supervision mechanism was sufficient to meet the minimum standard. China's implementation remains unchanged, and therefore continues to meet the minimum standard.

258. China has met all of the ToR for the information gathering process and no recommendations are made.

Exchange of information (ToR II.B)

259. China has the necessary domestic legal basis to exchange information spontaneously. China notes that there are no legal or practical impediments that prevent the spontaneous exchange of information on rulings as contemplated in the Action 5 minimum standard.

260. China has international agreements permitting spontaneous exchange of information, including: (i) the *Multilateral Convention on Mutual Administrative Assistance in Tax Matters: Amended by the 2010 Protocol* (OECD/Council of Europe, 2011[2]) ("the Convention") and (ii) bilateral agreements in force with 101 jurisdictions.[1]

261. For the year in review, the timeliness of exchanges is as follows:

Future rulings within the scope of the transparency framework	Number of exchanges transmitted within three months of the information becoming available to the competent authority or immediately after legal impediments have been lifted	Delayed exchanges		
		Number of exchanges transmitted later than three months of the information on rulings becoming available to the competent authority	Reasons for the delays	Any other comments
	22	0	N/A	N/A

Follow-up requests received for exchange of the ruling	Number	Average time to provide response	Number of requests not answered
	0	N/A	N/A

262. In the prior years' peer review reports, it was determined that China's process for the completion and exchange of templates were sufficient to meet the minimum standard. With respect to past rulings, no further action was required. China's implementation in this regard remains unchanged and therefore continues to meet the minimum standard.

263. China has the necessary legal basis for spontaneous exchange of information, a process for completing the templates in a timely way and has completed all exchanges. China has met all of the ToR for the exchange of information process and no recommendations are made.

Statistics (ToR IV.D)

264. The statistics for the year in review are as follows:

Category of ruling	Number of exchanges	Jurisdictions exchanged with
Cross-border unilateral APAs and any other cross-border unilateral tax rulings (such as an advance tax ruling) covering transfer pricing or the application of transfer pricing principles	22	France, Hong Kong (China), Japan, Korea, Malaysia, Singapore, United States

Matters related to intellectual property regimes (ToR I.A.1.3)

265. China does not offer an intellectual property regime for which transparency requirements under the Action 5 Report (OECD, 2015[3]) were imposed.

Summary of recommendations on implementation of the transparency framework

Aspect of implementation of the transparency framework that should be improved	Recommendation for improvement
	No recommendations are made.

References

OECD (2021), *BEPS Action 5 on Harmful Tax Practices - Terms of Reference and Methodology for the Conduct of the Peer Reviews of the Action 5 Transparency Framework*, OECD Publishing, Paris, https://www.oecd.org/tax/beps/beps-action-5-harmful-tax-practices-peer-review-transparency-framework.pdf. [1]

OECD (2015), *Countering Harmful Tax Practices More Effectively, Taking into Account Transparency and Substance, Action 5 - 2015 Final Report*, OECD/G20 Base Erosion and Profit Shifting Project, OECD Publishing, Paris, https://doi.org/10.1787/9789264241190-en. [3]

OECD/Council of Europe (2011), *The Multilateral Convention on Mutual Administrative Assistance in Tax Matters: Amended by the 2010 Protocol*, OECD Publishing, Paris, https://doi.org/10.1787/9789264115606-en. [2]

Notes

[1] Participating jurisdictions to the Convention are available here: www.oecd.org/tax/exchange-of-tax-information/convention-on-mutual-administrative-assistance-in-tax-matters.htm. China also has bilateral agreements with Albania, Algeria, Armenia, Australia, Austria, Azerbaijan, Bahrain, Bangladesh, Barbados, Belarus, Belgium, Bosnia and Herzegovina, Brazil, Brunei Darussalam, Bulgaria, Cambodia, Canada, Chile, Croatia, Cuba, Cyprus, Czechia, Denmark, Ecuador, Egypt, Estonia, Ethiopia, Finland, France,, Georgia, Germany, Greece, Hong Kong (China), Hungary, Iceland, India, Indonesia, Iran, Ireland, Israel, Italy, Jamaica, Japan, Kazakhstan, Korea, Kuwait, Kyrgyzstan, Lao People's Democratic Republic, Latvia, Lithuania, Luxembourg, Macao (China), Malaysia, Malta, Mauritius, Mexico, Moldova, Mongolia, Montenegro, Morocco, Nepal, Netherlands, New Zealand, Nigeria, North Macedonia, Norway, Oman, Pakistan, Papua New Guinea, Philippines, Poland, Portugal, Qatar, Romania, Russia, Saudi Arabia, Serbia, Seychelles, Singapore, Slovenia, South Africa, Spain, Sri Lanka, Sudan, Sweden, Switzerland, Syrian Arab Republic, Tajikistan, Thailand, Trinidad and Tobago, Tunisia, Türkiye, Turkmenistan, Ukraine, United Arab Emirates, United Kingdom, United States, Uzbekistan, Venezuela, Viet Nam, Zambia and Zimbabwe.

Colombia

Colombia has met all aspects of the terms of reference (OECD, 2021[1]) (ToR) for the calendar year 2022 (year in review), and no recommendations are made.

Colombia can legally issue one type of rulings within the scope of the transparency framework.

In practice, Colombia issued rulings within the scope of the transparency framework as follows:

Type of ruling	Number of rulings
Past rulings	1
Future rulings in the period 1 April 2016 – 31 December 2016	0
Future rulings in the calendar year 2017	0
Future rulings in the calendar year 2018	0
Future rulings in the calendar year 2019	0
Future rulings in the calendar year 2020	0
Future rulings in the calendar year 2021	0
Future rulings in the year in review	0

As no exchanges were required to take place, no peer input was received in respect of the exchanges of information on rulings received from Colombia.

Information gathering process (ToR I.A)

266. Colombia can legally issue the following type of rulings within the scope of the transparency framework: cross-border unilateral APAs and any other cross-border unilateral tax rulings (such as an advance tax ruling) covering transfer pricing or the application of transfer pricing principles.

267. For Colombia, past rulings are any tax rulings within scope that are issued either: (i) on or after 1 January 2014 but before 1 April 2016; or (ii) on or after 1 January 2010 but before 1 January 2014, provided they were still in effect as at 1 January 2014. Future rulings are any tax rulings within scope that are issued on or after 1 April 2016.

268. In the prior years' peer review reports, it was determined that Colombia's undertakings to identify past and future rulings and all potential exchange jurisdictions were sufficient to meet the minimum standard. In addition, it was determined that Colombia's review and supervision mechanism was sufficient to meet the minimum standard. Colombia's implementation remains unchanged, and therefore continues to meet the minimum standard.

269. Colombia has met all of the ToR for the information gathering process and no recommendations are made.

Exchange of information (ToR II.B)

270. Colombia has the necessary domestic legal basis to exchange information spontaneously. Colombia notes that there are no legal or practical impediments that prevent the spontaneous exchange of information on rulings as contemplated in the Action 5 minimum standard.

271. Colombia has international agreements permitting spontaneous exchange of information, including: (i) the Multilateral Convention on Mutual Administrative Assistance in Tax Matters: Amended by the 2010 Protocol (OECD/Council of Europe, 2011[2]) ("the Convention"), (ii) bilateral agreements in force with 13 jurisdictions, (iii) regional instruments in force with three jurisdictions and (iv) tax information exchange agreements with one jurisdiction.[1]

272. During the year in review, no exchanges were required to take place and no data on the timeliness of exchanges is reported.

273. In the prior years' peer review reports, it was determined that Colombia's process for the completion and exchange of templates were sufficient to meet the minimum standard. With respect to past rulings, no further action was required. Colombia's implementation in this regard remains unchanged and therefore continues to meet the minimum standard.

274. Colombia has the necessary legal basis for spontaneous exchange of information, a process for completing the templates in a timely way and has completed all exchanges. Colombia has met all of the ToR for the exchange of information process and no recommendations are made.

Statistics (ToR IV.D)

275. As no rulings were issued, no statistics can be reported.

Matters related to intellectual property regimes (ToR I.A.1.3)

276. Colombia does not offer an intellectual property regime for which transparency requirements under the Action 5 Report (OECD, 2015[3]) were imposed.

Summary of recommendations on implementation of the transparency framework

Aspect of implementation of the transparency framework that should be improved	Recommendation for improvement
	No recommendations are made.

References

OECD (2021), *BEPS Action 5 on Harmful Tax Practices - Terms of Reference and Methodology for the Conduct of the Peer Reviews of the Action 5 Transparency Framework*, OECD Publishing, Paris, https://www.oecd.org/tax/beps/beps-action-5-harmful-tax-practices-peer-review-transparency-framework.pdf. [1]

OECD (2015), *Countering Harmful Tax Practices More Effectively, Taking into Account Transparency and Substance, Action 5 - 2015 Final Report*, OECD/G20 Base Erosion and Profit Shifting Project, OECD Publishing, Paris, https://doi.org/10.1787/9789264241190-en. [3]

OECD/Council of Europe (2011), *The Multilateral Convention on Mutual Administrative Assistance in Tax Matters: Amended by the 2010 Protocol*, OECD Publishing, Paris, https://doi.org/10.1787/9789264115606-en. [2]

Note

[1] Participating jurisdictions to the Convention are available here: www.oecd.org/tax/exchange-of-tax-information/convention-on-mutual-administrative-assistance-in-tax-matters.htm. Colombia also has bilateral agreements with Canada, Chile, Czechia, France, India, Italy, Japan, Korea, Mexico, Portugal, Spain, Switzerland and United Kingdom; regional instruments with Bolivia, Ecuador and Peru; and a tax information exchange agreement with the United States.

Congo

Congo did not provide a completed peer review questionnaire to the Secretariat. It is not known whether Congo has implemented the transparency framework in line with the terms of reference (OECD, 2021[1]) ToR) for the calendar year 2022 (year in review). Congo receives two recommendations covering the information gathering process (ToR I.A) and exchange of information (ToR II.B) for the year in review.

In the prior year report, as well as in the 2017-2020 peer reviews, Congo had received the same recommendations. As they have not been addressed, the recommendations remain in place.

Congo can legally issue two types of rulings within the scope of the transparency framework.

In practice, Congo did not issue any type of rulings within the scope of the transparency framework in previous years. For the year in review, as well as for the three prior years, it is not known whether Congo issued any type of rulings within the scope of the transparency framework.

No peer input was received in respect of the exchanges of information on rulings received from Congo.

Information gathering process (ToR I.A)

277. Congo can legally issue the following two types of rulings within the scope of the transparency framework: (i) cross-border unilateral APAs and any other cross-border unilateral tax rulings (such as an advance tax ruling) covering transfer pricing or the application of transfer pricing principles; (ii) permanent establishment rulings.

Past rulings (ToR I.A.1.1, I.A.1.2, I.A.2.1, I.A.2.2)

278. For Congo, past rulings are any tax rulings within scope that are issued either (i) on or after 1 January 2015 but before 1 April 2017; and (ii) on or after 1 January 2012 but before 1 January 2015, provided they were still in effect as at 1 January 2015.

279. In the 2018 peer review report, it was determined that Congo issued no past rulings in scope of the transparency framework. As such, this section is not assessed.

Future rulings (ToR I.A.1.1, I.A.1.2, I.A.2.1)

280. For Congo, future rulings are any tax rulings within scope that are issued on or after 1 April 2017.

281. In the 2018 peer review report, Congo indicated that there were no processes in place for the record keeping of rulings for the purposes of the transparency framework. It was noted that Congo intended to implement guidelines and practices to make sure the necessary information to meet the requirements of the transparency framework is required in all cases. Congo was recommended to finalise its information gathering process as soon as possible.

282. During the year in review, as it is not known whether Congo has finalised its information gathering process, the recommendation remains in place.

Review and supervision (ToR I.A.3)

283. In the 2018 peer review report, it was determined that Congo did not yet have a review and supervision mechanism under the transparency framework. Congo was in the process of considering the implementation of a revision and supervision mechanism for ensuring implementation of the transparency framework. As it is not known whether Congo has put in place a review and supervision mechanism under the transparency framework for the year in review, the recommendation remains in place.

Conclusion on section A

284. Congo is recommended to finalise its information gathering process, with a review and supervision mechanism, as soon as possible (ToR I.A).

Exchange of information (ToR II.B)

285. In the 2018 peer review report, it was determined that Congo was in the process of putting in place the necessary domestic legal basis to exchange information spontaneously. It is not known whether Congo has already put in place the necessary domestic legal basis to exchange information spontaneously for the year in review.

286. Congo has international agreements permitting spontaneous exchange of information, including bilateral agreements in force with 3 jurisdictions.[1] Congo is not a party to the *Multilateral Convention on Mutual Administrative Assistance in Tax Matters: Amended by the 2010 Protocol* (OECD/Council of Europe, 2011[2]) ("the Convention"). Congo is encouraged to continue its efforts to expand its international exchange of information instruments to be able to exchange information on rulings. It is noted, however, that jurisdictions are assessed on their compliance with the transparency framework in respect of the exchange of information network in effect for the year of the particular annual review.

Completion and exchange of templates (ToR II.B.3, II.B.4, II.B.5, II.B.6, II.B.7)

287. In the 2018 peer review report, it was determined that Congo was developing a process to complete the templates on relevant rulings, to make them available to the Competent Authority for exchange of information, and to exchange them with relevant jurisdictions. It is not known whether Congo has already put in place such a process for the year in review.

288. As it is not known whether exchanges took place in the year of review, no data on the timeliness of exchanges can be reported.

Conclusion on section B

289. Congo is recommended to put in place a domestic legal framework allowing spontaneous exchange of information on rulings and to continue its efforts to complete the templates for all relevant rulings and to ensure that the exchanges of information on rulings occur as soon as possible (ToR II.B).

Statistics (ToR IV.D)

290. As it is not known whether information on rulings was exchanged by Congo for the year in review, no statistics can be reported.

Matters related to intellectual property regimes (ToR I.A.1.3)

291. Congo does not offer an intellectual property regime for which transparency requirements under the Action 5 Report (OECD, 2015[3]) were imposed.

Summary of recommendations on implementation of the transparency framework

Aspect of implementation of the transparency framework that should be improved	Recommendation for improvement
It is not known whether Congo has finalised the steps to have in place its necessary information and gathering process.	Congo is recommended to finalise its information gathering process, with a review and supervision mechanism, as soon as possible. This recommendation remains unchanged since the 2017, 2018, 2019, 2020 and 2021 peer review reports.
It is not known whether Congo has finalised the steps to have effective compulsory spontaneous exchange of information on the tax rulings within the scope of the transparency framework.	Congo is recommended to continue to put in place a domestic legal framework allowing spontaneous exchange of information on rulings and to continue its efforts to complete the templates for all relevant rulings and to ensure that the exchanges of information on rulings occur as soon as possible. This recommendation remains unchanged since the 2017, 2018, 2019, 2020 and 2021 peer review reports.

References

OECD (2021), *BEPS Action 5 on Harmful Tax Practices - Terms of Reference and Methodology for the Conduct of the Peer Reviews of the Action 5 Transparency Framework*, OECD Publishing, Paris, https://www.oecd.org/tax/beps/beps-action-5-harmful-tax-practices-peer-review-transparency-framework.pdf. [1]

OECD (2015), *Countering Harmful Tax Practices More Effectively, Taking into Account Transparency and Substance, Action 5 - 2015 Final Report*, OECD/G20 Base Erosion and Profit Shifting Project, OECD Publishing, Paris, https://doi.org/10.1787/9789264241190-en. [3]

OECD/Council of Europe (2011), *The Multilateral Convention on Mutual Administrative Assistance in Tax Matters: Amended by the 2010 Protocol*, OECD Publishing, Paris, https://doi.org/10.1787/9789264115606-en. [2]

Note

[1] Participating jurisdictions to the Convention are available here: www.oecd.org/tax/exchange-of-tax-information/convention-on-mutual-administrative-assistance-in-tax-matters.htm. Congo also has bilateral agreements with France, Italy and Mauritius.

Costa Rica

Costa Rica has met all aspects of the terms of reference (OECD, 2021[1]) (ToR) for the calendar year 2022 (year in review), and no recommendations are made.

Costa Rica can legally issue two types of rulings within the scope of the transparency framework.

In practice, Costa Rica issued rulings within the scope of the transparency framework as follows:

Type of ruling	Number of rulings
Past rulings	6
Future rulings in the period 1 April 2017 – 31 December 2017	3
Future rulings in the calendar year 2018	4
Future rulings in the calendar year 2019	0
Future rulings in the calendar year 2020	3
Future rulings in the calendar year 2021	9
Future rulings in the year in review	3

No peer input was received in respect of the exchanges of information on rulings received from Costa Rica.

Information gathering process (ToR I.A)

292. Costa Rica can legally issue the following two types of rulings within the scope of the transparency framework: (i) cross-border unilateral APAs and any other cross-border unilateral tax rulings (such as an advance tax ruling) covering transfer pricing or the application of transfer pricing principles; and (ii) permanent establishment rulings.

293. For Costa Rica, past rulings are any tax rulings within scope that are issued either: (i) on or after 1 January 2015 but before 1 April 2017; or (ii) on or after 1 January 2012 but before 1 January 2015, provided they were still in effect as at 1 January 2015. Future rulings are any tax rulings within scope that are issued on or after 1 April 2017.

294. In the prior years' peer review reports, it was determined that Costa Rica's undertakings to identify past and future rulings and all potential exchange jurisdictions were sufficient to meet the minimum standard. In addition, it was determined that Costa Rica's review and supervision mechanism was sufficient to meet the minimum standard. Costa Rica notes that during the year in review, changes were introduced regarding the information gathering process on permanent establishment (PE) rulings. More specifically, the territorial tax administrations and the Large Taxpayers Directorate are now in charge of issuing these rulings. Furthermore, taxpayers are required to notify if there are any changes regarding the head office and the intermediate and ultimate parent entities. Costa Rica also notes that with these changes, the review and supervision mechanism has also changed. An official within the Taxpayer Service Management Area of the territorial tax administration and the Large Taxpayers Directorate reviews the information on the PE ruling and sends the draft ruling for approval and signature to the Deputy Manager. Afterwards, the Manager of the Territorial Tax Administration or Director of the Large Taxpayers Directorate issues the ruling. The template for the PE ruling will then be sent to the Competent Authority for the exchange. Costa Rica's implementation continues to meet the minimum standard.

295. Costa Rica has met all of the ToR for the information gathering process and no recommendations are made.

Exchange of information (ToR II.B)

296. Costa Rica has the necessary domestic legal basis to exchange information spontaneously. Costa Rica notes that there are no legal or practical impediments that prevent the spontaneous exchange of information on rulings as contemplated in the Action 5 minimum standard.

297. Costa Rica has international agreements permitting spontaneous exchange of information, including: (i) the *Multilateral Convention on Mutual Administrative Assistance in Tax Matters: Amended by the 2010 Protocol* (OECD/Council of Europe, 2011[2]) ("the Convention"), (ii) the Convention on Mutual Assistance and Technical Cooperation between Tax and Customs Administrations of Central America, (iii) bilateral agreements in force with four jurisdictions and (iv) tax information exchange agreements in force with two jurisdictions.[1]

298. For the year in review, the timeliness of exchanges is as follows:

Future rulings within the scope of the transparency framework	Number of exchanges transmitted within three months of the information becoming available to the competent authority or immediately after legal impediments have been lifted	Delayed exchanges		
		Number of exchanges transmitted later than three months of the information on rulings becoming available to the competent authority	Reasons for the delays	Any other comments
	6	0	N/A	N/A

Follow-up requests received for exchange of the ruling	Number	Average time to provide response	Number of requests not answered
	0	N/A	N/A

299. In the prior years' peer review reports, it was determined that Costa Rica's process for the completion and exchange of templates were sufficient to meet the minimum standard. With respect to past rulings, no further action was required. Costa Rica's implementation in this regard remains unchanged and therefore continues to meet the minimum standard.

300. Costa Rica has the necessary legal basis for spontaneous exchange of information, a process for completing the templates in a timely way and has completed all exchanges. Costa Rica has met all of the ToR for the exchange of information process and no recommendations are made.

Statistics (ToR IV.D)

301. The statistics for the year in review are as follows:

Category of ruling	Number of exchanges	Jurisdictions exchanged with
Cross-border unilateral APAs and any other cross-border unilateral tax rulings (such as an advance tax ruling) covering transfer pricing or the application of transfer pricing principles	0	N/A
Permanent establishment rulings	*De minimis* rule applies	N/A
De minimis rule	6	
Total	6	

Matters related to intellectual property regimes (ToR I.A.1.3)

302. Costa Rica does not offer an intellectual property regime for which transparency requirements under the Action 5 Report (OECD, 2015[3]) were imposed.

Summary of recommendations on implementation of the transparency framework

Aspect of implementation of the transparency framework that should be improved	Recommendation for improvement
	No recommendations are made.

References

OECD (2021), *BEPS Action 5 on Harmful Tax Practices - Terms of Reference and Methodology for the Conduct of the Peer Reviews of the Action 5 Transparency Framework*, OECD Publishing, Paris, https://www.oecd.org/tax/beps/beps-action-5-harmful-tax-practices-peer-review-transparency-framework.pdf. [1]

OECD (2015), *Countering Harmful Tax Practices More Effectively, Taking into Account Transparency and Substance, Action 5 - 2015 Final Report*, OECD/G20 Base Erosion and Profit Shifting Project, OECD Publishing, Paris, https://doi.org/10.1787/9789264241190-en. [3]

OECD/Council of Europe (2011), *The Multilateral Convention on Mutual Administrative Assistance in Tax Matters: Amended by the 2010 Protocol*, OECD Publishing, Paris, https://doi.org/10.1787/9789264115606-en. [2]

Note

[1] Participating jurisdictions to the Convention are available here: www.oecd.org/tax/exchange-of-tax-information/convention-on-mutual-administrative-assistance-in-tax-matters.htm. Costa Rica is also party to the Convention on Mutual Assistance and Technical Cooperation between Tax and Customs Administrations of Central America including El Salvador, Guatemala, Honduras and Nicaragua. Costa Rica has bilateral tax agreements with Germany, Mexico, Spain, and United Arab Emirates, and tax information exchange agreements with Argentina and the United States. All these agreements allow spontaneous exchange of information.

Croatia

Croatia has met all aspects of the terms of reference (OECD, 2021[1]) (ToR) for the calendar year 2022 (year in review), and no recommendations are made.

Croatia can legally issue four types of rulings within the scope of the transparency framework.

In practice, Croatia issued rulings within the scope of the transparency framework as follows:

Type of ruling	Number of rulings
Past rulings	0
Future rulings in the period 1 April 2017 – 31 December 2017	0
Future rulings in the calendar year 2018	1
Future rulings in the calendar year 2019	0
Future rulings in the calendar year 2020	0
Future rulings in the calendar year 2021	1
Future rulings in the year in review	1

No peer input was received in respect of the exchanges of information on rulings received from Croatia.

Information gathering process (ToR I.A)

303. Croatia can legally issue the following four types of rulings within the scope of the transparency framework: (i) cross-border unilateral APAs and any other cross-border unilateral tax rulings (such as an advance tax ruling) covering transfer pricing or the application of transfer pricing principles; (ii) rulings providing for unilateral downward adjustments; (iii) permanent establishment rulings; and (iv) related party conduit rulings.

304. For Croatia, past rulings are any tax rulings within scope that are issued either: (i) on or after 1 January 2015 but before 1 April 2017; or (ii) on or after 1 January 2012 but before 1 January 2015, provided they were still in effect as at 1 January 2014. Future rulings are any tax rulings within scope that are issued on or after 1 April 2017.

305. In the prior years' peer review reports, it was determined that Croatia's undertakings to identify past and future rulings and all potential exchange jurisdictions were sufficient to meet the minimum standard. In addition, it was determined that Croatia's review and supervision mechanism was sufficient to meet the minimum standard. Croatia's implementation remains unchanged, and therefore continues to meet the minimum standard.

306. Croatia has met all of the ToR for the information gathering process and no recommendations are made.

Exchange of information (ToR II.B)

307. Croatia has the necessary domestic legal basis to exchange information spontaneously. Croatia notes that there are no legal or practical impediments that prevent the spontaneous exchange of information on rulings as contemplated in the Action 5 minimum standard.

308. Croatia has international agreements permitting spontaneous exchange of information, including: (i) the *Multilateral Convention on Mutual Administrative Assistance in Tax Matters: Amended by the 2010 Protocol* (OECD/Council of Europe, 2011[2]) ("the Convention"), (ii) the Directive 2011/16/EU with all other European Union Member States and (iii) bilateral agreements in force with 66 jurisdictions.[1]

309. For the year in review, the timeliness of exchanges is as follows:

Future rulings within the scope of the transparency framework	Number of exchanges transmitted within three months of the information becoming available to the competent authority or immediately after legal impediments have been lifted	Delayed exchanges		
		Number of exchanges transmitted later than three months of the information on rulings becoming available to the competent authority	Reasons for the delays	Any other comments
	1	1	A delay occurred in 2021 that was solved in 2022, as described in the previous year's peer review report.	N/A

Follow-up requests received for exchange of the ruling	Number	Average time to provide response	Number of requests not answered
	0	N/A	N/A

310. In the prior years' peer review reports, it was determined that Croatia's process for the completion and exchange of templates were sufficient to meet the minimum standard. With respect to past rulings, no further action was required. Croatia's implementation in this regard remains unchanged and therefore continues to meet the minimum standard.

311. Croatia has the necessary legal basis for spontaneous exchange of information, a process for completing the templates in a timely way and has completed all exchanges. Croatia has met all of the ToR for the exchange of information process and no recommendations are made.

Statistics (ToR IV.D)

312. The statistics for the year in review are as follows:

Category of ruling	Number of exchanges	Jurisdictions exchanged with
Cross-border unilateral APAs and any other cross-border unilateral tax rulings (such as an advance tax ruling) covering transfer pricing or the application of transfer pricing principles	0	N/A
Cross-border rulings providing for a unilateral downward adjustment to the taxpayer's taxable profits that is not directly reflected in the taxpayer's financial / commercial accounts	0	N/A
Permanent establishment rulings	*De minimis* rule applies	N/A
Related party conduit rulings	0	N/A
De minimis rule	2	N/A
Total	2	

Matters related to intellectual property regimes (ToR I.A.1.3)

313. Croatia does not offer an intellectual property regime for which transparency requirements under the Action 5 Report (OECD, 2015[3]) were imposed.

Summary of recommendations on implementation of the transparency framework

Aspect of implementation of the transparency framework that should be improved	Recommendation for improvement
	No recommendations are made.

References

OECD (2021), *BEPS Action 5 on Harmful Tax Practices - Terms of Reference and Methodology for the Conduct of the Peer Reviews of the Action 5 Transparency Framework*, OECD Publishing, Paris, https://www.oecd.org/tax/beps/beps-action-5-harmful-tax-practices-peer-review-transparency-framework.pdf. [1]

OECD (2015), *Countering Harmful Tax Practices More Effectively, Taking into Account Transparency and Substance, Action 5 - 2015 Final Report*, OECD/G20 Base Erosion and Profit Shifting Project, OECD Publishing, Paris, https://doi.org/10.1787/9789264241190-en. [3]

OECD/Council of Europe (2011), *The Multilateral Convention on Mutual Administrative Assistance in Tax Matters: Amended by the 2010 Protocol*, OECD Publishing, Paris, https://doi.org/10.1787/9789264115606-en. [2]

Note

[1] Participating jurisdictions to the Convention are available here: www.oecd.org/tax/exchange-of-tax-information/convention-on-mutual-administrative-assistance-in-tax-matters.htm. Croatia also has bilateral agreements with Albania, Armenia, Austria, Azerbaijan, Belarus, Belgium, Bosnia and Herzegovina, Bulgaria, Canada, Chile, China (People's Republic of), Czechia, Denmark, Estonia, Finland, France, Georgia, Germany, Greece, Hungary, Iceland, India, Indonesia, Iran, Ireland, Israel, Italy, Japan, Jordan, Kazakhstan, Korea, Kosovo, Kuwait, Latvia, Lithuania, Luxembourg, Malaysia, Malta, Mauritius, Morocco, Moldova, Montenegro, Netherlands, North Macedonia, Norway, Oman, Poland, Portugal, Qatar, Romania, Russia, San Marino, Serbia, Slovak Republic, Slovenia, South Africa, Spain, Syrian Arab Republic, Sweden, Switzerland, Türkiye, Turkmenistan, Ukraine, United Arab Emirates, United Kingdom and Viet Nam.

Curaçao

Curaçao has met all aspects of the terms of reference (OECD, 2021[1]) (ToR) for the calendar year 2022 (year in review), except for identifying rulings within the scope of the transparency framework and under which category of rulings they fall (ToR I.A.1.1 and ToR I.A.1.2) and completing exchanges of information on rulings in accordance with the timelines (ToR II.B.5 and II.B.6). Curaçao receives two recommendations on these points for the year in review.

In the prior year report, as well as in the 2017-2020 peer reviews, Curaçao received the same two recommendations. As they have not yet been fully addressed, the recommendations remain in place.

Curaçao can legally issue five types of rulings within the scope of the transparency framework.

In practice, Curaçao issued rulings within the scope of the transparency framework as follows:

Type of ruling	Number of rulings
Past rulings	2414
Future rulings in the period 1 April 2017 – 31 December 2017	320
Future rulings in the calendar year 2018	48
Future rulings in the calendar year 2019	40
Future rulings in the calendar year 2020	20
Future rulings in the calendar year 2021	0
Future rulings in the year in review	0

As no exchanges took place, no peer input was received in respect of the exchanges of information on rulings received from Curaçao.

Information gathering process (ToR I.A)

314. Curaçao can legally issue the following five types of rulings within the scope of the transparency framework: (i) preferential regimes;[1] (ii) cross-border unilateral APAs and any other cross-border unilateral tax rulings (such as an advance tax ruling) covering transfer pricing or the application of transfer pricing principles; (iii) rulings providing for unilateral downward adjustments; (iv) permanent establishment rulings; and (v) related party conduit rulings.

Past rulings (ToR I.A.1.1, I.A.1.2, I.A.2.1, I.A.2.2)

315. For Curaçao, past rulings are any tax rulings within scope that are issued either (i) on or after 1 January 2015 but before 1 April 2017; and (ii) on or after 1 January 2012 but before 1 January 2015, provided they were still in effect as at 1 January 2015.

316. In the prior years' peer review reports, it was determined that Curaçao's undertakings to identify past rulings and all potential exchange jurisdictions have met all the ToR, except for completing the process of reviewing the templates to confirm that all past rulings identified are cross-border rulings and therefore within the scope of the transparency framework, and to identify which category of rulings they fall under (ToR I.4.1.2). In the 2021 peer review report, it was determined that the process was still ongoing given the large number of rulings, many of which fall into more than one category. It was also noted that Curaçao was identifying the potential exchange jurisdictions. Therefore, Curaçao was recommended to continue its work to complete its information gathering process on past rulings as soon as possible.

317. During the year in review, Curaçao continued this work and accordingly provided new statistics on past rulings, as part of the previously identified past rulings do not fall within the scope of one of the categories of the transparency framework. Curaçao anticipates that this process will be completed by the end of 2023. Therefore, the prior years' recommendation remains.

Future rulings (ToR I.A.1.1, I.A.1.2, I.A.2.1)

318. For Curaçao, future rulings are any tax rulings within scope that are issued on or after 1 April 2017.

319. In the prior years' peer review reports, it was determined that Curaçao's undertakings to identify future rulings and all potential exchange jurisdictions have met all the ToR, except for completing the process of reviewing the templates to confirm that all future rulings identified are cross border rulings and therefore within the scope of the transparency framework, and to identify which category each ruling falls under (ToR I.4.1.2). In the 2021 peer review report, it was noted that Curaçao was identifying the potential exchange jurisdictions. This process was still ongoing with respect to future rulings issued before July 2018, when a new procedure requiring future rulings and potential exchange jurisdictions to be immediately identified at the point of issue was put in place. Therefore, Curaçao was recommended to continue its work to complete its information-gathering process on future rulings as soon as possible.

320. In the prior years' peer review reports, it was also noted that Curaçao developing an electronic online system to digitalise the ruling request process. This new electronic procedure was intended to further increase the speed and accuracy of the information gathering process in future. Curaçao noted that this electronic system is expected to be in place in 2023.

321. During the year in review, Curaçao continued this work and it anticipates that this process will be completed by the end of 2023. Therefore, the prior years' recommendation remains.

Review and supervision (ToR I.A.3)

322. In the prior years' peer review reports, it was determined that Curaçao's review and supervision mechanism was sufficient to meet the minimum standard. Curaçao's implementation in this regard remains unchanged, and therefore continues to meet the minimum standard.

Conclusion on section A

323. Curaçao has met all of the ToR for the information gathering process except for identifying rulings within the scope of the transparency framework and under which category of rulings they fall (ToR I.A.1). Curaçao is recommended to finalise its information gathering process for identifying all past and future rulings within the scope of the transparency framework as soon as possible.

Exchange of information (ToR II.B)

Legal basis for spontaneous exchange of information (ToR II.B.1, II.B.2)

324. Curaçao has the necessary domestic legal basis to exchange information spontaneously. Curaçao notes that there are no legal or practical impediments that prevent the spontaneous exchange of information on rulings as contemplated in the Action 5 minimum standard.

325. Curaçao has international agreements permitting spontaneous exchange of information, including:(i) the *Multilateral Convention on Mutual Administrative Assistance in Tax Matters: Amended by the 2010 Protocol* (OECD/Council of Europe, 2011[2]) ("the Convention") and (ii) bilateral agreements in force with two jurisdictions.[2]

Completion and exchange of templates (ToR II.B.3, II.B.4, II.B.5, II.B.6, II.B.7)

326. In the prior years' peer review reports, it was determined that Curaçao's process for the completion and exchange of templates met all the ToR, except for the timely exchange of information on past and future rulings (ToR II.5.6). In the prior year's peer review report, it was determined that Curaçao still needed to identify which of the approximately 3 500 rulings issued in previous years meet the conditions to be exchanged. Therefore, Curaçao was recommended to continue its work to continue its efforts to ensure all information on past and future rulings is exchanged as soon as possible.

327. During the year in review, as noted above, Curaçao continued this work but was not able to finalise this process. Curaçao confirms that there were no rulings to be exchanged for the year in review and also anticipates completing the exchange of information process for previous years' rulings by the end of 2023. Therefore, the prior years' recommendation remains.

Conclusion on section B

328. Curaçao has met all of the ToR for the information gathering process except for completing exchanges of information on rulings in accordance with the timelines (ToR II.B.5 and II.B.6) and Curaçao is recommended to continue its efforts to ensure that all information on past and future rulings is exchanged as soon as possible.

Statistics (ToR IV.D)

329. As there was no information on rulings exchanged by Curaçao for the year in review, no statistics can be reported.

Matters related to intellectual property regimes (ToR I.A.1.3)

330. In the prior years' peer review reports, it was determined that Curaçao's information gathering and exchange of information processes for matters related to intellectual property regimes[3] were sufficient to meet the minimum standard. Curaçao's implementation in this regard remains unchanged and therefore continues to meet the minimum standard.

Summary of recommendations on implementation of the transparency framework

Aspect of implementation of the transparency framework that should be improved	Recommendation for improvement
The information gathering process is still underway in Curaçao with respect to past and future rulings within the scope of the transparency framework and the classification of these rulings under each category.	Curaçao is recommended to finalise its information gathering process for identifying all past and future rulings within the scope of the transparency framework as soon as possible. This recommendation remains unchanged since the 2017, 2018, 2019, 2020 and 2021 peer review reports.
Curaçao experienced delays in exchanging information on past and future rulings.	Curaçao is recommended to continue its efforts to ensure that all information on past and future rulings is exchanged as soon as possible. This recommendation remains unchanged since the 2017, 2018, 2019, 2020 and 2021 peer review reports.

References

OECD (2021), *BEPS Action 5 on Harmful Tax Practices - Terms of Reference and Methodology for the Conduct of the Peer Reviews of the Action 5 Transparency Framework*, OECD Publishing, Paris, https://www.oecd.org/tax/beps/beps-action-5-harmful-tax-practices-peer-review-transparency-framework.pdf. [1]

OECD (2015), *Countering Harmful Tax Practices More Effectively, Taking into Account Transparency and Substance, Action 5 - 2015 Final Report*, OECD/G20 Base Erosion and Profit Shifting Project, OECD Publishing, Paris, https://doi.org/10.1787/9789264241190-en. [3]

OECD/Council of Europe (2011), *The Multilateral Convention on Mutual Administrative Assistance in Tax Matters: Amended by the 2010 Protocol*, OECD Publishing, Paris, https://doi.org/10.1787/9789264115606-en. [2]

Notes

[1] 1) Export facility; 2) Tax exempt entity; 3) Free zone; and 4) Offshore regime. The offshore regime has been abolished in 2001 and is grandfathered for fiscal years preceding 30 June 2019.

[2] Participating jurisdictions to the Convention are available here: www.oecd.org/tax/exchange-of-tax-information/convention-on-mutual-administrative-assistance-in-tax-matters.htm. Curaçao also has bilateral agreements with the Netherlands and Norway.

[3] One regime that was abolished and not subject to the transparency framework: Export facility; and two regimes that are subject to the transparency framework: 1) Curaçao investment company (formerly Tax exempt entity); and 2) Innovation box.

Czechia

Czechia has met all aspects of the terms of reference (OECD, 2021[1]) (ToR) for the calendar year 2022 (year in review), and no recommendations are made.

In the prior year report, as well as in the 2017-2020 peer reviews, Czechia had received a recommendation regarding the timely exchange of information on rulings (ToR II.B.6). Czechia has resolved this issue and therefore the recommendation is now removed.

Czechia can legally issue two types of rulings within the scope of the transparency framework.

In practice, Czechia issued rulings within the scope of the transparency framework as follows:

Type of ruling	Number of rulings
Past rulings	48
Future rulings in the period 1 April 2016 – 31 December 2016	5
Future rulings in the calendar year 2017	11
Future rulings in the calendar year 2018	7
Future rulings in the calendar year 2019	19
Future rulings in the calendar year 2020	15
Future rulings in the calendar year 2021	25
Future rulings in the year in review	17

Peer input was received from one jurisdiction in respect of the exchanges of information on rulings received from Czechia. The input was positive, noting that information was complete, in a correct format and received in a timely manner.

Information gathering process (ToR I.A)

331. Czechia can legally issue the following two types of rulings within the scope of the transparency framework: (i) cross-border unilateral APAs and any other cross-border unilateral tax rulings (such as an advance tax ruling) covering transfer pricing or the application of transfer pricing principles and (ii) permanent establishment rulings.

332. For Czechia, past rulings are any tax rulings within scope that are issued either: (i) on or after 1 January 2014 but before 1 April 2016; or (ii) on or after 1 January 2010 but before 1 January 2014, provided they were still in effect as at 1 January 2014. Future rulings are any tax rulings within scope that are issued on or after 1 April 2016.

333. In the prior years' peer review reports, it was determined that Czechia's undertakings to identify past and future rulings and all potential exchange jurisdictions were sufficient to meet the minimum standard. In addition, it was determined that Czechia's review and supervision mechanism was sufficient to meet the minimum standard. Czechia's implementation remains unchanged, and therefore continues to meet the minimum standard.

334. Czechia has met all of the ToR for the information gathering process and no recommendations are made.

Exchange of information (ToR II.B)

Legal basis for spontaneous exchange of information (ToR II.B.1, II.B.2)

335. Czechia has the necessary domestic legal basis to exchange information spontaneously. Czechia notes that there are no legal or practical impediments that prevent the spontaneous exchange of information on rulings as contemplated in the Action 5 minimum standard.

336. Czechia has international agreements permitting spontaneous exchange of information, including: (i) the *Multilateral Convention on Mutual Administrative Assistance in Tax Matters: Amended by the 2010 Protocol* (OECD/Council of Europe, 2011[2]) ("the Convention"), (ii) the Directive 2011/16/EU with all other European Union Member States and (iii) bilateral agreements in force with 96 jurisdictions.[1]

Completion and exchange of templates (ToR II.B.3, II.B.4, II.B.5, II.B.6, II.B.7)

337. In the prior years' peer review reports, it was determined that Czechia's process for the completion and exchange of templates were sufficient to meet the minimum standard. With respect to past rulings, no further action was required. In the prior year's and 2020 peer review reports, it was determined that Czechia continued to apply the European Union (EU) timelines for the exchange of information on future rulings (EU Directive 2011/16/EU), i.e. exchanges of information on future rulings are carried out within three months after the end of the calendar half-year in which these rulings were issued, regardless of whether the exchange is transmitted to EU Member States or other jurisdictions. Despite the best efforts to meet the timelines under the Action 5 transparency framework (and to therefore exchange faster than the domestic legislation and EU Directive would require), in the prior year's report, Czechia continued to experience some delays in the exchange of information on future rulings and as a consequence, some exchanges were performed later than three months after the tax ruling became available to the Competent Authority. As noted in the prior year's peer review report, this delay was also a result of the limited activities carried out by the Czech Tax Authorities due to the Covid-19 pandemic.

338. To avoid delays, Czechia has held discussions with regional tax offices responsible regarding on the issuance of tax rulings. The staff members of the tax offices have been made aware of the timelines under the Action 5 transparency framework. Czechia has also strengthened its supervision mechanism. As the exchange process has now been following the FHTP timelines, Czechia is doing random check-

ups on the timeliness of the exchanges. As the measures of Czechia have been efficient and based on the statistics, no delays regarding the exchanges occurred in the year of review, the recommendation is now removed.

339. For the year in review, the timeliness of exchanges is as follows:

Future rulings within the scope of the transparency framework	Number of exchanges transmitted within three months of the information becoming available to the competent authority or immediately after legal impediments have been lifted	Delayed exchanges		
		Number of exchanges transmitted later than three months of the information on rulings becoming available to the competent authority	Reasons for the delays	Any other comments
	38	0	N/A	N/A

Follow-up requests received for exchange of the ruling	Number	Average time to provide response	Number of requests not answered
	0	N/A	N/A

Conclusion on section B

340. Czechia has met all of the ToR for the exchange of information process. Czechia has implemented a process for completing the exchanges in a timely way and no delays occurred in the year of review. Therefore, no recommendations are made.

Statistics (ToR IV.D)

341. The statistics for the year in review are as follows:

Category of ruling	Number of exchanges	Jurisdictions exchanged with
Cross-border unilateral APAs and any other cross-border unilateral tax rulings (such as an advance tax ruling) covering transfer pricing or the application of transfer pricing principles	33	Austria, Belgium, Belize, Cyprus, Finland, France, Germany, Korea, Netherlands, Spain, Switzerland, United Kingdom, Switzerland, Poland, United States
Permanent establishment rulings	5	Austria, Belgium, Germany, Switzerland
Total	38	

Matters related to intellectual property regimes (ToR I.A.1.3)

342. Czechia does not offer an intellectual property regime for which transparency requirements under the Action 5 Report (OECD, 2015[3]) were imposed.

Summary of recommendations on implementation of the transparency framework

Aspect of implementation of the transparency framework that should be improved	Recommendation for improvement
	No recommendations.

References

OECD (2021), *BEPS Action 5 on Harmful Tax Practices - Terms of Reference and Methodology for the Conduct of the Peer Reviews of the Action 5 Transparency Framework*, OECD Publishing, Paris, https://www.oecd.org/tax/beps/beps-action-5-harmful-tax-practices-peer-review-transparency-framework.pdf. [1]

OECD (2015), *Countering Harmful Tax Practices More Effectively, Taking into Account Transparency and Substance, Action 5 - 2015 Final Report*, OECD/G20 Base Erosion and Profit Shifting Project, OECD Publishing, Paris, https://doi.org/10.1787/9789264241190-en. [3]

OECD/Council of Europe (2011), *The Multilateral Convention on Mutual Administrative Assistance in Tax Matters: Amended by the 2010 Protocol*, OECD Publishing, Paris, https://doi.org/10.1787/9789264115606-en. [2]

Note

[1] Participating jurisdictions to the Convention are available here: www.oecd.org/tax/exchange-of-tax-information/convention-on-mutual-administrative-assistance-in-tax-matters.htm. Czechia also has bilateral agreements with Albania, Azerbaijan, Armenia, Australia, Austria, Bahrain, Bangladesh, Barbados, Belarus, Belgium, Bosnia and Herzegovina, Botswana, Brazil, Bulgaria, Canada, Chile, China (People's Republic of), Colombia, Croatia, Cyprus, Democratic People's Republic of Korea, Denmark, Egypt, Estonia, Ethiopia, Finland, France, Georgia, Germany, Ghana, Greece, Hong Kong (China), Hungary, Iceland, India, Indonesia, Iran, Ireland, Israel, Italy, Japan, Jordan, Kazakhstan, Korea, Kuwait, Kyrgyzstan, Latvia, Lebanon, Liechtenstein, Lithuania, Luxembourg, Malaysia, Malta, Mexico, Moldovia, Mongolia, Montenegro, Morocco, Netherlands, New Zealand, Nigeria, North Macedonia, Norway, Pakistan, Panama, Philippines, Poland, Portugal, Qatar, Romania, Russia, San Marino, Saudi Arabia, Senegal, Serbia, Singapore, Slovak Republic, Slovenia, South Africa, Spain, Sri Lanka, Sweden, Switzerland, Syrian Arab Republic, Tajikistan, Thailand, Tunisia, Türkiye, Turkmenistan, Ukraine, United Arab Emirates, United Kingdom, United States, Uzbekistan, Venezuela and Viet Nam. Czechia has a tax information exchange agreement (TIEA) with Aruba.

Democratic Republic of Congo

The Democratic Republic of the Congo did not provide a completed peer review questionnaire to the Secretariat. It is not known whether the Democratic Republic of the Congo has implemented the transparency framework in line with the terms of reference (OECD, 2021[1]) (ToR) for the calendar year 2022 (year in review). The Democratic Republic of the Congo receives two recommendations covering the information gathering process (ToR I.A) and exchange of information (ToR II.B) for the year in review.

In the prior year's report, as well as in the 2020 peer review report, the Democratic Republic of the Congo had received the same recommendations. As they have not been addressed, the recommendations remain in place.

It is not known which types of rulings the Democratic Republic of the Congo can legally issue within the scope of the transparency framework.

In practice, the Democratic Republic of the Congo did not issue any type of rulings within the scope of the transparency framework in previous years. For the year in review, as well as for the prior year, is not known whether the Democratic Republic of the Congo issued any such rulings.

No peer input was received in respect of the exchanges of information on rulings received from the Democratic Republic of the Congo.

Information gathering process (ToR I.A)

343. It is not known which types of rulings the Democratic Republic of the Congo can legally issue within the scope of the transparency framework.

Past rulings (ToR I.A.1.1, I.A.1.2, I.A.2.1, I.A.2.2)

344. For the Democratic Republic of the Congo, past rulings are any tax rulings within scope that are issued either (i) on or after 1 January 2015 but before 1 April 2017; and (ii) on or after 1 January 2012 but before 1 January 2015, provided they were still in effect as at 1 January 2015.

345. In the prior years' peer review reports, it was determined that the Democratic Republic of the Congo issued no past rulings in scope of the transparency framework. As such, this section is not assessed.

Future rulings (ToR I.A.1.1, I.A.1.2, I.A.2.1)

346. For the Democratic Republic of the Congo, future rulings are any tax rulings within scope that are issued on or after 1 April 2017.

347. In the prior year's peer review report, the Democratic Republic of the Congo was recommended to put in place an information gathering process for future rulings as soon as possible.

348. During the year in review, as it is not known whether the Democratic Republic of the Congo has finalised its information gathering process, the recommendation remains in place.

Review and supervision (ToR I.A.3)

349. In the prior years' peer review report, the Democratic Republic of the Congo was recommended to have in place a review and supervision mechanism to ensure that all relevant information is captured adequately. As it is not known whether the Democratic Republic of the Congo has put in place a review and supervision mechanism under the transparency framework for the year in review, the recommendation remains in place.

Conclusion on section A

350. The Democratic Republic of the Congo is recommended to put in place an information gathering process, with a review and supervision mechanism, as soon as possible (ToR I.A).

Exchange of information (ToR II.B)

Legal basis for spontaneous exchange of information (ToR II.B.1, II.B.2)

351. It is not known whether the Democratic Republic of the Congo has the necessary domestic legal basis to exchange information spontaneously.

352. The Democratic Republic of the Congo is not a party to the (i) the *Multilateral Convention on Mutual Administrative Assistance in Tax Matters: Amended by the 2010 Protocol* (OECD/Council of Europe, 2011[2]) ("the Convention"). The Democratic Republic of the Congo is encouraged to continue its efforts to expand its international exchange of information instruments to be able to exchange information on rulings. It is noted, however, that jurisdictions are assessed on their compliance with the transparency framework in respect of the exchange of information network in effect for the year of the particular annual review.

Completion and exchange of templates (ToR II.B.3, II.B.4, II.B.5, II.B.6, II.B.7)

353. In the prior years' peer review reports, the Democratic Republic of the Congo is recommended to put in place a process to complete the templates for all relevant rulings and to ensure that the exchanges

of information on rulings occur as soon as possible. It is not known whether the Democratic Republic of the Congo has already put in place such a process for the year in review.

354. As it is not known whether exchanges took place in the year of review, no data on the timeliness of exchanges can be reported.

Conclusion on section B

355. The Democratic Republic of the Congo is recommended to put in place a domestic legal framework allowing spontaneous exchange of information on rulings and to put in place a process to complete the templates for all relevant rulings and to ensure that the exchanges of information on rulings occur as soon as possible (ToR II.B).

Statistics (ToR IV.D)

356. As it is not known whether information on rulings was exchanged by the Democratic Republic of the Congo for the year in review, no statistics can be reported.

Matters related to intellectual property regimes (ToR I.A.1.3)

357. The Democratic Republic of the Congo does not offer an intellectual property regime for which transparency requirements under the Action 5 Report (OECD, 2015[3]) were imposed.

Summary of recommendations on implementation of the transparency framework

Aspect of implementation of the transparency framework that should be improved	Recommendation for improvement
It is not known whether the Democratic Republic of the Congo has put in place the necessary information and gathering process.	The Democratic Republic of the Congo is recommended to finalise its information gathering process, with a review and supervision mechanism, as soon as possible. This recommendation remains unchanged since the 2020 and 2021 peer review reports.
It is not known whether the Democratic Republic of the Congo has put in place an effective compulsory spontaneous exchange of information on the tax rulings within the scope of the transparency framework.	The Democratic Republic of the Congo is recommended to continue to put in place a domestic legal framework allowing spontaneous exchange of information on rulings and to continue its efforts to complete the templates for all relevant rulings and to ensure that the exchanges of information on rulings occur as soon as possible. This recommendation remains unchanged since the 2020 and 2021 peer review reports.

References

OECD (2021), *BEPS Action 5 on Harmful Tax Practices - Terms of Reference and Methodology for the Conduct of the Peer Reviews of the Action 5 Transparency Framework*, OECD Publishing, Paris, https://www.oecd.org/tax/beps/beps-action-5-harmful-tax-practices-peer-review-transparency-framework.pdf. [1]

OECD (2015), *Countering Harmful Tax Practices More Effectively, Taking into Account Transparency and Substance, Action 5 - 2015 Final Report*, OECD/G20 Base Erosion and Profit Shifting Project, OECD Publishing, Paris, https://doi.org/10.1787/9789264241190-en. [3]

OECD/Council of Europe (2011), *The Multilateral Convention on Mutual Administrative Assistance in Tax Matters: Amended by the 2010 Protocol*, OECD Publishing, Paris, https://doi.org/10.1787/9789264115606-en. [2]

Denmark

Denmark has met all aspects of the terms of reference (OECD, 2021[1]) (ToR) for the calendar year 2022 (year in review), and no recommendations are made.

Denmark can legally issue five types of rulings within the scope of the transparency framework.

In practice, Denmark issued rulings within the scope of the transparency framework as follows:

Type of ruling	Number of rulings
Past rulings	43
Future rulings in the period 1 April 2016 – 31 December 2016	7
Future rulings in the calendar year 2017	17
Future rulings in the calendar year 2018	13
Future rulings in the calendar year 2019	14
Future rulings in the calendar year 2020	9
Future rulings in the calendar year 2021	19
Future rulings in the year in review	22

No peer input was received in respect of the exchanges of information on rulings received from Denmark.

Information gathering process (ToR I.A)

358. Denmark can legally issue the following five types of rulings within the scope of the transparency framework: (i) preferential regimes;[1] (ii) cross-border unilateral APAs and any other cross-border unilateral tax rulings (such as an advance tax ruling) covering transfer pricing or the application of transfer pricing principles; (iii) rulings providing for unilateral downward adjustments; (iv) permanent establishment rulings; and (v) related party conduit rulings.

359. For Denmark, past rulings are any tax rulings within scope that are issued either: (i) on or after 1 January 2014 but before 1 April 2016; or (ii) on or after 1 January 2010 but before 1 January 2014, provided they were still in effect as at 1 January 2014. Future rulings are any tax rulings within scope that are issued on or after 1 April 2016.

360. In the prior years' peer review reports, it was determined that Denmark's undertakings to identify past and future rulings and all potential exchange jurisdictions were sufficient to meet the minimum standard. In addition, it was determined that Denmark's review and supervision mechanism was sufficient to meet the minimum standard. Denmark's implementation remains unchanged, and therefore continues to meet the minimum standard.

361. Denmark has met all of the ToR for the information gathering process and no recommendations are made.

Exchange of information (ToR II.B)

362. Denmark has the necessary domestic legal basis to exchange information spontaneously. Denmark notes that there are no legal or practical impediments that prevent the spontaneous exchange of information on rulings as contemplated in the Action 5 minimum standard.

363. Denmark has international agreements permitting spontaneous exchange of information, including: (i) the *Multilateral Convention on Mutual Administrative Assistance in Tax Matters: Amended by the 2010 Protocol* (OECD/Council of Europe, 2011[2]) ("the Convention"), (ii) the Directive 2011/16/EU with all other European Union Member States, (iii) the Nordic Convention on Assistance in Tax Matters and (iv) bilateral agreements in force with 70 jurisdictions.[2]

364. For the year in review, the timeliness of exchanges is as follows:

Future rulings within the scope of the transparency framework	Number of exchanges transmitted within three months of the information becoming available to the competent authority or immediately after legal impediments have been lifted	Delayed exchanges		
		Number of exchanges transmitted later than three months of the information on rulings becoming available to the competent authority	Reasons for the delays	Any other comments
	32	0	N/A	N/A

Follow-up requests received for exchange of the ruling	Number	Average time to provide response	Number of requests not answered
	0	N/A	N/A

365. In the prior years' peer review reports, it was determined that Denmark's process for the completion and exchange of templates were sufficient to meet the minimum standard. With respect to past rulings, no further action was required. Denmark's implementation in this regard remains unchanged and therefore continues to meet the minimum standard.

366. Denmark has the necessary legal basis for spontaneous exchange of information, a process for completing the templates in a timely way and has completed all exchanges. Denmark has met all of the ToR for the exchange of information process and no recommendations are made.

Statistics (ToR IV.D)

367. The statistics for the year in review are as follows:

Category of ruling	Number of exchanges	Jurisdictions exchanged with
Ruling related to a preferential regime	4	*De minimis* rule applies
Cross-border unilateral APAs and any other cross-border unilateral tax rulings (such as an advance tax ruling) covering transfer pricing or the application of transfer pricing principles	0	N/A
Cross-border rulings providing for a unilateral downward adjustment to the taxpayer's taxable profits that is not directly reflected in the taxpayer's financial / commercial accounts	0	N/A
Permanent establishment rulings	22	Australia, Estonia, France, Germany, Ireland, Norway, Slovak Republic, Sweden, United States
Related party conduit rulings	6	Germany, Gibraltar, Luxembourg, Malta, United Kingdom, United States
Total	32	

Matters related to intellectual property regimes (ToR I.A.1.3)

368. Denmark does not offer an intellectual property regime for which transparency requirements under the Action 5 Report (OECD, 2015[3]) were imposed.

Summary of recommendations on implementation of the transparency framework

Aspect of implementation of the transparency framework that should be improved	Recommendation for improvement
	No recommendations are made.

References

OECD (2021), *BEPS Action 5 on Harmful Tax Practices - Terms of Reference and Methodology for the Conduct of the Peer Reviews of the Action 5 Transparency Framework*, OECD Publishing, Paris, https://www.oecd.org/tax/beps/beps-action-5-harmful-tax-practices-peer-review-transparency-framework.pdf. [1]

OECD (2015), *Countering Harmful Tax Practices More Effectively, Taking into Account Transparency and Substance, Action 5 - 2015 Final Report*, OECD/G20 Base Erosion and Profit Shifting Project, OECD Publishing, Paris, https://doi.org/10.1787/9789264241190-en. [3]

OECD/Council of Europe (2011), *The Multilateral Convention on Mutual Administrative Assistance in Tax Matters: Amended by the 2010 Protocol*, OECD Publishing, Paris, https://doi.org/10.1787/9789264115606-en. [2]

Notes

[1] Tonnage tax.

[2] Participating jurisdictions to the Convention are available here: www.oecd.org/tax/exchange-of-tax-information/convention-on-mutual-administrative-assistance-in-tax-matters.htm. Denmark also has bilateral agreements with Argentina, Armenia, Aruba, Australia, Austria, Azerbaijan, Bangladesh, Belarus, Belgium, Brazil, Bulgaria, Canada, Chile, China (People's Republic of), Croatia, Cyprus, Czechia, Egypt, Estonia, Georgia, Germany, Ghana, Greece, Hungary, India, Indonesia, Ireland, Israel, Italy, Jamaica, Japan, Kenya, Korea, Kuwait, Latvia, Lithuania, Luxembourg, Malaysia, Malta, Mexico, Montenegro, Morocco, Netherlands, New Zealand, North Macedonia, Pakistan, Philippines, Poland, Portugal, Romania, Russia, Serbia, Singapore, Slovak Republic, Slovenia, South Africa, Sri Lanka, Switzerland, Chinese Taipei, Tanzania, Thailand, Tunisia, Türkiye, Uganda, Ukraine, United Kingdom, United States, Venezuela, Viet Nam and Zambia. Agreements have been concluded with Algeria and France but are not yet in force.

Dominican Republic

The Dominican Republic has met all aspects of the terms of reference (OECD, 2021[1]) (ToR) for the calendar year 2022 (year in review), and no recommendations are made.

The Dominican Republic can legally issue five types of rulings within the scope of the transparency framework.

In practice, the Dominican Republic issued rulings within the scope of the transparency framework as follows:

Type of ruling	Number of rulings
Future rulings in the period 1 March 2019 – 31 December 2019	23
Future rulings in the calendar year 2020	57
Future rulings in the calendar year 2021	83
Future rulings in the year in review	17

Peer input was received from one jurisdiction in respect of the exchanges of information on rulings received from the Dominican Republic. The input was positive, noting that information was complete, in a correct format and received in a timely manner.

Information gathering process (ToR I.A)

369. The Dominican Republic can legally issue the following five types of rulings within the scope of the transparency framework: (i) preferential regimes;[1] (ii) cross-border unilateral APAs and any other cross-border unilateral tax rulings (such as an advance tax ruling) covering transfer pricing or the application of transfer pricing principles; (iii) rulings providing for unilateral downward adjustments; (iv) permanent establishment rulings; and (v) related party conduit rulings.

370. For the Dominican Republic, past rulings are any tax rulings within scope that are issued prior to 1 March 2019. However, there is no obligation for the Dominican Republic to conduct spontaneous exchange information on past rulings. Future rulings are any tax rulings within scope that are issued on or after 1 March 2019.

371. In the prior years' peer review reports, it was determined that the Dominican Republic's undertakings to identify past and future rulings and all potential exchange jurisdictions were sufficient to meet the minimum standard. In addition, it was determined that the Dominican Republic's review and supervision mechanism was sufficient to meet the minimum standard. The Dominican Republic's implementation remains unchanged, and therefore continues to meet the minimum standard.

372. The Dominican Republic has met all of the ToR for the information gathering process and no recommendations are made.

Exchange of information (ToR II.B)

373. The Dominican Republic has the necessary domestic legal basis to exchange information spontaneously. The Dominican Republic notes that there are no legal or practical impediments that prevent the spontaneous exchange of information on rulings as contemplated in the Action 5 minimum standard.

374. The Dominican Republic has international agreements permitting spontaneous exchange of information, including: (i) the *Multilateral Convention on Mutual Administrative Assistance in Tax Matters: Amended by the 2010 Protocol* (OECD/Council of Europe, 2011[2]) ("the Convention") and (ii) bilateral agreements in force with three jurisdictions.[2]

375. For the year in review, the timeliness of exchanges is as follows:

Future rulings within the scope of the transparency framework	Number of exchanges transmitted within three months of the information becoming available to the competent authority or immediately after legal impediments have been lifted	Delayed exchanges		
		Number of exchanges transmitted later than three months of the information on rulings becoming available to the competent authority	Reasons for the delays	Any other comments
	66	0	N/A	N/A
Total	66	0		

Follow-up requests received for exchange of the ruling	Number	Average time to provide response	Number of requests not answered
	0	N/A	N/A

376. The Dominican Republic has the necessary legal basis for spontaneous exchange of information, a process for completing the templates in a timely way and has completed all exchanges. The Dominican Republic has met all of the ToR for the exchange of information process and no recommendations are made.

Statistics (ToR IV.D)

377. The statistics for the year in review are as follows:

Category of ruling	Number of exchanges	Jurisdictions exchanged with
Ruling related to a preferential regime	0	N/A
Cross-border unilateral APAs and any other cross-border unilateral tax rulings (such as an advance tax ruling) covering transfer pricing or the application of transfer pricing principles	65	Barbados, Canada, Curaçao, France, Ireland, Luxembourg, Mexico, Netherlands, Panama, Paraguay, Saint Kitts and Nevis, Spain, Switzerland, United States, and Uruguay
Cross-border rulings providing for a unilateral downward adjustment to the taxpayer's taxable profits that is not directly reflected in the taxpayer's financial / commercial accounts	0	N/A
Permanent establishment rulings	0	N/A
Related party conduit rulings	0	N/A
Total	65	

Matters related to intellectual property regimes (ToR I.A.1.3)

378. The Dominican Republic does not offer an intellectual property regime for which transparency requirements under the Action 5 Report (OECD, 2015[3]) were imposed.

Summary of recommendations on implementation of the transparency framework

Aspect of implementation of the transparency framework that should be improved	Recommendation for improvement
	No recommendations are made.

References

OECD (2021), *BEPS Action 5 on Harmful Tax Practices - Terms of Reference and Methodology for the Conduct of the Peer Reviews of the Action 5 Transparency Framework*, OECD Publishing, Paris, https://www.oecd.org/tax/beps/beps-action-5-harmful-tax-practices-peer-review-transparency-framework.pdf. [1]

OECD (2015), *Countering Harmful Tax Practices More Effectively, Taking into Account Transparency and Substance, Action 5 - 2015 Final Report*, OECD/G20 Base Erosion and Profit Shifting Project, OECD Publishing, Paris, https://doi.org/10.1787/9789264241190-en. [3]

OECD/Council of Europe (2011), *The Multilateral Convention on Mutual Administrative Assistance in Tax Matters: Amended by the 2010 Protocol*, OECD Publishing, Paris, https://doi.org/10.1787/9789264115606-en. [2]

Notes

[1] i) Border development and ii) Logistics centres. It should be noted that FHTP has not yet concluded if these regimes are in scope. If the FHTP decides that these regimes are out of scope for the FHTP, then exchange of information on rulings with respect to these regimes would no longer be required under the Action 5 transparency framework. However, until then, the Dominican Republic has committed to do the spontaneous exchange of information on rulings related to these regimes.

[2] Participating jurisdictions to the Convention are available here: www.oecd.org/tax/exchange-of-tax-information/convention-on-mutual-administrative-assistance-in-tax-matters.htm. The Dominican Republic also has bilateral agreements with Canada, Spain and United States.

Egypt

Egypt did not provide a completed peer review questionnaire to the Secretariat. Egypt is taking steps to implement the legal basis for exchange of information under the transparency framework, and has commenced administrative preparations to ensure that information on rulings will be exchanged. Egypt has met all aspects of the terms of reference (OECD, 2021[1]) (ToR) for the calendar year 2022 (year in review), except for identifying all potential exchange jurisdictions (ToR I.A.2), having in place a review and supervision mechanism (ToR I.A.3) and having in place a process to ensure the timely exchange of information on rulings in the form required by the transparency framework (ToR II.B). Egypt receives two recommendations on these points for the year in review.

In the prior year report, as well as in the 2018-2020 peer reviews, Egypt had received the same two recommendations. As they have not been addressed, the recommendations remain in place.

Egypt can legally issue three types of rulings within the scope of the transparency framework.

In practice, Egypt issued rulings within the scope of the transparency framework as follows:

Type of ruling	Number of rulings
Past rulings	31
Future rulings in the period 1 April 2018 – 31 December 2018	3
Future rulings in the calendar year 2019	11
Future rulings in the calendar year 2020	2
Future rulings in the calendar year 2021	1
Future rulings in the year in review	*Unknown*

As no exchanges took place, no peer input was received in respect of the exchanges of information on rulings received from Egypt.

Information gathering process (ToR I.A)

379. Egypt can legally issue the following three types of rulings within the scope of the transparency framework: (i) cross-border unilateral APAs and any other cross-border unilateral tax rulings (such as an advance tax ruling) covering transfer pricing or the application of transfer pricing principles; (ii) permanent establishment rulings; and (iii) related party conduit rulings.

Past rulings (ToR I.A.1.1, I.A.1.2, I.A.2.1, I.A.2.2)

380. For Egypt, past rulings are any tax rulings within scope that are issued either (i) on or after 1 January 2016 but before 1 April 2018; and (ii) on or after 1 January 2014 but before 1 January 2016, provided still in effect as at 1 January 2016.

381. In the prior years' peer review reports, it was determined that Egypt's undertakings to identify past rulings and all potential exchange jurisdictions have met all the ToR, except for identifying all potential exchange jurisdictions for past rulings (ToR I.A.2.2). Therefore, Egypt was recommended to apply the "best efforts approach" to identify potential exchange jurisdictions for past rulings.

382. During the year in review, it is not known if whether Egypt has identified the potential exchange jurisdictions for all past rulings, and therefore the recommendation remains in place.

Future rulings (ToR I.A.1.1, I.A.1.2, I.A.2.1)

383. For Egypt, future rulings are any tax rulings within scope that are issued on or after 1 April 2018.

384. In the prior years' peer review reports, it was also noted that Egypt did not yet have a process in place for the identification of potential exchange jurisdictions for future rulings other than APAs. Therefore, it was determined that Egypt's undertakings to identify future rulings and all potential exchange jurisdictions have met all the ToR, except for identifying all potential exchange jurisdictions for future rulings other than APAs (ToR I.A.2.1). Egypt was recommended to ensure that all potential exchange jurisdictions are identified swiftly for all future rulings other than APAs.

385. During the year in review, it is not known whether Egypt has put in place a process to identify the potential exchange jurisdictions for all future rulings other than APAs, and therefore the recommendation remains in place.

Review and supervision (ToR I.A.3)

386. Egypt does not yet have in place a review and supervision mechanism for the identification of rulings and potential exchange jurisdictions (ToR I.A.3), and therefore the recommendation remains in place.

387. As noted in the prior years' peer review reports, Egypt envisages that supervision on the identification of rulings and potential exchange jurisdictions will take place by the managers of the relevant departments. Egypt also intends to issue internal guidance for staff on the identification process.

Conclusion on section A

388. Egypt has met the ToR for the information gathering process except for identifying all potential exchange jurisdictions for past and future rulings (ToR I.A.2) and having in place a review and supervision mechanism (ToR I.A.3). Egypt is recommended to continue its efforts to identify all potential exchange jurisdictions for both past and future rulings and to implement a review and supervision mechanism, as soon as possible.

Exchange of information (ToR II.B)

Legal basis for spontaneous exchange of information (ToR II.B.1, II.B.2)

389. Egypt has the necessary domestic legal basis to exchange information spontaneously. Egypt notes that there are no legal or practical impediments that prevent the spontaneous exchange of information on rulings as contemplated in the Action 5 minimum standard.

390. Egypt has international agreements permitting spontaneous exchange of information, including bilateral agreements in force with 58 jurisdictions.[1] Egypt is not a party to the *Multilateral Convention on Mutual Administrative Assistance in Tax Matters: Amended by the 2010 Protocol* (OECD/Council of Europe, 2011[2]) ("the Convention"). Egypt is encouraged to continue its efforts to expand its international exchange of information instruments to be able to exchange information on tax rulings. Egypt notes that it is planning to become a party to the Convention in the near future. It is noted, however, that jurisdictions are assessed on their compliance with the transparency framework in respect of the exchange of information network in effect for the year of the particular annual review.

Completion and exchange of templates (ToR II.B.3, II.B.4, II.B.5, II.B.6, II.B.7)

391. In the prior years' peer review reports, it was determined that Egypt did not have a process for the completion and exchange of templates. Therefore, Egypt was recommended to develop a process to complete the templates on relevant rulings and to ensure that the exchanges of information on rulings occur in accordance with the form and timelines under the transparency framework (ToR II.B). As it is not known whether action has been undertaken on this aspect during the year in review, the recommendation remains in place.

392. It is not known whether Egypt issued rulings during the year in review. Therefore, no data can be reported on the timeliness of exchanges of information.

Conclusion on section B

393. Egypt has the necessary legal basis for spontaneous exchange of information. Egypt is recommended to swiftly implement its process to complete the templates on relevant rulings and to ensure that the exchanges of information on rulings occur as soon as possible (ToR II.B).

Statistics (ToR IV)

394. As there was no information on rulings exchanged by Egypt for the year in review, no statistics can be reported.

Matters related to intellectual property regimes (ToR I.A.1.3)

395. Egypt does not offer an intellectual property regime for which transparency requirements under the Action 5 Report (OECD, 2015[3]) were imposed.

Summary of recommendations on implementation of the transparency framework

Aspect of implementation of the transparency framework that should be improved	Recommendation for improvement
Egypt has not yet identified all potential exchange jurisdictions for both past and future rulings and does not have a review and supervision mechanism in place to ensure that all relevant information on the identification of rulings and potential exchange jurisdictions is captured adequately.	Egypt is recommended to continue its efforts to identify all potential exchange jurisdictions for both past and future rulings and to implement a review and supervision mechanism, as soon as possible. This recommendation remains unchanged since the 2018, 2019, 2020 and 2021 review reports.
Egypt does not have in place a process to ensure the timely exchange of information on rulings in the form required by the transparency framework.	Egypt is recommended to swiftly implement its process to complete the templates on relevant rulings and to ensure that the exchanges of information on rulings occur as soon as possible. This recommendation remains unchanged since the 2018, 2019, 2020 and 2021 peer review reports.

References

OECD (2021), *BEPS Action 5 on Harmful Tax Practices - Terms of Reference and Methodology for the Conduct of the Peer Reviews of the Action 5 Transparency Framework*, OECD Publishing, Paris, https://www.oecd.org/tax/beps/beps-action-5-harmful-tax-practices-peer-review-transparency-framework.pdf. [1]

OECD (2015), *Countering Harmful Tax Practices More Effectively, Taking into Account Transparency and Substance, Action 5 - 2015 Final Report*, OECD/G20 Base Erosion and Profit Shifting Project, OECD Publishing, Paris, https://doi.org/10.1787/9789264241190-en. [3]

OECD/Council of Europe (2011), *The Multilateral Convention on Mutual Administrative Assistance in Tax Matters: Amended by the 2010 Protocol*, OECD Publishing, Paris, https://doi.org/10.1787/9789264115606-en. [2]

Note

[1] Albania, Algeria, Austria, Bahrain, Belarus, Belgium, Bulgaria, Canada, China (People's Republic of), Cyprus, Czechia, Denmark, Ethiopia, Finland, France, Georgia, Germany, Greece, Hungary, India, Indonesia, Iraq, Ireland, Italy, Japan, Jordan, Korea, Kuwait, Lebanon, Libya, Malaysia, Malta, Mauritius, Morocco, Netherlands, Norway, Pakistan, Palestinian Authority, Poland, Romania, Russia, Saudi Arabia, Serbia, Singapore, Spain, South Africa, Sudan, Sweden, Syrian Arab Republic, Tunisia, Türkiye, Ukraine, United Arab Emirates, United Kingdom, United States, Uzbekistan and Yemen. Egypt also has an agreement with the Council of Arab Economic Unity permitting spontaneous exchange of information.

Estonia

Estonia has met all aspects of the terms of reference (OECD, 2021[1]) (ToR) for the calendar year 2022 (year in review), and no recommendations are made.

Estonia can legally issue two types of rulings within the scope of the transparency framework.

In practice, Estonia issued rulings within the scope of the transparency framework as follows:

Type of ruling	Number of rulings
Past rulings	20
Future rulings in the period 1 April 2016 – 31 December 2016	8
Future rulings in the calendar year 2017	11
Future rulings in the calendar year 2018	9
Future rulings in the calendar year 2019	9
Future rulings in the calendar year 2020	7
Future rulings in the calendar year 2021	3
Future rulings in the year in review	9

As no exchanges took place, no peer input was received in respect of the exchanges of information on rulings received from Estonia.

Information gathering process (ToR I.A)

396. Estonia can legally issue the following two types of rulings within the scope of the transparency framework: (i) permanent establishment rulings and (ii) related party conduit rulings.

397. For Estonia, past rulings are any tax rulings within scope that are issued either: (i) on or after 1 January 2014 but before 1 April 2016; or (ii) on or after 1 January 2010 but before 1 January 2014, provided they were still in effect as at 1 January 2014. Future rulings are any tax rulings within scope that are issued on or after 1 April 2016.

398. In the prior years' peer review reports, it was determined that Estonia's undertakings to identify past and future rulings and all potential exchange jurisdictions were sufficient to meet the minimum standard. In addition, it was determined that Estonia's review and supervision mechanism was sufficient to meet the minimum standard. Estonia's implementation remains unchanged, and therefore continues to meet the minimum standard.

399. Estonia has met all of the ToR for the information gathering process and no recommendations are made.

Exchange of information (ToR II.B)

400. Estonia has the necessary domestic legal basis to exchange information spontaneously. Estonia notes that there are no legal or practical impediments that prevent the spontaneous exchange of information on rulings as contemplated in the Action 5 minimum standard.

401. Estonia has international agreements permitting spontaneous exchange of information, including: (i) the *Multilateral Convention on Mutual Administrative Assistance in Tax Matters: Amended by the 2010 Protocol* (OECD/Council of Europe, 2011[2]) ("the Convention"), (ii) the Directive 2011/16/EU with all other European Union Member States and (iii) bilateral agreements in force with 60 jurisdictions.[1]

402. For the year in review, the timeliness of exchanges is as follows:

Future rulings within the scope of the transparency framework	Number of exchanges transmitted within three months of the information becoming available to the competent authority or immediately after legal impediments have been lifted	Delayed exchanges		
		Number of exchanges transmitted later than three months of the information on rulings becoming available to the competent authority	Reasons for the delays	Any other comments
	5	4	See below	N/A

Follow-up requests received for exchange of the ruling	Number	Average time to provide response	Number of requests not answered
	0	N/A	N/A

403. The reason that four exchanges were not transmitted timely was because of a temporary lack of employees. Estonia confirms that new employees have been hired, and therefore, this was a temporary issue for which no recommendation needs to be made.

404. In the prior years' peer review reports, it was determined that Estonia's process for the completion and exchange of templates were sufficient to meet the minimum standard. With respect to past rulings, no further action was required from Estonia. Estonia's implementation in this regard remains unchanged and therefore continues to meet the minimum standard.

405. Estonia has the necessary legal basis for spontaneous exchange of information, a process for completing the templates in a timely way and has completed all exchanges. Estonia has met all of the ToR for the exchange of information process and no recommendations are made.

Statistics (ToR IV.D)

406. The statistics for the year in review are as follows:

Category of ruling	Number of exchanges	Jurisdictions exchanged with
Permanent establishment rulings	*De minimis* rule applies	N/A
Related party conduit rulings	7	Denmark, Finland, Germany, Gibraltar, Latvia, Lithuania, Luxembourg, Poland, United States
De minimis rule	2	
Total	9	

Matters related to intellectual property regimes (ToR I.A.1.3)

407. Estonia does not offer an intellectual property regime for which transparency requirements under the Action 5 Report (OECD, 2015[3]) were imposed.

Summary of recommendations on implementation of the transparency framework

Aspect of implementation of the transparency framework that should be improved	Recommendation for improvement
	No recommendations are made.

References

OECD (2021), *BEPS Action 5 on Harmful Tax Practices - Terms of Reference and Methodology for the Conduct of the Peer Reviews of the Action 5 Transparency Framework*, OECD Publishing, Paris, https://www.oecd.org/tax/beps/beps-action-5-harmful-tax-practices-peer-review-transparency-framework.pdf. [1]

OECD (2015), *Countering Harmful Tax Practices More Effectively, Taking into Account Transparency and Substance, Action 5 - 2015 Final Report*, OECD/G20 Base Erosion and Profit Shifting Project, OECD Publishing, Paris, https://doi.org/10.1787/9789264241190-en. [3]

OECD/Council of Europe (2011), *The Multilateral Convention on Mutual Administrative Assistance in Tax Matters: Amended by the 2010 Protocol*, OECD Publishing, Paris, https://doi.org/10.1787/9789264115606-en. [2]

Note

[1] Participating jurisdictions to the Convention are available here: www.oecd.org/tax/exchange-of-tax-information/convention-on-mutual-administrative-assistance-in-tax-matters.htm. Estonia also has bilateral agreements with Albania, Armenia, Azerbaijan, Austria, Bahrain, Belarus, Belgium, Bulgaria, Canada, China (People's Republic of), Croatia, Cyprus, Czechia, Denmark, Finland, France, Georgia, Germany, Greece, Hungary, Hong Kong (China), Iceland, India, Ireland, Isle of Man, Israel, Italy, Japan, Jersey, Kazakhstan, Korea, Kyrgyzstan, Latvia, Lithuania, Luxembourg, Malta, Mexico, Moldova, Netherlands, North Macedonia, Norway, Poland, Portugal, Romania, Serbia, Singapore, Slovak Republic, Slovenia, Spain, Sweden, Switzerland, Thailand, Türkiye, Turkmenistan, Ukraine, United Arab Emirates, United Kingdom, United States, Uzbekistan and Viet Nam.

Eswatini

Eswatini is taking steps to implement the aspects of the terms of reference (OECD, 2021[3]) (ToR) for the transparency framework and to commence administrative preparations to ensure that it establishes an information gathering process (ToR I.A) and that information on rulings will be identified and exchanged in a timely manner (ToR II.B). Eswatini receives two recommendations on these points for the year in review.

In the prior year report, as well as in the 2020 peer review report, Eswatini had received the same two recommendations. As they have not been addressed, the recommendations remain in place.

Eswatini can legally issue four types of rulings within the scope of the transparency framework.

In practice, Eswatini issued no rulings within the scope of the transparency framework.

As no exchanges were required to take place, no peer input was received in respect of the exchanges of information on rulings received from Eswatini.

Information gathering process (ToR I.A)

408. Eswatini can legally issue the following four types of rulings within the scope of the transparency framework: (i) rulings on preferential regimes;[1] (ii) rulings providing for unilateral downward adjustments; (iii) permanent establishment rulings; and (iv) related party conduit rulings. According to the Income Tax Order, the Commissioner General can issue private rulings regarding the application of the Order to a transaction proposed by the taxpayer.

Past rulings (ToR I.A.1.1, I.A.1.2, I.A.2.1, I.A.2.2)

409. For Eswatini, past rulings are any tax rulings issued prior to 1 March 2020. However, there is no obligation for Eswatini to conduct spontaneous exchange information on past rulings.

Future rulings (ToR I.A.1.1, I.A.1.2, I.A.2.1)

410. For Eswatini, future rulings are any tax rulings within scope that are issued on or after 1 March 2020.

411. Eswatini does not yet have processes in place to ensure the identification of all relevant rulings and all potential exchange jurisdictions but is currently taking steps to ensure the implementation of the obligations relating to the transparency framework.

Review and supervision (ToR I.A.3)

412. Eswatini does not yet have a review and supervision mechanism under the transparency framework but is currently taking steps to ensure the implementation of the obligations relating to the transparency framework.

Conclusion on section A

413. Eswatini is currently taking steps to ensure the identification of all relevant rulings and all potential exchange jurisdictions as well as to have a review and supervision mechanism under the transparency framework.

414. Eswatini is recommended to put in place its information gathering process for identifying all relevant rulings and all potential exchange jurisdictions, with a review and supervision mechanism, as soon as possible (ToR I.A).

Exchange of information (ToR II.B)

415. Eswatini has the necessary domestic legal basis to exchange information spontaneously. Eswatini notes that there are no legal or practical impediments that prevent the spontaneous exchange of information on rulings as contemplated in the Action 5 minimum standard.

416. Eswatini has international agreements permitting spontaneous exchange of information, including: (i) the *Multilateral Convention on Mutual Administrative Assistance in Tax Matters: Amended by the 2010 Protocol* (OECD/Council of Europe, 2011[2]) ("the Convention"), (ii) bilateral agreements in force with seven jurisdictions and (iii) tax information exchange agreements in force with two jurisdictions.[2]

Completion and exchange of templates (ToR II.B.3, II.B.4, II.B.5, II.B.6, II.B.7)

417. Eswatini does not yet have a process in place for the completion and exchange of information on rulings in accordance with the form and timelines required by the transparency framework but is currently taking steps to ensure the implementation of the obligations relating to the transparency framework.

418. During the year in review, no exchanges were required to take place and no data on the timeliness of exchanges is reported.

Conclusion on section B

419. Eswatini has the necessary legal basis for spontaneous exchange of information. Eswatini has met all of the ToR for the exchange of information process except for having a process in place for the completion and exchange of information on rulings. Eswatini is recommended to develop a process to complete the templates on relevant rulings and to ensure that the exchanges of information on rulings occur in accordance with the form and timelines under the transparency framework (ToR II.B).

Statistics (ToR IV)

420. As no rulings were issued, no statistics can be reported.

Matters related to intellectual property regimes (ToR I.A.1.3)

421. Eswatini does not offer an intellectual property regime for which transparency requirements under the Action 5 Report (OECD, 2015[3]) were imposed.

Summary of recommendations on implementation of the transparency framework

Aspect of implementation of the transparency framework that should be improved	Recommendation for improvement
Eswatini is currently taking steps to ensure the identification of all relevant rulings and all potential exchange jurisdictions as well as to have a review and supervision mechanism under the transparency framework.	Eswatini is recommended to put in place its information gathering process for identifying all relevant rulings and all potential exchange jurisdictions, with a review and supervision mechanism, as soon as possible. This recommendation remains unchanged since the 2020 and 2021 peer review reports.
Eswatini is currently taking steps to put a process in place for the completion and exchange of information on rulings in accordance with the form and timelines required by the transparency framework.	Eswatini is recommended to develop a process to complete the templates on relevant rulings and to ensure that the exchanges of information on rulings occur in accordance with the form and timelines under the transparency framework. This recommendation remains unchanged since the 2020 and 2021 peer review reports.

References

OECD (2021), *BEPS Action 5 on Harmful Tax Practices - Terms of Reference and Methodology for the Conduct of the Peer Reviews of the Action 5 Transparency Framework*, OECD Publishing, Paris, https://www.oecd.org/tax/beps/beps-action-5-harmful-tax-practices-peer-review-transparency-framework.pdf. [1]

OECD (2015), *Countering Harmful Tax Practices More Effectively, Taking into Account Transparency and Substance, Action 5 - 2015 Final Report*, OECD/G20 Base Erosion and Profit Shifting Project, OECD Publishing, Paris, https://doi.org/10.1787/9789264241190-en. [3]

OECD/Council of Europe (2011), *The Multilateral Convention on Mutual Administrative Assistance in Tax Matters: Amended by the 2010 Protocol*, OECD Publishing, Paris, https://doi.org/10.1787/9789264115606-en. [2]

Notes

[1] Special Economic Zones regime.

[2] Participating jurisdictions to the Convention are available here: www.oecd.org/tax/exchange-of-tax-information/convention-on-mutual-administrative-assistance-in-tax-matters.htm. Eswatini also has bilateral agreements with Botswana, Lesotho, Mauritius, Seychelles, South Africa, Chinese Taipei, United Kingdom. The TIEA with Guernsey also permits for the spontaneous exchange of information.

Faroe Islands

The Faroe Islands has met all aspects of the terms of reference (OECD, 2021[1]) (ToR) for the calendar year 2022 (year in review), except for identifying all potential exchange jurisdictions for permanent establishment rulings (ToR I.A.2.1) and the timely exchange of information on future rulings (ToR II.B.6.2). The Faroe Islands receives two recommendations these points for the year in review.

In the prior year report, as well as in the 2019-2020 peer reviews, the Faroe Islands had received the same recommendations. The recommendations have been partially addressed, and are now targeted to specific ToR.

The Faroe Islands can legally issue two types of rulings within the scope of the transparency framework.

In practice, The Faroe Islands issued rulings within the scope of the transparency framework as follows:

Type of ruling	Number of rulings
Past rulings	0
Future rulings in the period 1 September 2019 – 31 December 2019	0
Future rulings in the calendar year 2020	1
Future rulings in the calendar year 2021	0
Future rulings in the year in review	0

As no exchanges took place, no peer input was received in respect of the exchanges of information on rulings received from the Faroe Islands.

Information gathering process (ToR I.A)

422. The Faroe Islands can legally issue the following five types of rulings within the scope of the transparency framework: (i) preferential regimes[1] and (ii) permanent establishment rulings.

Past rulings (ToR I.A.1.1, I.A.1.2, I.A.2.1, I.A.2.2)

423. For the Faroe Islands, past rulings are any tax rulings issued prior to 1 September 2019. However, there is no obligation for the Faroe Islands to conduct spontaneous exchange information on past rulings.

424. For the Faroe Islands, future rulings are any tax rulings within scope that are issued on or after 1 September 2019.

425. In the prior years' peer review reports, it was determined that the Faroe Islands had no processes in place for the record keeping of rulings for the purposes of the transparency framework. The Faroe Islands indicates that during the year in review, the Faroe Islands' tax administration TAKS implemented a rulings manual. TAKS is keeping record of all rulings that are issued and in scope of the Action 5 transparency framework. It now requires all taxpayers that apply for a rulings on preferential regimes to provide information on the related parties, the immediate parent entity and the ultimate parent entity. However, this information is not required for permanent establishment rulings. The Faroe Islands is therefore recommended to identify potential exchange jurisdictions with respect to permanent establishment rulings, as soon as possible (ToR I.A.1.2).

Review and supervision (ToR I.A.3)

426. In the prior year's peer review report, it was determined that the Faroe Islands did not yet have a review and supervision mechanism under the transparency framework. During the year in review, the Faroe Islands took steps to implement a review and supervision mechanism. There are two departments within TAKS responsible for the issuing of rulings. Department managers are responsible for ensuring that the rulings and exchange jurisdictions are correctly identified. The prior year's recommendation can therefore be removed.

Conclusion on section A

427. The Faroe Islands is recommended to put in place a process to identify all potential exchange jurisdictions for permanent establishment rulings (ToR I.A.1.2).

Exchange of information (ToR II.B)

Legal basis for spontaneous exchange of information (ToR II.B.1, II.B.2)

428. The Faroe Islands has the necessary domestic legal basis to exchange information spontaneously. The Faroe Islands notes that there are no legal or practical impediments that prevent the spontaneous exchange of information on rulings as contemplated in the Action 5 minimum standard.

429. The Faroe Islands has international agreements permitting spontaneous exchange of information, including being a participating jurisdiction in (i) the *Multilateral Convention on Mutual Administrative Assistance in Tax Matters: Amended by the 2010 Protocol* (OECD/Council of Europe, 2011[2]) ("the Convention"), (ii) the Nordic Convention on Assistance in Tax Matters and (iii) bilateral agreements in force with four jurisdictions.[2]

Completion and exchange of templates (ToR II.B.3, II.B.4, II.B.5, II.B.6, II.B.7)

430. In the prior years' peer review reports, it was determined that the Faroe Islands is still developing a process to complete the templates on relevant rulings, to make them available to the Competent Authority for exchange of information, and to exchange them with relevant jurisdictions. Therefore, the Faroe Islands

was recommended to develop a process to complete the templates for all relevant rulings and to ensure that the exchanges of information on rulings occur in accordance with the form and timelines under the transparency framework going forward.

431. During the year in review, the Faroe Islands took steps to implement a process on the completion and exchange of templates. TAKS requires the department issuing the ruling to complete the Annex C template. Department managers are responsible that the template is filled out correctly, and that the summary section of the Annex C template is in line with the internal FHTP suggested guidance. The Competent Authority is responsible for the exchanges. The Faroe Islands does not yet have put timelines in place for the exchange of the information on rulings in line with the Action 5 transparency framework.

432. As no exchanges took place in the year of review, no data on the timeliness of exchanges can be reported.

Conclusion on section B

433. The Faroe Islands is recommended to put in place a process to ensure that the exchanges of information on rulings occur in accordance with the form and timelines under the transparency framework going forward (ToR II.B.6).

Statistics (ToR IV)

434. As there was no information on rulings exchanged by the Faroe Islands for the year in review, no statistics can be reported.

Matters related to intellectual property regimes (ToR I.A.1.3)

435. The Faroe Islands does not offer an intellectual property regime for which transparency requirements under the Action 5 Report (OECD, 2015[3]) were imposed.

Summary of recommendations on implementation of the transparency framework

Aspect of implementation of the transparency framework that should be improved	Recommendation for improvement
The Faroe Islands does not yet have a process in place to identify all potential exchange jurisdictions for permanent establishment rulings.	The Faroe Islands is recommended to put in place a process to identify all potential exchange jurisdictions for permanent establishment rulings. This recommendation remains unchanged since the 2019, 2020 and 2021 peer review reports, but is now targeted to the specific ToR that still needs to be put in place.
The Faroe Islands does not have a process for the timely exchange of information on rulings with relevant jurisdictions.	The Faroe Islands is recommended to put in place a process to ensure that the exchanges of information on rulings occur in accordance with the form and timelines under the transparency framework going forward This recommendation remains unchanged since the 2019, 2020 and 2021 peer review reports, but is now targeted to the specific ToR that still needs to be put in place.

References

OECD (2021), *BEPS Action 5 on Harmful Tax Practices - Terms of Reference and Methodology for the Conduct of the Peer Reviews of the Action 5 Transparency Framework*, OECD Publishing, Paris, https://www.oecd.org/tax/beps/beps-action-5-harmful-tax-practices-peer-review-transparency-framework.pdf. [1]

OECD (2015), *Countering Harmful Tax Practices More Effectively, Taking into Account Transparency and Substance, Action 5 - 2015 Final Report*, OECD/G20 Base Erosion and Profit Shifting Project, OECD Publishing, Paris, https://doi.org/10.1787/9789264241190-en. [3]

OECD/Council of Europe (2011), *The Multilateral Convention on Mutual Administrative Assistance in Tax Matters: Amended by the 2010 Protocol*, OECD Publishing, Paris, https://doi.org/10.1787/9789264115606-en. [2]

Notes

[1] 1) Tonnage tax regime; 2) International shipping regime.

[2] Parties to the Convention are available here: www.oecd.org/tax/exchange-of-tax-information/convention-on-mutual-administrative-assistance-in-tax-matters.htm. Parties to the Nordic Convention on Assistance in Tax Matters are Denmark, Finland, Iceland, Norway and Sweden. The Faroe Islands also has bilateral agreements with Greenland, India, Switzerland and the United Kingdom. The bilateral agreements with Switzerland and India are the Danish tax treaties, which are territorially extended to include the Faroe Islands.

Finland

Finland has met all aspects of the terms of reference (OECD, 2021[1]) (ToR) for the calendar year 2022 (year in review), and no recommendations are made.

Finland can legally issue four types of rulings within the scope of the transparency framework.

In practice, Finland issued rulings within the scope of the transparency framework as follows:

Type of ruling	Number of rulings
Past rulings	42
Future rulings in the period 1 April 2016 – 31 December 2016	13
Future rulings in the calendar year 2017	19
Future rulings in the calendar year 2018	8
Future rulings in the calendar year 2019	32
Future rulings in the calendar year 2020	27
Future rulings in the calendar year 2021	28
Future rulings in the year in review	33

Peer input was received from three jurisdictions in respect of the exchanges of information on rulings received from Finland. The input was generally positive, noting that overall information was complete and in a correct format. However, peer input indicated that exchanges on rulings were not timely.

Information gathering process (ToR I.A)

436. Finland can legally issue the following four types of rulings within the scope of the transparency framework: (i) preferential regimes;[1] (ii) cross-border unilateral APAs and any other cross-border unilateral tax rulings (such as an advance tax ruling) covering transfer pricing or the application of transfer pricing principles; (iii) permanent establishment rulings; and (iv) related party conduit rulings.

437. For Finland, past rulings are any tax rulings within scope that are issued either: (i) on or after 1 January 2014 but before 1 April 2016; or (ii) on or after 1 January 2010 but before 1 January 2014, provided they were still in effect as at 1 January 2014. Future rulings are any tax rulings within scope that are issued on or after 1 April 2016.

438. In the prior years' peer review reports, it was determined that Finland's undertakings to identify past and future rulings and all potential exchange jurisdictions were sufficient to meet the minimum standard. In addition, it was determined that Finland's review and supervision mechanism was sufficient to meet the minimum standard. Finland's implementation remains unchanged, and therefore continues to meet the minimum standard.

439. Finland has met all of the ToR for the information gathering process and no recommendations are made.

Exchange of information (ToR II.B)

440. Finland has the necessary domestic legal basis to exchange information spontaneously. Finland notes that there are no legal or practical impediments that prevent the spontaneous exchange of information on rulings as contemplated in the Action 5 minimum standard.

441. Finland has international agreements permitting spontaneous exchange of information, including: (i) the *Multilateral Convention on Mutual Administrative Assistance in Tax Matters: Amended by the 2010 Protocol* (OECD/Council of Europe, 2011[2]) ("the Convention"), (ii) the Directive 2011/16/EU with all other European Union Member States and (iii) bilateral agreements in force with 89 jurisdictions.[2]

442. For the year in review, the timeliness of exchanges is as follows:

Future rulings within the scope of the transparency framework	Number of exchanges transmitted within three months of the information becoming available to the competent authority or immediately after legal impediments have been lifted	Delayed exchanges		
		Number of exchanges transmitted later than three months of the information on rulings becoming available to the competent authority	Reasons for the delays	Any other comments
	142	0	N/A	N/A

Follow-up requests received for exchange of the ruling	Number	Average time to provide response	Number of requests not answered
	0	0	0

443. In the prior years' peer review reports, it was determined that Finland's process for the completion and exchange of templates were sufficient to meet the minimum standard. With respect to past rulings, no further action was required from Finland. Finland's implementation in this regard remains unchanged and therefore continues to meet the minimum standard.

444. Finland has the necessary legal basis for spontaneous exchange of information, a process for completing the templates in a timely way and has completed all exchanges. Finland has met all of the ToR for the exchange of information process and no recommendations are made.

Statistics (ToR IV.D)

445. The statistics for the year in review are as follows:

Category of ruling	Number of exchanges	Jurisdictions exchanged with
Ruling related to a preferential regime	0	N/A
Cross-border unilateral APAs and any other cross-border unilateral tax rulings (such as an advance tax ruling) covering transfer pricing or the application of transfer pricing principles	137	Australia, Austria, Belgium, Brazil, Bulgaria, China (People's Republic of), Croatia, Cyprus, Czechia, Denmark, Estonia, France, Georgia, Germany, Greece, Hong Kong (China), Hungary, India, Ireland, Italy, Japan, Kazakhstan, Korea, Latvia, Lithuania, Luxembourg, Malaysia, Netherlands, New Zealand, Norway, Poland, Portugal Romania, Serbia, Singapore, Slovak Republic, Slovenia, Spain, Sweden, Switzerland, Thailand, Ukraine, United Kingdom, United States,
Permanent establishment rulings	5	Belgium, Germany, Ireland, Netherlands, United States
Related party conduit rulings	0	N/A
Total	142	

Matters related to intellectual property regimes (ToR I.A.1.3)

446. Finland does not offer an intellectual property regime for which transparency requirements under the Action 5 Report (OECD, 2015[3]) were imposed.

Summary of recommendations on implementation of the transparency framework

Aspect of implementation of the transparency framework that should be improved	Recommendation for improvement
	No recommendations are made.

References

OECD (2021), *BEPS Action 5 on Harmful Tax Practices - Terms of Reference and Methodology for the Conduct of the Peer Reviews of the Action 5 Transparency Framework*, OECD Publishing, Paris, https://www.oecd.org/tax/beps/beps-action-5-harmful-tax-practices-peer-review-transparency-framework.pdf. [1]

OECD (2015), *Countering Harmful Tax Practices More Effectively, Taking into Account Transparency and Substance, Action 5 - 2015 Final Report*, OECD/G20 Base Erosion and Profit Shifting Project, OECD Publishing, Paris, https://doi.org/10.1787/9789264241190-en. [3]

OECD/Council of Europe (2011), *The Multilateral Convention on Mutual Administrative Assistance in Tax Matters: Amended by the 2010 Protocol*, OECD Publishing, Paris, https://doi.org/10.1787/9789264115606-en. [2]

Notes

[1] Shipping regime.

[2] Participating jurisdictions to the Convention are available here: www.oecd.org/tax/exchange-of-tax-information/convention-on-mutual-administrative-assistance-in-tax-matters.htm. Finland also has bilateral agreements with Argentina, Armenia, Aruba, Australia, Austria, Azerbaijan, Bailiwick of Jersey, Barbados, Belarus, Belgium Bermuda, Bosnia and Herzegovina, Brazil, British Virgin Islands, Bulgaria, Canada, Cayman Islands, China (People's Republic of), Cook Islands, Croatia, Cyprus, Czechia, Denmark, Egypt, Estonia, Faroe Islands, France, Georgia, Germany, Greece, Guatemala, Guernsey, Hungary, India, Indonesia, Ireland, Isle of Man, Israel, Italy, Japan, Kazakhstan, Korea, Kosovo, Kyrgyzstan, Latvia, Lebanon, Lithuania, Luxembourg, Malaysia, Malta, Mexico, Moldova, Monaco, Montenegro, Morocco, Netherlands, Netherlands Antilles, New Zealand, North Macedonia, Norway, Pakistan, Panama, Philippines, Poland, Portugal, Romania, Russia, Serbia, Singapore, Slovak Republic, Slovenia, South Africa, Spain, Sri Lanka, Sweden, Switzerland, Tajikistan, Tanzania, Thailand, Türkiye, Turkmenistan, Ukraine, United Arab Emirates, United Kingdom, United States, Uruguay, Uzbekistan, Viet Nam and Zambia.

France

France has met all aspects of the terms of reference (OECD, 2021[1]) (ToR) for the calendar year 2022 (year in review), and no recommendations are made.

In the prior year report, as well as in the 2016-2020 peer reviews, France had received a recommendation regarding identifying and exchanging information on new entrants to the grandfathered IP regime (ToR I.A.1.3). France has now exchanged all information on new entrants and the recommendation is resolved.

France can legally issue three types of rulings within the scope of the transparency framework.

In practice, France issued rulings within the scope of the transparency framework as follows:

Type of ruling	Number of rulings
Past rulings	45
Future rulings in the period 1 April 2016 – 31 December 2016	4
Future rulings in the calendar year 2017	6
Future rulings in the calendar year 2018	6
Future rulings in the calendar year 2019	16
Future rulings in the calendar year 2020	8
Future rulings in the calendar year 2021	16
Future rulings in the year in review	34[1]

No peer input was received in respect of the exchanges of information on rulings received from France.

Information gathering process (ToR I.A)

447. France can legally issue the following three types of rulings within the scope of the transparency framework: (i) preferential regimes;[2] (ii) cross-border unilateral APAs and any other cross-border unilateral tax rulings (such as an advance tax ruling) covering transfer pricing or the application of transfer pricing principles; and (iii) permanent establishment rulings.

448. For France, past rulings are any tax rulings within scope that are issued either: (i) on or after 1 January 2014 but before 1 April 2016; or (ii) on or after 1 January 2010 but before 1 January 2014, provided they were still in effect as at 1 January 2014. Future rulings are any tax rulings within scope that are issued on or after 1 April 2016.

449. In the prior years' peer review reports, it was determined that France's undertakings to identify past and future rulings and all potential exchange jurisdictions were sufficient to meet the minimum standard. In addition, it was determined that France's review and supervision mechanism was sufficient to meet the minimum standard. France's implementation remains unchanged, and therefore continues to meet the minimum standard.

450. France has met all of the ToR for the information gathering process and no recommendations are made.

Exchange of information (ToR II.B)

451. France has the necessary domestic legal basis to exchange information spontaneously. France notes that there are no legal or practical impediments that prevent the spontaneous exchange of information on rulings as contemplated in the Action 5 minimum standard.

452. France has international agreements permitting spontaneous exchange of information, including: (i) the *Multilateral Convention on Mutual Administrative Assistance in Tax Matters: Amended by the 2010 Protocol* (OECD/Council of Europe, 2011[2]) ("the Convention"), (ii) the Directive 2011/16/EU with all other European Union Member States and (iii) bilateral agreements in force with 126 jurisdictions.[3]

453. For the year in review, the timeliness of exchanges is as follows:

Future rulings within the scope of the transparency framework	Number of exchanges transmitted within three months of the information becoming available to the competent authority or immediately after legal impediments have been lifted	Delayed exchanges		
		Number of exchanges transmitted later than three months of the information on rulings becoming available to the competent authority	Reasons for the delays	Any other comments
	34	0	N/A	N/A

Follow-up requests received for exchange of the ruling	Number	Average time to provide response	Number of requests not answered
	3	2 months	0

454. In the prior years' peer review reports, it was determined that France's process for the completion and exchange of templates were sufficient to meet the minimum standard. With respect to past rulings, no further action was required. France's implementation in this regard remains unchanged and therefore continues to meet the minimum standard.

455. France has the necessary legal basis for spontaneous exchange of information, a process for completing the templates in a timely way and has completed all exchanges. France has met all of the ToR for the exchange of information process and no recommendations are made.

Statistics (ToR IV.D)

456. The statistics for the year in review are as follows:

Category of ruling	Number of exchanges	Jurisdictions exchanged with
Ruling related to a preferential regime	6	Belgium, Germany, Italy, Luxembourg, Netherlands, United Kingdom
Cross-border unilateral APAs and any other cross-border unilateral tax rulings (such as an advance tax ruling) covering transfer pricing or the application of transfer pricing principles	4	*De minimis* rule applies
Permanent establishment rulings	24	Canada, Denmark, Estonia, Germany, Ireland, Luxembourg, Netherlands, Spain, Sweden, Switzerland, United Kingdom
IP regimes: total exchanges on taxpayers benefitting from the third category of IP assets, new entrants benefitting from grandfathered IP regimes; and taxpayers making use of the option to treat the nexus ratio as a rebuttable presumption	41	Belgium, Germany, Italy, Japan, Luxembourg, Netherlands, Norway, Spain, Sweden, Switzerland, United Kingdom, United States
Total	75	

Matters related to intellectual property regimes (ToR I.A.1.3)

457. France offers an intellectual property regime (IP regime)[4] that is subject to the transparency requirements under the Action 5 Report (OECD, 2015[3]). This regime was amended with effect from 1 January 2019 and is compliant with the nexus approach. It states that the identification of the benefitting taxpayers will occur as follows:

- ***New entrants benefitting from the grandfathered IP regime:***

  With respect to the previous form of the regime that existed until 31 December 2018, France had not identified information on new entrants, and as such had not exchanged information. Therefore, France was recommended to identify and exchange information on all new entrants to the IP regime. In the prior year's report, it was noted that France identified those taxpayers that were owned for at least 25% by foreign residents among all new entrants to the regime between 2015 and 2018.

  During the year in review, France exchanged all information regarding the identified taxpayers. As all the information was identified and exchanged, the recommendation has now been resolved.

- ***Third category of IP assets:***

  In the previous year's report, it was noted that the third category of IP assets was not yet in effect. France has made amendments to its IP regimes by the Article 72 of Law no. 2022-1726 of 31 December 2022. As of 2023, the regime no longer provides benefits to the third category of IP assets.

- ***Taxpayers making use of the option to treat the nexus ratio as a rebuttable presumption***:

The amended IP regime allows for the option to treat the nexus ratio as a rebuttable presumption. Taxpayers opting to do so must obtain a ruling from the tax administration and are required to list the specific assets for which the presumption was rebutted in their tax return. France confirms that no taxpayer elected to treat the nexus approach as a rebuttable presumption.

Summary of recommendations on implementation of the transparency framework

Aspect of implementation of the transparency framework that should be improved	Recommendation for improvement
	No recommendations are made

References

OECD (2021), *BEPS Action 5 on Harmful Tax Practices - Terms of Reference and Methodology for the Conduct of the Peer Reviews of the Action 5 Transparency Framework*, OECD Publishing, Paris, https://www.oecd.org/tax/beps/beps-action-5-harmful-tax-practices-peer-review-transparency-framework.pdf. [1]

OECD (2015), *Countering Harmful Tax Practices More Effectively, Taking into Account Transparency and Substance, Action 5 - 2015 Final Report*, OECD/G20 Base Erosion and Profit Shifting Project, OECD Publishing, Paris, https://doi.org/10.1787/9789264241190-en. [3]

OECD/Council of Europe (2011), *The Multilateral Convention on Mutual Administrative Assistance in Tax Matters: Amended by the 2010 Protocol*, OECD Publishing, Paris, https://doi.org/10.1787/9789264115606-en. [2]

Notes

[1] During the year in review, France also issued three rulings relating to "other types of rulings" that fall outside of the scope of the transparency framework and exchanged information on these rulings.

[2] Shipping regime.

[3] Participating jurisdictions to the Convention are available here: www.oecd.org/tax/exchange-of-tax-information/convention-on-mutual-administrative-assistance-in-tax-matters.htm. France also has bilateral agreements with: Albania, Algeria, Andorra, Argentina, Armenia, Australia, Austria, Azerbaijan, Bahrain, Bangladesh, Belarus, Belgium, Benin, Bolivia, Bosnia and Herzegovina, Botswana, Brazil, Bulgaria, Burkina Faso, Cameroon, Canada, Central African Republic, Chile, China (People's Republic of), Colombia, Congo, Côte d'Ivoire, Croatia, Cyprus, Czechia, Ecuador, Egypt, Estonia, Ethiopia, Finland, French Polynesia, Gabon, Georgia, Germany, Ghana, Greece, Guinea, Hong Kong (China), Hungary, Iceland, India, Indonesia, Iran, Ireland, Israel, Italy, Jamaica, Japan, Jordan, Kazakhstan, Kenya, Korea, Kosovo, Kuwait, Kyrgyzstan, Latvia, Lebanon, Libya, Lithuania, Luxembourg, Madagascar, Malawi, Malaysia, Mali, Malta, Mauritania, Mauritius, Mexico, Monaco, Mongolia, Montenegro, Morocco, Namibia, Netherlands, New Caledonia, New Zealand, Niger, Nigeria, North Macedonia, Norway, Oman, Pakistan, Panama, Philippines, Poland, Portugal, Qatar, Romania, Russia, Saudi Arabia, Senegal, Serbia, Singapore, Slovak Republic, Slovenia, South Africa, Spain, Sri Lanka, Sint Maarten, Saint Pierre and Miquelon, Sweden, Switzerland, Syrian Arab Republic, Chinese Taipei, Thailand, Togo, Trinidad and Tobago, Tunisia, Türkiye, Turkmenistan, Ukraine, United Arab Emirates, United Kingdom, United States, Uzbekistan, Venezuela, Viet Nam, Zambia and Zimbabwe.

[4] Reduced corporation tax rate on IP income, formerly known as Reduced rate for long term capital gains and profits from the licensing of IP rights.

Gabon

Gabon did not provide a completed peer review questionnaire to the Secretariat. Gabon is taking steps to implement the aspects of the terms of reference (OECD, 2021[1]) (ToR) for the transparency framework and to commence administrative preparations to ensure that it establishes an information gathering process (ToR I.A) and that information on rulings will be identified and exchanged in a timely manner (ToR II.B). Gabon receives two recommendations on these points for the calendar year 2022 (year in review).

In the prior year report, as well as in the 2018-2020 peer reviews, Gabon had received the same two recommendations. As they have not been addressed, the recommendations remain in place.

Gabon can legally issue two types of rulings within the scope of the transparency framework.

In practice, Gabon issued no rulings within the scope of the transparency framework.

As no exchanges were required to take place, no peer input was received in respect of the exchanges of information on rulings received from Gabon.

Information gathering process (ToR I.A)

458. Gabon can legally issue the following two types of rulings within the scope of the transparency framework: (i) preferential regimes;[1] and (ii) cross-border unilateral APAs and any other cross-border unilateral tax rulings (such as an advance tax ruling) covering transfer pricing or the application of transfer pricing principles.

Past rulings (ToR I.A.1.1, I.A.1.2, I.A.2.1, I.A.2.2)

459. For Gabon, past rulings are any tax rulings within scope that are issued either (i) on or after 1 January 2016 but before 1 April 2018; and (ii) on or after 1 January 2014 but before 1 January 2016, provided they were still in effect as at 1 January 2016. Gabon issued no past rulings within the scope of the transparency framework. As such, there was no need to identify potential exchange jurisdictions.

Future rulings (ToR I.A.1.1, I.A.1.2, I.A.2.1)

460. For Gabon, future rulings are any tax rulings within scope that are issued on or after 1 April 2018.

461. In the prior years' peer review reports, Gabon indicated that there were no processes in place for the record keeping of rulings for the purposes of the transparency framework. It was noted that Gabon intended to implement guidelines and practices to make sure the necessary information to meet the requirements of the transparency framework is required in all cases. Therefore, Gabon was recommended to finalise its information gathering process for identifying all relevant rulings and potential exchange jurisdictions, as soon as possible.

462. It is not known whether during the year in review, additional steps to finalise its information gathering process were taken, and therefore the prior years' recommendation remains in place.

Review and supervision (ToR I.A.3)

463. In the prior years' peer review reports, it was determined that Gabon did not yet have a review and supervision mechanism under the transparency framework. Therefore, Gabon was recommended to put in place a review and supervision mechanism as soon as possible. Gabon was in the process of considering the implementation of a revision and supervision mechanism for ensuring implementation of the transparency framework. It is not known whether during the year in review, additional steps were taken, and therefore the prior year recommendation remains.

Conclusion on section A

464. Gabon is recommended to finalise its information gathering process for identifying all relevant rulings and all potential exchange jurisdictions, with a review and supervision mechanism, as soon as possible (ToR I.A).

Exchange of information (ToR II.B)

465. Gabon has the necessary domestic legal basis to exchange information spontaneously. Gabon notes that there are no legal or practical impediments that prevent the spontaneous exchange of information on rulings as contemplated in the Action 5 minimum standard.

466. Gabon has international agreements permitting spontaneous exchange of information, including bilateral agreements in force with six jurisdictions.[2] Gabon signed the *Multilateral Convention on Mutual Administrative Assistance in Tax Matters: Amended by the 2010 Protocol* (OECD/Council of Europe, 2011[2]) ("the Convention") in July 2014 but Gabon has not yet ratified the Convention. Gabon is encouraged to continue its efforts to ratify the Convention and expand its international exchange of information instruments to be able to exchange information on rulings. It is noted, however, that

jurisdictions are assessed on their compliance with the transparency framework in respect of the exchange of information network in effect for the year of the particular annual review.

Completion and exchange of templates (ToR II.B.3, II.B.4, II.B.5, II.B.6, II.B.7)

467. In the prior years' peer review reports, it was determined that Gabon was developing a process to complete the templates on relevant rulings, to make them available to the Competent Authority for exchange of information, and to exchange them with relevant jurisdictions.

468. It is not known whether during the year in review, additional steps were taken, and therefore the prior year recommendation remains.

469. As no exchanges were required to take place for the year in review, no data on the timeliness of exchanges can be reported.

Conclusion on section B

470. Gabon has the necessary legal basis for spontaneous exchange of information. Gabon is recommended to continue its efforts to put in place a process to complete the templates for all relevant rulings and to ensure that the exchanges of information on rulings occur as soon as possible (ToR II.B).

Statistics (ToR IV.D)

471. As no rulings were issued, no statistics can be reported.

Matters related to intellectual property regimes (ToR I.A.1.3)

472. Gabon does not offer an intellectual property regime for which transparency requirements under the Action 5 Report (OECD, 2015[3]) were imposed.

Summary of recommendations on implementation of the transparency framework

Aspect of implementation of the transparency framework that should be improved	Recommendation for improvement
It is not known whether Gabon has finalised the steps to have in place its necessary information gathering process, with a review and supervision mechanism.	Gabon is recommended to finalise its information gathering process for identifying all relevant rulings and all potential exchange jurisdictions, with a review and supervision mechanism, as soon as possible. This recommendation remains unchanged since the 2018, 2019, 2020 and 2021 peer review reports.
It is not known whether Gabon has finalised the steps to put in place a process to complete the templates for all relevant rulings and to ensure that the exchanges of information on rulings occur as soon as possible.	Gabon is recommended to continue its efforts to put in place a process to complete the templates for all relevant rulings and to ensure that the exchanges of information on rulings occur as soon as possible. This recommendation remains unchanged since the 2018, 2019, 2020 and 2021 peer review reports.

References

OECD (2021), *BEPS Action 5 on Harmful Tax Practices - Terms of Reference and Methodology for the Conduct of the Peer Reviews of the Action 5 Transparency Framework*, OECD Publishing, Paris, https://www.oecd.org/tax/beps/beps-action-5-harmful-tax-practices-peer-review-transparency-framework.pdf. [1]

OECD (2015), *Countering Harmful Tax Practices More Effectively, Taking into Account Transparency and Substance, Action 5 - 2015 Final Report*, OECD/G20 Base Erosion and Profit Shifting Project, OECD Publishing, Paris, https://doi.org/10.1787/9789264241190-en. [3]

OECD/Council of Europe (2011), *The Multilateral Convention on Mutual Administrative Assistance in Tax Matters: Amended by the 2010 Protocol*, OECD Publishing, Paris, https://doi.org/10.1787/9789264115606-en. [2]

Notes

[1] Special economic zone.

[2] Participating jurisdictions to the Convention are available here: www.oecd.org/tax/exchange-of-tax-information/convention-on-mutual-administrative-assistance-in-tax-matters.htm. Gabon also has bilateral agreements with Belgium, Canada, France, Korea, Morocco and Saudi Arabia.

Georgia

Georgia has met all aspects of the terms of reference (OECD, 2021[1]) (ToR) for the calendar year 2022 (year in review), and no recommendations are made.

Georgia can legally issue four types of rulings within the scope of the transparency framework.

In practice, Georgia issued no rulings within the scope of the transparency framework.

As no exchanges were required to take place, no peer input was received in respect of the exchanges of information on rulings received from Georgia.

Information gathering process (ToR I.A)

473. Georgia can legally issue the following four types of rulings within the scope of the transparency framework: (i) preferential regimes;[1] (ii) cross-border unilateral APAs and any other cross-border unilateral tax rulings (such as an advance tax ruling) covering transfer pricing or the application of transfer pricing principles; (iii) permanent establishment rulings; and (iv) related party conduit rulings.

474. For Georgia, past rulings are any tax rulings within scope that are issued either: (i) on or after 1 January 2016 but before 1 April 2018; or (ii) on or after 1 January 2014 but before 1 January 2016, provided they were still in effect as at 1 January 2016. Future rulings are any tax rulings within scope that are issued on or after 1 April 2018.

475. In the prior years' peer review reports, it was determined that Georgia's undertakings to identify past and future rulings and all potential exchange jurisdictions were sufficient to meet the minimum standard. In addition, it was determined that Georgia's review and supervision mechanism was sufficient to meet the minimum standard. Georgia's implementation remains unchanged, and therefore continues to meet the minimum standard.

476. Georgia has met all of the ToR for the information gathering process and no recommendations are made.

Exchange of information (ToR II.B)

477. Georgia has the necessary domestic legal basis to exchange information spontaneously. Georgia notes that there are no legal or practical impediments that prevent the spontaneous exchange of information on rulings as contemplated in the Action 5 minimum standard.

478. Georgia has international agreements permitting spontaneous exchange of information, including: (i) the *Multilateral Convention on Mutual Administrative Assistance in Tax Matters: Amended by the 2010 Protocol* (OECD/Council of Europe, 2011[2]) ("the Convention") and (ii) bilateral agreements in force with 58 jurisdictions.[2]

479. During the year in review, no exchanges were required to take place and no data on the timeliness of exchanges is reported.

480. In the prior years' peer review reports, it was determined that Georgia's process for the completion and exchange of templates were sufficient to meet the minimum standard. With respect to past rulings, no further action was required. Georgia's implementation in this regard remains unchanged and therefore continues to meet the minimum standard.

481. Georgia has met all of the ToR for the exchange of information process and no recommendations are made.

Statistics (ToR IV.D)

482. As no rulings were issued, no statistics can be reported.

Matters related to intellectual property regimes (ToR I.A.1.3)

483. Georgia does not offer an intellectual property regime for which transparency requirements under the Action 5 Report (OECD, 2015[3]) were imposed.

Summary of recommendations on implementation of the transparency framework

Aspect of implementation of the transparency framework that should be improved	Recommendation for improvement
	No recommendations are made.

References

OECD (2021), *BEPS Action 5 on Harmful Tax Practices - Terms of Reference and Methodology for the Conduct of the Peer Reviews of the Action 5 Transparency Framework*, OECD Publishing, Paris, https://www.oecd.org/tax/beps/beps-action-5-harmful-tax-practices-peer-review-transparency-framework.pdf. [1]

OECD (2015), *Countering Harmful Tax Practices More Effectively, Taking into Account Transparency and Substance, Action 5 - 2015 Final Report*, OECD/G20 Base Erosion and Profit Shifting Project, OECD Publishing, Paris, https://doi.org/10.1787/9789264241190-en. [3]

OECD/Council of Europe (2011), *The Multilateral Convention on Mutual Administrative Assistance in Tax Matters: Amended by the 2010 Protocol*, OECD Publishing, Paris, https://doi.org/10.1787/9789264115606-en. [2]

Notes

[1] International financial company and 2) Virtual zone person.

[2] Participating jurisdictions to the Convention are available here: www.oecd.org/tax/exchange-of-tax-information/convention-on-mutual-administrative-assistance-in-tax-matters.htm. Georgia also has bilateral agreements with Armenia, Austria, Azerbaijan, Bahamas, Bahrain, Belarus, Belgium, Bulgaria, China (People's Republic of), Croatia, Cyprus, Czechia, Denmark, Egypt, Estonia, Finland, France, Germany, Greece, Hungary, Iceland, India, Iran, Ireland, Israel, Italy, Japan, Kazakhstan, Korea, Kuwait, Latvia, Liechtenstein, Lithuania, Luxembourg, Malta, Moldova, Netherlands, Norway, Poland, Portugal, Qatar, Romania, San Marino, Saudi Arabia, Serbia, Seychelles, Singapore, Slovak Republic, Slovenia, Spain, Sweden, Switzerland, Türkiye, Turkmenistan, Ukraine, United Arab Emirates, United Kingdom and Uzbekistan.

Germany

Germany has met all aspects of the terms of reference (OECD, 2021[1]) (ToR) for the calendar year 2022 (year in review), and no recommendations are made.

Germany can legally issue five types of rulings within the scope of the transparency framework.

In practice, Germany issued rulings within the scope of the transparency framework as follows:

Type of ruling	Number of rulings
Past rulings	30
Future rulings in the period 1 April 2016 – 31 December 2016	7
Future rulings in the calendar year 2017	10
Future rulings in the calendar year 2018	10
Future rulings in the calendar year 2019	8
Future rulings in the calendar year 2020	13
Future rulings in the calendar year 2021	10
Future rulings in the year in review	5

No peer input was received in respect of the exchanges of information on rulings received from Germany.

Information gathering process (ToR I.A)

484. Germany can legally issue the following five types of rulings within the scope of the transparency framework: (i) preferential regimes;[1] (ii) cross-border unilateral APAs and any other cross-border unilateral tax rulings (such as an advance tax ruling) covering transfer pricing or the application of transfer pricing principles; (iii) rulings providing for unilateral downward adjustments; (iv) permanent establishment rulings; and (v) related party conduit rulings.

485. For Germany, past rulings are any tax rulings within scope that are issued either: (i) on or after 1 January 2014 but before 1 April 2016; or (ii) on or after 1 January 2010 but before 1 January 2014, provided they were still in effect as at 1 January 2014. Future rulings are any tax rulings within scope that are issued on or after 1 April 2016.

486. In the prior years' peer review reports, it was determined that Germany's undertakings to identify past and future rulings and all potential exchange jurisdictions were sufficient to meet the minimum standard. In addition, it was determined that Germany's review and supervision mechanism was sufficient to meet the minimum standard. Germany's implementation remains unchanged, and therefore continues to meet the minimum standard.

487. Germany has met all of the ToR for the information gathering process and no recommendations are made.

Exchange of information (ToR II.B)

488. Germany has the necessary domestic legal basis to exchange information spontaneously. Germany notes that there are no legal or practical impediments that prevent the spontaneous exchange of information on rulings as contemplated in the Action 5 minimum standard.

489. Germany has international agreements permitting spontaneous exchange of information, including: (i) the *Multilateral Convention on Mutual Administrative Assistance in Tax Matters: Amended by the 2010 Protocol* (OECD/Council of Europe, 2011[2]) ("the Convention"), (ii) the Directive 2011/16/EU with all other European Union Member States and (iii) bilateral agreements in force with 61 jurisdictions.[2]

490. For the year in review, the timeliness of exchanges is as follows:

Future rulings within the scope of the transparency framework	Number of exchanges transmitted within three months of the information becoming available to the competent authority or immediately after legal impediments have been lifted	Delayed exchanges		
		Number of exchanges transmitted later than three months of the information on rulings becoming available to the competent authority	Reasons for the delays	Any other comments
	5	0	N/A	N/A

Follow-up requests received for exchange of the ruling	Number	Average time to provide response	Number of requests not answered
	0	N/A	N/A

491. In the prior years' peer review reports, it was determined that Germany's process for the completion and exchange of templates were sufficient to meet the minimum standard. With respect to past rulings, no further action was required. Germany's implementation in this regard remains unchanged and therefore continues to meet the minimum standard.

492. Germany has the necessary legal basis for spontaneous exchange of information, a process for completing the templates in a timely way and has completed all exchanges. Germany has met all of the ToR for the exchange of information process and no recommendations are made.

Statistics (ToR IV.D)

493. The statistics for the year in review are as follows:

Category of ruling	Number of exchanges	Jurisdictions exchanged with
Ruling related to a preferential regime	1	*De minimis* rule applies
Cross-border unilateral APAs and any other cross-border unilateral tax rulings (such as an advance tax ruling) covering transfer pricing or the application of transfer pricing principles	0	N/A
Cross-border rulings providing for a unilateral downward adjustment to the taxpayer's taxable profits that is not directly reflected in the taxpayer's financial / commercial accounts	1	*De minimis* rule applies
Permanent establishment rulings	2	*De minimis* rule applies
Related party conduit rulings	1	*De minimis* rule applies
Total	5	

Matters related to intellectual property regimes (ToR I.A.1.3)

494. Germany does not offer an intellectual property regime for which transparency requirements under the Action 5 Report (OECD, 2015[3]) were imposed.

Summary of recommendations on implementation of the transparency framework

Aspect of implementation of the transparency framework that should be improved	Recommendation for improvement
	No recommendations are made.

References

OECD (2021), *BEPS Action 5 on Harmful Tax Practices - Terms of Reference and Methodology for the Conduct of the Peer Reviews of the Action 5 Transparency Framework*, OECD Publishing, Paris, https://www.oecd.org/tax/beps/beps-action-5-harmful-tax-practices-peer-review-transparency-framework.pdf. [1]

OECD (2015), *Countering Harmful Tax Practices More Effectively, Taking into Account Transparency and Substance, Action 5 - 2015 Final Report*, OECD/G20 Base Erosion and Profit Shifting Project, OECD Publishing, Paris, https://doi.org/10.1787/9789264241190-en. [3]

OECD/Council of Europe (2011), *The Multilateral Convention on Mutual Administrative Assistance in Tax Matters: Amended by the 2010 Protocol*, OECD Publishing, Paris, https://doi.org/10.1787/9789264115606-en. [2]

Notes

[1] Tonnage tax regime.

[2] Participating jurisdictions to the Convention are available here: www.oecd.org/tax/exchange-of-tax-information/convention-on-mutual-administrative-assistance-in-tax-matters.htm. Germany also has bilateral agreements with Albania, Algeria, Armenia, Australia, Austria, Azerbaijan, Belarus, Belgium, Bulgaria, Canada, China (People's Republic of), Costa Rica, Croatia, Cyprus, Denmark, Estonia, Finland, France, Georgia, Ghana, Hungary, Iceland, Ireland, Israel, Italy, Japan, Kazakhstan, Korea, Kyrgyzstan, Latvia, Liechtenstein, Lithuania, Luxembourg, Malaysia, Malta, Mauritius, Mexico, Netherlands, New Zealand, North Macedonia, Norway, Philippines, Poland, Portugal, Romania, Russia, Singapore, Slovenia, Spain, Sweden, Switzerland, Syrian Arab Republic, Tajikistan, Tunisia, Türkiye, Turkmenistan, United Arab Emirates, United Kingdom, United States, Uruguay, and Uzbekistan.

Gibraltar

Gibraltar has met all aspects of the terms of reference (OECD, 2021[1]) (ToR) for the calendar year 2022 (year in review), and no recommendations are made.

Gibraltar can legally issue four types of rulings within the scope of the transparency framework.

In practice, Gibraltar issued no rulings within the scope of the transparency framework.

As no rulings were issued, no exchanges were required to take place, and no peer input was received in respect of the exchanges of information on rulings received from Gibraltar.

Information gathering process (ToR I.A)

495. Gibraltar can legally issue the following four types of rulings within the scope of the transparency framework: (i) cross-border unilateral APAs and any other cross-border unilateral tax rulings (such as an advance tax ruling) covering transfer pricing or the application of transfer pricing principles; (ii) rulings providing for unilateral downward adjustments; (iii) permanent establishment rulings; and (iv) related party conduit rulings.

496. For Gibraltar, past rulings are any tax rulings issued prior to 1 March 2020. However, there is no obligation for Gibraltar to conduct spontaneous exchange information on past rulings. For Gibraltar, future rulings are any tax rulings within scope that are issued on or after 1 March 2020.

497. In the prior year's peer review report, it was determined that Gibraltar's undertakings to identify past and future rulings and all potential exchange jurisdictions were sufficient to meet the minimum standard. In addition, it was determined that Gibraltar's review and supervision mechanism was sufficient to meet the minimum standard. Gibraltar's implementation remains unchanged, and therefore continues to meet the minimum standard.

498. Gibraltar has met all of the ToR for the information gathering process and no recommendations are made.

Exchange of information (ToR II.B)

499. Gibraltar has the necessary domestic legal basis to exchange information spontaneously. Gibraltar notes that there are no legal or practical impediments that prevent the spontaneous exchange of information on rulings as contemplated in the Action 5 minimum standard.

500. Gibraltar has international agreements permitting spontaneous exchange of information, including being a jurisdiction participating in (i) the *Multilateral Convention on Mutual Administrative Assistance in Tax Matters: Amended by the 2010 Protocol* (OECD/Council of Europe, 2011[2]) ("the Convention"), following the territorial extension of this convention to Gibraltar by the United Kingdom, (ii) a bilateral agreement in force with one jurisdiction and (iii) tax information exchange agreements in force with four jurisdictions.[1]

501. During the year in review, no exchanges were required to take place and no data on the timeliness of exchanges is reported.

502. In the prior year's peer review report, it was determined that Gibraltar's process for the completion and exchange of templates were sufficient to meet the minimum standard. With respect to past rulings, no action was required. Gibraltar's implementation in this regard remains unchanged and therefore continues to meet the minimum standard.

503. Gibraltar has the necessary legal basis for spontaneous exchange of information, a process for completing the templates in a timely way and has completed all exchanges. Gibraltar has met all of the ToR for the exchange of information process and no recommendations are made.

Statistics (ToR IV.D)

504. As no rulings were issued, no statistics can be reported.

Matters related to intellectual property regimes (ToR I.A.1.3)

505. Gibraltar does not offer an intellectual property regime for which transparency requirements under the Action 5 Report (OECD, 2015[3]) were imposed.

Summary of recommendations on implementation of the transparency framework

Aspect of implementation of the transparency framework that should be improved	Recommendation for improvement
	No recommendations are made.

References

OECD (2021), *BEPS Action 5 on Harmful Tax Practices - Terms of Reference and Methodology for the Conduct of the Peer Reviews of the Action 5 Transparency Framework*, OECD Publishing, Paris, https://www.oecd.org/tax/beps/beps-action-5-harmful-tax-practices-peer-review-transparency-framework.pdf. [1]

OECD (2015), *Countering Harmful Tax Practices More Effectively, Taking into Account Transparency and Substance, Action 5 - 2015 Final Report*, OECD/G20 Base Erosion and Profit Shifting Project, OECD Publishing, Paris, https://doi.org/10.1787/9789264241190-en. [3]

OECD/Council of Europe (2011), *The Multilateral Convention on Mutual Administrative Assistance in Tax Matters: Amended by the 2010 Protocol*, OECD Publishing, Paris, https://doi.org/10.1787/9789264115606-en. [2]

Note

[1] Participating jurisdictions to the Convention are available here: www.oecd.org/tax/exchange-of-tax-information/convention-on-mutual-administrative-assistance-in-tax-matters.htm. Gibraltar also has bilateral agreements with the United Kingdom and tax information exchange agreements with Guernsey, Isle of Man, United Kingdom and United States.

Greece

Greece has met all aspects of the terms of reference (OECD, 2021[1]) (ToR) for the calendar year 2022 (year in review), and no recommendations are made.

Greece can legally issue one type of rulings within the scope of the transparency framework.

In practice, Greece issued rulings within the scope of the transparency framework as follows:

Type of ruling	Number of rulings
Past rulings	1
Future rulings in the period 1 April 2016 – 31 December 2016	0
Future rulings in the calendar year 2017	0
Future rulings in the calendar year 2018	2
Future rulings in the calendar year 2019	0
Future rulings in the calendar year 2020	1
Future rulings in the calendar year 2021	0
Future rulings in the year in review	1

No peer input was received in respect of the exchanges of information on rulings received from Greece.

Information gathering process (ToR I.A)

506. Greece can legally issue one type of ruling within the scope of the transparency framework: cross-border unilateral APAs and any other cross-border unilateral tax rulings (such as an advance tax ruling) covering transfer pricing or the application of transfer pricing principles.

507. For Greece, past rulings are any tax rulings within scope that are issued either: (i) on or after 1 January 2014 but before 1 April 2016; or (ii) on or after 1 January 2010 but before 1 January 2014, provided they were still in effect as at 1 January 2014. Future rulings are any tax rulings within scope that are issued on or after 1 April 2016.

508. In the prior years' peer review reports, it was determined that Greece's undertakings to identify past and future rulings and all potential exchange jurisdictions were sufficient to meet the minimum standard. In addition, it was determined that Greece's review and supervision mechanism was sufficient to meet the minimum standard. Greece's implementation remains unchanged, and therefore continues to meet the minimum standard.

509. Greece has met all of the ToR for the information gathering process and no recommendations are made.

Exchange of information (ToR II.B)

510. Greece has the necessary domestic legal basis to exchange information spontaneously. Greece notes that there are no legal or practical impediments that prevent the spontaneous exchange of information on rulings as contemplated in the Action 5 minimum standard.

511. Greece has international agreements permitting spontaneous exchange of information, including: (i) the *Multilateral Convention on Mutual Administrative Assistance in Tax Matters: Amended by the 2010 Protocol* (OECD/Council of Europe, 2011[2]) ("the Convention"), (ii) the Directive 2011/16/EU with all other European Union Member States and (iii) bilateral agreements in force with 57 jurisdictions.[1]

512. For the year in review, the timeliness of exchanges is as follows:

Future rulings within the scope of the transparency framework	Number of exchanges transmitted within three months of the information becoming available to the competent authority or immediately after legal impediments have been lifted	Delayed exchanges		
		Number of exchanges transmitted later than three months of the information on rulings becoming available to the competent authority	Reasons for the delays	Any other comments
	1	0	N/A	N/A

Follow-up requests received for exchange of the ruling	Number	Average time to provide response	Number of requests not answered
	0	N/A	N/A

513. In the prior years' peer review reports, it was determined that Greece's process for the completion and exchange of templates were sufficient to meet the minimum standard. With respect to past rulings, no further action was required. Greece's implementation in this regard remains unchanged and therefore continues to meet the minimum standard.

514. Greece has the necessary legal basis for spontaneous exchange of information, a process for completing the templates in a timely way and has completed all exchanges. Greece has met all of the ToR for the exchange of information process and no recommendations are made.

Statistics (ToR IV.D)

515. The statistics for the year in review are as follows:

Category of ruling	Number of exchanges	Jurisdictions exchanged with
Cross-border unilateral APAs and any other cross-border unilateral tax rulings (such as an advance tax ruling) covering transfer pricing or the application of transfer pricing principles	*De minimis* rule applies	N/A
De minimis rule	1	N/A

Matters related to intellectual property regimes (ToR I.A.1.3)

516. Greece does not offer an intellectual property regime for which transparency requirements under the Action 5 Report (OECD, 2015[3]) were imposed.

Summary of recommendations on implementation of the transparency framework

Aspect of implementation of the transparency framework that should be improved	Recommendation for improvement
	No recommendations are made.

References

OECD (2021), *BEPS Action 5 on Harmful Tax Practices - Terms of Reference and Methodology for the Conduct of the Peer Reviews of the Action 5 Transparency Framework*, OECD Publishing, Paris, https://www.oecd.org/tax/beps/beps-action-5-harmful-tax-practices-peer-review-transparency-framework.pdf. [1]

OECD (2015), *Countering Harmful Tax Practices More Effectively, Taking into Account Transparency and Substance, Action 5 - 2015 Final Report*, OECD/G20 Base Erosion and Profit Shifting Project, OECD Publishing, Paris, https://doi.org/10.1787/9789264241190-en. [3]

OECD/Council of Europe (2011), *The Multilateral Convention on Mutual Administrative Assistance in Tax Matters: Amended by the 2010 Protocol*, OECD Publishing, Paris, https://doi.org/10.1787/9789264115606-en. [2]

Note

[1] Participating jurisdictions to the Convention are available here: www.oecd.org/tax/exchange-of-tax-information/convention-on-mutual-administrative-assistance-in-tax-matters.htm. Greece also has bilateral agreements with Albania, Armenia, Austria, Azerbaijan, Belgium, Bosnia and Herzegovina, Bulgaria, Canada, China (People's Republic of), Croatia, Cyprus, Czechia, Denmark, Egypt, Estonia, Finland, France, Germany, Georgia, Hungary, Iceland, India, Ireland, Israel, Italy, Korea, Kuwait, Latvia, Lithuania, Luxembourg, Malta, Mexico, Moldova, Morocco, Netherlands, Norway, Poland, Portugal, Qatar, Romania, Russia, San Marino, Saudi Arabia, Serbia, Singapore, Slovak Republic, Slovenia, Spain, South Africa, Switzerland, Tunisia, Türkiye, Ukraine, United Arab Emirates, United Kingdom, Uzbekistan and United States.

Grenada

Grenada is taking steps to implement the aspects of the terms of reference (OECD, 2021[1]) (ToR) for the transparency framework and to commence administrative preparations to ensure that it establishes an information gathering process (ToR I.A) and that information on rulings will be identified and exchanged in a timely manner (ToR II.B). Grenada receives two recommendations on these points for the calendar year 2022 (year in review).

In the prior year report, as well as in the 2019 and 2020 peer review reports, Grenada had received the same recommendations. As they have not been addressed, the recommendations remain in place.

Grenada can legally issue five types of rulings within the scope of the transparency framework.

In practice, Grenada issued no rulings within the scope of the transparency framework.

As no exchanges were required to take place, no peer input was received in respect of the exchanges of information on rulings received from Grenada.

Information gathering process (ToR I.A)

517. Grenada can legally issue the following five types of rulings within the scope of the transparency framework: (i) preferential regimes; (ii) cross-border unilateral APAs and any other cross-border unilateral tax rulings (such as an advance tax ruling) covering transfer pricing or the application of transfer pricing principles; (iii) rulings providing for unilateral downward adjustments; (iv) permanent establishment rulings; and (v) related party conduit rulings.

Past rulings (ToR I.A.1.1, I.A.1.2, I.A.2.1, I.A.2.2)

518. For Grenada, past rulings are any tax rulings issued prior to 1 March 2019. However, there is no obligation for Grenada to conduct spontaneous exchange information on past rulings.

Future rulings (ToR I.A.1.1, I.A.1.2, I.A.2.1)

519. For Grenada, future rulings are any tax rulings within scope that are issued on or after 1 March 2019.

520. No rulings were issued by Grenada during the period in review. Grenada indicates that there are not yet processes in place to ensure the implementation of the obligations relating to the transparency framework such as the record keeping of rulings. It is noted that Grenada intends to implement appropriate processes to ensure the necessary information to meet the requirements of the transparency framework is required in all cases.

Review and supervision (ToR I.A.3)

521. In the prior years' peer review reports, it was determined that Grenada did not yet have a review and supervision mechanism for past rulings under the transparency framework. Therefore, Grenada was recommended to put in place a review and supervision mechanism as soon as possible. Grenada is discussing the implementation of a revision and supervision mechanism for ensuring implementation of the transparency framework.

Conclusion on section A

522. Grenada is recommended to finalise its information gathering process for identifying all past and future rulings and all potential exchange jurisdictions, with a review and supervision mechanism, as soon as possible (ToR I.A).

Exchange of information (ToR II.B)

Legal basis for spontaneous exchange of information (ToR II.B.1, II.B.2)

523. Grenada has the necessary domestic legal basis to exchange information spontaneously. Grenada notes that there are no legal or practical impediments that prevent the spontaneous exchange of information on rulings as contemplated in the Action 5 minimum standard.

524. Grenada has international agreements permitting spontaneous exchange of information, including: (i) the *Multilateral Convention on Mutual Administrative Assistance in Tax Matters: Amended by the 2010 Protocol* (OECD/Council of Europe, 2011[2]) ("the Convention") and (ii) bilateral agreements in force with 12 jurisdictions.[1]

Completion and exchange of templates (ToR II.B.3, II.B.4, II.B.5, II.B.6, II.B.7)

525. Grenada is still developing a process to complete the templates on relevant rulings, to make them available to the Competent Authority for exchange of information, and to exchange them with relevant jurisdictions.

526. During the year in review, no exchanges were required to take place and no data on the timeliness of exchanges is reported.

Conclusion on section B

527. Grenada is recommended to continue its efforts to put in place a process to complete the templates for all relevant rulings and to ensure that the exchanges of information on rulings occur as soon as possible (ToR II.B).

Statistics (ToR IV.D)

528. As no rulings were issued, no statistics can be reported.

Matters related to intellectual property regimes (ToR I.A.1.3)

529. Grenada does not offer an intellectual property regime for which transparency requirements under the Action 5 Report (OECD, 2015[3]) were imposed.

Summary of recommendations on implementation of the transparency framework

Aspect of implementation of the transparency framework that should be improved	Recommendation for improvement
Grenada has not put in place the necessary information gathering process.	Grenada is recommended to finalise its information gathering process for identifying all future rulings and potential exchange jurisdictions, with a review and supervision mechanism, as soon as possible. This recommendation remains unchanged since the 2019, 2020 and 2021 peer review reports.
Grenada does not have a process to complete the templates on relevant rulings, to make them available to the Competent Authority for exchange of information, and to exchange them with relevant jurisdictions.	Grenada is recommended to develop a process to complete the templates on relevant rulings and to ensure that the exchanges of information on rulings occur in accordance with the form and timelines under the transparency framework. This recommendation remains unchanged since the 2019, 2020 and 2021 peer review reports.

References

OECD (2021), *BEPS Action 5 on Harmful Tax Practices - Terms of Reference and Methodology for the Conduct of the Peer Reviews of the Action 5 Transparency Framework*, OECD Publishing, Paris, https://www.oecd.org/tax/beps/beps-action-5-harmful-tax-practices-peer-review-transparency-framework.pdf. [1]

OECD (2015), *Countering Harmful Tax Practices More Effectively, Taking into Account Transparency and Substance, Action 5 - 2015 Final Report*, OECD/G20 Base Erosion and Profit Shifting Project, OECD Publishing, Paris, https://doi.org/10.1787/9789264241190-en. [3]

OECD/Council of Europe (2011), *The Multilateral Convention on Mutual Administrative Assistance in Tax Matters: Amended by the 2010 Protocol*, OECD Publishing, Paris, https://doi.org/10.1787/9789264115606-en. [2]

Note

[1] Participating jurisdictions to the Convention are available here: www.oecd.org/tax/exchange-of-tax-information/convention-on-mutual-administrative-assistance-in-tax-matters.htm. Grenada also has bilateral agreements with South Africa, the United Kingdom, and jurisdictions party to the CARICOM agreement.

Guernsey

Guernsey has met all aspects of the terms of reference (OECD, 2021[1]) (ToR) for the calendar year 2022 (year in review), and no recommendations are made.

Guernsey can legally issue four types of rulings within the scope of the transparency framework.

In practice, Guernsey issued rulings within the scope of the transparency framework as follows:

Type of ruling	Number of rulings
Past rulings	5
Future rulings in the period 1 April 2017 – 31 December 2017	2
Future rulings in the calendar year 2018	3
Future rulings in the calendar year 2019	1
Future rulings in the calendar year 2020	0
Future rulings in the calendar year 2021	0
Future rulings in the year in review	1

No peer input was received in respect of the exchanges of information on rulings received from Guernsey.

Information gathering process (ToR I.A)

530. Guernsey can legally issue four types of rulings within the scope of the transparency framework: (i) cross-border unilateral APAs and any other cross-border unilateral tax rulings (such as an advance tax ruling) covering transfer pricing or the application of transfer pricing principles; (ii) rulings providing for unilateral downward adjustments; (iii) permanent establishment rulings; and (iv) related party conduit rulings.

531. For Guernsey, past rulings are any tax rulings within scope that are issued either: (i) on or after 1 January 2015 but before 1 April 2017; or (ii) on or after 1 January 2012 but before 1 January 2015, provided they were still in effect as at 1 January 2015. Future rulings are any tax rulings within scope that are issued on or after 1 April 2017.

532. In the prior years' peer review reports, it was determined that Guernsey's undertakings to identify past and future rulings and all potential exchange jurisdictions were sufficient to meet the minimum standard. In addition, it was determined that Guernsey's review and supervision mechanism was sufficient to meet the minimum standard. Guernsey's implementation remains unchanged, and therefore continues to meet the minimum standard.

533. Guernsey has met all of the ToR for the information gathering process and no recommendations are made.

Exchange of information (ToR II.B)

534. Guernsey has the necessary domestic legal basis to exchange information spontaneously. Guernsey notes that there are no legal or practical impediments that prevent the spontaneous exchange of information on rulings as contemplated in the Action 5 minimum standard.

535. Guernsey has international agreements permitting spontaneous exchange of information, including: (i) the *Multilateral Convention on Mutual Administrative Assistance in Tax Matters: Amended by the 2010 Protocol* (OECD/Council of Europe, 2011[2]) ("the Convention") and (ii) bilateral agreements in force with 19 jurisdictions.[1]

536. For the year in review, the timeliness of exchanges is as follows:

Future rulings within the scope of the transparency framework	Number of exchanges transmitted within three months of the information becoming available to the competent authority or immediately after legal impediments have been lifted	Delayed exchanges		
		Number of exchanges transmitted later than three months of the information on rulings becoming available to the competent authority	Reasons for the delays	Any other comments
	1	0	N/A	N/A

Follow-up requests received for exchange of the ruling	Number	Average time to provide response	Number of requests not answered
	0	N/A	N/A

537. In the prior years' peer review reports, it was determined that Guernsey's process for the completion and exchange of templates were sufficient to meet the minimum standard. With respect to past rulings, no further action was required. Guernsey's implementation in this regard remains unchanged and therefore continues to meet the minimum standard.

538. Guernsey has the necessary legal basis for spontaneous exchange of information, a process for completing the templates in a timely way and has completed all exchanges. Guernsey has met all of the ToR for the exchange of information process and no recommendations are made.

Statistics (ToR IV.D)

539. The statistics for the year in review are as follows:

Category of ruling	Number of exchanges	Jurisdictions exchanged with
Cross-border unilateral APAs and any other cross-border unilateral tax rulings (such as an advance tax ruling) covering transfer pricing or the application of transfer pricing principles	0	N/A
Cross-border rulings providing for a unilateral downward adjustment to the taxpayer's taxable profits that is not directly reflected in the taxpayer's financial / commercial accounts	0	N/A
Permanent establishment rulings	*De minimis* rule applies	N/A
Related party conduit rulings	0	N/A
De minimis rule	1	N/A
Total	1	

Matters related to intellectual property regimes (ToR I.A.1.3)

540. Guernsey does not offer an intellectual property regime for which transparency requirements under the Action 5 Report (OECD, 2015[3]) were imposed.

Summary of recommendations on implementation of the transparency framework

Aspect of implementation of the transparency framework that should be improved	Recommendation for improvement
	No recommendations are made.

References

OECD (2021), *BEPS Action 5 on Harmful Tax Practices - Terms of Reference and Methodology for the Conduct of the Peer Reviews of the Action 5 Transparency Framework*, OECD Publishing, Paris, https://www.oecd.org/tax/beps/beps-action-5-harmful-tax-practices-peer-review-transparency-framework.pdf. [1]

OECD (2015), *Countering Harmful Tax Practices More Effectively, Taking into Account Transparency and Substance, Action 5 - 2015 Final Report*, OECD/G20 Base Erosion and Profit Shifting Project, OECD Publishing, Paris, https://doi.org/10.1787/9789264241190-en. [3]

OECD/Council of Europe (2011), *The Multilateral Convention on Mutual Administrative Assistance in Tax Matters: Amended by the 2010 Protocol*, OECD Publishing, Paris, https://doi.org/10.1787/9789264115606-en. [2]

Note

[1] Participating jurisdictions to the Convention are available here: www.oecd.org/tax/exchange-of-tax-information/convention-on-mutual-administrative-assistance-in-tax-matters.htm. Guernsey also has bilateral agreements with British Virgin Islands, Cayman Islands, Cyprus, Estonia, Gibraltar, Hong Kong (China), Isle of Man, Jersey, Liechtenstein, Luxembourg, Malta, Mauritius, Monaco, Qatar, Seychelles, Singapore, Turks and Caicos Islands, United Kingdom and United States permitting spontaneous exchange of information.

Hong Kong (China)

Hong Kong (China) ("Hong Kong") has met all aspects of the terms of reference (OECD, 2021[1]) (ToR) for the calendar year 2022 (year in review), and no recommendations are made.

Hong Kong can legally issue four types of rulings within the scope of the transparency framework.

In practice, Hong Kong issued rulings within the scope of the transparency framework as follows:

Type of ruling	Number of rulings
Past rulings	1
Future rulings in the period 1 April 2017 – 31 December 2017	0
Future rulings in the calendar year 2018	0
Future rulings in the calendar year 2019	2
Future rulings in the calendar year 2020	1
Future rulings in the calendar year 2021	0
Future rulings in the year in review	0

As no exchanges were required to take place, no peer input was received in respect of the exchanges of information on rulings received from Hong Kong.

Information gathering process (ToR I.A)

541. Hong Kong can legally issue the following four types of rulings within the scope of the transparency framework: (i) preferential regimes;[1] (ii) cross-border unilateral APAs and any other cross-border unilateral tax rulings (such as an advance tax ruling) covering transfer pricing or the application of transfer pricing principles; (iii) permanent establishment rulings; and (iv) related party conduit rulings.

542. For Hong Kong, past rulings are any tax rulings within scope that are issued either: (i) on or after 1 January 2015 but before 1 April 2017; or (ii) on or after 1 January 2012 but before 1 January 2015, provided they were still in effect as at 1 January 2015. Future rulings are any tax rulings within scope that are issued on or after 1 April 2017.

543. In the prior years' peer review reports, it was determined that Hong Kong's undertakings to identify past and future rulings and all potential exchange jurisdictions were sufficient to meet the minimum standard. In addition, it was determined that Hong Kong's review and supervision mechanism was sufficient to meet the minimum standard. Hong Kong's implementation remains unchanged, and therefore continues to meet the minimum standard.

544. Hong Kong has met all of the ToR for the information gathering process and no recommendations are made.

Exchange of information (ToR II.B)

545. Hong Kong has the necessary domestic legal basis to exchange information spontaneously. Hong Kong notes that there are no legal or practical impediments that prevent the spontaneous exchange of information on rulings as contemplated in the Action 5 minimum standard.

546. Hong Kong has international agreements permitting spontaneous exchange of information, including being a jurisdiction participating in (i) the *Multilateral Convention on Mutual Administrative Assistance in Tax Matters: Amended by the 2010 Protocol* (OECD/Council of Europe, 2011[2]) ("the Convention") and (ii) bilateral agreements in force with 39 jurisdictions.[2]

547. During the year in review, no exchanges were required to take place and no data on the timeliness of exchanges is reported.

548. In the prior years' peer review reports, it was determined that Hong Kong's process for the completion and exchange of templates were sufficient to meet the minimum standard. With respect to past rulings, no further action was required. Hong Kong's implementation in this regard remains unchanged and therefore continues to meet the minimum standard.

549. Hong Kong has the necessary legal basis for spontaneous exchange of information, a process for completing the templates in a timely way and has completed all exchanges. Hong Kong has met all of the ToR for the exchange of information process and no recommendations are made.

Statistics (ToR IV.D)

550. As no rulings were issued, no statistics can be reported.

Matters related to intellectual property regimes (ToR I.A.1.3)

551. Hong Kong does not offer an intellectual property regime for which transparency requirements under the Action 5 Report (OECD, 2015[3]) were imposed.

Summary of recommendations on implementation of the transparency framework

Aspect of implementation of the transparency framework that should be improved	Recommendation for improvement
	No recommendations are made.

References

OECD (2021), *BEPS Action 5 on Harmful Tax Practices - Terms of Reference and Methodology for the Conduct of the Peer Reviews of the Action 5 Transparency Framework*, OECD Publishing, Paris, https://www.oecd.org/tax/beps/beps-action-5-harmful-tax-practices-peer-review-transparency-framework.pdf. [1]

OECD (2015), *Countering Harmful Tax Practices More Effectively, Taking into Account Transparency and Substance, Action 5 - 2015 Final Report*, OECD/G20 Base Erosion and Profit Shifting Project, OECD Publishing, Paris, https://doi.org/10.1787/9789264241190-en. [3]

OECD/Council of Europe (2011), *The Multilateral Convention on Mutual Administrative Assistance in Tax Matters: Amended by the 2010 Protocol*, OECD Publishing, Paris, https://doi.org/10.1787/9789264115606-en. [2]

Notes

[1] 1) Profits tax concession for corporate treasury centres; 2) profits tax concession for professional reinsurers; 3) profits tax concession for captive insurers; 4) profits tax exemptions for ship operators; 5) profits tax concessions for aircraft lessors and aircraft leasing managers; 6) profits tax concession for ship lessors and ship leasing managers, 7) profits tax concession for specified insurers and licensed insurance broker companies; and 8) profits tax concessions for carried interest.

[2] Participating jurisdictions to the Convention are available here: www.oecd.org/tax/exchange-of-tax-information/convention-on-mutual-administrative-assistance-in-tax-matters.htm. Hong Kong also has bilateral agreements with Austria, Belarus, Belgium, Cambodia, Canada, China (People's Republic of), Estonia, Finland, France, Georgia, Guernsey, Hungary, India, Indonesia, Ireland, Italy, Japan, Jersey, Korea, Latvia, Macau (China), Malaysia, Malta, Mexico, Netherlands, New Zealand, Pakistan, Portugal, Qatar, Romania, Saudi Arabia, Serbia, South Africa, Spain, Switzerland, Thailand, United Arab Emirates, United Kingdom and Viet Nam.

Hungary

Hungary has met all aspects of the terms of reference (OECD, 2021[1]) (ToR) for the calendar year 2022 (year in review), except for applying the "best efforts approach" to identify potential exchange jurisdictions for all past rulings (ToR I.A.2.2). Hungary receives one recommendation on this point for the year in review.

In the prior year report, as well as in the 2016-2020 peer reviews, Hungary has received the same recommendation. As it have not been addressed, the recommendation remains in place.

Hungary can legally issue four types of rulings within the scope of the transparency framework.

In practice, Hungary issued rulings within the scope of the transparency framework as follows:

Type of ruling	Number of rulings
Past rulings	77
Future rulings in the period 1 April 2016 – 31 December 2016	4
Future rulings in the calendar year 2017	9
Future rulings in the calendar year 2018	11
Future rulings in the calendar year 2019	21
Future rulings in the calendar year 2020	18
Future rulings in the calendar year 2021	27
Future rulings in the year in review	14

No peer input was received in respect of the exchanges of information on rulings received from Hungary.

Information gathering process (ToR I.A)

552. Hungary can legally issue the following four types of rulings within the scope of the transparency framework: (i) preferential regimes;[1] (ii) cross-border unilateral APAs and any other cross-border unilateral tax rulings (such as an advance tax ruling) covering transfer pricing or the application of transfer pricing principles; (iii) permanent establishment rulings; and (iv) related party conduit rulings.

Past rulings (ToR I.A.1.1, I.A.1.2, I.A.2.1, I.A.2.2)

553. For Hungary, past rulings are any tax rulings within scope that are issued either: (i) on or after 1 January 2014 but before 1 April 2016; or (ii) on or after 1 January 2010 but before 1 January 2014, provided they were still in effect as at 1 January 2014.

554. In the prior years' peer review reports, it was determined that Hungary had not used the "best efforts approach" to identify potential exchange jurisdictions, meaning that Hungary had only identified potential exchange jurisdictions for around half of the past ATRs, although it had identified most potential exchange jurisdictions for APAs but not necessarily the ultimate parent company jurisdiction. Therefore, Hungary was recommended to continue to apply the "best efforts approach" to identify potential exchange jurisdictions for all past rulings.

555. During the year in review, Hungary has not been able to take additional steps. As such, the recommendation remains.

Future rulings (ToR I.A.1.1, I.A.1.2, I.A.2.1)

556. For Hungary, future rulings are any tax rulings within scope that are issued on or after 1 April 2016.

557. In the prior year peer review report, it was determined that Hungary's undertakings to identify future rulings and all potential exchange jurisdictions was sufficient to meet the minimum standard. Hungary's implementation in this regard remains and continues to meet the minimum standard.

Review and supervision (ToR I.A.3)

558. In the prior years' peer review reports, it was determined that Hungary's review and supervision mechanism was sufficient to meet the minimum standard. Hungary's implementation in this regard remains unchanged, and therefore continues to meet the minimum standard.

Conclusion on section A

559. Hungary has met all of the ToR for the information gathering process except for applying the "best efforts approach" for past rulings (ToR I.A.2.2) and Hungary is recommended to continue to apply the "best efforts approach" to identify potential exchange jurisdictions for all past rulings.

Exchange of information (ToR II.B)

560. Hungary has the necessary domestic legal basis to exchange information spontaneously. Hungary notes that there are no legal or practical impediments that prevent the spontaneous exchange of information on rulings as contemplated in the Action 5 minimum standard.

561. Hungary has international agreements permitting spontaneous exchange of information, including (i) being a party to the *Multilateral Convention on Mutual Administrative Assistance in Tax Matters: Amended by the 2010 Protocol* (OECD/Council of Europe, 2011[2]) ("the Convention"), (ii) the Directive 2011/16/EU with all other European Union Member States and (iii) bilateral agreements in force with 83 jurisdictions.[2]

562. For the year in review, the timeliness of exchanges is as follows:

Future rulings within the scope of the transparency framework	Number of exchanges transmitted within three months of the information becoming available to the competent authority or immediately after legal impediments have been lifted	Delayed exchanges		
		Number of exchanges transmitted later than three months of the information on rulings becoming available to the competent authority	Reasons for the delays	Any other comments
	8	2	Due to an organisational restructuring in the National Tax and Customs Administration and Ministry of Finance of Hungary, a temporary interruption in the workflow occurred when issuing the APAs.	

Follow-up requests received for exchange of the ruling	Number	Average time to provide response	Number of requests not answered
	0	N/A	N/A

563. Hungary notes that exchanges of information regarding the issued permanent establishment rulings (nine issued rulings) have not yet been made. It is not known what the reason for the delay is. This will be assessed in next year's peer review.

564. In the prior year's peer review report, it was determined that Hungary's process for the completion and exchange of templates were sufficient to meet the minimum standard. With respect to past rulings, no further action was required. Hungary's implementation in this regard remains unchanged and therefore continues to meet the minimum standard.

565. Hungary has the necessary legal basis for spontaneous exchange of information, a process for completing the templates in a timely way and has completed all exchanges. Hungary has met all of the ToR for the exchange of information process and no recommendations are made.

Statistics (ToR IV.D)

566. The statistics for the year in review are as follows:

Category of ruling	Number of exchanges	Jurisdictions exchanged with
Ruling related to a preferential regime	0	N/A
Cross-border unilateral APAs and any other cross-border unilateral tax rulings (such as an advance tax ruling) covering transfer pricing or the application of transfer pricing principles	10	Canada, Cyprus, Czechia, Hong Kong (China), Germany, Romania, Slovak Republic, Switzerland, United Kingdom, Uruguay
Permanent establishment rulings	0	N/A
Related party conduit rulings	0	N/A
IP regimes: total exchanges on taxpayers benefitting from the third category of IP assets, new entrants	0	N/A

benefitting from grandfathered IP regimes; and taxpayers making use of the option to treat the nexus ratio as a rebuttable presumption		
Total	10	

Matters related to intellectual property regimes (ToR I.A.1.3)

567. In the prior year's peer review report, it was determined that Hungary's information gathering and exchange of information processes for matters related to intellectual property regimes[3] were sufficient to meet the minimum standard. Hungary's implementation in this regard remains unchanged and therefore continues to meet the minimum standard.

Summary of recommendations on implementation of the transparency framework

Aspect of implementation of the transparency framework that should be improved	Recommendation for improvement
Hungary did not yet apply the "best efforts approach" to identify potential exchange jurisdictions for all past rulings.	Hungary is recommended to continue to apply the "best efforts approach" to identify potential exchange jurisdictions for all past rulings. This recommendation remains unchanged since the 2016, 2017, 2018, 2019, 2020 and 2021 peer review reports

References

OECD (2021), *BEPS Action 5 on Harmful Tax Practices - Terms of Reference and Methodology for the Conduct of the Peer Reviews of the Action 5 Transparency Framework*, OECD Publishing, Paris, https://www.oecd.org/tax/beps/beps-action-5-harmful-tax-practices-peer-review-transparency-framework.pdf. [1]

OECD (2015), *Countering Harmful Tax Practices More Effectively, Taking into Account Transparency and Substance, Action 5 - 2015 Final Report*, OECD/G20 Base Erosion and Profit Shifting Project, OECD Publishing, Paris, https://doi.org/10.1787/9789264241190-en. [3]

OECD/Council of Europe (2011), *The Multilateral Convention on Mutual Administrative Assistance in Tax Matters: Amended by the 2010 Protocol*, OECD Publishing, Paris, https://doi.org/10.1787/9789264115606-en. [2]

Notes

[1] IP regime for royalties and capital gains.

[2] Participating jurisdictions to the Convention are available here: www.oecd.org/tax/exchange-of-tax-information/convention-on-mutual-administrative-assistance-in-tax-matters.htm. Hungary also has bilateral agreements with Albania, Armenia, Australia, Austria, Azerbaijan, Bahrain, Belarus, Belgium, Bosnia and Herzegovina, Brazil, Bulgaria, Canada, China (People's Republic of), Croatia, Cyprus, Czechia, Denmark, Egypt, Estonia, Finland, France, Georgia, Germany, Greece, Hong Kong (China), Iceland, India, Indonesia, Iran, Iraq, Ireland, Israel, Italy, Japan, Kazakhstan, Korea, Kosovo, Kuwait, Kyrgyzstan, Latvia, Liechtenstein, Lithuania, Luxembourg, Malaysia, Malta, Mexico, Moldova, Mongolia, Montenegro, Morocco, Netherlands, North Macedonia, Norway, Oman, Pakistan, Philippines, Poland, Portugal, Qatar, Romania, Russia, San Marino, Saudi Arabia, Serbia, Singapore, Slovak Republic, Slovenia, South Africa, Spain, Sweden, Switzerland, Chinese Taipei, Thailand, Tunisia, Türkiye, Turkmenistan, Ukraine, United Arab Emirates, United Kingdom, United States, Uruguay, Uzbekistan and Viet Nam.

[3] IP regime for royalties and capital gains.

Iceland

Iceland has met all aspects of the terms of reference (OECD, 2021[1]) (ToR) for the calendar year 2022 (year in review), and no recommendations are made.

Iceland can legally issue two types of rulings within the scope of the transparency framework.

In practice, Iceland issued rulings within the scope of the transparency framework as follows:

Type of ruling	Number of rulings
Past rulings	1
Future rulings in the period 1 April 2016 – 31 December 2016	0
Future rulings in the calendar year 2017	0
Future rulings in the calendar year 2018	0
Future rulings in the calendar year 2019	0
Future rulings in the calendar year 2020	0
Future rulings in the calendar year 2021	0
Future rulings in the year in review	0

As no exchanges were required to take place, no peer input was received in respect of the exchanges of information on rulings received from Iceland.

Information gathering process (ToR I.A)

568. Iceland can legally issue the following two types of rulings within the scope of the transparency framework: (i) permanent establishment rulings and (ii) related party conduit rulings.

569. For Iceland, past rulings are any tax rulings within scope that are issued either: (i) on or after 1 January 2014 but before 1 April 2016; or (ii) on or after 1 January 2010 but before 1 January 2014, provided they were still in effect as at 1 January 2014. Future rulings are any tax rulings within scope that are issued on or after 1 April 2016.

570. In the prior years' peer review reports, it was determined that Iceland's undertakings to identify past and future rulings and all potential exchange jurisdictions were sufficient to meet the minimum standard. In addition, it was determined that Iceland's review and supervision mechanism was sufficient to meet the minimum standard. Iceland's implementation remains unchanged, and therefore continues to meet the minimum standard.

571. Iceland has met all of the ToR for the information gathering process and no recommendations are made.

Exchange of information (ToR II.B)

572. Iceland has the necessary domestic legal basis to exchange information spontaneously. Iceland notes that there are no legal or practical impediments that prevent the spontaneous exchange of information on rulings as contemplated in the Action 5 minimum standard.

573. Iceland has international agreements permitting spontaneous exchange of information, including: (i) the *Multilateral Convention on Mutual Administrative Assistance in Tax Matters: Amended by the 2010 Protocol* (OECD/Council of Europe, 2011[2]) ("the Convention"), (ii) the Nordic Convention on Assistance in Tax Matters and (iii) bilateral agreements in force with 40 jurisdictions.[1]

574. During the year in review, no exchanges were required to take place and no data on the timeliness of exchanges is reported.

575. In the prior years' peer review reports, it was determined that Iceland's process for the completion and exchange of templates were sufficient to meet the minimum standard. With respect to past rulings, no further action was required. Iceland's implementation in this regard remains unchanged and therefore continues to meet the minimum standard.

576. Iceland has the necessary legal basis for spontaneous exchange of information, a process for completing the templates in a timely way and has completed all exchanges. Iceland has met all of the ToR for the exchange of information process and no recommendations are made.

Statistics (ToR IV.D)

577. As no rulings were issued, no statistics can be reported.

Matters related to intellectual property regimes (ToR I.A.1.3)

578. Iceland does not offer an intellectual property regime for which transparency requirements under the Action 5 Report (OECD, 2015[3]) were imposed.

Summary of recommendations on implementation of the transparency framework

Aspect of implementation of the transparency framework that should be improved	Recommendation for improvement
	No recommendations are made.

References

OECD (2021), *BEPS Action 5 on Harmful Tax Practices - Terms of Reference and Methodology for the Conduct of the Peer Reviews of the Action 5 Transparency Framework*, OECD Publishing, Paris, https://www.oecd.org/tax/beps/beps-action-5-harmful-tax-practices-peer-review-transparency-framework.pdf. [1]

OECD (2015), *Countering Harmful Tax Practices More Effectively, Taking into Account Transparency and Substance, Action 5 - 2015 Final Report*, OECD/G20 Base Erosion and Profit Shifting Project, OECD Publishing, Paris, https://doi.org/10.1787/9789264241190-en. [3]

OECD/Council of Europe (2011), *The Multilateral Convention on Mutual Administrative Assistance in Tax Matters: Amended by the 2010 Protocol*, OECD Publishing, Paris, https://doi.org/10.1787/9789264115606-en. [2]

Note

[1] Participating jurisdictions to the Convention are available here: www.oecd.org/tax/exchange-of-tax-information/convention-on-mutual-administrative-assistance-in-tax-matters.htm. Parties to the Nordic Double Taxation Convention and the Nordic Convention on Assistance in tax matters are Denmark, the Faroe Islands, Finland, Iceland, Norway and Sweden. Iceland also has bilateral agreements with Albania, Austria, Barbados, Belgium, Canada, China (People's Republic of), Croatia, Cyprus, Czechia, Estonia, France, Georgia, Greece, Greenland, Germany, Hungary, India, Ireland, Italy, Japan, Korea, Latvia, Liechtenstein, Lithuania, Luxembourg, Malta, Mexico, Netherlands, Poland, Portugal, Romania, Russia, Slovak Republic, Slovenia, Spain, Switzerland, Ukraine, United Kingdom, United States, Viet Nam.

India

India has met all aspects of the terms of reference (OECD, 2021[1]) (ToR) for the calendar year 2022 (year in review), except for the timely exchange of information on future rulings (ToR II.B.6.2). India receives one recommendation on this point for the year in review.

In the prior year report, as well as in the 2017-2020 peer reviews, India had received the same recommendation. During the year in review, a number of exchanges remained delayed, and therefore the recommendation remains in place.

India can legally issue two types of rulings within the scope of the transparency framework.

In practice, India issued rulings within the scope of the transparency framework as follows:

Type of ruling	Number of rulings
Past rulings	69
Future rulings in the period 1 April 2016 – 31 December 2016	55
Future rulings in the calendar year 2017	73
Future rulings in the calendar year 2018	44
Future rulings in the calendar year 2019	137
Future rulings in the calendar year 2020	28
Future rulings in the calendar year 2021	37
Future rulings in the year in review	51

Peer input was received from nine jurisdictions in respect of the exchanges of information on rulings received from India. The input was generally positive, noting that overall information was complete and in a correct format. However, one peer indicated that information included in the summary section of Annex C of the Action 5 report (OECD, 2015[3]) was not sufficient. This issue will be reassessed in next year's peer review. Furthermore, five peers indicated that and exchanges on rulings were not timely.

Information gathering process (ToR I.A)

579. India can legally issue the following two types of rulings within the scope of the transparency framework: (i) cross-border unilateral APAs and any other cross-border unilateral tax rulings (such as an advance tax ruling) covering transfer pricing or the application of transfer pricing principles and (ii) permanent establishment rulings.

580. For India, past rulings are any tax rulings within scope that are issued either: (i) on or after 1 January 2014 but before 1 April 2016; or (ii) on or after 1 January 2010 but before 1 January 2014, provided they were still in effect as at 1 January 2014. Future rulings are any tax rulings within scope that are issued on or after 1 April 2016.

581. In the prior year peer review report, it was determined that India's undertakings to identify past and future rulings and all potential exchange jurisdictions were sufficient to meet the minimum standard. In addition, it was determined that India's review and supervision mechanism was sufficient to meet the minimum standard. India's implementation remains unchanged, and therefore continues to meet the minimum standard.

582. India has met all of the ToR for the information gathering process and no recommendations are made.

Exchange of information (ToR II.B)

Legal basis for spontaneous exchange of information (TOR II.B.1, II.B.2)

583. India has the necessary domestic legal basis to exchange information spontaneously. India notes that there are no legal or practical impediments that prevent the spontaneous exchange of information on rulings as contemplated in the Action 5 minimum standard.

584. India has international agreements permitting spontaneous exchange of information, including: (i) the *Multilateral Convention on Mutual Administrative Assistance in Tax Matters: Amended by the 2010 Protocol* (OECD/Council of Europe, 2011[2]) ("the Convention"), (ii) the South Asian Association for Regional Cooperation (SAARC) Agreement and (iii) bilateral agreements in force with 101 jurisdictions.[1]

Completion and exchange of templates (ToR II.B.3, II.B.4, II.B.5, II.B.6, II.B.7)

585. In the prior years' peer review reports, it was determined that India's process for the completion and exchange of templates met all the ToR, except for ensuring that information on future APA rulings is exchanged as soon as possible (ToR II.B.6). Therefore, India was recommended to ensure the timely exchange of information on future APA rulings. With respect to past rulings, no further action was required.

586. For the year in review, the timeliness of exchanges is as follows:

Future rulings within the scope of the transparency framework	Number of exchanges transmitted within three months of the information becoming available to the competent authority or immediately after legal impediments have been lifted	Delayed exchanges		
		Number of exchanges transmitted later than three months of the information on rulings becoming available to the competent authority	Reasons for the delays	Any other comments
	197	113	See below.	N/A

Follow-up requests received for exchange of the ruling	Number	Average time to provide response	Number of requests not answered
	1	N/A as the request is still processed.	N/A as the request is still processed.

Conclusion on section B

587. During the year in review, India continued to encounter delays with respect to the exchange of information on future APAs. This was due to the fact that India had to use the "best efforts approach" to identify potential exchange jurisdictions for APAs filed before 16 June 2017. Therefore, India is still recommended to continue to ensure the timely exchange of information on future APA rulings (ToR II.B.6).

Statistics (ToR IV.D)

588. The statistics for the year in review are as follows:

Category of ruling	Number of exchanges	Jurisdictions exchanged with
Cross-border unilateral APAs and any other cross-border unilateral tax rulings (such as an advance tax ruling) covering transfer pricing or the application of transfer pricing principles	310	Australia, Austria, Belgium, Bulgaria, Canada, China (People's Republic of), Costa Rica, Croatia, Czechia, Denmark, Dominican Republic, El Salvador, Finland, France, Germany, Greece, Honduras, Hong Kong (China), Hungary, Indonesia, Ireland, Italy, Japan, Korea, Lithuania, Luxembourg, Macedonia, Malaysia, Malta, Mexico, Netherlands, New Zealand, Norway, Panama, Poland, Portugal, Puerto Rico, Romania, Russia, Serbia, Singapore, Slovak Republic, Slovenia, Spain, Sweden, Switzerland, Trinidad and Tobago, Türkiye, Ukraine, United Kingdom, United States
Permanent establishment rulings	0	N/A
Total	310	

Matters related to intellectual property regimes (ToR I.A.1.3)

589. In the prior years' peer review reports, it was determined that the India's information gathering and exchange of information processes for matters related to intellectual property regimes[2] were sufficient to meet the minimum standard. India's implementation in this regard remains unchanged and therefore continues to meet the minimum standard.

Summary of recommendations on implementation of the transparency framework

Aspect of implementation of the transparency framework that should be improved	Recommendation for improvement
India experienced delays in the exchange of information on future APAs.	India is recommended to continue its efforts to ensure that all information on future APAs is exchanged as soon as possible. This recommendation remains unchanged since the 2017, 2018, 2019, 2020 and 2021 peer review reports.

References

OECD (2021), *BEPS Action 5 on Harmful Tax Practices - Terms of Reference and Methodology for the Conduct of the Peer Reviews of the Action 5 Transparency Framework*, OECD Publishing, Paris, https://www.oecd.org/tax/beps/beps-action-5-harmful-tax-practices-peer-review-transparency-framework.pdf. [1]

OECD (2015), *Countering Harmful Tax Practices More Effectively, Taking into Account Transparency and Substance, Action 5 - 2015 Final Report*, OECD/G20 Base Erosion and Profit Shifting Project, OECD Publishing, Paris, https://doi.org/10.1787/9789264241190-en. [3]

OECD/Council of Europe (2011), *The Multilateral Convention on Mutual Administrative Assistance in Tax Matters: Amended by the 2010 Protocol*, OECD Publishing, Paris, https://doi.org/10.1787/9789264115606-en. [2]

Notes

[1] Participating jurisdictions to the Convention are available here: www.oecd.org/tax/exchange-of-tax-information/convention-on-mutual-administrative-assistance-in-tax-matters.htm. India also has bilateral agreements with Albania, Armenia, Australia, Austria, Bangladesh, Belarus, Belgium, Bhutan, Botswana, Brazil,10 Bulgaria, Canada, China (People's Republic of), Chile, Colombia, Croatia, Cyprus, Czechia, Denmark, Egypt, Estonia, Ethiopia, Fiji, Finland, France, Georgia, Germany, Greece, Hong Kong (China), Hungary, Iceland, Indonesia, Iran, Ireland, Israel, Italy, Japan, Jordan, Kazakhstan, Kenya, Korea, Kuwait, Kyrgyzstan, Latvia, Libya, Lithuania, Luxembourg, Malaysia, Malta, Mauritius, Mexico, Mongolia, Morocco, Montenegro, Mozambique, Myanmar, Namibia, Nepal, Netherlands, New Zealand, North Macedonia, Norway, Oman, Philippines, Poland, Portugal, Qatar, Romania, Russia, Saudi Arabia, Serbia, Singapore, Slovak Republic, Slovenia, South Africa, Spain, Sri Lanka, Sudan, Sweden, Switzerland, Syrian Arab Republic, Chinese Taipei, Tajikistan, Tanzania, Thailand, Trinidad and Tobago, Türkiye, Turkmenistan, Uganda, Ukraine, United Arab Emirates, United Kingdom, United States, Uruguay, Uzbekistan, Viet Nam, and Zambia. The SAARC was entered into force on 19 May 2010 and provides for exchanges with Bangladesh, Bhutan, Maldives, Nepal, Pakistan and Sri Lanka.

[2] Tax on income from patents.

Indonesia

Indonesia has met all aspects of the terms of reference (OECD, 2021[1]) (ToR) for the calendar year 2022 (year in review), and no recommendations are made.

Indonesia can legally issue one type of rulings within the scope of the transparency framework.

In practice, Indonesia issued rulings within the scope of the transparency framework as follows:

Type of ruling	Number of rulings
Past rulings	0
Future rulings in the period 1 April 2016 – 31 December 2016	0
Future rulings in the calendar year 2017	0
Future rulings in the calendar year 2018	0
Future rulings in the calendar year 2019	1
Future rulings in the calendar year 2020	1
Future rulings in the calendar year 2021	2
Future rulings in the year in review	0

Peer input was received from one jurisdiction in respect of the exchanges of information on rulings received from Indonesia. The input was positive, noting that information was complete and in a correct format.[1]

Information gathering process (ToR I.A)

590. Indonesia can legally issue one type of ruling within the scope of the transparency framework: (i) cross-border unilateral APAs and any other cross-border unilateral tax rulings (such as an advance tax ruling) covering transfer pricing or the application of transfer pricing principles.

591. For Indonesia, past rulings are any tax rulings within scope that are issued either: (i) on or after 1 January 2014 but before 1 April 2016; or (ii) on or after 1 January 2010 but before 1 January 2014, provided they were still in effect as at 1 January 2014. Future rulings are any tax rulings within scope that are issued on or after 1 April 2016.

592. In the prior years' peer review reports, it was determined that Indonesia's undertakings to identify past and future rulings and all potential exchange jurisdictions were sufficient to meet the minimum standard. In addition, it was determined that Indonesia's review and supervision mechanism was sufficient to meet the minimum standard. Indonesia's implementation remains unchanged, and therefore continues to meet the minimum standard.

593. Indonesia has met all of the ToR for the information gathering process and no recommendations are made.

Exchange of information (ToR II.B)

594. Indonesia has the necessary domestic legal basis to exchange information spontaneously. Indonesia notes that there are no legal or practical impediments that prevent the spontaneous exchange of information on rulings as contemplated in the Action 5 minimum standard.

595. Indonesia has international agreements permitting spontaneous exchange of information, including: (i) the *Multilateral Convention on Mutual Administrative Assistance in Tax Matters: Amended by the 2010 Protocol* (OECD/Council of Europe, 2011[2]) ("the Convention") and (ii) bilateral agreements in force with 69 jurisdictions.[2]

596. During the year in review, no exchanges were required to take place and no data on the timeliness of exchanges is reported.

597. In the prior years' peer review reports, it was determined that Indonesia's process for the completion and exchange of templates were sufficient to meet the minimum standard. With respect to past rulings, no action was required. Indonesia's implementation in this regard remains unchanged and therefore continues to meet the minimum standard.

598. Indonesia has the necessary legal basis for spontaneous exchange of information, a process for completing the templates in a timely way and has completed all exchanges. Indonesia has met all of the ToR for the exchange of information process and no recommendations are made.

Statistics (ToR IV.D)

599. As no rulings were issued, no statistics can be reported.

Matters related to intellectual property regimes (ToR I.A.1.3)

600. Indonesia does not offer an intellectual property regime for which transparency requirements under the Action 5 Report (OECD, 2015[3]) were imposed.

Summary of recommendations on implementation of the transparency framework

Aspect of implementation of the transparency framework that should be improved	Recommendation for improvement
	No recommendations are made.

References

OECD (2021), *BEPS Action 5 on Harmful Tax Practices - Terms of Reference and Methodology for the Conduct of the Peer Reviews of the Action 5 Transparency Framework*, OECD Publishing, Paris, https://www.oecd.org/tax/beps/beps-action-5-harmful-tax-practices-peer-review-transparency-framework.pdf. [1]

OECD (2015), *Countering Harmful Tax Practices More Effectively, Taking into Account Transparency and Substance, Action 5 - 2015 Final Report*, OECD/G20 Base Erosion and Profit Shifting Project, OECD Publishing, Paris, https://doi.org/10.1787/9789264241190-en. [3]

OECD/Council of Europe (2011), *The Multilateral Convention on Mutual Administrative Assistance in Tax Matters: Amended by the 2010 Protocol*, OECD Publishing, Paris, https://doi.org/10.1787/9789264115606-en. [2]

Notes

[1] The peer input relates to rulings that Indonesia reported as exchanged in the prior year's peer review report, but were exchanged in the first quarter of the year in review. Indonesia confirms that no rulings were issued in the year in review.

[2] Participating jurisdictions to the Convention are available here: www.oecd.org/tax/exchange-of-tax-information/convention-on-mutual-administrative-assistance-in-tax-matters.htm. Indonesia also has bilateral agreements with Algeria, Armenia, Australia, Austria, Bangladesh, Belarus, Belgium, Brunei Darussalam, Bulgaria, Cambodia, Canada, China (People's Republic of), Croatia, Czechia, Democratic People's Republic of Korea, Denmark, Egypt, Finland, France, Germany, Hong Kong (China), Hungary, India, Iran, Italy, Japan, Jordan, Korea, Kuwait, Lao People's Democratic Republic, Luxembourg, Malaysia, Mexico, Mongolia, Morocco, Netherlands, New Zealand, Norway, Pakistan, Papua New Guinea, Philippines, Poland, Portugal, Qatar, Romania, Russia, Serbia, Seychelles, Singapore, Slovak Republic, South Africa, Spain, Sri Lanka, Sudan, Suriname, Sweden, Syrian Arab Republic, Chinese Taipei, Tajikistan, Thailand, Tunisia, Türkiye, Ukraine, United Arab Emirates, United Kingdom, United States, Uzbekistan, Venezuela, Viet Nam.

Ireland

Ireland has met all aspects of the terms of reference (OECD, 2021[1]) (ToR) for the calendar year 2022 (year in review), and no recommendations are made.

Ireland can legally issue three types of rulings within the scope of the transparency framework.

In practice, Ireland issued rulings within the scope of the transparency framework as follows:

Type of ruling	Number of rulings
Past rulings	29
Future rulings in the period 1 April 2016 – 31 December 2016	0
Future rulings in the calendar year 2017	2
Future rulings in the calendar year 2018	39
Future rulings in the calendar year 2019	5
Future rulings in the calendar year 2020	4
Future rulings in the calendar year 2021	2
Future rulings in the year in review	0

No peer input was received in respect of the exchanges of information on rulings received from Ireland.

Information gathering process (ToR I.A)

601. Ireland can legally issue three types of rulings within the scope of the transparency framework: (i) preferential regimes;[1] (ii) cross-border unilateral APAs and any other cross-border unilateral tax rulings (such as an advance tax ruling) covering transfer pricing or the application of transfer pricing principles; and (iii) permanent establishment rulings.

602. For Ireland, past rulings are any tax rulings within scope that are issued either: (i) on or after 1 January 2014 but before 1 April 2016; or (ii) on or after 1 January 2010 but before 1 January 2014, provided they were still in effect as at 1 January 2014. Future rulings are any tax rulings within scope that are issued on or after 1 April 2016.

603. In the prior years' peer review reports, it was determined that Ireland's undertakings to identify past and future rulings and all potential exchange jurisdictions were sufficient to meet the minimum standard. In addition, it was determined that Ireland's review and supervision mechanism was sufficient to meet the minimum standard. Ireland's implementation remains unchanged, and therefore continues to meet the minimum standard.

604. Ireland has met all of the ToR for the information gathering process and no recommendations are made.

Exchange of information (ToR II.B)

605. Ireland has the necessary domestic legal basis to exchange information spontaneously. Ireland notes that there are no legal or practical impediments that prevent the spontaneous exchange of information on rulings as contemplated in the Action 5 minimum standard.

606. Ireland has international agreements permitting spontaneous exchange of information, including: (i) the *Multilateral Convention on Mutual Administrative Assistance in Tax Matters: Amended by the 2010 Protocol* (OECD/Council of Europe, 2011[2]) ("the Convention"), (ii) the Directive 2011/16/EU with all other European Union Member States and (iii) bilateral agreements in force with 73 jurisdictions.[2]

607. For the year in review, the timeliness of exchanges is as follows:

Past rulings within the scope of the transparency framework	Number of exchanges transmitted by 31 December 2022	Delayed exchanges		
		Number of exchanges not transmitted by 31 December 2022	Reasons for the delays	Any other comments
	5	0	N/A	N/A

Follow-up requests received for exchange of the ruling	Number	Average time to provide response	Number of requests not answered
	0	N/A	N/A

608. In the prior years' peer review reports, it was determined that Ireland's process for the completion and exchange of templates were sufficient to meet the minimum standard. With respect to past rulings, no further action was required. Ireland's implementation in this regard remains unchanged and therefore continues to meet the minimum standard.

609. Ireland has the necessary legal basis for spontaneous exchange of information, a process for completing the templates in a timely way and has completed all exchanges. Ireland has met all of the ToR for the exchange of information process and no recommendations are made.

Statistics (ToR IV.D)

610. The statistics for the year in review are as follows:

Category of ruling	Number of exchanges	Jurisdictions exchanged with
Ruling related to a preferential regime	0	N/A
Cross-border unilateral APAs and any other cross-border unilateral tax rulings (such as an advance tax ruling) covering transfer pricing or the application of transfer pricing principles	0	N/A
Permanent establishment rulings	*De minimis* rule applies	N/A
IP regimes: total exchanges on taxpayers benefitting from the third category of IP assets, new entrants benefitting from grandfathered IP regimes; and taxpayers making use of the option to treat the nexus ratio as a rebuttable presumption	0	N/A
De minimis rule	5	
Total	5	

Matters related to intellectual property regimes (ToR I.A.1.3)

611. In the prior years' peer review reports, it was determined that Ireland's information gathering and exchange of information processes for matters related to intellectual property regimes[3] were sufficient to meet the minimum standard. Ireland's implementation in this regard remains unchanged and therefore continues to meet the minimum standard.

Summary of recommendations on implementation of the transparency framework

Aspect of implementation of the transparency framework that should be improved	Recommendation for improvement
	No recommendations are made.

References

OECD (2021), *BEPS Action 5 on Harmful Tax Practices - Terms of Reference and Methodology for the Conduct of the Peer Reviews of the Action 5 Transparency Framework*, OECD Publishing, Paris, https://www.oecd.org/tax/beps/beps-action-5-harmful-tax-practices-peer-review-transparency-framework.pdf. [1]

OECD (2015), *Countering Harmful Tax Practices More Effectively, Taking into Account Transparency and Substance, Action 5 - 2015 Final Report*, OECD/G20 Base Erosion and Profit Shifting Project, OECD Publishing, Paris, https://doi.org/10.1787/9789264241190-en. [3]

OECD/Council of Europe (2011), *The Multilateral Convention on Mutual Administrative Assistance in Tax Matters: Amended by the 2010 Protocol*, OECD Publishing, Paris, https://doi.org/10.1787/9789264115606-en. [2]

Notes

[1] 1) Shipping regime and 2) Knowledge development box.

[2] Participating jurisdictions to the Convention are available here: www.oecd.org/tax/exchange-of-tax-information/convention-on-mutual-administrative-assistance-in-tax-matters.htm. Ireland also has bilateral agreements with Albania, Armenia, Australia, Austria, Bahrain, Belarus, Belgium, Bosnia and Herzegovina, Botswana, Bulgaria, Canada, Chile, China (People's Republic of), Croatia, Cyprus, Czechia, Denmark, Egypt, Estonia, Ethiopia, Finland, France, Georgia, Germany, Greece, Hong Kong (China), Hungary, Iceland, India, Israel, Italy, Japan, Kazakhstan, Korea, Kuwait, Latvia, Lithuania, Luxembourg, Malaysia, Malta, Mexico, Moldova, Montenegro, Morocco, Netherlands, New Zealand, North Macedonia, Norway, Pakistan, Panama, Poland, Portugal, Qatar, Romania, Russia, Saudi Arabia, Serbia, Singapore, Slovak Republic, Slovenia, South Africa, Spain, Sweden, Switzerland, Thailand, Türkiye, United Arab Emirates, Ukraine, United Kingdom, United States, Uzbekistan, Viet Nam, and Zambia.

[3] Knowledge development box.

Isle of Man

Isle of Man has met all aspects of the terms of reference (OECD, 2021[1]) (ToR) for the calendar year 2022 (year in review), and no recommendations are made.

Isle of Man can legally issue two types of rulings within the scope of the transparency framework.

In practice, Isle of Man issued rulings within the scope of the transparency framework as follows:

Type of ruling	Number of rulings
Past rulings	2
Future rulings in the period 1 April 2017 – 31 December 2017	0
Future rulings in the calendar year 2017	0
Future rulings in the calendar year 2018	0
Future rulings in the calendar year 2019	0
Future rulings in the calendar year 2020	0
Future rulings in the calendar year 2021	1
Future rulings in the year in review	0

As no exchanges were required to take place, no peer input was received in respect of the exchanges of information on rulings received from Isle of Man.

Information gathering process (ToR I.A)

612. The Isle of Man can legally issue two types of rulings within the scope of the transparency framework: (i) rulings providing for unilateral downward adjustments and (ii) permanent establishment rulings.

613. For the Isle of Man, past rulings are any tax rulings within scope that are issued either: (i) on or after 1 January 2015 but before 1 April 2017; or (ii) on or after 1 January 2012 but before 1 January 2015, provided they were still in effect as at 1 January 2015. Future rulings are any tax rulings within scope that are issued on or after 1 April 2017.

614. In the prior years' peer review reports, it was determined that the Isle of Man's undertakings to identify past and future rulings and all potential exchange jurisdictions were sufficient to meet the minimum standard. In addition, it was determined that the Isle of Man's review and supervision mechanism was sufficient to meet the minimum standard. The Isle of Man's implementation remains unchanged, and therefore continues to meet the minimum standard.

615. The Isle of Man has met all of the ToR for the information gathering process and no recommendations are made.

Exchange of information (ToR II.B)

616. The Isle of Man has the necessary domestic legal basis to exchange information spontaneously. The Isle of Man notes that there are no legal or practical impediments that prevent the spontaneous exchange of information on rulings as contemplated in the Action 5 minimum standard.

617. The Isle of Man has international agreements permitting spontaneous exchange of information, including: (i) the *Multilateral Convention on Mutual Administrative Assistance in Tax Matters: Amended by the 2010 Protocol* (OECD/Council of Europe, 2011[2]) ("the Convention") and (ii) bilateral agreements in force with 16 jurisdictions.[1]

618. During the year in review, no exchanges were required to take place and no data on the timeliness of exchanges is reported.

619. In the prior years' peer review reports, it was determined that the Isle of Man's process for the completion and exchange of templates were sufficient to meet the minimum standard. With respect to past rulings, no further action was required. The Isle of Man's implementation in this regard remains unchanged and therefore continues to meet the minimum standard.

620. The Isle of Man has the necessary legal basis for spontaneous exchange of information, a process for completing the templates in a timely way and has completed all exchanges. The Isle of Man has met all of the ToR for the exchange of information process and no recommendations are made.

Statistics (ToR IV.D)

621. As no rulings were issued, no statistics can be reported.

Matters related to intellectual property regimes (ToR I.A.1.3)

622. The Isle of Man does not offer an intellectual property regime for which transparency requirements under the Action 5 Report (OECD, 2015[3]) were imposed.

Summary of recommendations on implementation of the transparency framework

Aspect of implementation of the transparency framework that should be improved	Recommendation for improvement
	No recommendations are made.

References

OECD (2021), *BEPS Action 5 on Harmful Tax Practices - Terms of Reference and Methodology for the Conduct of the Peer Reviews of the Action 5 Transparency Framework*, OECD Publishing, Paris, https://www.oecd.org/tax/beps/beps-action-5-harmful-tax-practices-peer-review-transparency-framework.pdf. [1]

OECD (2015), *Countering Harmful Tax Practices More Effectively, Taking into Account Transparency and Substance, Action 5 - 2015 Final Report*, OECD/G20 Base Erosion and Profit Shifting Project, OECD Publishing, Paris, https://doi.org/10.1787/9789264241190-en. [3]

OECD/Council of Europe (2011), *The Multilateral Convention on Mutual Administrative Assistance in Tax Matters: Amended by the 2010 Protocol*, OECD Publishing, Paris, https://doi.org/10.1787/9789264115606-en. [2]

Note

[1] Participating jurisdictions to the Convention are available here: www.oecd.org/tax/exchange-of-tax-information/convention-on-mutual-administrative-assistance-in-tax-matters.htm. The Isle of Man also has bilateral agreements with Anguilla, Bahrain, British Virgin Islands, Cayman Islands, Estonia, Gibraltar, Guernsey, Jersey, Luxembourg, Malta, Qatar, Seychelles, Singapore, Turks and Caicos Islands, United Kingdom and United States permitting spontaneous exchange of information.

Israel

Israel has met all aspects of the terms of reference (OECD, 2021[1]) (ToR) for the calendar year 2022 (year in review), and no recommendations are made.

Israel can legally issue five types of rulings within the scope of the transparency framework.

In practice, Israel issued rulings within the scope of the transparency framework as follows:

Type of ruling	Number of rulings
Past rulings	79
Future rulings in the period 1 April 2016 – 31 December 2016	5
Future rulings in the calendar year 2017	3
Future rulings in the calendar year 2018	15
Future rulings in the calendar year 2019	30
Future rulings in the calendar year 2020	15
Future rulings in the calendar year 2021	47
Future rulings in the year in review	24

Peer input was received from one jurisdiction in respect of the exchanges of information on rulings received from Israel. The input was positive, noting that overall information was complete, in a correct format and received in a timely manner.

Information gathering process (ToR I.A)

623. Israel can legally issue the following five types of rulings within the scope of the transparency framework: (i) preferential regimes;[1] (ii) cross-border unilateral APAs and any other cross-border unilateral tax rulings (such as an advance tax ruling) covering transfer pricing or the application of transfer pricing principles; (iii) rulings providing for unilateral downward adjustments; (iv) permanent establishment rulings; and (v) related party conduit rulings.

624. For Israel, past rulings are any tax rulings within scope that are issued either: (i) on or after 1 January 2014 but before 1 April 2016; or (ii) on or after 1 January 2010 but before 1 January 2014, provided they were still in effect as at 1 January 2014. Future rulings are any tax rulings within scope that are issued on or after 1 April 2016.

625. In the prior year peer review report, it was determined that Israel's undertakings to identify past and future rulings and all potential exchange jurisdictions were sufficient to meet the minimum standard. In addition, it was determined that Israel's review and supervision mechanism was sufficient to meet the minimum standard. Israel's implementation remains unchanged, and therefore continues to meet the minimum standard.

626. Israel has met all of the ToR for the information gathering process and no recommendations are made.

Exchange of information (ToR II.B)

627. Israel has the necessary domestic legal basis to exchange information spontaneously. Israel notes that there are no legal or practical impediments that prevent the spontaneous exchange of information on rulings as contemplated in the Action 5 minimum standard.

628. Israel has international agreements permitting spontaneous exchange of information, including being a party to (i) the *Multilateral Convention on Mutual Administrative Assistance in Tax Matters: Amended by the 2010 Protocol* (OECD/Council of Europe, 2011[2]) ("the Convention") and (ii) bilateral agreements in force with jurisdictions.[2]

629. For the year in review, the timeliness of exchanges is as follows:

Future rulings within the scope of the transparency framework	Number of exchanges transmitted within three months of the information becoming available to the competent authority or immediately after legal impediments have been lifted	Delayed exchanges		
		Number of exchanges transmitted later than three months of the information on rulings becoming available to the competent authority	Reasons for the delays	Any other comments
	95	0	N/A	N/A

Follow-up requests received for exchange of the ruling	Number	Average time to provide response	Number of requests not answered
	0	N/A	N/A

630. In the prior year's peer review report, it was determined that Israel's process for the completion and exchange of templates were sufficient to meet the minimum standard. With respect to past rulings, no further action was required. Israel's implementation in this regard remains unchanged and therefore continues to meet the minimum standard. Israel has the necessary legal basis for spontaneous exchange

of information, a process for completing the templates in a timely way and has completed all exchanges. Israel has met all of the ToR for the exchange of information process and no recommendations are made.

Statistics (ToR IV.D)

631. The statistics for the year in review are as follows:

Category of ruling	Number of exchanges	Jurisdictions exchanged with
Ruling related to a preferential regime	95	Australia, Belarus, Belgium, Brazil, Bulgaria, Canada, China (People's Republic of), Croatia, Cyprus, Czechia, Denmark, Estonia, France, Germany, Hungary, India, Ireland, Italy, Korea, Lithuania, New Zealand, Poland, Romania, Serbia, Singapore, Slovakia, Spain, Sweden, Türkiye, Ukraine, United Arab Emirates, United Kingdom, United States, Uruguay
Cross-border unilateral APAs and any other cross-border unilateral tax rulings (such as an advance tax ruling) covering transfer pricing or the application of transfer pricing principles	0	N/A
Cross-border rulings providing for a unilateral downward adjustment to the taxpayer's taxable profits that is not directly reflected in the taxpayer's financial / commercial accounts	0	N/A
Permanent establishment rulings	0	N/A
Related party conduit rulings	0	N/A
IP regimes: total exchanges on taxpayers benefitting from the third category of IP assets, new entrants benefitting from grandfathered IP regimes; and taxpayers making use of the option to treat the nexus ratio as a rebuttable presumption	0	N/A
Total	97	

Matters related to intellectual property regimes (ToR I.A.1.3)

632. In the prior years' peer review reports, it was determined that Israel's information gathering and exchange of information processes for matters related to intellectual property regimes[3] were sufficient to meet the minimum standard. Israel's implementation in this regard remains unchanged and therefore continues to meet the minimum standard.

Summary of recommendations on implementation of the transparency framework

Aspect of implementation of the transparency framework that should be improved	Recommendation for improvement
	No recommendations are made.

References

OECD (2021), *BEPS Action 5 on Harmful Tax Practices - Terms of Reference and Methodology for the Conduct of the Peer Reviews of the Action 5 Transparency Framework*, OECD Publishing, Paris, https://www.oecd.org/tax/beps/beps-action-5-harmful-tax-practices-peer-review-transparency-framework.pdf. [1]

OECD (2015), *Countering Harmful Tax Practices More Effectively, Taking into Account Transparency and Substance, Action 5 - 2015 Final Report*, OECD/G20 Base Erosion and Profit Shifting Project, OECD Publishing, Paris, https://doi.org/10.1787/9789264241190-en. [3]

OECD/Council of Europe (2011), *The Multilateral Convention on Mutual Administrative Assistance in Tax Matters: Amended by the 2010 Protocol*, OECD Publishing, Paris, https://doi.org/10.1787/9789264115606-en. [2]

Notes

[1] With respect to the following preferential regimes: Preferred company regime and Preferred technological enterprise regime.

[2] Participating jurisdictions to the Convention are available here: www.oecd.org/tax/exchange-of-tax-information/convention-on-mutual-administrative-assistance-in-tax-matters.htm. Israel also has bilateral agreements with Australia, Austria, Belarus, Belgium, Brazil, Bulgaria, Canada, China (People's Republic of), Croatia, Czechia, Denmark, Estonia, Ethiopia, Finland, France, Georgia, Germany, Greece, Hungary, India, Ireland, Italy, Jamaica, Japan, Korea, Latvia, Lithuania, Luxembourg, Malta, Mexico, Moldova, Netherlands, Norway, Panama, Philippines, Poland, Portugal, Romania, Russia, Serbia, Singapore, Slovak Republic, Slovenia, South Africa, Spain, Sweden, Switzerland, Chinese Taipei, Thailand, Türkiye, Ukraine, United Kingdom, United States, Uzbekistan and Viet Nam.

Italy

Italy has met all aspects of the terms of reference (OECD, 2021[1]) (ToR) for the calendar year 2022 (year in review), and no recommendations are made.

Italy can legally issue three types of rulings within the scope of the transparency framework.

In practice, Italy issued rulings within the scope of the transparency framework as follows:

Type of ruling	Number of rulings
Past rulings	53
Future rulings in the period 1 April 2016 – 31 December 2016	39
Future rulings in the calendar year 2017	123
Future rulings in the calendar year 2018	308
Future rulings in the calendar year 2019	206
Future rulings in the calendar year 2020	224
Future rulings in the calendar year 2021	273
Future rulings in the year in review	136

Peer input was received from six jurisdictions in respect of the exchanges of information on rulings received from Italy. The input was generally positive, noting that overall information was complete, in a correct format and received in a timely manner.

Information gathering process (ToR I.A)

633. Italy can legally issue the following three types of rulings within the scope of the transparency framework: (i) preferential regimes;[1] (ii) cross-border unilateral APAs and any other cross-border unilateral tax rulings (such as an advance tax ruling) covering transfer pricing or the application of transfer pricing principles; and (iii) permanent establishment rulings.

634. For Italy, past rulings are any tax rulings within scope that are issued either: (i) on or after 1 January 2014 but before 1 April 2016; or (ii) on or after 1 January 2010 but before 1 January 2014, provided they were still in effect as at 1 January 2014. Future rulings are any tax rulings within scope that are issued on or after 1 April 2016.

635. In the prior years' peer review reports, it was determined that Italy's undertakings to identify past and future rulings and all potential exchange jurisdictions were sufficient to meet the minimum standard. In addition, it was determined that Italy's review and supervision mechanism was sufficient to meet the minimum standard. Italy's implementation remains unchanged, and therefore continues to meet the minimum standard.

636. Italy has met all of the ToR for the information gathering process and no recommendations are made.

Exchange of information (ToR II.B)

637. Italy has the necessary domestic legal basis to exchange information spontaneously. Italy notes that there are no legal or practical impediments that prevent the spontaneous exchange of information on rulings as contemplated in the Action 5 minimum standard.

638. Italy has international agreements permitting spontaneous exchange of information, including: (i) the *Multilateral Convention on Mutual Administrative Assistance in Tax Matters: Amended by the 2010 Protocol* (OECD/Council of Europe, 2011[2]) ("the Convention"), (ii) the Directive 2011/16/EU with all other European Union Member States and (iii) bilateral agreements in force with 104 jurisdictions.[2]

639. For the year in review, the timeliness of exchanges is as follows:

Future rulings within the scope of the transparency framework	Number of exchanges transmitted within three months of the information becoming available to the competent authority or immediately after legal impediments have been lifted	Delayed exchanges		
		Number of exchanges transmitted later than three months of the information on rulings becoming available to the competent authority	Reasons for the delays	Any other comments
	712	0	N/A	N/A

Follow-up requests received for exchange of the ruling	Number	Average time to provide response	Number of requests not answered
	9	95 days	0

640. Italy comments that in two cases the delays in responding to follow-up requests occurred due to difficulties in processing the requests. In one case the request of the ruling was part of a wider request and the information collection process involved more than one tax administration office. In the other case clarifications were needed from the requesting jurisdiction to identify which ruling was sought. In both cases, the requesting jurisdictions were informed during the information collection process.

641. In the prior years' peer review reports, it was determined that Italy's process for the completion and exchange of templates were sufficient to meet the minimum standard. With respect to past rulings, no further action was required. Italy's implementation in this regard remains unchanged and therefore continues to meet the minimum standard.

642. Italy has the necessary legal basis for spontaneous exchange of information, a process for completing the templates in a timely way and has completed all exchanges. Italy has met all of the ToR for the exchange of information process and no recommendations are made.

Statistics (ToR IV.D)

643. The statistics for the year in review are as follows:

Category of ruling	Number of exchanges	Jurisdictions exchanged with
Ruling related to a preferential regime	500	Argentina, Australia, Austria, Belgium, Brazil, Bulgaria, Cabo Verde, Canada, China, Chile, Colombia, Croatia, Czechia, Denmark, Dominican Republic, Egypt, Finland, France, Germany, Greece, Hong Kong (China), Hungary, India, Indonesia, Ireland, Japan, Kazakhstan, Korea, Luxembourg, Macedonia, Malaysia, Maldives, Mexico, Moldova, Morocco, Netherlands, Oman, Paraguay, Poland, Portugal, Romania, Slovak Republic, San Marino, Singapore, Slovenia, Spain, Sweden, Thailand, Tunisia, Türkiye, United Kingdom, United States
Cross-border unilateral APAs and any other cross-border unilateral tax rulings (such as an advance tax ruling) covering transfer pricing or the application of transfer pricing principles	207	Andorra, Australia, Austria, Belgium, Brazil, Bulgaria, Canada, China, Croatia, Czechia, Denmark, France, Germany, Greece, Hong Kong (China), Hungary, India, Ireland, Japan, Korea, Luxembourg, Macao (China), Malaysia, Mexico, Monaco, Netherlands, New Zealand, Pakistan, Panama, Poland, Portugal, Romania, Serbia, Singapore, Slovak Republic, Spain, Sweden, Switzerland, Thailand, Türkiye, United Kingdom, United States, Viet Nam
Permanent establishment rulings	5	France, Malta, Qatar, San Marino, United Kingdom
IP regimes: total exchanges on taxpayers benefitting from the third category of IP assets, new entrants benefitting from grandfathered IP regimes; and taxpayers making use of the option to treat the nexus ratio as a rebuttable presumption	0	N/A
Total	712	

Matters related to intellectual property regimes (ToR I.A.1.3)

644. In the prior years' peer review reports, it was determined that Italy's information gathering and exchange of information processes for matters related to intellectual property regimes[3] were sufficient to

meet the minimum standard. Italy's implementation in this regard remains unchanged and therefore continues to meet the minimum standard.

Summary of recommendations on implementation of the transparency framework

Aspect of implementation of the transparency framework that should be improved	Recommendation for improvement
	No recommendations are made.

References

OECD (2021), *BEPS Action 5 on Harmful Tax Practices - Terms of Reference and Methodology for the Conduct of the Peer Reviews of the Action 5 Transparency Framework*, OECD Publishing, Paris, https://www.oecd.org/tax/beps/beps-action-5-harmful-tax-practices-peer-review-transparency-framework.pdf. [1]

OECD (2015), *Countering Harmful Tax Practices More Effectively, Taking into Account Transparency and Substance, Action 5 - 2015 Final Report*, OECD/G20 Base Erosion and Profit Shifting Project, OECD Publishing, Paris, https://doi.org/10.1787/9789264241190-en. [3]

OECD/Council of Europe (2011), *The Multilateral Convention on Mutual Administrative Assistance in Tax Matters: Amended by the 2010 Protocol*, OECD Publishing, Paris, https://doi.org/10.1787/9789264115606-en. [2]

Notes

[1] 1) International shipping and 2) Patent Box.

[2] Participating jurisdictions to the Convention are available here: www.oecd.org/tax/exchange-of-tax-information/convention-on-mutual-administrative-assistance-in-tax-matters.htm. Italy also has bilateral agreements with Albania, Algeria, Argentina, Armenia, Australia, Austria, Azerbaijan, Bangladesh, Barbados, Belarus, Belgium, Bosnia and Herzegovina, Brazil, Bulgaria, Canada, Chile, China (People's Republic of), Colombia, Congo, Côte d'Ivoire, Croatia, Cyprus, Czechia, Denmark, Ecuador, Egypt, Estonia, Ethiopia, Finland, North Macedonia, France, Georgia, Germany, Ghana, Greece, Hong Kong (China), Hungary, Iceland, India, Indonesia, Ireland, Israel, Jamaica, Japan, Jordan, Kazakhstan, Korea, Kuwait, Kyrgyzstan, Latvia, Lebanon, Lithuania, Luxembourg, Malaysia, Malta, Mauritius, Mexico, Moldova, Mongolia, Montenegro, Morocco, Mozambique, Netherlands, New Zealand, Norway, Oman, Panama, Pakistan, Philippines, Poland, Portugal, Qatar, Romania, Russia, San Marino, Saudi Arabia, Senegal, Serbia, Singapore, Slovak Republic, Slovenia, South Africa, Spain, Sri Lanka, Sweden, Switzerland, Syrian Arab Republic, Chinese Taipei, Tajikistan, Tanzania, Thailand, Trinidad and Tobago, Tunisia, Türkiye, Uganda, Ukraine, United Arab Emirates, United Kingdom, United States, Uruguay, Uzbekistan, Venezuela, Viet Nam and Zambia.

[3] Partial exemption for income/gains derived from certain IP rights.

Jamaica

Jamaica has met all aspects of the terms of reference (OECD, 2021[1]) (ToR) for the calendar year 2022 (year in review), and no recommendations are made.

Jamaica can legally issue five types of rulings within the scope of the transparency framework.

In practice, Jamaica issued no rulings within the scope of the transparency framework.

As no exchanges were required to take place, no peer input was received in respect of the exchanges of information on rulings received from Jamaica.

Information gathering process (ToR I.A)

645. Jamaica can legally issue the following five types of rulings within the scope of the transparency framework: (i) preferential regimes;[1] (ii) cross-border unilateral APAs and any other cross-border unilateral tax rulings (such as an advance tax ruling) covering transfer pricing or the application of transfer pricing principles; (iii) rulings providing for unilateral downward adjustments; (iv) permanent establishment rulings; and (v) related party conduit rulings.

646. For Jamaica, past rulings are any tax rulings within scope that are issued either (i) on or after 1 January 2015 but before 1 April 2017; and (ii) on or after 1 January 2012 but before 1 January 2015, provided they were still in effect as at 1 January 2015. Future rulings are any tax rulings within scope that are issued on or after 1 April 2017.

647. In the prior years' peer review reports, it was determined that Jamaica's undertakings to identify past and future rulings and all potential exchange jurisdictions were sufficient to meet the minimum standard. In the prior year's peer review report, it was also noted that Jamaica was preparing a more formal procedure to issue and review rulings for the purposes of the transparency framework, including guidelines to specify which information must be included in rulings applications. During the year in review, there have been no further developments. In addition, it was determined that Jamaica's review and supervision mechanism was sufficient to meet the minimum standard. Jamaica's implementation in this regard remains unchanged, and therefore continues to meet the minimum standard.

648. Jamaica has met all of the ToR for the information gathering process and no recommendations are made.

Exchange of information (ToR II.B)

649. Jamaica has the necessary domestic legal basis to exchange information spontaneously. Jamaica notes that there are no legal or practical impediments that prevent the spontaneous exchange of information on rulings as contemplated in the Action 5 minimum standard.

650. Jamaica has international agreements permitting spontaneous exchange of information, including: (i) the *Multilateral Convention on Mutual Administrative Assistance in Tax Matters: Amended by the 2010 Protocol* (OECD/Council of Europe, 2011[2]) ("the Convention") and (ii) agreements in force with 28 jurisdictions.[2]

651. As Jamaica did not issue any rulings within the scope of the transparency framework in the relevant period, Jamaica was not required to exchange any information on rulings in the year in review and no data on the timeliness of exchanges can be reported.

652. In the prior years' peer review reports, it was determined that Jamaica's process for the completion and exchange of templates were sufficient to meet the minimum standard. Jamaica's implementation in this regard remains unchanged and therefore continues to meet the minimum standard.

653. Jamaica has the necessary legal basis for spontaneous exchange of information, a process for completing the templates in a timely way and has completed all exchanges. Jamaica has met all of the ToR for the exchange of information process and no recommendations are made.

Statistics (ToR IV.D)

654. As no rulings were issued, no statistics can be reported.

Matters related to intellectual property regimes (ToR I.A.1.3)

655. Jamaica does not offer an intellectual property regime for which transparency requirements under the Action 5 Report (OECD, 2015[3]) were imposed.

Summary of recommendations on implementation of the transparency framework

Aspect of implementation of the transparency framework that should be improved	Recommendation for improvement
	No recommendations are made.

References

OECD (2021), *BEPS Action 5 on Harmful Tax Practices - Terms of Reference and Methodology for the Conduct of the Peer Reviews of the Action 5 Transparency Framework*, OECD Publishing, Paris, https://www.oecd.org/tax/beps/beps-action-5-harmful-tax-practices-peer-review-transparency-framework.pdf. [1]

OECD (2015), *Countering Harmful Tax Practices More Effectively, Taking into Account Transparency and Substance, Action 5 - 2015 Final Report*, OECD/G20 Base Erosion and Profit Shifting Project, OECD Publishing, Paris, https://doi.org/10.1787/9789264241190-en. [3]

OECD/Council of Europe (2011), *The Multilateral Convention on Mutual Administrative Assistance in Tax Matters: Amended by the 2010 Protocol*, OECD Publishing, Paris, https://doi.org/10.1787/9789264115606-en. [2]

Notes

[1] Special economic zones.

[2] Participating jurisdictions to the Convention are available here: www.oecd.org/tax/exchange-of-tax-information/convention-on-mutual-administrative-assistance-in-tax-matters.htm. Jamaica also has bilateral agreements with Antigua and Barbuda, Barbados, Belize, Brazil, Canada, China (People's Republic of), Denmark, Dominica, Faroe Islands, Finland, France, Germany, Greenland, Grenada, Guyana, Iceland, Israel, Japan, Mexico, Norway, Saint Kitts and Nevis, Saint Lucia, Saint Vincent and the Grenadines, Spain, Sweden, Trinidad and Tobago, United Kingdom and United States.

Japan

Japan has met all aspects of the terms of reference (OECD, 2021[1]) (ToR) for the calendar year 2022 (year in review), and no recommendations are made.

Japan can legally issue three types of rulings within the scope of the transparency framework.

In practice, Japan issued rulings within the scope of the transparency framework as follows:

Type of ruling	Number of rulings
Past rulings	51
Future rulings in the period 1 April 2016 – 31 December 2016	12
Future rulings in the calendar year 2017	14
Future rulings in the calendar year 2018	16
Future rulings in the calendar year 2019	4
Future rulings in the calendar year 2020	29
Future rulings in the calendar year 2021	6
Future rulings in the year in review	57

Peer input was received from three jurisdictions in respect of the exchanges of information on rulings received from Japan. The input was positive, noting that information was complete, in a correct format and received in a timely manner.

Information gathering process (ToR I.A)

656. Japan can legally issue the following three types of rulings within the scope of the transparency framework: (i) cross-border unilateral APAs and any other cross-border unilateral tax rulings (such as an advance tax ruling) covering transfer pricing or the application of transfer pricing principles; (ii) permanent establishment rulings; and (iii) related party conduit rulings.

657. For Japan, past rulings are any tax rulings within scope that are issued either: (i) on or after 1 January 2014 but before 1 April 2016; or (ii) on or after 1 January 2010 but before 1 January 2014, provided they were still in effect as at 1 January 2014. Future rulings are any tax rulings within scope that are issued on or after 1 April 2016.

658. In the prior years' peer review reports, it was determined that Japan's undertakings to identify past and future rulings and all potential exchange jurisdictions were sufficient to meet the minimum standard. In addition, it was determined that Japan's review and supervision mechanism was sufficient to meet the minimum standard. Japan's implementation remains unchanged, and therefore continues to meet the minimum standard.

659. Japan has met all of the ToR for the information gathering process and no recommendations are made.

Exchange of information (ToR II.B)

660. Japan has the necessary domestic legal basis to exchange information spontaneously. Japan notes that there are no legal or practical impediments that prevent the spontaneous exchange of information on rulings as contemplated in the Action 5 minimum standard.

661. Japan has international agreements permitting spontaneous exchange of information, including: (i) the *Multilateral Convention on Mutual Administrative Assistance in Tax Matters: Amended by the 2010 Protocol* (OECD/Council of Europe, 2011[2]) ("the Convention") and (ii) bilateral agreements in force with 79 jurisdictions.[1]

662. For the year in review, the timeliness of exchanges is as follows:

Future rulings within the scope of the transparency framework	Number of exchanges transmitted within three months of the information becoming available to the competent authority or immediately after legal impediments have been lifted	Delayed exchanges		
		Number of exchanges transmitted later than three months of the information on rulings becoming available to the competent authority	Reasons for the delays	Any other comments
	50	0	N/A	N/A

Follow-up requests received for exchange of the ruling	Number	Average time to provide response	Number of requests not answered
	0	N/A	N/A

663. In the prior years' peer review reports, it was determined that Japan's process for the completion and exchange of templates were sufficient to meet the minimum standard. With respect to past rulings, no further action was required. Japan's implementation in this regard remains unchanged and therefore continues to meet the minimum standard.

664. Japan has the necessary legal basis for spontaneous exchange of information, a process for completing the templates in a timely way and has completed all exchanges. Japan has met all of the ToR for the exchange of information process and no recommendations are made.

Statistics (ToR IV.D)

665. The statistics for the year in review are as follows:

Category of ruling	Number of exchanges	Jurisdictions exchanged with
Cross-border unilateral APAs and any other cross-border unilateral tax rulings (such as an advance tax ruling) covering transfer pricing or the application of transfer pricing principles	50	Belgium, Brazil, Canada, China, France, Germany, Hungary, India, Indonesia, Ireland, Israel, Italy, Malta, Mexico, Netherlands, Poland, Romania, Serbia, Singapore, Spain, Switzerland, Thailand, United States
Permanent establishment rulings	0	N/A
Related party conduit rulings	0	N/A
Total	50	

Matters related to intellectual property regimes (ToR I.A.1.3)

666. Japan does not offer an intellectual property regime for which transparency requirements under the Action 5 Report (OECD, 2015[3]) were imposed.

Summary of recommendations on implementation of the transparency framework

Aspect of implementation of the transparency framework that should be improved	Recommendation for improvement
	No recommendations are made.

References

OECD (2021), *BEPS Action 5 on Harmful Tax Practices - Terms of Reference and Methodology for the Conduct of the Peer Reviews of the Action 5 Transparency Framework*, OECD Publishing, Paris, https://www.oecd.org/tax/beps/beps-action-5-harmful-tax-practices-peer-review-transparency-framework.pdf. [1]

OECD (2015), *Countering Harmful Tax Practices More Effectively, Taking into Account Transparency and Substance, Action 5 - 2015 Final Report*, OECD/G20 Base Erosion and Profit Shifting Project, OECD Publishing, Paris, https://doi.org/10.1787/9789264241190-en. [3]

OECD/Council of Europe (2011), *The Multilateral Convention on Mutual Administrative Assistance in Tax Matters: Amended by the 2010 Protocol*, OECD Publishing, Paris, https://doi.org/10.1787/9789264115606-en. [2]

Note

[1] Parties to the Convention are available here: www.oecd.org/tax/exchange-of-tax-information/convention-on-mutual-administrative-assistance-in-tax-matters.htm. Japan also has bilateral agreements in force with Armenia, Australia, Austria, Azerbaijan, Bangladesh, Belarus, Belgium, Brazil, Brunei Darussalam, Bulgaria, Canada, Chile, China (People's Republic of), Colombia, Croatia, Czechia, Denmark, Ecuador, Egypt, Estonia, Fiji, Finland, France, Georgia, Germany, Hong Kong (China), Hungary, Iceland, India, Indonesia, Ireland, Israel, Italy, Jamaica, Kazakhstan, Korea, Kuwait, Kyrgyzstan, Latvia, Lithuania, Luxembourg, Malaysia, Mexico, Moldova, Morocco, Netherlands, New Zealand, Norway, Oman, Pakistan, Peru, Philippines, Poland, Portugal, Qatar, Romania, Russia, Saudi Arabia, Serbia, Singapore, Slovak Republic, Slovenia, South Africa, Spain, Sri Lanka, Sweden, Switzerland, Tajikistan, Thailand, Türkiye, Turkmenistan, Ukraine, United Arab Emirates, United Kingdom, United States, Uruguay, Uzbekistan, Viet Nam, Zambia.

Jersey

Jersey has met all aspects of the terms of reference (OECD, 2021[1]) (ToR) for the calendar year 2022 (year in review), and no recommendations are made.

Jersey can legally issue four types of rulings within the scope of the transparency framework.

In practice, Jersey issued rulings within the scope of the transparency framework as follows:

Type of ruling	Number of rulings
Past rulings	16
Future rulings in the period 1 April 2017 – 31 December 2017	1
Future rulings in the calendar year 2018	0
Future rulings in the calendar year 2019	1
Future rulings in the calendar year 2020	0
Future rulings in the calendar year 2021	1
Future rulings in the year in review	0

No peer input was received in respect of the exchanges of information on rulings received from Jersey.

Information gathering process (ToR I.A)

667. Jersey can legally issue four types of rulings within the scope of the transparency framework: (i) cross-border unilateral APAs and any other cross-border unilateral tax rulings (such as an advance tax ruling) covering transfer pricing or the application of transfer pricing principles; (ii) rulings providing for unilateral downward adjustments; (iii) permanent establishment rulings; and (iv) related party conduit rulings.

668. For Jersey, past rulings are any tax rulings within scope that are issued either: (i) on or after 1 January 2015 but before 1 April 2017; or (ii) on or after 1 January 2012 but before 1 January 2015, provided they were still in effect as at 1 January 2015. Future rulings are any tax rulings within scope that are issued on or after 1 April 2017.

669. In the prior years' peer review reports, it was determined that Jersey's undertakings to identify past and future rulings and all potential exchange jurisdictions were sufficient to meet the minimum standard. In addition, it was determined that Jersey's review and supervision mechanism was sufficient to meet the minimum standard. Jersey's implementation remains unchanged, and therefore continues to meet the minimum standard.

670. Jersey has met all of the ToR for the information gathering process and no recommendations are made.

Exchange of information (ToR II.B)

671. Jersey has the necessary domestic legal basis to exchange information spontaneously. Jersey notes that there are no legal or practical impediments that prevent the spontaneous exchange of information on rulings as contemplated in the Action 5 minimum standard.

672. Jersey has international agreements permitting spontaneous exchange of information, including: (i) being a jurisdiction participating in the *Multilateral Convention on Mutual Administrative Assistance in Tax Matters: Amended by the 2010 Protocol* (OECD/Council of Europe, 2011[2]) ("the Convention") and (ii) bilateral agreements in force with 16 jurisdictions.[1]

673. For the year in review, the timeliness of exchanges is as follows:

Future rulings within the scope of the transparency framework	Number of exchanges transmitted within three months of the information becoming available to the competent authority or immediately after legal impediments have been lifted	Delayed exchanges		
		Number of exchanges transmitted later than three months of the information on rulings becoming available to the competent authority	Reasons for the delays	Any other comments
	1	0	N/A	N/A

Follow-up requests received for exchange of the ruling	Number	Average time to provide response	Number of requests not answered
	0	N/A	N/A

674. In the prior years' peer review reports, it was determined that Jersey's process for the completion and exchange of templates were sufficient to meet the minimum standard. With respect to past rulings, no further action was required. Jersey's implementation in this regard remains unchanged and therefore continues to meet the minimum standard.

675. Jersey has the necessary legal basis for spontaneous exchange of information, a process for completing the templates in a timely way and has completed all exchanges. Jersey has met all of the ToR for the exchange of information process and no recommendations are made.

Statistics (ToR IV.D)

676. The statistics for the year in review are as follows:

Category of ruling	Number of exchanges	Jurisdictions exchanged with
Cross-border unilateral APAs and any other cross-border unilateral tax rulings (such as an advance tax ruling) covering transfer pricing or the application of transfer pricing principles	0	N/A
Cross-border rulings providing for a unilateral downward adjustment to the taxpayer's taxable profits that is not directly reflected in the taxpayer's financial / commercial accounts	0	N/A
Permanent establishment rulings	*De minimis* rule applies	N/A
Related party conduit rulings	0	N/A
De minimis rule	1	The exchange related to a ruling issued in 2021
Total	1	

Matters related to intellectual property regimes (ToR I.A.1.3)

677. Jersey does not offer an intellectual property regime for which transparency requirements under the Action 5 Report (OECD, 2015[3]) were imposed.

Summary of recommendations on implementation of the transparency framework

Aspect of implementation of the transparency framework that should be improved	Recommendation for improvement
	No recommendations are made.

References

OECD (2021), *BEPS Action 5 on Harmful Tax Practices - Terms of Reference and Methodology for the Conduct of the Peer Reviews of the Action 5 Transparency Framework*, OECD Publishing, Paris, https://www.oecd.org/tax/beps/beps-action-5-harmful-tax-practices-peer-review-transparency-framework.pdf. [1]

OECD (2015), *Countering Harmful Tax Practices More Effectively, Taking into Account Transparency and Substance, Action 5 - 2015 Final Report*, OECD/G20 Base Erosion and Profit Shifting Project, OECD Publishing, Paris, https://doi.org/10.1787/9789264241190-en. [3]

OECD/Council of Europe (2011), *The Multilateral Convention on Mutual Administrative Assistance in Tax Matters: Amended by the 2010 Protocol*, OECD Publishing, Paris, https://doi.org/10.1787/9789264115606-en. [2]

Note

[1] Participating jurisdictions to the Convention are available here: www.oecd.org/tax/exchange-of-tax-information/convention-on-mutual-administrative-assistance-in-tax-matters.htm. Jersey also has bilateral agreements with Cyprus, Estonia, Guernsey, Hong Kong (China), Isle of Man, Liechtenstein, Luxembourg, Malta, Mauritius, Qatar, Rwanda, Seychelles, Singapore, United Arab Emirates, United Kingdom and United States.

Jordan

Jordan has met all aspects of the terms of reference (OECD, 2021[1]) (ToR) for the calendar year 2021 (year in review), except for having the necessary information gathering process in place (ToR I.A), having a domestic legal basis for spontaneous exchange of information and exchanging information on the tax rulings in accordance with the form and timelines under the transparency framework (ToR II.B) and for identifying and exchanging information on all new entrants to the IP regime (ToR I.A.1.3). Jordan receives three recommendations on these points for the year in review.

In the prior year report, as well as in the 2019 and 2020 and partly in the 2017 and 2018 peer reviews, Jordan had received the same three recommendations. As they have not been addressed, the recommendations remain in place.

Jordan can legally issue one type of rulings within the scope of the transparency framework.

In practice, Jordan issued rulings within the scope of the transparency framework as follows:

Type of ruling	Number of rulings
Past rulings	0
Future rulings in the period 1 September 2017 – 31 December 2017	0
Future rulings in the calendar year 2018	0
Future rulings in the calendar year 2019	7
Future rulings in the calendar year 2020	6
Future rulings in the calendar year 2021	3
Future rulings in the year in review	17

As no exchanges took place, no peer input was received in respect of the exchanges of information on rulings received from Jordan.

Information gathering process (ToR I.A)

678. Jordan can legally issue the following one type of rulings within the scope of the transparency framework: (i) preferential regimes.[1]

Past rulings (ToR I.A.1.1Jor, I.A.1.2, I.A.2.1, I.A.2.2)

679. For Jordan, past rulings are any tax rulings within scope that are issued either (i) on or after 1 January 2015 but before 1 September 2017; and (ii) and on or after 1 January 2012 but before 1 January 2015, provided still in effect as at 1 January 2015. However, as Jordan put in place an administrative process to issue rulings in 2019, there are no past rulings that have been issued by Jordan in the relevant period.

Future rulings (ToR I.A.1.1, I.A.1.2, I.A.2.1)

680. For Jordan, future rulings are any tax rulings within scope that are issued on or after 1 September 2017. Jordan only put in place an administrative process to issue rulings in 2019.

681. In the prior year's peer review report, it was determined that Jordan did not yet have specific mechanisms in place for identifying future rulings and potential exchange jurisdictions within the scope of the transparency framework. During the year in review, Jordan did not implement such mechanisms, and therefore the recommendation remains in place. The Income and Sales Tax Department (ISTD) within the Ministry of Finance is currently working on introducing a mechanism to identify future rulings that are in the scope of the transparency framework and all jurisdictions for which the tax ruling would be relevant. Jordan indicated that detailed procedures and guidance are expected to be developed in 2023.

Review and supervision (ToR I.A.3)

682. In the prior year's peer review report, it was determined that Jordan did not yet have a review and supervision mechanism under the transparency framework. During the year in review, Jordan did not implement such a review and supervision mechanism, and therefore the recommendation remains in place. Jordan is currently considering the implementation of review and supervision mechanisms within ISTD to ensure that all relevant information related to future rulings is captured adequately.

Conclusion on section A

683. Jordan does not have specific mechanisms in place for identifying relevant rulings and potential exchange jurisdictions within the scope of the transparency framework as well as for reviewing and supervising that all relevant information is captured adequately. Jordan is recommended to ensure that it has put in place an effective information gathering process to identify all relevant rulings and potential exchange jurisdictions, with a review and supervision mechanism, as soon as possible (ToR I.A).

Exchange of information (ToR II.B)

Legal basis for spontaneous exchange of information (ToR II.B.1, II.B.2)

684. In the prior years' peer review reports, it was determined that Jordan did not yet have the necessary domestic legal basis to exchange information spontaneously. During the year in review, Jordan did not introduce such a domestic legal framework, and therefore the recommendation remains in place. ISTD is currently in the process of putting in place the necessary domestic legal basis to exchange information spontaneously and this is expected to be completed in 2023. Jordan notes that there is legislation being drafted in the Jordan parliament regarding spontaneous exchange of information. Jordan can only exchange information on request.

685. Jordan has international agreements permitting spontaneous exchange of information, including: (i) the *Multilateral Convention on Mutual Administrative Assistance in Tax Matters: Amended by the 2010 Protocol* (OECD/Council of Europe, 2011[2]) ("the Convention").

Completion and exchange of templates (ToR II.B.3, II.B.4, II.B.5, II.B.6, II.B.7)

686. In the prior years' peer review reports, it was determined that Jordan did not yet have a process to exchange information on rulings in accordance with the form and timelines required by the transparency framework. During the year in review, Jordan did not introduce such a process, and therefore the recommendation remains in place. Jordan is currently considering the implementation of a process within ISTD to ensure the timely exchange of information on future rulings.

Conclusion on section B

687. Jordan does not yet have the necessary domestic legal basis to exchange information spontaneously and a process to exchange information on rulings in the required format and timelines. Jordan is recommended to put in place a domestic legal framework allowing spontaneous exchange of information on the relevant tax rulings and to ensure the timely exchange of information on rulings in the form required by the transparency framework, as soon as possible (ToR II.B).

Statistics (ToR IV.D)

688. As no rulings were issued, no statistics can be reported.

Matters related to intellectual property regimes (ToR I.A.1.3)

689. Jordan offers one intellectual property regime (IP regime).[2] The assessment of transparency requirements under the Action 5 Report (OECD, 2015[3]), is as follows.

- ***New entrants benefitting from the grandfathered IP regime***: the Development zone regime was reported in the year 2019 as actually harmful. In January 2021, Jordan issued regulation as well as a legally binding opinion and an administrative act, both annexed to the regulation, amending the regime as of 1 January 2021 with no grandfathering provided to existing taxpayers. The FHTP approved these documents and concluded that the regime was compliant with the FHTP standard and therefore updated the conclusion to "not harmful (amended)". Throughout the period in which the regime is considered "harmful", Jordan is expected to have information available and to have exchanged information on new entrants as of the relevant date from which the enhanced transparency obligations apply (i.e. 16 October 2017) until the date the regime is amended (i.e. 1 January 2021). During the year in review, Jordan has not identified information on new entrants to the Development zone regime for the relevant period indicated above, and as such has not exchanged information on these taxpayers. Jordan has indicated that a process to identify new entrants to the Development zone regime for the relevant period will be developed in 2023. Therefore, Jordan is recommended to identify information and to put in place a domestic legal framework allowing spontaneous exchange of information on all new entrants to the IP regime, as soon as possible (ToR I.A.1.3).
- ***Third category of IP assets***: not applicable to this regime.
- ***Taxpayers making the use of the option to treat the nexus ratio as a rebuttable presumption:*** not applicable to this regime.

Summary of recommendations on implementation of the transparency framework

Aspect of implementation of the transparency framework that should be improved	Recommendation for improvement
Jordan does not have specific mechanisms in place for identifying relevant rulings and potential exchange jurisdictions within the scope of the transparency framework as well as for reviewing and supervising that all relevant information is captured adequately.	Jordan is recommended to ensure that it has put in place an effective information gathering process to identify all relevant rulings and potential exchange jurisdictions, with a review and supervision mechanism, as soon as possible. This recommendation remains unchanged since the 2019, 2020 and 2021 peer review reports.
Jordan does not yet have the necessary domestic legal basis to exchange information spontaneously and a process to exchange information on rulings in the required format and timelines.	Jordan is recommended to put in place a domestic legal framework allowing spontaneous exchange of information on the relevant tax rulings and to ensure the timely exchange of information on rulings in the form required by the transparency framework, as soon as possible. This recommendation remains unchanged since the 2019, 2020 and 2021 peer review reports.
Jordan has not identified information on new entrants to the Development zone IP regime during the relevant period and has not exchanged information on these taxpayers.	Jordan is recommended to identify information and to put in place a domestic legal framework allowing spontaneous exchange of information on all new entrants to the IP regime, as soon as possible. This recommendation remains unchanged since the prior year's peer review report. This recommendation remains unchanged since the 2019, 2020 and 2021 peer review reports.

References

OECD (2021), *BEPS Action 5 on Harmful Tax Practices - Terms of Reference and Methodology for the Conduct of the Peer Reviews of the Action 5 Transparency Framework*, OECD Publishing, Paris, https://www.oecd.org/tax/beps/beps-action-5-harmful-tax-practices-peer-review-transparency-framework.pdf. [1]

OECD (2015), *Countering Harmful Tax Practices More Effectively, Taking into Account Transparency and Substance, Action 5 - 2015 Final Report*, OECD/G20 Base Erosion and Profit Shifting Project, OECD Publishing, Paris, https://doi.org/10.1787/9789264241190-en. [3]

OECD/Council of Europe (2011), *The Multilateral Convention on Mutual Administrative Assistance in Tax Matters: Amended by the 2010 Protocol*, OECD Publishing, Paris, https://doi.org/10.1787/9789264115606-en. [2]

Notes

[1] 1) Development zone regime; 2) Aqaba special economic zone; and 3) the tax preference (i.e. 5% income tax rate on information technology services performed inside or outside the development zones) granted to the information technology sector by the Investment law and included in the Cabinet Decision no. 14883 of 2016.

[2] Development zone regime.

Kazakhstan

Kazakhstan is taking steps to implement the legal basis for the transparency framework and to commence administrative preparations in line with the terms of reference (OECD, 2021[1]) (ToR) to ensure that it finalises information gathering process (ToR I.A) and that information on rulings will be identified and exchanged in a timely manner (ToR II.B). Kazakhstan receives two recommendations on these points for the calendar year 2022 (year in review).

In the prior year report, as well as in the 2018-2020 peer reviews, Kazakhstan had received two recommendations. As they have not yet been addressed, the recommendations remain in place.

Kazakhstan can legally issue one type of ruling within the scope of the transparency framework.

In practice, Kazakhstan issued one past ruling and no future rulings within the scope of the transparency framework.

As no exchanges took place, no peer input was received in respect of the exchanges of information on rulings received from Kazakhstan.

Information gathering process (ToR I.A)

690. Kazakhstan can legally issue the following two types of rulings within the scope of the transparency framework: (i) cross-border unilateral APAs and any other cross-border unilateral tax rulings (such as an advance tax ruling) covering transfer pricing or the application of transfer pricing principles.

Past rulings (ToR I.A.1.1, I.A.1.2, I.A.2.1, I.A.2.2)

691. For Kazakhstan, past rulings are any tax rulings issued either (i) on or after 1 January 2016 but before 1 April 2018; and (ii) on or after 1 January 2014 but before 1 January 2016, provided still in effect as at 1 January 2016.

692. In the prior years' peer review reports, it was noted that Kazakhstan issued one past ruling and that the responsible team is continuing to put in place guidelines and practices to collect and record the relevant information for the purposes of the transparency framework. As Kazakhstan has not finalised this process for the year in review, the recommendation remains in place.

Future rulings (ToR I.A.1.1, I.A.1.2, I.A.2.1)

693. For Kazakhstan, future rulings are any tax rulings within scope that are issued on or after 1 April 2018.

694. In the prior years' peer review reports, Kazakhstan noted that when requesting an APA, the taxpayer must identify all transactions that will be covered by the agreement and provide all necessary information about these related parties. However, for the year in review, it is still not clear whether information on the immediate parent and ultimate parent is being collected. Kazakhstan notes that guidelines and practices are being implemented to make sure that the relevant information is adequately processed for the purposes of the transparency framework. However, as this process has not yet been completed, the recommendation remains in place.

Review and supervision (ToR I.A.3)

695. In the prior years' peer review reports, it was determined that Kazakhstan was in the process of implementing a review and supervision mechanism. Once issued by the transfer pricing division, rulings should be reviewed by the non-residents taxation division, which will be responsible to collect the relevant information and to make sure that all relevant information is captured adequately and submitted to all relevant jurisdictions without delay. Kazakhstan is still implementing the process and therefore, the recommendation remains in place.

Conclusion on section A

696. Kazakhstan is recommended to finalise its information gathering process, with a review and supervision mechanism, as soon as possible (ToR I.A).

Exchange of information (ToR II.B)

Legal basis for spontaneous exchange of information (ToR II.B.1, II.B.2)

697. In the prior years' peer review reports, it was determined that Kazakhstan did not have the necessary domestic legal basis to exchange information spontaneously. Kazakhstan intends to draft regulations that will allow for the spontaneous exchange of information on tax rulings in future. However, for the year in review, Kazakhstan has not yet put in place the necessary domestic legal basis to exchange information spontaneously.

698. Kazakhstan has international agreements permitting spontaneous exchange of information, including being a party to (i) the *Multilateral Convention on Mutual Administrative Assistance in Tax*

Matters: Amended by the 2010 Protocol (OECD/Council of Europe, 2011[2]) ("the Convention"), (ii) and bilateral agreements in force with 59 jurisdictions.[1]

Completion and exchange of templates (ToR II.B.3, II.B.4, II.B.5, II.B.6, II.B.7)

699. In the prior years' peer review reports, it was determined that Kazakhstan was still developing a process to complete the templates on relevant rulings, to make them available to the Competent Authority for exchange of information, and to exchange them with relevant jurisdictions. Kazakhstan has not yet put in place such a process for the year in review.

700. During the year in review, no exchanges took place and no data on the timeliness of exchanges is reported.

Conclusion on section B

701. Kazakhstan is recommended to put in place a domestic legal framework allowing spontaneous exchange of information on rulings and to continue its efforts to complete the templates for all relevant rulings and to ensure that the exchanges of information on rulings occur as soon as possible (ToR II.B).

Statistics (ToR IV.D)

702. As there was no information on rulings exchanged by Kazakhstan for the year in review, no statistics can be reported.

Matters related to intellectual property regimes (ToR I.A.1.3)

703. Kazakhstan does not offer an intellectual property regime for which transparency requirements under the Action 5 Report (OECD, 2015[3]) were imposed.

Summary of recommendations on implementation of the transparency framework

Aspect of implementation of the transparency framework that should be improved	Recommendation for improvement
Kazakhstan has not yet finalised the steps to have in place its necessary information and gathering process.	Kazakhstan is recommended to finalise its information gathering process, with a review and supervision mechanism, as soon as possible. This recommendation remains unchanged since the 2018, 2019, 2020 and 2021 peer review reports.
Kazakhstan has not yet finalised the steps to have effective compulsory spontaneous exchange of information on the tax rulings within the scope of the transparency framework.	Kazakhstan is recommended to continue to put in place a domestic legal framework allowing spontaneous exchange of information on rulings and to continue its efforts to complete the templates for all relevant rulings and to ensure that the exchanges of information on rulings occur as soon as possible. This recommendation remains unchanged since the 2018, 2019, 2020 and 2021 peer review reports

References

OECD (2021), *BEPS Action 5 on Harmful Tax Practices - Terms of Reference and Methodology for the Conduct of the Peer Reviews of the Action 5 Transparency Framework*, OECD Publishing, Paris, https://www.oecd.org/tax/beps/beps-action-5-harmful-tax-practices-peer-review-transparency-framework.pdf. [1]

OECD (2015), *Countering Harmful Tax Practices More Effectively, Taking into Account Transparency and Substance, Action 5 - 2015 Final Report*, OECD/G20 Base Erosion and Profit Shifting Project, OECD Publishing, Paris, https://doi.org/10.1787/9789264241190-en. [3]

OECD/Council of Europe (2011), *The Multilateral Convention on Mutual Administrative Assistance in Tax Matters: Amended by the 2010 Protocol*, OECD Publishing, Paris, https://doi.org/10.1787/9789264115606-en. [2]

Note

[1] Participating jurisdictions to the Convention are available here: www.oecd.org/tax/exchange-of-tax-information/convention-on-mutual-administrative-assistance-in-tax-matters.htm. Kazakhstan also has bilateral agreements with Albania, Armenia, Austria, Azerbaijan, Belarus, Belgium, Bulgaria, Canada, China (People's Republic of), Croatia, Czechia, Denmark, Estonia, Finland, France, Georgia, Germany, Hungary, Iceland, India, Iran, Ireland, Italy, Japan, Korea, Kyrgyzstan, Latvia, Lithuania, Luxembourg, Malaysia, Moldova, Mongolia, Montenegro, Morocco, Netherlands, North Macedonia, Norway, Pakistan, Poland, Portugal, Qatar, Romania, Russian Federation, Saudi Arabia, Serbia, Singapore, Slovak Republic, Slovenia, Spain, Sweden, Switzerland, Tajikistan, Turkey, Turkmenistan, Ukraine, United Arab Emirates, United Kingdom, United States and Uzbekistan.

Kenya

Kenya has met all aspects of the terms of reference (OECD, 2021[1]) (ToR) for the calendar year 2022 (year in review), and no recommendations are made.

Kenya can legally issue four types of rulings within the scope of the transparency framework.

In practice, Kenya issued no rulings within the scope of the transparency framework.

As no exchanges were required to take place, no peer input was received in respect of the exchanges of information on rulings received from Kenya.

Information gathering process (ToR I.A)

704. Kenya can legally issue the following four types of rulings within the scope of the transparency framework: (i) preferential regimes;[1] (ii) rulings providing for unilateral downward adjustments; (iii) permanent establishment rulings; and (iv) related party conduit rulings.

705. For Kenya, past rulings are any tax rulings within scope that are issued either: (i) on or after 1 January 2016 but before 1 April 2018; or (ii) on or after 1 January 2014 but before 1 January 2016, provided they were still in effect as at 1 January 2016. Future rulings are any tax rulings within scope that are issued on or after 1 April 2018.

706. In the prior years' peer review reports, it was determined that Kenya's undertakings to identify past and future rulings and all potential exchange jurisdictions were sufficient to meet the minimum standard. In addition, it was determined that Kenya's review and supervision mechanism was sufficient to meet the minimum standard. Kenya's implementation remains unchanged, and therefore continues to meet the minimum standard.

707. Kenya has met all of the ToR for the information gathering process and no recommendations are made.

Exchange of information (ToR II.B)

708. Kenya has the necessary domestic legal basis to exchange information spontaneously. Kenya notes that there are no legal or practical impediments that prevent the spontaneous exchange of information on rulings as contemplated in the Action 5 minimum standard.

709. Kenya has international agreements permitting spontaneous exchange of information, including: (i) the *Multilateral Convention on Mutual Administrative Assistance in Tax Matters: Amended by the 2010 Protocol* (OECD/Council of Europe, 2011[2]) ("the Convention") and (ii) bilateral agreements in force with 15 jurisdictions.[2]

710. As no rulings are issued in practice, no data on the timeliness of exchanges can be reported.

711. In the prior years' peer review reports, it was determined that Kenya's process for the completion and exchange of templates were sufficient to meet the minimum standard. With respect to past rulings, no further action was required. Kenya's implementation in this regard remains unchanged and therefore continues to meet the minimum standard.

712. Kenya has the necessary legal basis for spontaneous exchange of information and a process for completing the templates in a timely way. Kenya has met all of the ToR for the exchange of information process and no recommendations are made.

Statistics (ToR IV.D)

713. As no rulings were issued, no statistics can be reported.

Matters related to intellectual property regimes (ToR I.A.1.3)

714. Kenya does not offer an intellectual property regime for which transparency requirements under the Action 5 Report (OECD, 2015[3]) were imposed.

Summary of recommendations on implementation of the transparency framework

Aspect of implementation of the transparency framework that should be improved	Recommendation for improvement
	No recommendations are made.

References

OECD (2021), *BEPS Action 5 on Harmful Tax Practices - Terms of Reference and Methodology for the Conduct of the Peer Reviews of the Action 5 Transparency Framework*, OECD Publishing, Paris, https://www.oecd.org/tax/beps/beps-action-5-harmful-tax-practices-peer-review-transparency-framework.pdf. [1]

OECD (2015), *Countering Harmful Tax Practices More Effectively, Taking into Account Transparency and Substance, Action 5 - 2015 Final Report*, OECD/G20 Base Erosion and Profit Shifting Project, OECD Publishing, Paris, https://doi.org/10.1787/9789264241190-en. [3]

OECD/Council of Europe (2011), *The Multilateral Convention on Mutual Administrative Assistance in Tax Matters: Amended by the 2010 Protocol*, OECD Publishing, Paris, https://doi.org/10.1787/9789264115606-en. [2]

Notes

[1] 1) Export processing zone and 2) Special economic zone.

[2] Participating jurisdictions to the Convention are available here: www.oecd.org/tax/exchange-of-tax-information/convention-on-mutual-administrative-assistance-in-tax-matters.htm. Kenya also has bilateral agreements with Canada, Denmark, France, Germany, India, Iran, Korea, Norway, Qatar, Seychelles, South Africa, Sweden, United Arab Emirates, United Kingdom and Zambia.

Korea

Korea has met all aspects of the terms of reference (OECD, 2021[1]) (ToR) for the calendar year 2022 (year in review), and no recommendations are made.

Korea can legally issue one type of rulings within the scope of the transparency framework.

In practice, Korea issued rulings within the scope of the transparency framework as follows:

Type of ruling	Number of rulings
Past rulings	45
Future rulings in the period 1 April 2016 – 31 December 2016	1
Future rulings in the calendar year 2017	4
Future rulings in the calendar year 2018	5
Future rulings in the calendar year 2019	5
Future rulings in the calendar year 2020	12
Future rulings in the calendar year 2021	4
Future rulings in the year in review	7

Peer input was received from two jurisdictions in respect of the exchanges of information on rulings received from Korea. The input was positive, noting that information was complete, in a correct format and received in a timely manner.

Information gathering process (ToR I.A)

715. Korea can legally issue the following type of ruling within the scope of the transparency framework: cross-border unilateral APAs and any other cross-border unilateral tax rulings (such as an advance tax ruling) covering transfer pricing or the application of transfer pricing principles.

716. For Korea, past rulings are any tax rulings within scope that are issued either: (i) on or after 1 January 2014 but before 1 April 2016; or (ii) on or after 1 January 2010 but before 1 January 2014, provided they were still in effect as at 1 January 2014. Future rulings are any tax rulings within scope that are issued on or after 1 April 2016.

717. In the prior years' peer review reports, it was determined that Korea's undertakings to identify past and future rulings and all potential exchange jurisdictions were sufficient to meet the minimum standard. In addition, it was determined that Korea's review and supervision mechanism was sufficient to meet the minimum standard. Korea's implementation remains unchanged, and therefore continues to meet the minimum standard.

718. Korea has met all of the ToR for the information gathering process and no recommendations are made.

Exchange of information (ToR II.B)

719. Korea has the necessary domestic legal basis to exchange information spontaneously. Korea notes that there are no legal or practical impediments that prevent the spontaneous exchange of information on rulings as contemplated in the Action 5 minimum standard.

720. Korea has international agreements permitting spontaneous exchange of information, including: (i) the *Multilateral Convention on Mutual Administrative Assistance in Tax Matters: Amended by the 2010 Protocol* (OECD/Council of Europe, 2011[2]) ("the Convention") and (ii) bilateral agreements in force with 93 jurisdictions.[1]

721. For the year in review, the timeliness of exchanges is as follows:

Future rulings within the scope of the transparency framework	Number of exchanges transmitted within three months of the information becoming available to the competent authority or immediately after legal impediments have been lifted	Delayed exchanges		
		Number of exchanges transmitted later than three months of the information on rulings becoming available to the competent authority	Reasons for the delays	Any other comments
	26	0	N/A	N/A

Follow-up requests received for exchange of the ruling	Number	Average time to provide response	Number of requests not answered
	0	N/A	N/A

722. In the prior years' peer review reports, it was determined that Korea's process for the completion and exchange of templates were sufficient to meet the minimum standard. With respect to past rulings, no further action was required. Korea's implementation in this regard remains unchanged and therefore continues to meet the minimum standard.

723. Korea has the necessary legal basis for spontaneous exchange of information, a process for completing the templates in a timely way and has completed all exchanges. Korea has met all of the ToR for the exchange of information process and no recommendations are made.

Statistics (ToR IV.D)

724. The statistics for the year in review are as follows:

Category of ruling	Number of exchanges	Jurisdictions exchanged with
Cross-border unilateral APAs and any other cross-border unilateral tax rulings (such as an advance tax ruling) covering transfer pricing or the application of transfer pricing principles	26	Australia, Canada, Germany, Hong Kong (China), Indonesia, Japan, Malaysia, Mauritius, Netherlands, Russia, Singapore, Thailand, United Kingdom, United States
IP regimes: total exchanges on taxpayers benefitting from the third category of IP assets, new entrants benefitting from grandfathered IP regimes; and taxpayers making use of the option to treat the nexus ratio as a rebuttable presumption	0	N/A
Total	26	

Matters related to intellectual property regimes (ToR I.A.1.3)

725. In the prior years' peer review reports, it was determined that Korea's information gathering and exchange of information processes for matters related to intellectual property regimes[2] were sufficient to meet the minimum standard. Korea's implementation in this regard remains unchanged and therefore continues to meet the minimum standard.

Summary of recommendations on implementation of the transparency framework

Aspect of implementation of the transparency framework that should be improved	Recommendation for improvement
	No recommendations are made.

References

OECD (2021), *BEPS Action 5 on Harmful Tax Practices - Terms of Reference and Methodology for the Conduct of the Peer Reviews of the Action 5 Transparency Framework*, OECD Publishing, Paris, https://www.oecd.org/tax/beps/beps-action-5-harmful-tax-practices-peer-review-transparency-framework.pdf. [1]

OECD (2015), *Countering Harmful Tax Practices More Effectively, Taking into Account Transparency and Substance, Action 5 - 2015 Final Report*, OECD/G20 Base Erosion and Profit Shifting Project, OECD Publishing, Paris, https://doi.org/10.1787/9789264241190-en. [3]

OECD/Council of Europe (2011), *The Multilateral Convention on Mutual Administrative Assistance in Tax Matters: Amended by the 2010 Protocol*, OECD Publishing, Paris, https://doi.org/10.1787/9789264115606-en. [2]

Notes

[1] Participating jurisdictions to the Convention are available here: www.oecd.org/tax/exchange-of-tax-information/convention-on-mutual-administrative-assistance-in-tax-matters.htm. Korea also has bilateral agreements with Albania, Algeria, Australia, Austria, Azerbaijan, Bahrain, Bangladesh, Belarus, Belgium, Brazil, Brunei Darussalam, Bulgaria, Canada, Chile, China (People's Republic of), Colombia, Croatia, Czechia, Denmark, Ecuador, Egypt, Estonia, Ethiopia, Fiji, Finland, France, Gabon, Georgia, Germany, Greece, Hong Kong (China), Hungary, Iceland, India, Indonesia, Iran, Ireland, Israel, Italy, Japan, Jordan, Kazakhstan, Kenya, Kuwait, Kyrgyzstan, Lao People's Democratic Republic, Latvia, Lithuania, Luxembourg, Malaysia, Malta, Mexico, Mongolia, Morocco, Myanmar, Nepal, Netherlands, New Zealand, Norway, Oman, Pakistan, Panama, Papua New Guinea, Peru, Philippines, Poland, Portugal, Qatar, Romania, Russia, Saudi Arabia, Serbia, Singapore, Slovak Republic, Slovenia, South Africa, Spain, Sri Lanka, Sweden, Switzerland, Tajikistan, Thailand, Tunisia, Türkiye, Turkmenistan, Ukraine, United Arab Emirates, United Kingdom, United States, Uruguay, Uzbekistan, Venezuela and Viet Nam.

[2] Special taxation for transfer, acquisition, etc. of technology.

Latvia

Latvia has met all aspects of the terms of reference (OECD, 2021[1]) (ToR) for the calendar year 2022 (year in review), and no recommendations are made.

Latvia can legally issue three types of rulings within the scope of the transparency framework.

In practice, Latvia issued rulings within the scope of the transparency framework as follows:

Type of ruling	Number of rulings
Past rulings	1
Future rulings in the period 1 April 2016 – 31 December 2016	1
Future rulings in the calendar year 2017	2
Future rulings in the calendar year 2018	3
Future rulings in the calendar year 2019	4
Future rulings in the calendar year 2020	4
Future rulings in the calendar year 2021	2
Future rulings in the year in review	4

No peer input was received in respect of the exchanges of information on rulings received from Latvia.

Information gathering process (ToR I.A)

726. Latvia can legally issue the following three types of rulings within the scope of the transparency framework: (i) preferential regimes;[1] (ii) cross-border unilateral APAs and any other cross-border unilateral tax rulings (such as an advance tax ruling) covering transfer pricing or the application of transfer pricing principles; and (iii) permanent establishment rulings.

727. For Latvia, past rulings are any tax rulings within scope that are issued either: (i) on or after 1 January 2014 but before 1 April 2016; or (ii) on or after 1 January 2010 but before 1 January 2014, provided they were still in effect as at 1 January 2014. Future rulings are any tax rulings within scope that are issued on or after 1 April 2016.

728. In the prior years' peer review reports, it was determined that Latvia's undertakings to identify past and future rulings and all potential exchange jurisdictions were sufficient to meet the minimum standard. In addition, it was determined that Latvia's review and supervision mechanism was sufficient to meet the minimum standard. Latvia's implementation remains unchanged, and therefore continues to meet the minimum standard.

729. Latvia has met all of the ToR for the information gathering process and no recommendations are made.

Exchange of information (ToR II.B)

730. Latvia has the necessary domestic legal basis to exchange information spontaneously. Latvia notes that there are no legal or practical impediments that prevent the spontaneous exchange of information on rulings as contemplated in the Action 5 minimum standard.

731. Latvia has international agreements permitting spontaneous exchange of information, including: (i) the *Multilateral Convention on Mutual Administrative Assistance in Tax Matters: Amended by the 2010 Protocol* (OECD/Council of Europe, 2011[2]) ("the Convention"), (ii) the Directive 2011/16/EU with all other European Union Member States and (iii) bilateral agreements in force with 63 jurisdictions.[2]

732. For the year in review, the timeliness of exchanges is as follows:

Future rulings within the scope of the transparency framework	Number of exchanges transmitted within three months of the information becoming available to the competent authority or immediately after legal impediments have been lifted	Delayed exchanges		
		Number of exchanges transmitted later than three months of the information on rulings becoming available to the competent authority	Reasons for the delays	Any other comments
	4	0	N/A	N/A

Follow-up requests received for exchange of the ruling	Number	Average time to provide response	Number of requests not answered
	0	N/A	N/A

733. In the prior years' peer review reports, it was determined that Latvia's process for the completion and exchange of templates were sufficient to meet the minimum standard. With respect to past rulings, no further action was required. Latvia's implementation in this regard remains unchanged and therefore continues to meet the minimum standard.

734. Latvia has the necessary legal basis for spontaneous exchange of information, a process for completing the templates in a timely way and has completed all exchanges. Latvia has met all of the ToR for the exchange of information process and no recommendations are made.

Statistics (ToR IV.D)

735. The statistics for the year in review are as follows:

Category of ruling	Number of exchanges	Jurisdictions exchanged with
Ruling related to a preferential regime	0	N/A
Cross-border unilateral APAs and any other cross-border unilateral tax rulings (such as an advance tax ruling) covering transfer pricing or the application of transfer pricing principles	*De minimis* rule applies	N/A
Permanent establishment rulings	0	N/A
De minimis rule	4	N/A
Total	4	

Matters related to intellectual property regimes (ToR I.A.1.3)

736. Latvia does not offer an intellectual property regime for which transparency requirements under the Action 5 Report (OECD, 2015[3]) were imposed.

Summary of recommendations on implementation of the transparency framework

Aspect of implementation of the transparency framework that should be improved	Recommendation for improvement
	No recommendations are made.

References

OECD (2021), *BEPS Action 5 on Harmful Tax Practices - Terms of Reference and Methodology for the Conduct of the Peer Reviews of the Action 5 Transparency Framework*, OECD Publishing, Paris, https://www.oecd.org/tax/beps/beps-action-5-harmful-tax-practices-peer-review-transparency-framework.pdf. [1]

OECD (2015), *Countering Harmful Tax Practices More Effectively, Taking into Account Transparency and Substance, Action 5 - 2015 Final Report*, OECD/G20 Base Erosion and Profit Shifting Project, OECD Publishing, Paris, https://doi.org/10.1787/9789264241190-en. [3]

OECD/Council of Europe (2011), *The Multilateral Convention on Mutual Administrative Assistance in Tax Matters: Amended by the 2010 Protocol*, OECD Publishing, Paris, https://doi.org/10.1787/9789264115606-en. [2]

Notes

[1] 1) Shipping tax regime and 2) Special economic zones.

[2] Participating jurisdictions to the Convention are available here: www.oecd.org/tax/exchange-of-tax-information/convention-on-mutual-administrative-assistance-in-tax-matters.htm. Latvia also has bilateral agreements with Albania, Armenia, Austria, Azerbaijan, Belarus, Belgium, Bulgaria, Canada, China (People's Republic of), Croatia, Cyprus, Czechia, Denmark, Estonia, Finland, France, Georgia, Germany, Greece, Hong Kong (China), Hungary, Iceland, India, Ireland, Israel, Italy, Japan, Kazakhstan, Korea, Kosovo, Kuwait, Kyrgyzstan, Lithuania, Luxembourg, Malta, Mexico, Moldova, Montenegro, Morocco, Netherlands, North Macedonia, Norway, Poland, Portugal, Qatar, Romania, Saudi Arabia, Serbia, Singapore, Slovak Republic, Slovenia, Spain, Sweden, Switzerland, Tajikistan, Türkiye, Turkmenistan, Ukraine, United Arab Emirates, United Kingdom, United States, Uzbekistan and Viet Nam.

Liberia

Liberia is taking steps to implement the aspects of the terms of reference (OECD, 2021[1]) (ToR) for the transparency framework and to commence administrative preparations to ensure that it establishes an information gathering process (ToR I.A) and information on rulings will be identified and exchanged in a timely manner (ToR II.B). Liberia receives two recommendations on these points for the year in review.

In the prior year report, Liberia had received the same two recommendations. As they have not been addressed, the recommendations remain in place.

Liberia can legally issue one type of ruling within the scope of the transparency framework.

In practice, Liberia issued rulings within the scope of the transparency framework as follows:

Type of ruling	Number of rulings
Past rulings	0
Future rulings in the period 1 April 2017 – 31 December 2017	0
Future rulings in the calendar year 2018	0
Future rulings in the calendar year 2019	1
Future rulings in the calendar year 2020	0
Future rulings in the calendar year 2021	0
Future rulings in the year in review	0

As no exchanges took place, no peer input was received in respect of the exchanges of information on rulings received from Liberia.

Information gathering process (ToR I.A)

737. Liberia can legally issue the following type of ruling within the scope of the transparency framework: cross-border unilateral APAs and any other cross-border unilateral tax rulings (such as an advance tax ruling) covering transfer pricing or the application of transfer pricing principles.

Past rulings (ToR I.A.1.1, I.A.1.2, I.A.2.1, I.A.2.2)

738. For Liberia, past rulings are any tax rulings within scope that are issued either (i) on or after 1 January 2015 but before 1 April 2017; and (ii) on or after 1 January 2012 but before 1 January 2015, provided they were still in effect as at 1 January 2015.

739. Liberia confirms that no past rulings have been issued, as its administrative framework for issuing rulings only took effect at a later stage. Therefore, no recommendations are made regarding past rulings.

Future rulings (ToR I.A.1.1, I.A.1.2, I.A.2.1)

740. For Liberia, future rulings are any tax rulings within scope that are issued on or after 1 April 2017.

741. Liberia indicates that there are not yet processes in place to ensure the implementation of the obligations relating to the transparency framework.

Review and supervision (ToR I.A.3)

742. Liberia did not yet have a review and supervision mechanism under the transparency framework for the year in review.

Conclusion on section A

743. Liberia is recommended to ensure that it has put in place an effective information gathering process to identify all relevant future rulings and all potential exchange jurisdictions and to implement a review and supervision mechanism, as soon as possible (ToR I.A).

Exchange of information (ToR II.B)

Legal basis for spontaneous exchange of information (ToR II.B.1, II.B.2)

744. Liberia has the necessary domestic legal basis to exchange information spontaneously. Liberia notes that there are no legal or practical impediments that prevent the spontaneous exchange of information on rulings as contemplated in the Action 5 minimum standard.

745. Liberia has international agreements permitting spontaneous exchange of information, including being a party to (i) the *Multilateral Convention on Mutual Administrative Assistance in Tax Matters: Amended by the 2010 Protocol* (OECD/Council of Europe, 2011[2]) ("the Convention") and (ii) bilateral agreements in force with two jurisdictions.[1]

Completion and exchange of templates (ToR II.B.3, II.B.4, II.B.5, II.B.6, II.B.7)

746. Liberia does not yet have a process to complete the templates on all relevant rulings, to make them available to the Competent Authority for exchange of information, and to exchange them with relevant jurisdictions.

747. During the year in review, no exchanges took place and no data on the timeliness of exchanges is reported.

Conclusion on section B

748. Liberia is recommended to develop a process to complete the templates for all relevant rulings and to ensure that the exchanges of information on rulings occur in accordance with the form and timelines under the transparency framework going forward (ToR II.B).

Statistics (ToR IV.D)

749. As there was no information on rulings exchanged by Liberia for the year in review, no statistics can be reported.

Matters related to intellectual property regimes (ToR I.A.1.3)

750. Liberia does not offer an intellectual property regime for which transparency requirements under the Action 5 Report (OECD, 2015[3]) were imposed.

Summary of recommendations on implementation of the transparency framework

Aspect of implementation of the transparency framework that should be improved	Recommendation for improvement
Liberia does not yet have the necessary information gathering process in place.	Liberia is recommended to ensure that it has put in place an effective information gathering process to identify all relevant past and future rulings and all potential exchange jurisdictions and to implement a review and supervision mechanism, as soon as possible.
Liberia does not yet have a process to complete the templates on relevant rulings, to make them available to the Competent Authority for exchange of information, and to exchange them with relevant jurisdictions.	Liberia is recommended to develop a process to complete the templates for all relevant rulings and to ensure that the exchanges of information on rulings occur in accordance with the form and timelines under the transparency framework going forward.

References

OECD (2021), *BEPS Action 5 on Harmful Tax Practices - Terms of Reference and Methodology for the Conduct of the Peer Reviews of the Action 5 Transparency Framework*, OECD Publishing, Paris, https://www.oecd.org/tax/beps/beps-action-5-harmful-tax-practices-peer-review-transparency-framework.pdf. [1]

OECD (2015), *Countering Harmful Tax Practices More Effectively, Taking into Account Transparency and Substance, Action 5 - 2015 Final Report*, OECD/G20 Base Erosion and Profit Shifting Project, OECD Publishing, Paris, https://doi.org/10.1787/9789264241190-en. [3]

OECD/Council of Europe (2011), *The Multilateral Convention on Mutual Administrative Assistance in Tax Matters: Amended by the 2010 Protocol*, OECD Publishing, Paris, https://doi.org/10.1787/9789264115606-en. [2]

Note

[1] Participating jurisdictions to the Convention are available here: www.oecd.org/tax/exchange-of-tax-information/convention-on-mutual-administrative-assistance-in-tax-matters.htm. Liberia also has bilateral agreements with Germany and Morocco.

Liechtenstein

Liechtenstein has met all aspects of the terms of reference (OECD, 2021[1]) (ToR) for the calendar year 2022 (year in review), and no recommendations are made.

Liechtenstein can legally issue four types of rulings within the scope of the transparency framework.

In practice, Liechtenstein issued rulings within the scope of the transparency framework as follows:

Type of ruling	Number of rulings
Past rulings	18
Future rulings in the period 1 April 2017 – 31 December 2017	6
Future rulings in the calendar year 2018	5
Future rulings in the calendar year 2019	3
Future rulings in the calendar year 2020	14
Future rulings in the calendar year 2021	6
Future rulings in the year in review	8

Peer input was received from one jurisdiction in respect of the exchanges of information on rulings received from Liechtenstein. The input was positive, noting that information was complete, in a correct format and received in a timely manner.

Information gathering process (ToR I.A)

751. Liechtenstein can legally issue the following four types of rulings within the scope of the transparency framework: (i) cross-border unilateral APAs and any other cross-border unilateral tax rulings (such as an advance tax ruling) covering transfer pricing or the application of transfer pricing principles; (ii) rulings providing for unilateral downward adjustments; (iii) permanent establishment rulings; and (iv) related party conduit rulings.

752. For Liechtenstein, past rulings are any tax rulings within scope that are issued either: (i) on or after January 2015 but before 1 April 2017; or (ii) on or after 1 January 2012 but before 1 January 2015, provided they were still in effect as at 1 January 2017. Future rulings are any tax rulings within scope that are issued on or after 1 April 2017.

753. In the prior years' peer review reports, it was determined that Liechtenstein's undertakings to identify past and future rulings and all potential exchange jurisdictions were sufficient to meet the minimum standard. In addition, it was determined that Liechtenstein's review and supervision mechanism was sufficient to meet the minimum standard. Liechtenstein's implementation remains unchanged, and therefore continues to meet the minimum standard.

754. Liechtenstein has met all of the ToR for the information gathering process and no recommendations are made.

Exchange of information (ToR II.B)

755. Liechtenstein has the necessary domestic legal basis to exchange information spontaneously. Liechtenstein notes that there are no legal or practical impediments that prevent the spontaneous exchange of information on rulings as contemplated in the Action 5 minimum standard.

756. Liechtenstein has international agreements permitting spontaneous exchange of information, including: (i) the *Multilateral Convention on Mutual Administrative Assistance in Tax Matters: Amended by the 2010 Protocol* (OECD/Council of Europe, 2011[2]) ("the Convention") and (ii) bilateral agreements in force with 15 jurisdictions.[1]

757. For the year in review, the timeliness of exchanges is as follows:

Future rulings within the scope of the transparency framework	Number of exchanges transmitted within three months of the information becoming available to the competent authority or immediately after legal impediments have been lifted	Delayed exchanges		
		Number of exchanges transmitted later than three months of the information on rulings becoming available to the competent authority	Reasons for the delays	Any other comments
	13	0	N/A	N/A

Follow-up requests received for exchange of the ruling	Number	Average time to provide response	Number of requests not answered
	0	N/A	N/A

758. In the prior years' peer review reports, it was determined that Liechtenstein's process for the completion and exchange of templates were sufficient to meet the minimum standard. With respect to past rulings, no further action was required from Liechtenstein. Liechtenstein's implementation in this regard remains unchanged and therefore continues to meet the minimum standard.

759. Liechtenstein has the necessary legal basis for spontaneous exchange of information, a process for completing the templates in a timely way and has completed all exchanges. Liechtenstein has met all of the ToR for the exchange of information process and no recommendations are made.

Statistics (ToR IV.D)

760. The statistics for the year in review are as follows:

Category of ruling	Number of exchanges	Jurisdictions exchanged with
Cross-border unilateral APAs and any other cross-border unilateral tax rulings (such as an advance tax ruling) covering transfer pricing or the application of transfer pricing principles	10	Austria, Germany, Ireland, Netherlands, Romania, Sweden, Switzerland
Cross-border rulings providing for a unilateral downward adjustment to the taxpayer's taxable profits that is not directly reflected in the taxpayer's financial / commercial accounts	0	N/A
Permanent establishment rulings	4	*De minimis* rule applies
Related party conduit rulings	0	N/A
Total	14[2]	

Matters related to intellectual property regimes (ToR I.A.1.3)

761. Liechtenstein does not offer an intellectual property regime for which transparency requirements under the Action 5 Report (OECD, 2015[3]) were imposed.

Summary of recommendations on implementation of the transparency framework

Aspect of implementation of the transparency framework that should be improved	Recommendation for improvement
	No recommendations are made.

References

OECD (2021), *BEPS Action 5 on Harmful Tax Practices - Terms of Reference and Methodology for the Conduct of the Peer Reviews of the Action 5 Transparency Framework*, OECD Publishing, Paris, https://www.oecd.org/tax/beps/beps-action-5-harmful-tax-practices-peer-review-transparency-framework.pdf. [1]

OECD (2015), *Countering Harmful Tax Practices More Effectively, Taking into Account Transparency and Substance, Action 5 - 2015 Final Report*, OECD/G20 Base Erosion and Profit Shifting Project, OECD Publishing, Paris, https://doi.org/10.1787/9789264241190-en. [3]

OECD/Council of Europe (2011), *The Multilateral Convention on Mutual Administrative Assistance in Tax Matters: Amended by the 2010 Protocol*, OECD Publishing, Paris, https://doi.org/10.1787/9789264115606-en. [2]

Notes

[1] Participating jurisdictions to the Convention are available here: www.oecd.org/tax/exchange-of-tax-information/convention-on-mutual-administrative-assistance-in-tax-matters.htm. Liechtenstein also has bilateral agreements with Andorra, Austria, Czechia, Germany, Hungary, Iceland, Jersey, Lithuania, Luxembourg, Monaco, Netherlands, San Marino, Singapore, United Arab Emirates, and United Kingdom.

[2] Including one ruling that fell into more than one category and was exchanged with more than one jurisdiction under the BEPS Action 5 report (OECD, 2015[3]).

Lithuania

Lithuania has met all aspects of the terms of reference (OECD, 2021[1]) (ToR) for the calendar year 2022 (year in review), and no recommendations are made.

Lithuania can legally issue five types of rulings within the scope of the transparency framework.

In practice, Lithuania issued rulings within the scope of the transparency framework as follows:

Type of ruling	Number of rulings
Past rulings	5
Future rulings in the period 1 April 2017 – 31 December 2017	6
Future rulings in the calendar year 2018	5
Future rulings in the calendar year 2019	9
Future rulings in the calendar year 2020	4
Future rulings in the calendar year 2021	5
Future rulings in the year in review	3

No peer input was received in respect of the exchanges of information on rulings received from Lithuania.

Information gathering process (ToR I.A)

762. Lithuania can legally issue the following five types of rulings within the scope of the transparency framework: (i) preferential regimes;[1] (ii) cross-border unilateral APAs and any other cross-border unilateral tax rulings (such as an advance tax ruling) covering transfer pricing or the application of transfer pricing principles; (iii) rulings providing for unilateral downward adjustments; (iv) permanent establishment rulings; and (v) related party conduit rulings.

763. For Lithuania, past rulings are any tax rulings within scope that are issued either: (i) on or after 1 January 2015 but before 1 April 2017; or (ii) on or after 1 January 2012 but before 1 January 2015, provided they were still in effect as at 1 January 2015. Future rulings are any tax rulings within scope that are issued on or after 1 April 2017.

764. In the prior years' peer review reports, it was determined that Lithuania's undertakings to identify past and future rulings and all potential exchange jurisdictions were sufficient to meet the minimum standard. In addition, it was determined that Lithuania's review and supervision mechanism was sufficient to meet the minimum standard. For past rulings, Lithuania's implementation remains unchanged, and therefore continues to meet the minimum standard.

765. Lithuania has met all of the ToR for the information gathering process and no recommendations are made.

Exchange of information (ToR II.B)

766. Lithuania has the necessary domestic legal basis to exchange information spontaneously. Lithuania notes that there are no legal or practical impediments that prevent the spontaneous exchange of information on rulings as contemplated in the Action 5 minimum standard.

767. Lithuania has international agreements permitting spontaneous exchange of information, including: (i) the *Multilateral Convention on Mutual Administrative Assistance in Tax Matters: Amended by the 2010 Protocol* (OECD/Council of Europe, 2011[2]) ("the Convention"), (ii) the Directive 2011/16/EU with all other European Union Member States and (iii) bilateral agreements in force with 57 jurisdictions.[2]

768. For the year in review, the timeliness of exchanges is as follows:

Future rulings within the scope of the transparency framework	Number of exchanges transmitted within three months of the information becoming available to the competent authority or immediately after legal impediments have been lifted	Delayed exchanges		
		Number of exchanges transmitted later than three months of the information on rulings becoming available to the competent authority	Reasons for the delays	Any other comments
	4	0	N/A	N/A

Follow-up requests received for exchange of the ruling	Number	Average time to provide response	Number of requests not answered
	0	N/A	N/A

769. In the prior years' peer review reports, it was determined that Lithuania's process for the completion and exchange of templates were sufficient to meet the minimum standard. With respect to past rulings, no further action was required. Lithuania's implementation in this regard remains unchanged and therefore continues to meet the minimum standard.

770. Lithuania has the necessary legal basis for spontaneous exchange of information, a process for completing the templates in a timely way and has completed all exchanges. Lithuania has met all of the ToR for the exchange of information process and no recommendations are made.

Statistics (ToR IV.D)

771. The statistics for the year in review are as follows:

Category of ruling	Number of exchanges	Jurisdictions exchanged with
Ruling related to a preferential regime	0	N/A
Cross-border unilateral APAs and any other cross-border unilateral tax rulings (such as an advance tax ruling) covering transfer pricing or the application of transfer pricing principles	*De minimis* rule applies	N/A
Cross-border rulings providing for a unilateral downward adjustment to the taxpayer's taxable profits that is not directly reflected in the taxpayer's financial / commercial accounts	0	N/A
Permanent establishment rulings	*De minimis* rule applies	N/A
Related party conduit rulings	0	N/A
De minimis rule	4	
Total	4	

Matters related to intellectual property regimes (ToR I.A.1.3)

772. In the prior years' peer review reports, it was determined that Lithuania's information gathering and exchange of information processes for matters related to intellectual property regimes[3] were sufficient to meet the minimum standard. Lithuania's implementation in this regard remains unchanged and therefore continues to meet the minimum standard.

Summary of recommendations on implementation of the transparency framework

Aspect of implementation of the transparency framework that should be improved	Recommendation for improvement
	No recommendations are made.

References

OECD (2021), *BEPS Action 5 on Harmful Tax Practices - Terms of Reference and Methodology for the Conduct of the Peer Reviews of the Action 5 Transparency Framework*, OECD Publishing, Paris, https://www.oecd.org/tax/beps/beps-action-5-harmful-tax-practices-peer-review-transparency-framework.pdf. [1]

OECD (2015), *Countering Harmful Tax Practices More Effectively, Taking into Account Transparency and Substance, Action 5 - 2015 Final Report*, OECD/G20 Base Erosion and Profit Shifting Project, OECD Publishing, Paris, https://doi.org/10.1787/9789264241190-en. [3]

OECD/Council of Europe (2011), *The Multilateral Convention on Mutual Administrative Assistance in Tax Matters: Amended by the 2010 Protocol*, OECD Publishing, Paris, https://doi.org/10.1787/9789264115606-en. [2]

Notes

[1] 1) Free economic zone taxation regime, 2) Tonnage tax regime and 3) IP regime.

[2] Participating jurisdictions to the Convention are available here: www.oecd.org/tax/exchange-of-tax-information/convention-on-mutual-administrative-assistance-in-tax-matters.htm. Lithuania also has bilateral agreements with Armenia, Austria, Azerbaijan, Belarus, Belgium, Bulgaria, Canada, China (People's Republic of), Croatia, Czechia, Cyprus, Denmark, Estonia, Finland, France, Georgia, Germany, Greece, Hungary, Iceland, India, Ireland, Israel, Italy, Japan, Kazakhstan, Korea, Kosovo, Kuwait, Kyrgyzstan, Latvia, Liechtenstein, Luxembourg, Malta, Mexico, Moldova, Netherlands, North Macedonia, Norway, Poland, Portugal, Romania, Russia, Serbia, Singapore, Slovak Republic, Slovenia, Spain, Sweden, Switzerland, Türkiye, Turkmenistan, Ukraine, United Arab Emirates, United Kingdom, United States and Uzbekistan.

[3] IP regime.

Luxembourg

Luxembourg has met all aspects of the terms of reference (OECD, 2021[1]) (ToR) for the calendar year 2022 (year in review), and no recommendations are made.

Luxembourg can legally issue four types of rulings within the scope of the transparency framework.

In practice, Luxembourg issued rulings within the scope of the transparency framework as follows:

Type of ruling	Number of rulings
Past rulings	1922
Future rulings in the period 1 April 2016 – 31 December 2016	73
Future rulings in the calendar year 2017	18
Future rulings in the calendar year 2018	9
Future rulings in the calendar year 2019	3
Future rulings in the calendar year 2020	0
Future rulings in the calendar year 2021	6
Future rulings in the year in review	0

Peer input was received from four jurisdictions in respect of the exchanges of information on rulings received from Luxembourg. The input was generally positive, noting that overall information was complete, in a correct format and received in a timely manner.

Information gathering process (ToR I.A)

773. Luxembourg can legally issue the following four types of rulings within the scope of the transparency framework: (i) preferential regimes;[1] (ii) cross-border unilateral APAs and any other cross-border unilateral tax rulings (such as an advance tax ruling) covering transfer pricing or the application of transfer pricing principles; (iii) rulings providing for unilateral downward adjustments; and (iv) permanent establishment rulings.

774. For Luxembourg, past rulings are any tax rulings within scope that are issued either: (i) on or after 1 January 2014 but before 1 April 2016; or (ii) on or after 1 January 2010 but before 1 January 2014, provided they were still in effect as at 1 January 2014. Future rulings are any tax rulings within scope that are issued on or after 1 April 2016.

775. In the prior years' peer review reports, it was determined that Luxembourg's undertakings to identify past and future rulings and all potential exchange jurisdictions were sufficient to meet the minimum standard. In addition, it was determined that Luxembourg's review and supervision mechanism was sufficient to meet the minimum standard. Luxembourg's implementation remains unchanged, and therefore continues to meet the minimum standard.

776. Luxembourg has met all of the ToR for the information gathering process and no recommendations are made.

Exchange of information (ToR II.B)

777. Luxembourg has the necessary domestic legal basis to exchange information spontaneously. Luxembourg notes that there are no legal or practical impediments that prevent the spontaneous exchange of information on rulings as contemplated in the Action 5 minimum standard.

778. Luxembourg has international agreements permitting spontaneous exchange of information, including: (i) the *Multilateral Convention on Mutual Administrative Assistance in Tax Matters: Amended by the 2010 Protocol* (OECD/Council of Europe, 2011[2]) ("the Convention"), (ii) the Directive 2011/16/EU with all other European Union Member States and (iii) bilateral agreements in force with 83 jurisdictions.[2]

779. For the year in review, the timeliness of exchanges is as follows:

Future rulings within the scope of the transparency framework	Number of exchanges transmitted within three months of the information becoming available to the competent authority or immediately after legal impediments have been lifted	Delayed exchanges		
		Number of exchanges transmitted later than three months of the information on rulings becoming available to the competent authority	Reasons for the delays	Any other comments
	0[3]	0	N/A	N/A

Follow-up requests received for exchange of the ruling	Number	Average time to provide response	Number of requests not answered
	2	One month	0

780. In the prior years' peer review reports, it was determined that Luxembourg's process for the completion and exchange of templates were sufficient to meet the minimum standard. With respect to past rulings, no further action was required. Luxembourg's implementation in this regard remains unchanged and therefore continues to meet the minimum standard.

781. Luxembourg has the necessary legal basis for spontaneous exchange of information, a process for completing the templates in a timely way and has completed all exchanges. Luxembourg has met all of the ToR for the exchange of information process and no recommendations are made.

Statistics (ToR IV.D)

782. The statistics for the year in review are as follows:

Category of ruling	Number of exchanges	Jurisdictions exchanged with
Ruling related to a preferential regime	0	N/A
Cross-border unilateral APAs and any other cross-border unilateral tax rulings (such as an advance tax ruling) covering transfer pricing or the application of transfer pricing principles	0	N/A
Cross-border rulings providing for a unilateral downward adjustment to the taxpayer's taxable profits that is not directly reflected in the taxpayer's financial / commercial accounts	0	N/A
Permanent establishment rulings	0	N/A
IP regimes: total exchanges on taxpayers benefitting from the third category of IP assets, new entrants benefitting from grandfathered IP regimes; and taxpayers making use of the option to treat the nexus ratio as a rebuttable presumption	2	*De minimis* rule applies
Total	2[4]	

Matters related to intellectual property regimes (ToR I.A.1.3)

783. In the prior years' peer review reports, it was determined that Luxembourg's information gathering and exchange of information processes for matters related to intellectual property regimes[5] were sufficient to meet the minimum standard. Luxembourg's implementation in this regard remains unchanged and therefore continues to meet the minimum standard.

Summary of recommendations on implementation of the transparency framework

Aspect of implementation of the transparency framework that should be improved	Recommendation for improvement
	No recommendations are made.

References

OECD (2021), *BEPS Action 5 on Harmful Tax Practices - Terms of Reference and Methodology for the Conduct of the Peer Reviews of the Action 5 Transparency Framework*, OECD Publishing, Paris, https://www.oecd.org/tax/beps/beps-action-5-harmful-tax-practices-peer-review-transparency-framework.pdf. [1]

OECD (2015), *Countering Harmful Tax Practices More Effectively, Taking into Account Transparency and Substance, Action 5 - 2015 Final Report*, OECD/G20 Base Erosion and Profit Shifting Project, OECD Publishing, Paris, https://doi.org/10.1787/9789264241190-en. [3]

OECD/Council of Europe (2011), *The Multilateral Convention on Mutual Administrative Assistance in Tax Matters: Amended by the 2010 Protocol*, OECD Publishing, Paris, https://doi.org/10.1787/9789264115606-en. [2]

Notes

[1] 1) Private asset management company, 2) Investment company in risk capital, 3) Provision for fluctuations in reinsurance companies, and 4) Informal capital and partial exemption for income/gains derived from certain IP rights.

[2] Participating jurisdictions to the Convention are available here: www.oecd.org/tax/exchange-of-tax-information/convention-on-mutual-administrative-assistance-in-tax-matters.htm. Luxembourg also has bilateral agreements with Andorra, Armenia, Austria, Azerbaijan, Bahrain, Guernsey, Barbados, Belgium, Botswana, Brazil, Brunei Darussalam, Bulgaria, Canada, China (People's Republic of), Croatia, Cyprus, Czechia, Denmark, Estonia, Finland, France, Georgia, Germany, Greece, Hungary, Iceland, India, Indonesia, Ireland, Isle of Man, Israel, Italy, Japan, Jersey, Kazakhstan, Korea, Kosovo, Lao People's Democratic Republic, Latvia, Liechtenstein, Lithuania, Malaysia, Malta, Mauritius, Mexico, Moldova, Monaco, Morocco, Netherlands, North Macedonia, Norway, Panama, Poland, Portugal, Qatar, Romania, Russia, San Marino, Saudi Arabia, Senegal, Serbia, Seychelles, Singapore, Slovak Republic, Slovenia, South Africa, Spain, Sri Lanka, Sweden, Switzerland, Chinese Taipei, Tajikistan, Thailand, Trinidad and Tobago, Tunisia, Türkiye, Ukraine, United Arab Emirates, United Kingdom, United States, Uruguay, Uzbekistan and Viet Nam.

[3] During the year in review, Luxembourg also transmitted an additional 23 exchanges of "other types of rulings" that fall outside of the scope of the transparency framework.

[4] During the year in review, Luxembourg transmitted additional 23 exchanges of "other types of rulings" to the following countries: Argentina, Brazil, France, Germany, Italy, Netherlands, Singapore, Spain, Sweden, Switzerland, United Kingdom and United States.

[5] Informal capital and partial exemption for income/gains derived from certain IP rights.

Malaysia

Malaysia has met all aspects of the terms of reference (OECD, 2021[1]) (ToR) for the calendar year 2022 (year in review), except for identifying all potential exchange jurisdictions for future rulings (ToR I.A.2.1) and for providing information on rulings to the Competent Authority without undue delay and undertaking spontaneous exchange of information on all future tax rulings within the scope of the transparency framework (ToR II.B). Malaysia receives two recommendations on these points for the year in review.

In the prior year report, as well as in the 2019 and 2020 peer reviews, Malaysia had received the same recommendations. As they have not been addressed, the recommendations remain in place.

Malaysia can legally issue five types of rulings within the scope of the transparency framework.

In practice, Malaysia issued rulings within the scope of the transparency framework as follows:

Type of ruling	Number of rulings
Past rulings	249
Future rulings in the period 1 April 2017 – 31 December 2017	23
Future rulings in the calendar year 2018	51
Future rulings in the calendar year 2019	69
Future rulings in the calendar year 2020	40
Future rulings in the calendar year 2021	3
Future rulings in the year in review	0

No peer input was received in respect of the exchanges of information on rulings received from Malaysia.

Information gathering process (ToR I.A)

784. Malaysia can legally issue the following five types of rulings within the scope of the transparency framework: (i) preferential regimes;[1] (ii) cross-border unilateral APAs and any other cross-border unilateral tax rulings (such as an advance tax ruling) covering transfer pricing or the application of transfer pricing principles; (iii) rulings providing for unilateral downward adjustments; (iv) permanent establishment rulings; and (v) related party conduit rulings.

Past rulings (ToR I.A.1.1, I.A.1.2, I.A.2.1, I.A.2.2)

785. For Malaysia, past rulings are any tax rulings within scope that are issued either (i) on or after 1 January 2015 but before 1 September 2017; and (ii) on or after 1 January 2012 but before 1 January 2015, provided they were still in effect as at 1 January 2015.

786. In the prior years' peer review reports, it was determined that Malaysia's undertakings to identify past rulings and all potential exchange jurisdictions were sufficient to meet the minimum standard. Malaysia's implementation in this regard remains unchanged, and therefore continues to meet the minimum standard.

Future rulings (ToR I.A.1.1, I.A.1.2, I.A.2.1)

787. For Malaysia, future rulings are any tax rulings within scope that are issued on or after 1 September 2017.

788. In the prior years' peer review reports, it was determined that Malaysia's undertakings to identify past and future rulings and all potential exchange jurisdictions have met all the ToR, except for identifying all potential exchange jurisdictions for future rulings (ToR I.A.2.1). Therefore, Malaysia was recommended to ensure that all potential exchange jurisdictions are identified swiftly for all future rulings.

789. Malaysia notes that during the year in review, a process has been created for identifying potential exchange jurisdictions. Taxpayers need to provide the information required in the Annex C template upon approval of the preferential regime. The promotional agency of Malaysia will monitor the information provided by the taxpayer. However, Malaysia notes that in case taxpayers do not provide the information required in the Annex C template, it will identify potential exchange jurisdictions using the "best efforts approach". As Malaysia cannot ensure that potential exchange jurisdictions are always identified through the process of requiring taxpayers to provide the Annex C template, the recommendation is not yet resolved. Malaysia is therefore recommended to continue its efforts to ensure that all potential exchange jurisdictions are identified swiftly for all future rulings. Malaysia notes that it started improving this process in 2023, and this will be taken into account in next year's peer review.

Review and supervision (ToR I.A.3)

790. In the prior years' peer review reports, it was determined that Malaysia's review and supervision mechanism was sufficient to meet the minimum standard. Malaysia's implementation in this regard remains unchanged, and therefore continues to meet the minimum standard.

Conclusion on section A

791. Malaysia has met all of the ToR for the information gathering process except for identifying all potential exchange jurisdictions for future rulings (ToR I.A.2.1). Malaysia is recommended to ensure that all potential exchange jurisdictions are identified swiftly for all future rulings.

Exchange of information (ToR II.B)

Legal basis for spontaneous exchange of information (ToR II.B.1, II.B.2)

792. Malaysia has the necessary domestic legal basis to exchange information spontaneously. Malaysia notes that there are no legal or practical impediments that prevent the spontaneous exchange of information on rulings as contemplated in the Action 5 minimum standard.

793. Malaysia has international agreements permitting spontaneous exchange of information, including: (i) the *Multilateral Convention on Mutual Administrative Assistance in Tax Matters: Amended by the 2010 Protocol* (OECD/Council of Europe, 2011[2]) ("the Convention") and (ii) bilateral agreements in force with 73 jurisdictions.[2]

Completion and exchange of templates (ToR II.B.3, II.B.4, II.B.5, II.B.6, II.B.7)

794. In the prior year's peer review report, it was determined that Malaysia's internal policies, processes and procedures for the completion and exchange of templates were sufficient to meet the minimum standard, except for the provision of information on rulings to the Competent Authority without undue delay, and the timely spontaneous exchange of information on future rulings (ToR II.B).

795. Malaysia's internal procedures and timelines to provide information on rulings to the Competent Authority remain unchanged, and therefore the recommendation to reduce the timelines for providing information on rulings to the Competent Authority without undue delay remains.

796. During the year in review, no exchanges were required to take place and no data on the timeliness of exchanges is reported. However, as there were delays on the exchange of information on future rulings in previous years and Malaysia reports that internal processes to ensure timely exchanges still need to be further developed, the recommendation to ensure that the exchanges of information on future rulings occur as soon as possible remains. This will be reassessed in next year's peer review.

Conclusion on section B

797. Malaysia has the necessary legal basis to undertake spontaneous exchange of information. Malaysia is recommended to continue its efforts to reduce the timeliness for providing the information on rulings to the Competent Authority and to complete the templates for all relevant future rulings and to ensure that the exchanges of information on future rulings occur as soon as possible (ToR II.B).

Statistics (ToR IV.D)

798. As no rulings were issued, no statistics can be reported.

Matters related to intellectual property regimes (ToR I.A.1.3)

799. Malaysia does not offer an intellectual property regime for which transparency requirements under the Action 5 Report (OECD, 2015[3]) were imposed.

Summary of recommendations on implementation of the transparency framework

Aspect of implementation of the transparency framework that should be improved	Recommendation for improvement
Malaysia experienced difficulties in identifying all potential exchange jurisdictions for future rulings.	Malaysia is recommended to continue its efforts to ensure that all potential exchange jurisdictions are identified swiftly for all future rulings. This recommendation remains unchanged since the 2019, 2020 and 2021 year peer review reports.
Malaysia experienced delays in the provision of rulings to the Competent Authority and did not undertake spontaneous exchange of information on all future tax rulings within the scope of the transparency framework during the year in review. Malaysia is in process of identifying future rulings that need to be exchanged and is estimating that the rulings will be exchanged via OECD XML Schema in 2023.	Malaysia is recommended to continue its efforts to reduce the timeliness for providing the information on rulings to the Competent Authority and to complete the templates for all relevant future rulings and to ensure that the exchanges of information on future rulings occur as soon as possible. This recommendation remains unchanged since the 2017, 2018, 2019, 2020 and 2021 peer review reports.

References

OECD (2021), *BEPS Action 5 on Harmful Tax Practices - Terms of Reference and Methodology for the Conduct of the Peer Reviews of the Action 5 Transparency Framework*, OECD Publishing, Paris, https://www.oecd.org/tax/beps/beps-action-5-harmful-tax-practices-peer-review-transparency-framework.pdf. [1]

OECD (2015), *Countering Harmful Tax Practices More Effectively, Taking into Account Transparency and Substance, Action 5 - 2015 Final Report*, OECD/G20 Base Erosion and Profit Shifting Project, OECD Publishing, Paris, https://doi.org/10.1787/9789264241190-en. [3]

OECD/Council of Europe (2011), *The Multilateral Convention on Mutual Administrative Assistance in Tax Matters: Amended by the 2010 Protocol*, OECD Publishing, Paris, https://doi.org/10.1787/9789264115606-en. [2]

Notes

[1] 1) Pioneer status – contract R&D, 2) Biotechnology industry, 3) Principal hub, 4) MSC Malaysia, 5) Green technology services and 6) Special economic regions, 7) High technology regime and 8) Treasury management centre.

[2] Participating jurisdictions to the Convention are available here: www.oecd.org/tax/exchange-of-tax-information/convention-on-mutual-administrative-assistance-in-tax-matters.htm. Malaysia also has bilateral agreements with Albania, Argentina, Australia, Austria, Bahrain, Bangladesh, Belgium, Bosnia and Herzegovina, Brunei Darussalam, Canada, Chile, China (People's Republic of), Croatia, Czechia, Denmark, Egypt, Fiji, Finland, France, Germany, Hong Kong (China), Hungary, India, Indonesia, Iran, Ireland, Italy, Japan, Jordan, Kazakhstan, Korea, Kuwait, Kyrgyzstan, Laos, Lebanon, Luxembourg, Malta, Mauritius, Mongolia, Morocco, Myanmar, Namibia, Netherlands, New Zealand, Norway, Pakistan, Papua New Guinea, Philippines, Poland, Qatar, Romania, Russia, San Marino, Saudi Arabia, Seychelles, Singapore, South Africa, Spain, Slovak Republic, Sri Lanka, Sudan, Sweden, Switzerland, Syrian Arab Republic, Thailand, Türkiye, Turkmenistan, United Arab Emirates, United Kingdom, Uzbekistan, Venezuela, Viet Nam, Zimbabwe.

Malta

Malta has met all aspects of the terms of reference (OECD, 2021[1]) (ToR) for the calendar year 2022 (year in review), and no recommendations are made.

Malta can legally issue four types of rulings within the scope of the transparency framework.

In practice, Malta issued rulings within the scope of the transparency framework as follows:

Type of ruling	Number of rulings
Past rulings	7
Future rulings in the period 1 April 2017 – 31 December 2017	4
Future rulings in the calendar year 2018	7
Future rulings in the calendar year 2019	15
Future rulings in the calendar year 2020	17
Future rulings in the calendar year 2021	13
Future rulings in the year in review	33

Peer input was received from two jurisdictions in respect of the exchanges of information on rulings received from Malta. The input was positive, noting that information was complete, in a correct format and received in a timely manner.

Information gathering process (ToR I.A)

800. Malta can legally issue the following four types of rulings within the scope of the transparency framework: (i) cross-border unilateral APAs and any other cross-border unilateral tax rulings (such as an advance tax ruling) covering transfer pricing or the application of transfer pricing principles; (ii) rulings providing for unilateral downward adjustments; (iii) permanent establishment rulings; and (iv) related party conduit rulings.

801. For Malta, past rulings are any tax rulings within scope that are issued either: (i) on or after 1 January 2015 but before 1 April 2017; and (ii) on or after 1 January 2012 but before 1 January 2015, provided they were still in effect as at 1 January 2015. Future rulings are any tax rulings within scope that are issued on or after 1 April 2017.

802. In the prior years' peer review reports, it was determined that Malta's undertakings to identify past and future rulings and all potential exchange jurisdictions were sufficient to meet the minimum standard. In addition, it was determined that Malta's review and supervision mechanism was sufficient to meet the minimum standard. Malta's implementation remains unchanged, and therefore continues to meet the minimum standard.

803. Malta has met all of the ToR for the information gathering process and no recommendations are made.

Exchange of information (ToR II.B)

804. Malta has the necessary domestic legal basis to exchange information spontaneously. Malta notes that there are no legal or practical impediments that prevent the spontaneous exchange of information on rulings as contemplated in the Action 5 minimum standard.

805. Malta has international agreements permitting spontaneous exchange of information, including: (i) the *Multilateral Convention on Mutual Administrative Assistance in Tax Matters: Amended by the 2010 Protocol* (OECD/Council of Europe, 2011[2]) ("the Convention"), (ii) Directive 2011/16/EU with all other EU Member States and (iii) bilateral agreements in force with 78 jurisdictions.[1]

806. For the year in review, the timeliness of exchanges is as follows:

Future rulings within the scope of the transparency framework	Number of exchanges transmitted within three months of the information becoming available to the competent authority or immediately after legal impediments have been lifted	Delayed exchanges		
		Number of exchanges transmitted later than three months of the information on rulings becoming available to the competent authority	Reasons for the delays	Any other comments
	62	0	N/A	N/A

Follow-up requests received for exchange of the ruling	Number	Average time to provide response	Number of requests not answered
	0	N/A	N/A

807. In the prior years' peer review reports, it was determined that Malta's process for the completion and exchange of templates were sufficient to meet the minimum standard. With respect to past rulings, no further action was required. Malta's implementation in this regard remains unchanged and therefore continues to meet the minimum standard.

808. Malta has the necessary legal basis for spontaneous exchange of information, a process for completing the templates in a timely way and has completed all exchanges. Malta has met all of the ToR for the exchange of information process and no recommendations are made.

Statistics (ToR IV.D)

809. The statistics for the year in review are as follows:

Category of ruling	Number of exchanges	Jurisdictions exchanged with
Cross-border unilateral APAs and any other cross-border unilateral tax rulings (such as an advance tax ruling) covering transfer pricing or the application of transfer pricing principles	2	*De minimis* rule applies
Cross-border rulings providing for a unilateral downward adjustment to the taxpayer's taxable profits that is not directly reflected in the taxpayer's financial / commercial accounts	0	N/A
Permanent establishment rulings	6	Curacao, Germany, Hungary, Malaysia, Netherlands, United Kingdom
Related party conduit rulings	54	Austria, Belgium, Cyprus, Czechia, Germany, Gibraltar, Hungary, Ireland, Isle of Man, Italy, Jersey, Luxembourg, Mexico, Netherlands, Panama, Poland, Singapore, Switzerland, Türkiye, United Kingdom, United States
IP regimes: total exchanges on taxpayers benefitting from the third category of IP assets, new entrants benefitting from grandfathered IP regimes; and taxpayers making use of the option to treat the nexus ratio as a rebuttable presumption	0	N/A
Total	62	

Matters related to intellectual property regimes (ToR I.A.1.3)

810. In the prior years' peer review reports, it was determined that Malta's information gathering and exchange of information processes for matters related to intellectual property regimes[2] were sufficient to meet the minimum standard. Malta's implementation in this regard remains unchanged and therefore continues to meet the minimum standard.

Summary of recommendations on implementation of the transparency framework

Aspect of implementation of the transparency framework that should be improved	Recommendation for improvement
	No recommendations are made.

References

OECD (2021), *BEPS Action 5 on Harmful Tax Practices - Terms of Reference and Methodology for the Conduct of the Peer Reviews of the Action 5 Transparency Framework*, OECD Publishing, Paris, https://www.oecd.org/tax/beps/beps-action-5-harmful-tax-practices-peer-review-transparency-framework.pdf. [1]

OECD (2015), *Countering Harmful Tax Practices More Effectively, Taking into Account Transparency and Substance, Action 5 - 2015 Final Report*, OECD/G20 Base Erosion and Profit Shifting Project, OECD Publishing, Paris, https://doi.org/10.1787/9789264241190-en. [3]

OECD/Council of Europe (2011), *The Multilateral Convention on Mutual Administrative Assistance in Tax Matters: Amended by the 2010 Protocol*, OECD Publishing, Paris, https://doi.org/10.1787/9789264115606-en. [2]

Notes

[1] Participating jurisdictions to the Convention are available here: www.oecd.org/tax/exchange-of-tax-information/convention-on-mutual-administrative-assistance-in-tax-matters.htm. Malta also has bilateral agreements with Albania, Andorra, Armenia, Australia, Austria, Azerbaijan, Bahrain, Barbados, Belgium, Botswana, Bulgaria, Canada, China (People's Republic of), Croatia, Cyprus, Czechia, Denmark, Egypt, Estonia, Finland, France, Georgia, Germany, Greece, Guernsey, Hong Kong (China), Hungary, Iceland, India, Ireland, Isle of Man, Israel, Italy, Jersey, Jordan, Korea, Kosovo, Kuwait, Latvia, Lebanon, Libya, Liechtenstein, Lithuania, Luxembourg, Malaysia, Mauritius, Mexico, Moldova, Monaco, Montenegro, Morocco, Netherlands, Norway, Pakistan, Poland, Portugal, Qatar, Romania, Russia, San Marino, Saudi Arabia, Serbia, Singapore, Slovak Republic, Slovenia, South Africa, Spain, Sweden, Switzerland, Syrian Arab Republic, Tunisia, Türkiye, Ukraine, United Arab Emirates, United Kingdom, United States, Uruguay and Viet Nam.

[2] Patent box deduction rules.

Mauritius

Mauritius has met all aspects of the terms of reference (OECD, 2021[1]) (ToR) for the calendar year 2022 (year in review), and no recommendations are made.

Mauritius can legally issue three types of rulings within the scope of the transparency framework.

In practice, Mauritius issued rulings within the scope of the transparency framework as follows:

Type of ruling	Number of rulings
Past rulings	20
Future rulings in the period 1 September 2017 – 31 December 2017	0
Future rulings in the calendar year 2018	1
Future rulings in the calendar year 2019	1
Future rulings in the calendar year 2020	10
Future rulings in the calendar year 2021	6
Future rulings in the year in review	2

No peer input was received in respect of the exchanges of information on rulings received from Mauritius.

Information gathering process (ToR I.A)

811. Mauritius can legally issue the following three types of rulings within the scope of the transparency framework: (i) preferential regimes;[1] (ii) cross-border unilateral APAs and any other cross-border unilateral tax rulings (such as an advance tax ruling) covering transfer pricing or the application of transfer pricing principles; and (iii) permanent establishment rulings.

812. For Mauritius, past rulings are any tax rulings within scope that are issued either: (i) on or after 1 January 2015 but before 1 September 2017; and (ii) on or after 1 January 2012 but before 1 January 2015, provided they were still in effect as at 1 January 2015. Future rulings are any tax rulings within scope that are issued on or after 1 September 2017.

813. In the prior years' peer review reports, it was determined that Mauritius' undertakings to identify past and future rulings and all potential exchange jurisdictions were sufficient to meet the minimum standard. In addition, it was determined that Mauritius' review and supervision mechanism was sufficient to meet the minimum standard. Mauritius' implementation remains unchanged, and therefore continues to meet the minimum standard.

814. Mauritius has met all of the ToR for the information gathering process and no recommendations are made.

Exchange of information (ToR II.B)

815. Mauritius has the necessary domestic legal basis to exchange information spontaneously. Mauritius notes that there are no legal or practical impediments that prevent the spontaneous exchange of information on rulings as contemplated in the Action 5 minimum standard.

816. Mauritius has international agreements permitting spontaneous exchange of information, including: (i) the *Multilateral Convention on Mutual Administrative Assistance in Tax Matters: Amended by the 2010 Protocol* (OECD/Council of Europe, 2011[2]) ("the Convention") and (ii) bilateral agreements in force with 46 jurisdictions.[2]

817. For the year in review, the timeliness of exchanges is as follows:

Future rulings within the scope of the transparency framework	Number of exchanges transmitted within three months of the information becoming available to the competent authority or immediately after legal impediments have been lifted	Delayed exchanges		
		Number of exchanges transmitted later than three months of the information on rulings becoming available to the competent authority	Reasons for the delays	Any other comments
	3	0	N/A	N/A

Follow-up requests received for exchange of the ruling	Number	Average time to provide response	Number of requests not answered
	0	N/A	N/A

818. In the prior years' peer review reports, it was determined that Mauritius' process for the completion and exchange of templates were sufficient to meet the minimum standard. With respect to past rulings, no further action was required. Mauritius' implementation in this regard remains unchanged and therefore continues to meet the minimum standard.

819. Mauritius has the necessary legal basis for spontaneous exchange of information, a process for completing the templates in a timely way and has completed all exchanges. Mauritius has met all of the ToR for the exchange of information process and no recommendations are made.

Statistics (ToR IV.D)

820. The statistics for the year in review are as follows:

Category of ruling	Number of exchanges	Jurisdictions exchanged with
Ruling related to a preferential regime	*De minimis* rule applies	N/A
Cross-border unilateral APAs and any other cross-border unilateral tax rulings (such as an advance tax ruling) covering transfer pricing or the application of transfer pricing principles	0	N/A
Permanent establishment rulings	0	N/A
IP regimes: total exchanges on taxpayers benefitting from the third category of IP assets, new entrants benefitting from grandfathered IP regimes; and taxpayers making use of the option to treat the nexus ratio as a rebuttable presumption	0	N/A
De minimis rule	3	
Total	3	

Matters related to intellectual property regimes (ToR I.A.1.3)

821. In the prior years' peer review reports, it was determined that Mauritius's information gathering and exchange of information processes for matters related to intellectual property regimes[3] were sufficient to meet the minimum standard. Mauritius's implementation in this regard remains unchanged and therefore continues to meet the minimum standard.

Summary of recommendations on implementation of the transparency framework

Aspect of implementation of the transparency framework that should be improved	Recommendation for improvement
	No recommendations are made.

References

OECD (2021), *BEPS Action 5 on Harmful Tax Practices - Terms of Reference and Methodology for the Conduct of the Peer Reviews of the Action 5 Transparency Framework*, OECD Publishing, Paris, https://www.oecd.org/tax/beps/beps-action-5-harmful-tax-practices-peer-review-transparency-framework.pdf. [1]

OECD (2015), *Countering Harmful Tax Practices More Effectively, Taking into Account Transparency and Substance, Action 5 - 2015 Final Report*, OECD/G20 Base Erosion and Profit Shifting Project, OECD Publishing, Paris, https://doi.org/10.1787/9789264241190-en. [3]

OECD/Council of Europe (2011), *The Multilateral Convention on Mutual Administrative Assistance in Tax Matters: Amended by the 2010 Protocol*, OECD Publishing, Paris, https://doi.org/10.1787/9789264115606-en. [2]

Notes

[1] 1) Global headquarters administration regime, 2) Global treasury activities, 3) Captive insurance, 4) Freeport zone, 5) Shipping regime, 6) Innovation box, 7) Partial exemption system, 8) Trusts and 9) Foundations.

[2] Parties to the Convention are available here: www.oecd.org/tax/exchange-of-tax-information/convention-on-mutual-administrative-assistance-in-tax-matters.htm. Mauritius also has bilateral agreements in force with Australia, Bangladesh, Barbados, Belgium, Botswana, Cabo Verde, China (People's Republic of), Congo, Croatia, Cyprus, Egypt, Estonia, Eswatini, France, Germany, Ghana, Guernsey, India, Italy, Jersey, Kuwait, Lesotho, Luxembourg, Madagascar, Malaysia, Malta, Monaco, Mozambique, Namibia, Nepal, Oman, Pakistan, Qatar, Rwanda, Seychelles, Singapore, South Africa, Sri Lanka, Sweden, Thailand, Tunisia, Uganda, United Arab Emirates, United Kingdom, Zimbabwe. In addition, Mauritius' TIEA with the United States permits for the spontaneous exchange of information.

[3] Innovation box.

Mexico

Mexico has met all aspects of the terms of reference (OECD, 2021[1]) (ToR) for the calendar year 2022 (year in review), and no recommendations are made.

Mexico can legally issue two types of rulings within the scope of the transparency framework.

In practice, Mexico issued rulings within the scope of the transparency framework as follows:

Type of ruling	Number of rulings
Past rulings	13
Future rulings in the period 1 April 2016 – 31 December 2016	1
Future rulings in the calendar year 2017	328
Future rulings in the calendar year 2018	294
Future rulings in the calendar year 2019	48
Future rulings in the calendar year 2020	44
Future rulings in the calendar year 2021	80
Future rulings in the year in review	119

No peer input was received in respect of the exchanges of information on rulings received from Mexico.

Information gathering process (ToR I.A)

822. Mexico can legally issue the following two types of rulings within the scope of the transparency framework: (i) cross-border unilateral APAs and any other cross-border unilateral tax rulings (such as an advance tax ruling) covering transfer pricing or the application of transfer pricing principles and (ii) permanent establishment rulings.

823. For Mexico, past rulings are any tax rulings within scope that are issued either: (i) on or after 1 January 2014 but before 1 April 2016; or (ii) on or after 1 January 2010 but before 1 January 2014, provided they were still in effect as at 1 January 2014. Future rulings are any tax rulings within scope that are issued on or after 1 April 2016.

824. In the prior years' peer review reports, it was determined that Mexico's undertakings to identify past and future rulings and all potential exchange jurisdictions were sufficient to meet the minimum standard. In addition, it was determined that Mexico's review and supervision mechanism was sufficient to meet the minimum standard. Mexico's implementation remains unchanged, and therefore continues to meet the minimum standard.

825. Mexico has met all of the ToR for the information gathering process and no recommendations are made.

Exchange of information (ToR II.B)

826. Mexico has the necessary domestic legal basis to exchange information spontaneously. Mexico notes that there are no legal or practical impediments that prevent the spontaneous exchange of information on rulings as contemplated in the Action 5 minimum standard.

827. Mexico has international agreements permitting spontaneous exchange of information, including: (i) the *Multilateral Convention on Mutual Administrative Assistance in Tax Matters: Amended by the 2010 Protocol* (OECD/Council of Europe, 2011[2]) ("the Convention"), (ii) bilateral agreements in force with seven jurisdictions and (iii) tax information exchange agreements in force with three jurisdictions.[1]

828. For the year in review, the timeliness of exchanges is as follows:

Future rulings within the scope of the transparency framework	Number of exchanges transmitted within three months of the information becoming available to the competent authority or immediately after legal impediments have been lifted	Delayed exchanges		
		Number of exchanges transmitted later than three months of the information on rulings becoming available to the competent authority	Reasons for the delays	Any other comments
	55	119	See below	N/A

Follow-up requests received for exchange of the ruling	Number	Average time to provide response	Number of requests not answered
	0	N/A	0

829. Mexico indicates that the main reason for the delay is that a significant number of rulings was issued in the year in review, and that therefore, the timelines could not be met. Mexico also notes that more than 95% of these rulings needed to be exchanged with the United States, and that there has been coordination and communication between both authorities. Finally, Mexico indicates that it designed and implemented an IT solution to exchange information on rulings on a monthly basis, and that the issue has been resolved. Therefore, no recommendation is made at this stage.

830. In the prior years' peer review reports, it was determined that Mexico's process for the completion and exchange of templates were sufficient to meet the minimum standard. With respect to past rulings, no further action was required. Mexico's implementation in this regard remains unchanged and therefore continues to meet the minimum standard.

831. Mexico has the necessary legal basis for spontaneous exchange of information, a process for completing the templates in a timely way and has completed all exchanges. Mexico has met all of the ToR for the exchange of information process and no recommendations are made.

Statistics (ToR IV.D)

832. The statistics for the year in review are as follows:

Category of ruling	Number of exchanges	Jurisdictions exchanged with
Cross-border unilateral APAs and any other cross-border unilateral tax rulings (such as an advance tax ruling) covering transfer pricing or the application of transfer pricing principles	174	Barbados, Canada, China (People's Republic of), Denmark, Hong Kong (China), Korea, Luxembourg, Netherlands, Singapore, Spain, Switzerland, Türkiye, United States
Permanent establishment rulings	0	N/A
Total	174	

Matters related to intellectual property regimes (ToR I.A.1.3)

833. Mexico does not offer an intellectual property regime for which transparency requirements under the Action 5 Report (OECD, 2015[3]) were imposed.

Summary of recommendations on implementation of the transparency framework

Aspect of implementation of the transparency framework that should be improved	Recommendation for improvement
	No recommendations are made.

References

OECD (2021), *BEPS Action 5 on Harmful Tax Practices - Terms of Reference and Methodology for the Conduct of the Peer Reviews of the Action 5 Transparency Framework*, OECD Publishing, Paris, https://www.oecd.org/tax/beps/beps-action-5-harmful-tax-practices-peer-review-transparency-framework.pdf. [1]

OECD (2015), *Countering Harmful Tax Practices More Effectively, Taking into Account Transparency and Substance, Action 5 - 2015 Final Report*, OECD/G20 Base Erosion and Profit Shifting Project, OECD Publishing, Paris, https://doi.org/10.1787/9789264241190-en. [3]

OECD/Council of Europe (2011), *The Multilateral Convention on Mutual Administrative Assistance in Tax Matters: Amended by the 2010 Protocol*, OECD Publishing, Paris, https://doi.org/10.1787/9789264115606-en. [2]

Note

[1] Participating jurisdictions to the Convention are available here: www.oecd.org/tax/exchange-of-tax-information/convention-on-mutual-administrative-assistance-in-tax-matters.htm. Mexico also has bilateral agreements with Austria, Canada, Hong Kong (China), Russia, South Africa, Ukraine and the United States. In addition, Mexico has tax information exchange agreements permitting spontaneous exchange of information with Aruba, Canada and the United States.

Morocco

Morocco has met all aspects of the terms of reference (OECD, 2021[1]) (ToR) for the calendar year 2022 (year in review), and no recommendations are made.

Morocco can legally issue one type of rulings within the scope of the transparency framework.

In practice, Morocco issued rulings within the scope of the transparency framework as follows:

Type of ruling	Number of rulings
Future rulings in the calendar year 2019	0
Future rulings in the calendar year 2020	4
Future rulings in the calendar year 2021	0
Future rulings in the year in review	0

As no exchanges took place, no peer input was received in respect of the exchanges of information on rulings received from Morocco.

Information gathering process (ToR I.A)

834. Morocco can legally issue the following type of ruling within the scope of the transparency framework: cross-border unilateral APAs and any other cross-border unilateral tax rulings (such as an advance tax ruling) covering transfer pricing or the application of transfer pricing principles.

835. For Morocco, past rulings are any tax rulings issued prior to 1 September 2019. However, there is no obligation for Morocco to conduct spontaneous exchange information on past rulings. Future rulings are any tax rulings within scope that are issued on or after 1 September 2019.

836. In the prior years' peer review reports, it was determined that Morocco's undertakings to identify past and future rulings and all potential exchange jurisdictions were sufficient to meet the minimum standard. In addition, it was determined that Morocco's review and supervision mechanism was sufficient to meet the minimum standard. Morocco's implementation remains unchanged, and therefore continues to meet the minimum standard.

837. Morocco has met all of the ToR for the information gathering process and no recommendations are made.

Exchange of information (ToR II.B)

838. Morocco has the necessary domestic legal basis to exchange information spontaneously. Morocco notes that there are no legal or practical impediments that prevent the spontaneous exchange of information on rulings as contemplated in the Action 5 minimum standard.

839. Morocco has international agreements permitting spontaneous exchange of information, including: (i) the *Multilateral Convention on Mutual Administrative Assistance in Tax Matters: Amended by the 2010 Protocol* (OECD/Council of Europe, 2011[2]) ("the Convention") and (ii) bilateral agreements in force with 64 jurisdictions.[1]

840. During the year in review, no exchanges were required to take place and no data on the timeliness of exchanges is reported.

841. In the prior year's peer review report, it was determined that Morocco's process for the completion and exchange of templates were sufficient to meet the minimum standard. With respect to past rulings, no action was required. Morocco's implementation in this regard remains unchanged and therefore continues to meet the minimum standard.

842. Morocco has the necessary legal basis for spontaneous exchange of information, a process for completing the templates in a timely way and has completed all exchanges. Morocco has met all of the ToR for the exchange of information process and no recommendations are made.

Statistics (ToR IV.D)

843. As no rulings were issued, no statistics can be reported.

Matters related to intellectual property regimes (ToR I.A.1.3)

844. Morocco does not offer an intellectual property regime for which transparency requirements under the Action 5 Report (OECD, 2015[3]) were imposed.

Summary of recommendations on implementation of the transparency framework

Aspect of implementation of the transparency framework that should be improved	Recommendation for improvement
	No recommendations are made.

References

OECD (2021), *BEPS Action 5 on Harmful Tax Practices - Terms of Reference and Methodology for the Conduct of the Peer Reviews of the Action 5 Transparency Framework*, OECD Publishing, Paris, https://www.oecd.org/tax/beps/beps-action-5-harmful-tax-practices-peer-review-transparency-framework.pdf. [1]

OECD (2015), *Countering Harmful Tax Practices More Effectively, Taking into Account Transparency and Substance, Action 5 - 2015 Final Report*, OECD/G20 Base Erosion and Profit Shifting Project, OECD Publishing, Paris, https://doi.org/10.1787/9789264241190-en. [3]

OECD/Council of Europe (2011), *The Multilateral Convention on Mutual Administrative Assistance in Tax Matters: Amended by the 2010 Protocol*, OECD Publishing, Paris, https://doi.org/10.1787/9789264115606-en. [2]

Note

[1] Participating jurisdictions to the Convention are available here: www.oecd.org/tax/exchange-of-tax-information/convention-on-mutual-administrative-assistance-in-tax-matters.htm. Morocco also has bilateral agreements with Arab Maghreb Union jurisdictions and Austria, Bahrain, Belgium, Benin, Bulgaria, Cameroon, Canada, China (People's Republic of), Côte d'Ivoire, Croatia, Czechia, Denmark, Egypt, Ethiopia, Finland, France, Gabon, Germany, Ghana, Greece, Guinea, Hungary, India, Indonesia, Ireland, Italy, Japan, Jordan, Korea, Kuwait, Latvia, Lebanon, Luxembourg, Madagascar, Malaysia, Mali, Malta, Netherlands, North Macedonia, Norway, Oman, Pakistan, Poland, Portugal, Qatar, Romania, Russia, Rwanda, Saudi Arabia, Senegal, Serbia, Singapore, Slovenia, Spain, Syrian Arab Republic, Türkiye, Ukraine, United Arab Emirates, United Kingdom, United States, Viet Nam, Zambia.

Namibia

Namibia is taking steps to implement the aspects of the terms of reference (OECD, 2021[1]) (ToR) for the transparency framework and to commence administrative preparations to ensure that it establishes an information gathering process (ToR I.A) and that information on rulings will be identified and exchanged in a timely manner (ToR II.B). Namibia receives two recommendations on these points for the year in review.

In the prior year report, Namibia had received the same recommendations. As they have not been addressed, the recommendations remain in place.

Namibia can legally issue four types of rulings within the scope of the transparency framework.

In practice, Namibia issued no rulings within the scope of the transparency framework.

As no exchanges took place, no peer input was received in respect of the exchanges of information on rulings received from Namibia.

Information gathering process (ToR I.A)

845. Namibia can legally issue the following four types of rulings within the scope of the transparency framework: (i) cross-border unilateral APAs and any other cross-border unilateral tax rulings (such as an advance tax ruling) covering transfer pricing or the application of transfer pricing principles; (ii) rulings providing for unilateral downward adjustments; (iii) permanent establishment rulings; and (iv) related party conduit rulings.

Past rulings (ToR I.A.1.1, I.A.1.2, I.A.2.1, I.A.2.2)

846. For Namibia, past rulings are any tax rulings issued prior to 1 March 2020. However, there is no obligation for Namibia to conduct spontaneous exchange information on past rulings.

Future rulings (ToR I.A.1.1, I.A.1.2, I.A.2.1)

847. For Namibia, future rulings are any tax rulings within scope that are issued on or after 1 March 2020.

848. No rulings were issued by Namibia during the future rulings period in the year in review. However, in the prior year's and 2020 peer review report, it was determined that Namibia did not yet have processes in place to ensure the implementation of the obligations relating to the transparency framework. During year 2021, Namibia started to develop a process, but did not yet implement such a process, and therefore the recommendation remains in place.

Review and supervision (ToR I.A.3)

849. In the prior year's peer review report, it was determined that Namibia did not yet have a review and supervision mechanism under the transparency framework. During the year in review, Namibia did not implement such a review and supervision mechanism, and therefore the recommendation remains in place.

Conclusion on section A

850. Namibia is recommended to ensure that it has put in place an effective information gathering process to identify all relevant future rulings and all potential exchange jurisdictions and to implement a review and supervision mechanism, as soon as possible (ToR I.A).

Exchange of information (ToR II.B)

851. In the prior years' peer review reports, it was noted that although Namibia does not have an explicit domestic legal basis to exchange information spontaneously, international agreements can override secrecy provisions prohibiting the exchange of information. Therefore, Namibia will be able to exchange information on rulings with jurisdictions that are treaty partners. Furthermore, there are no legal or practical impediments that prevent the spontaneous exchange of information on rulings as contemplated in the Action 5 minimum standard.

852. Namibia has international agreements permitting spontaneous exchange of information, including: (i) the *Multilateral Convention on Mutual Administrative Assistance in Tax Matters: Amended by the 2010 Protocol* (OECD/Council of Europe, 2011[2]) ("the Convention") which entered into force in 2021, and (ii) bilateral agreements in force with 11 jurisdictions.[1]

Completion and exchange of templates (ToR II.B.3, II.B.4, II.B.5, II.B.6, II.B.7)

853. In the prior year's peer review report, it was determined that Namibia did not yet have a process to complete the templates on all relevant rulings, to make them available to the Competent Authority for exchange of information, and to exchange them with relevant jurisdictions. During the prior year, the

Exchange of Information Unit within the Namibia Revenue Agency has been set up and Namibia started to develop a process for the spontaneous exchange of information on rulings. However, as Namibia is still in a process of implementing a process for exchange of information, the previous years' recommendation remains in place.

854. During the year in review, no exchanges were required to take place and no data on the timeliness of exchanges is reported.

Conclusion on section B

855. Namibia is recommended to develop a process to complete the templates for all relevant rulings and to ensure that the exchanges of information on rulings occur in accordance with the form and timelines under the transparency framework going forward (ToR II.B).

Statistics (ToR IV.D)

856. As no rulings were issued, no statistics can be reported.

Matters related to intellectual property regimes (ToR I.A.1.3)

857. Namibia does not offer an intellectual property regime for which transparency requirements under the Action 5 Report (OECD, 2015[3]) were imposed.

Summary of recommendations on implementation of the transparency framework

Aspect of implementation of the transparency framework that should be improved	Recommendation for improvement
Namibia does not yet have the necessary information gathering process in place.	Namibia is recommended to ensure that it has put in place an effective information gathering process to identify all relevant past and future rulings and all potential exchange jurisdictions and to implement a review and supervision mechanism, as soon as possible. This recommendation remains unchanged since the 2020 and 2021 peer reviews.
Namibia does not yet have a process to complete the templates on relevant rulings, to make them available to the Competent Authority for exchange of information, and to exchange them with relevant jurisdictions.	Namibia is recommended to develop a process to complete the templates for all relevant rulings and to ensure that the exchanges of information on rulings occur in accordance with the form and timelines under the transparency framework going forward. This recommendation remains unchanged since the 2020 and 2021 peer reviews.

References

OECD (2021), *BEPS Action 5 on Harmful Tax Practices - Terms of Reference and Methodology for the Conduct of the Peer Reviews of the Action 5 Transparency Framework*, OECD Publishing, Paris, https://www.oecd.org/tax/beps/beps-action-5-harmful-tax-practices-peer-review-transparency-framework.pdf. [1]

OECD (2015), *Countering Harmful Tax Practices More Effectively, Taking into Account Transparency and Substance, Action 5 - 2015 Final Report*, OECD/G20 Base Erosion and Profit Shifting Project, OECD Publishing, Paris, https://doi.org/10.1787/9789264241190-en. [3]

OECD/Council of Europe (2011), *The Multilateral Convention on Mutual Administrative Assistance in Tax Matters: Amended by the 2010 Protocol*, OECD Publishing, Paris, https://doi.org/10.1787/9789264115606-en. [2]

Note

[1] Participating jurisdictions to the Convention are available here: www.oecd.org/tax/exchange-of-tax-information/convention-on-mutual-administrative-assistance-in-tax-matters.htm. Namibia also has bilateral agreements with Botswana, France, Germany, India, Malaysia, Mauritius, Romania, Russia, South Africa, Sweden, United Kingdom.

Netherlands

The Netherlands has met all aspects of the terms of reference (OECD, 2021[1]) (ToR) for the calendar year 2022 (year in review), and no recommendations are made.

In the prior year report, as well as the 2020 peer review report, the Netherlands had received a recommendation regarding the timely provision of information on rulings to the Competent Authority for exchange of information (ToR II.B.5). The Netherlands has resolved this issue and therefore the recommendation is now removed.

The Netherlands can legally issue four types of rulings within the scope of the transparency framework.

In practice, The Netherlands issued rulings within the scope of the transparency framework as follows:

Type of ruling	Number of rulings
Past rulings	2 206
Future rulings in the period 1 April 2016 – 31 December 2016	297
Future rulings in the calendar year 2017	214
Future rulings in the calendar year 2018	272
Future rulings in the calendar year 2019	403
Future rulings in the calendar year 2020	263
Future rulings in the calendar year 2021	299
Future rulings in the year in review	234

Peer input was received from eleven jurisdictions in respect of the exchanges of information on rulings received from the Netherlands. The input was generally positive, noting that the exchanges on rulings were received in a timely manner and the information was in correct format. However, one peer indicated that the information was not presented in a correct format.

Information gathering process (ToR I.A)

858. The Netherlands can legally issue the following four types of rulings within the scope of the transparency framework: (i) preferential regimes;[1] (ii) cross-border unilateral APAs and any other cross-border unilateral tax rulings (such as an advance tax ruling) covering transfer pricing or the application of transfer pricing principles; (iii) rulings providing for unilateral downward adjustments; (iv) permanent establishment rulings.

859. For the Netherlands, past rulings are any tax rulings within scope that are issued either: (i) on or after 1 January 2014 but before 1 April 2016; or (ii) on or after 1 January 2010 but before 1 January 2014, provided they were still in effect as at 1 January 2014. Future rulings are any tax rulings within scope that are issued on or after 1 April 2016.

860. In the prior years' peer review reports, it was determined that the Netherlands' undertakings to identify past and future rulings and all potential exchange jurisdictions were sufficient to meet the minimum standard. In addition, it was determined that the Netherlands' review and supervision mechanism was sufficient to meet the minimum standard. The Netherlands' implementation remains unchanged, and therefore continues to meet the minimum standard.

861. The Netherlands has met all of the ToR for the information gathering process and no recommendations are made.

Exchange of information (ToR II.B)

Legal basis for spontaneous exchange of information (ToR II.B.1, II.B.2)

862. The Netherlands has the necessary domestic legal basis to exchange information spontaneously. The Netherlands notes that there are no legal or practical impediments that prevent the spontaneous exchange of information on rulings as contemplated in the Action 5 minimum standard.

863. The Netherlands has international agreements permitting spontaneous exchange of information, including: (i) the *Multilateral Convention on Mutual Administrative Assistance in Tax Matters: Amended by the 2010 Protocol* (OECD/Council of Europe, 2011[2]) ("the Convention"), (ii) the Directive 2011/16/EU with all other European Union Member States and (iii) bilateral agreements in force with 95 jurisdictions.[2]

Completion and exchange of templates (ToR II.B.3, II.B.4, II.B.5, II.B.6, II.B.7)

864. In the prior years' peer review reports, it was determined that the Netherlands' process for the completion and exchange of templates met all the ToR, except for the timely provision of information on rulings to the competent authority for exchange of information (ToR II.B.5). Therefore, the Netherlands was recommended to ensure that information is made available to the competent authority without undue delay.

865. The Netherlands indicates that it has taken steps to address this issue. As of 1 January 2022, a ruling can only be issued once all information to complete the Annex C template is available. In addition, all templates need to be sent to the Competent Authority every two months. The Netherlands has not reported any delays for the year in review and therefore, the recommendation is now removed.

866. For the year in review, the timeliness of exchanges is as follows:

Future rulings within the scope of the transparency framework	Number of exchanges transmitted within three months of the information becoming available to the competent authority or immediately after legal impediments have been lifted	Delayed exchanges		
		Number of exchanges transmitted later than three months of the information on rulings becoming available to the competent authority	Reasons for the delays	Any other comments
	829	0	N/A	N/A

Follow-up requests received for exchange of the ruling	Number	Average time to provide response	Number of requests not answered
	0	N/A	N/A

Conclusion on section B

867. The Netherlands has the necessary legal basis for spontaneous exchange of information, a process for completing the templates in a timely way and has completed all exchanges. The Netherlands has met all of the ToR for the exchange of information process and no recommendations are made.

Statistics (ToR IV.D)

868. The statistics for the year in review are as follows:

Category of ruling	Number of exchanges	Jurisdictions exchanged with
Ruling related to a preferential regime	607	Argentina, Aruba, Australia, Bangladesh, Belgium, Bosnia and Herzegovina, Brazil, Brunei Darussalam, Canada, Chile, China (People's Republic of), Curaçao, Colombia, Costa Rica, Czechia, Denmark, Dominican Republic, Ecuador, Egypt, El Salvador, Ethiopia, Finland, France, Germany, Ghana, Hong Kong (China), Iceland, India, Indonesia, Israel, Italy, Jamaica, Japan, Jersey, Jordan, Kazakhstan, Kenya, Korea, Lebanon, Lithuania, Malaysia, Mauritius, Mexico, Moldova, Morocco, New Zealand, Nigeria, North Macedonia, Norway, Oman, Pakistan, Panama, Peru, Philippines, Poland, Portugal, Puerto Rico, Saint Lucia, Saudi Arabia, Serbia, Singapore, South Africa, Sri Lanka, Suriname, Sweden, Switzerland, Chinese Taipei, Thailand, Tunisia, Türkiye, Uganda, United Kingdom, United States, Uruguay, Viet Nam, Zambia
Cross-border unilateral APAs and any other cross-border unilateral tax rulings (such as an advance tax ruling) covering transfer pricing or the application of transfer pricing principles	210	Argentina, Australia, Bosnia and Herzegovina, Brazil, Canada, Chile, China (People's Republic of), Colombia, Costa Rica, Dominican Republic, Ecuador, Egypt, Ghana, Guatemala, Hong Kong (China), Iceland, India, Indonesia, Israel, Japan, Jordan, Kazakhstan, Kenya, Korea, Malaysia, Mauritius, Mexico,

		Monaco, Morocco, New Zealand, Nigeria, Norway, Panama, Peru, Philippines, Puerto Rico, Saudi Arabia, Singapore, South Africa, Sri Lanka, Switzerland, Chinese Taipei, Thailand, Tunisia, Türkiye, United Kingdom, United States, Uruguay, Viet Nam
Cross-border rulings providing for a unilateral downward adjustment to the taxpayer's taxable profits that is not directly reflected in the taxpayer's financial / commercial accounts	0[3]	N/A
Permanent establishment rulings	12	Curaçao, Singapore, Switzerland, United Kingdom, United States
Related party conduit rulings	0	N/A
IP regimes: total exchanges on taxpayers benefitting from the third category of IP assets, new entrants benefitting from grandfathered IP regimes; and taxpayers making use of the option to treat the nexus ratio as a rebuttable presumption	Included in 'rulings related to a preferential regime'	N/A
Total	829	

Matters related to intellectual property regimes (ToR I.A.1.3)

869. In the prior years' peer review reports, it was determined that the Netherlands' information gathering and exchange of information processes for matters related to intellectual property regimes[4] were sufficient to meet the minimum standard. The Netherlands' implementation in this regard remains unchanged and therefore continues to meet the minimum standard.

Summary of recommendations on implementation of the transparency framework

Aspect of implementation of the transparency framework that should be improved	Recommendation for improvement
	No recommendations are made.

References

OECD (2021), *BEPS Action 5 on Harmful Tax Practices - Terms of Reference and Methodology for the Conduct of the Peer Reviews of the Action 5 Transparency Framework*, OECD Publishing, Paris, https://www.oecd.org/tax/beps/beps-action-5-harmful-tax-practices-peer-review-transparency-framework.pdf. [1]

OECD (2015), *Countering Harmful Tax Practices More Effectively, Taking into Account Transparency and Substance, Action 5 - 2015 Final Report*, OECD/G20 Base Erosion and Profit Shifting Project, OECD Publishing, Paris, https://doi.org/10.1787/9789264241190-en. [3]

OECD/Council of Europe (2011), *The Multilateral Convention on Mutual Administrative Assistance in Tax Matters: Amended by the 2010 Protocol*, OECD Publishing, Paris, https://doi.org/10.1787/9789264115606-en. [2]

Notes

[1] 1) Innovation box and 2) International shipping.

[2] Participating jurisdictions to the Convention are available here: www.oecd.org/tax/exchange-of-tax-information/convention-on-mutual-administrative-assistance-in-tax-matters.htm. The Netherlands also has bilateral agreements with Albania, Algeria, Argentina, Armenia, Australia, Austria, Azerbaijan, Bahrain, Bangladesh, Barbados, Belarus, Belgium, Bermuda, Bosnia and Herzegovina, Brazil, Bulgaria, Canada, China (People's Republic of), Croatia, Curaçao, Czechia, Denmark, Egypt, Estonia, Ethiopia, Finland, France, Georgia, Germany, Ghana, Greece, Hong Kong (China), Hungary, Iceland, India, Indonesia, Ireland, Israel, Italy, Japan, Jordan, Kazakhstan, Kenya, Korea, Kosovo, Kuwait, Latvia, Lithuania, Luxembourg, Malaysia, Malta, Mexico, Moldova, Montenegro, Morocco, New Zealand, Nigeria, North Macedonia, Norway, Oman, Pakistan, Panama, Philippines, Poland, Portugal, Qatar, Romania, Russia, Sint Maarten, Saudi Arabia, Serbia, Singapore, Slovak Republic, Slovenia, South Africa, Spain, Sri Lanka, Suriname, Sweden, Switzerland, Chinese Taipei, Tajikistan, Thailand, Tunisia, Türkiye, Uganda, Ukraine, United Arab Emirates, United Kingdom, United States, Uzbekistan, Venezuela, Viet Nam, Zambia and Zimbabwe.

[3] From 1 July 2019, a new ruling policy is in place which no longer allows rulings with regard to unilateral downward adjustments to be concluded.

[4] Innovation box.

New Zealand

New Zealand has met all aspects of the terms of reference (OECD, 2021[1]) (ToR) for the calendar year 2022 (year in review), and no recommendations are made.

New Zealand can legally issue five types of rulings within the scope of the transparency framework.

In practice, New Zealand issued rulings within the scope of the transparency framework as follows:

Type of ruling	Number of rulings
Past rulings	69
Future rulings in the period 1 April 2016 – 31 December 2016	14
Future rulings in the calendar year 2017	15
Future rulings in the calendar year 2018	8
Future rulings in the calendar year 2019	21
Future rulings in the calendar year 2020	18
Future rulings in the calendar year 2021	20
Future rulings in the year in review	29

Peer input was received from one jurisdiction in respect of the exchanges of information on rulings received from New Zealand. The input was positive, noting that information was complete, in a correct format and received in a timely manner.

Information gathering process (ToR I.A)

870. New Zealand can legally issue five types of rulings within the scope of the transparency framework, but in practice issues the three following types of rulings within the scope of the transparency framework: (i) cross-border unilateral APAs and any other cross-border unilateral tax rulings (such as an advance tax ruling) covering transfer pricing or the application of transfer pricing principles; (ii) permanent establishment rulings; and (iii) related party conduit rulings.

871. For New Zealand, past rulings are any tax rulings within scope that are issued either: (i) on or after 1 January 2014 but before 1 April 2016; or (ii) on or after 1 January 2010 but before 1 January 2014, provided they were still in effect as at 1 January 2014. Future rulings are any tax rulings within scope that are issued on or after 1 April 2016.

872. In the prior years' peer review reports, it was determined that New Zealand's undertakings to identify past and future rulings and all potential exchange jurisdictions were sufficient to meet the minimum standard. In addition, it was determined that New Zealand's review and supervision mechanism was sufficient to meet the minimum standard. New Zealand's implementation remains unchanged, and therefore continues to meet the minimum standard.

873. New Zealand has met all of the ToR for the information gathering process and no recommendations are made.

Exchange of information (ToR II.B)

874. New Zealand has the necessary domestic legal basis to exchange information spontaneously. New Zealand notes that there are no legal or practical impediments that prevent the spontaneous exchange of information on rulings as contemplated in the Action 5 minimum standard.

875. New Zealand has international agreements permitting spontaneous exchange of information, including: (i) the *Multilateral Convention on Mutual Administrative Assistance in Tax Matters: Amended by the 2010 Protocol* (OECD/Council of Europe, 2011[2]) ("the Convention") and (ii) bilateral agreements in force with 40 jurisdictions.[1]

876. For the year in review, the timeliness of exchanges is as follows:

Future rulings within the scope of the transparency framework	Number of exchanges transmitted within three months of the information becoming available to the competent authority or immediately after legal impediments have been lifted	Delayed exchanges		
		Number of exchanges transmitted later than three months of the information on rulings becoming available to the competent authority	Reasons for the delays	Any other comments
	75	0	N/A	N/A

Follow-up requests received for exchange of the ruling	Number	Average time to provide response	Number of requests not answered
	0	N/A	N/A

877. In the prior years' peer review reports, it was determined that New Zealand's process for the completion and exchange of templates were sufficient to meet the minimum standard. With respect to past rulings, no further action was required. New Zealand's implementation in this regard remains unchanged and therefore continues to meet the minimum standard.

878. New Zealand has the necessary legal basis for spontaneous exchange of information, a process for completing the templates in a timely way and has completed all exchanges. New Zealand has met all of the ToR for the exchange of information process and no recommendations are made.

Statistics (ToR IV.D)

879. The statistics for the year in review are as follows:

Category of ruling	Number of exchanges	Jurisdictions exchanged with
Ruling related to a preferential regime	0	N/A
Cross-border unilateral APAs and any other cross-border unilateral tax rulings (such as an advance tax ruling) covering transfer pricing or the application of transfer pricing principles	65	Australia, Belgium, Canada, China (People's Republic of), France, Germany, India, Japan, Korea, Malaysia, Mexico, Netherlands, Philippines, Singapore, Spain, Sweden, Switzerland, United Kingdom, United States, Viet Nam
Cross-border rulings providing for a unilateral downward adjustment to the taxpayer's taxable profits that is not directly reflected in the taxpayer's financial / commercial accounts	0	N/A
Permanent establishment rulings	10	Australia, Jersey, Netherlands, Singapore, United Kingdom, United States
Related party conduit rulings	0	N/A
Total	75	

Matters related to intellectual property regimes (ToR I.A.1.3)

880. New Zealand does not offer an intellectual property regime for which transparency requirements under the Action 5 Report (OECD, 2015[3]) were imposed.

Summary of recommendations on implementation of the transparency framework

Aspect of implementation of the transparency framework that should be improved	Recommendation for improvement
	No recommendations are made.

References

OECD (2021), *BEPS Action 5 on Harmful Tax Practices - Terms of Reference and Methodology for the Conduct of the Peer Reviews of the Action 5 Transparency Framework*, OECD Publishing, Paris, https://www.oecd.org/tax/beps/beps-action-5-harmful-tax-practices-peer-review-transparency-framework.pdf. [1]

OECD (2015), *Countering Harmful Tax Practices More Effectively, Taking into Account Transparency and Substance, Action 5 - 2015 Final Report*, OECD/G20 Base Erosion and Profit Shifting Project, OECD Publishing, Paris, https://doi.org/10.1787/9789264241190-en. [3]

OECD/Council of Europe (2011), *The Multilateral Convention on Mutual Administrative Assistance in Tax Matters: Amended by the 2010 Protocol*, OECD Publishing, Paris, https://doi.org/10.1787/9789264115606-en. [2]

Note

[1] Participating jurisdictions to the Convention are available here: www.oecd.org/tax/exchange-of-tax-information/convention-on-mutual-administrative-assistance-in-tax-matters.htm. New Zealand also has bilateral agreements with Australia, Austria, Belgium, Canada, Chile, China (People's Republic of), Czechia, Denmark, Fiji, Finland, France, Germany, Hong Kong (China), India, Indonesia, Ireland, Italy, Japan, Korea, Malaysia, Mexico, Netherlands, Norway, Papua New Guinea, Philippines, Poland, Russia, Samoa, Singapore, South Africa, Spain, Sweden, Switzerland, Chinese Taipei, Thailand, Türkiye, United Arab Emirates, United Kingdom, United States, Viet Nam.

Nigeria

Nigeria is taking steps to implement the aspects of the terms of reference (OECD, 2021[1]) (ToR) for the transparency framework and to commence administrative preparations to ensure that it establishes an information gathering process (ToR I.A) and information on rulings will be identified and exchanged in a timely manner (ToR II.B). Nigeria receives two recommendations on these points for the year in review.

In the prior year report, Nigeria had received the same two recommendations. As they have not been addressed, the recommendations remain in place.

Nigeria can legally issue four types of rulings within the scope of the transparency framework.

In practice, Nigeria issued rulings within the scope of the transparency framework. However, as Nigeria does not yet have administrative processes in place to identify the relevant rulings, it is unknown how many rulings in scope of the transparency framework have been issued.

As no exchanges took place, no peer input was received in respect of the exchanges of information on rulings received from Nigeria.

Information gathering process (ToR I.A)

881. Nigeria can legally issue the following four types of rulings within the scope of the transparency framework: (i) preferential regimes;[1] (ii) rulings providing for unilateral downward adjustments; (iii) permanent establishment rulings; and (iv) related party conduit rulings.

Past rulings (ToR I.A.1.1, I.A.1.2, I.A.2.1, I.A.2.2)

882. For Nigeria, past rulings are any tax rulings within scope that are issued either (i) on or after 1 January 2015 but before 1 April 2017; and (ii) on or after 1 January 2012 but before 1 January 2015, provided they were still in effect as at 1 January 2015.

883. Nigeria confirms that no past rulings have been issued, as its administrative framework for issuing rulings only took effect at a later stage. Therefore, this section is not assessed.

Future rulings (ToR I.A.1.1, I.A.1.2, I.A.2.1)

884. For Nigeria, future rulings are any tax rulings within scope that are issued on or after 1 April 2017.

885. Nigeria indicates that there are not yet processes in place to ensure the implementation of the obligations relating to the transparency framework. However, Nigeria notes that it is currently in the process of putting in place the administrative framework which would enable identifying and keeping track of the relevant future rulings.

Review and supervision (ToR I.A.3)

886. In the year of review, Nigeria did not yet have a review and supervision mechanism under the transparency framework. However, Nigeria notes that it is is currently establishing an administrative framework which ensures an efficient review and supervision mechanism.

Conclusion on section A

887. As Nigeria has not yet completed their process on establishing an administrative framework, Nigeria is recommended to ensure that it has put in place an effective information gathering process to identify all relevant future rulings and all potential exchange jurisdictions and to implement a review and supervision mechanism, as soon as possible (ToR I.A).

Exchange of information (ToR II.B)

Legal basis for spontaneous exchange of information (ToR II.B.1, II.B.2)

888. Nigeria has the necessary domestic legal basis to exchange information spontaneously. Nigeria notes that there are no legal or practical impediments that prevent the spontaneous exchange of information on rulings as contemplated in the Action 5 minimum standard.

889. Nigeria has international agreements permitting spontaneous exchange of information, including: (i) the *Multilateral Convention on Mutual Administrative Assistance in Tax Matters: Amended by the 2010 Protocol* (OECD/Council of Europe, 2011[2]) ("the Convention") and (ii) bilateral agreements in force with 15 jurisdictions.[2]

Completion and exchange of templates (ToR II.B.3, II.B.4, II.B.5, II.B.6, II.B.7)

890. Nigeria does not yet have a process to complete the templates on all relevant rulings, to make them available to the Competent Authority for exchange of information, and to exchange them with relevant jurisdictions. Nigeria is currently creating a process for making the information on rulings available to the competent authority responsible for exchanges as well as taking action to ensure that the exchange

process is managed without undue delay. It notes that it will use its current exchange of information platform for the spontaneous exchange of information on rulings.

891. During the year in review, no exchanges took place and no data on the timeliness of exchanges is reported.

Conclusion on section B

892. As Nigeria has not yet completed their process on establishing administrative framework, Nigeria is recommended to develop a process to complete the templates for all relevant rulings and to ensure that the exchanges of information on rulings occur in accordance with the form and timelines under the transparency framework going forward (ToR II.B).

Statistics (ToR IV.D)

893. As there was no information on rulings exchanged by Nigeria for the year in review, no statistics can be reported.

Matters related to intellectual property regimes (ToR I.A.1.3)

894. Nigeria does not offer an intellectual property regime for which transparency requirements under the Action 5 Report (OECD, 2015[3]) were imposed.

Summary of recommendations on implementation of the transparency framework

Aspect of implementation of the transparency framework that should be improved	Recommendation for improvement
Nigeria does not yet have the necessary information gathering process in place. Nigeria is currently in the process of putting in place the administrative framework which would enable identifying and keeping track on the relevant future rulings as well as ensuring efficient review and supervision mechanism. As the process has not yet been completed, the recommendation remains in place.	Nigeria is recommended to ensure that it has put in place an effective information gathering process to identify all relevant past and future rulings and all potential exchange jurisdictions and to implement a review and supervision mechanism, as soon as possible. This recommendation remains unchanged since the 2021 peer review report.
Nigeria does not yet have a process to complete the templates on relevant rulings, to make them available to the Competent Authority for exchange of information, and to exchange them with relevant jurisdictions. Nigeria is currently in the process of putting in place the administrative framework which ensures a process for making the information on rulings available to the competent authority. As the process has not yet been completed, the recommendation remains in place.	Nigeria is recommended to develop a process to complete the templates for all relevant rulings and to ensure that the exchanges of information on rulings occur in accordance with the form and timelines under the transparency framework going forward. This recommendation remains unchanged since the 2021 peer review report.

References

OECD (2021), *BEPS Action 5 on Harmful Tax Practices - Terms of Reference and Methodology for the Conduct of the Peer Reviews of the Action 5 Transparency Framework*, OECD Publishing, Paris, https://www.oecd.org/tax/beps/beps-action-5-harmful-tax-practices-peer-review-transparency-framework.pdf. [1]

OECD (2015), *Countering Harmful Tax Practices More Effectively, Taking into Account Transparency and Substance, Action 5 - 2015 Final Report*, OECD/G20 Base Erosion and Profit Shifting Project, OECD Publishing, Paris, https://doi.org/10.1787/9789264241190-en. [3]

OECD/Council of Europe (2011), *The Multilateral Convention on Mutual Administrative Assistance in Tax Matters: Amended by the 2010 Protocol*, OECD Publishing, Paris, https://doi.org/10.1787/9789264115606-en. [2]

Notes

[1] Free trade zones.

[2] Participating jurisdictions to the Convention are available here: www.oecd.org/tax/exchange-of-tax-information/convention-on-mutual-administrative-assistance-in-tax-matters.htm. Nigeria also has bilateral agreements with Belgium, Canada, China (People's Republic of), Czechia, France, Netherlands, Pakistan, Philippines, Romania, Slovak Republic, Spain, Sweden, Singapore, South Africa, and United Kingdom.

Norway

Norway has met all aspects of the terms of reference (OECD, 2021[1]) (ToR) for the calendar year 2022 (year in review), and no recommendations are made.

Norway can legally issue three types of rulings within the scope of the transparency framework.

In practice, Norway issued rulings within the scope of the transparency framework as follows:

Type of ruling	Number of rulings
Past rulings	1
Future rulings in the period 1 April 2016 – 31 December 2016	0
Future rulings in the calendar year 2017	1
Future rulings in the calendar year 2018	0
Future rulings in the calendar year 2019	0
Future rulings in the calendar year 2020	0
Future rulings in the calendar year 2021	0
Future rulings in the year in review	0

As no exchanges were required to take place, no peer input was received in respect of the exchanges of information on rulings received from Norway.

Information gathering process (ToR I.A)

895. Norway can legally issue the following three types of rulings within the scope of the transparency framework: (i) preferential regimes;[1] (ii) cross-border unilateral APAs covering transfer pricing or the application of transfer pricing principles in relation to realisation of natural gas for companies liable to tax under the Petroleum Tax Act; and (iii) related party conduit rulings.

896. For Norway, past rulings are any tax rulings within scope that are issued either: (i) on or after 1 January 2014 but before 1 April 2016; or (ii) on or after 1 January 2010 but before 1 January 2014, provided they were still in effect as at 1 January 2014. Future rulings are any tax rulings within scope that are issued on or after 1 April 2016.

897. In the prior years' peer review reports, it was determined that Norway's undertakings to identify past and future rulings and all potential exchange jurisdictions were sufficient to meet the minimum standard. In addition, it was determined that Norway's review and supervision mechanism was sufficient to meet the minimum standard. Norway's implementation remains unchanged, and therefore continues to meet the minimum standard.

898. Norway has met all of the ToR for the information gathering process and no recommendations are made.

Exchange of information (ToR II.B)

899. Norway has the necessary domestic legal basis to exchange information spontaneously. Norway notes that there are no legal or practical impediments that prevent the spontaneous exchange of information on rulings as contemplated in the Action 5 minimum standard.

900. Norway has international agreements permitting spontaneous exchange of information, including: (i) the *Multilateral Convention on Mutual Administrative Assistance in Tax Matters: Amended by the 2010 Protocol* (OECD/Council of Europe, 2011[2]) ("the Convention"), (ii) the Nordic Convention on Assistance in Tax Matters and (iii) bilateral agreements in force with 84 jurisdictions.[2]

901. During the year in review, no exchanges were required to take place and no data on the timeliness of exchanges is reported.

902. In the prior years' peer review reports, it was determined that Norway's process for the completion and exchange of templates were sufficient to meet the minimum standard. With respect to past rulings, no further action was required. Norway's implementation in this regard remains unchanged and therefore continues to meet the minimum standard.

903. Norway has the necessary legal basis for spontaneous exchange of information, a process for completing the templates in a timely way and has completed all exchanges. Norway has met all of the ToR for the exchange of information process and no recommendations are made.

Statistics (ToR IV.D)

904. As no rulings were issued, no statistics can be reported.

Matters related to intellectual property regimes (ToR I.A.1.3)

905. Norway does not offer an intellectual property regime for which transparency requirements under the Action 5 Report (OECD, 2015[3]) were imposed.

Summary of recommendations on implementation of the transparency framework

Aspect of implementation of the transparency framework that should be improved	Recommendation for improvement
	No recommendations are made.

References

OECD (2021), *BEPS Action 5 on Harmful Tax Practices - Terms of Reference and Methodology for the Conduct of the Peer Reviews of the Action 5 Transparency Framework*, OECD Publishing, Paris, https://www.oecd.org/tax/beps/beps-action-5-harmful-tax-practices-peer-review-transparency-framework.pdf. [1]

OECD (2015), *Countering Harmful Tax Practices More Effectively, Taking into Account Transparency and Substance, Action 5 - 2015 Final Report*, OECD/G20 Base Erosion and Profit Shifting Project, OECD Publishing, Paris, https://doi.org/10.1787/9789264241190-en. [3]

OECD/Council of Europe (2011), *The Multilateral Convention on Mutual Administrative Assistance in Tax Matters: Amended by the 2010 Protocol*, OECD Publishing, Paris, https://doi.org/10.1787/9789264115606-en. [2]

Notes

[1] International shipping.

[2] Participating jurisdictions to the Convention are available here: www.oecd.org/tax/exchange-of-tax-information/convention-on-mutual-administrative-assistance-in-tax-matters.htm. Parties to the Nordic Convention on Assistance in Tax Matters are Denmark, Faroe Islands, Finland, Iceland, Norway and Sweden. Norway also has bilateral agreements with Albania, Argentina, Australia, Austria, Azerbaijan, Bangladesh, Barbados, Belgium, Benin, Bonaire, Bosnia and Herzegovina, Brazil, Bulgaria, Canada, Chile, China (People's Republic of), Croatia, Curaçao, Cyprus, Czechia, Egypt, Estonia, France, Gambia, Georgia, Germany, Greece, Hungary, India, Indonesia, Ireland, Israel, Italy, Ivory Coast, Jamaica, Japan, Kazakhstan, Kenya, Korea, Latvia, Lithuania, Luxembourg, Malawi, Malaysia, Malta, Mexico, Montenegro, Morocco, Nepal, Netherlands, New Zealand, North Macedonia, Pakistan, Philippines, Poland, Portugal, Qatar, Romania, Russia, Saba, Senegal, Serbia, Sierra Leone, Singapore, Saint Eustatius, Sint Maarten, Slovak Republic, Slovenia, South Africa, Spain, Sri Lanka, Switzerland, Tanzania, Thailand, Tunisia, Türkiye, Uganda, Ukraine, United Kingdom, United States, Venezuela, Viet Nam, Zambia and Zimbabwe.

Pakistan

Pakistan is taking steps to implement the aspects of the terms of reference (OECD, 2021[1]) (ToR) for the transparency framework and to commence administrative preparations to ensure that it establishes an information gathering process (ToR I.A) and information on rulings will be identified and exchanged in a timely manner (ToR II.B). Pakistan receives two recommendations on these points for the year in review.

In the prior year report, Pakistan had received the same two recommendations. As they had not been fully addressed, the recommendations remain in place.

Pakistan can legally issue five types of rulings within the scope of the transparency framework.

In practice, Pakistan issued rulings within the scope of the transparency framework as follows:

Type of ruling	Number of rulings
Past rulings	0
Future rulings in the period 1 April 2017 – 31 December 2017	0
Future rulings in the calendar year 2018	1
Future rulings in the calendar year 2019	0
Future rulings in the calendar year 2020	0
Future rulings in the calendar year 2021	0
Future rulings in the year in review	0

As no exchanges took place, no peer input was received in respect of the exchanges of information on rulings received from Pakistan.

Information gathering process (ToR I.A)

906. Pakistan can legally issue the following five types of rulings within the scope of the transparency framework: (i) preferential regimes;[1] (ii) cross-border unilateral APAs and any other cross-border unilateral tax rulings (such as an advance tax ruling) covering transfer pricing or the application of transfer pricing principles; (iii) rulings providing for unilateral downward adjustments; (iv) permanent establishment rulings; and (v) related party conduit rulings.

Past rulings (ToR I.A.1.1, I.A.1.2, I.A.2.1, I.A.2.2)

907. For Pakistan, past rulings are any tax rulings within scope that are issued either (i) on or after 1 January 2015 but before 1 April 2017; and (ii) on or after 1 January 2012 but before 1 January 2015, provided they were still in effect as at 1 January 2015.

908. Pakistan confirms that no past rulings have been issued. Therefore, Pakistan is not required to ensure the implementation of the obligations relating to the transparency framework for past rulings.

Future rulings (ToR I.A.1.1, I.A.1.2, I.A.2.1)

909. For Pakistan, future rulings are any tax rulings within scope that are issued on or after 1 April 2017.

910. Pakistan can issue future rulings based on Section 206A of the Income Tax Ordinance 2001 and Section 231A of the Income Tax Rules 2002. There is a prescribed application form included in the Schedule to Section 231A of the Income Tax Rules 2002. The rulings that have been issued so far are available on the website of the Federal Board of Revenue.[2] The taxpayer can apply for a ruling to the Advance Ruling Committee, which is chaired by the Federal Board of Revenue.

911. Pakistan is currently taking steps to put a process in place to ensure the implementation of the obligations relating to the transparency framework.

Review and supervision (ToR I.A.3)

912. Pakistan did not yet have a review and supervision mechanism under the transparency framework for the year in review.

913. Pakistan is recommended to ensure that it has put in place an effective information gathering process to identify all relevant future rulings and all potential exchange jurisdictions and to implement a review and supervision mechanism, as soon as possible (ToR I.A).

Exchange of information (ToR II.B)

Legal basis for spontaneous exchange of information (ToR II.B.1, II.B.2)

914. Pakistan has the necessary domestic legal basis to exchange information spontaneously. Pakistan notes that there are no legal or practical impediments that prevent the spontaneous exchange of information on rulings as contemplated in the Action 5 minimum standard.

915. Pakistan has international agreements permitting spontaneous exchange of information, including: (i) the *Multilateral Convention on Mutual Administrative Assistance in Tax Matters: Amended by the 2010 Protocol* (OECD/Council of Europe, 2011[2]) ("the Convention") and (ii) bilateral agreements in force with 66 jurisdictions.[3]

Completion and exchange of templates (ToR II.B.3, II.B.4, II.B.5, II.B.6, II.B.7)

916. Pakistan is currently taking steps to put a process in place to complete the templates on all relevant rulings, to make them available to the Competent Authority for exchange of information, and to exchange them with relevant jurisdictions.

917. During the year in review, no exchanges took place and no data on the timeliness of exchanges is reported.

Conclusion on section B

918. Pakistan is recommended to develop a process to complete the templates for all relevant rulings and to ensure that the exchanges of information on rulings occur in accordance with the form and timelines under the transparency framework going forward (ToR II.B).

Statistics (ToR IV.D)

919. As there was no information on rulings exchanged by Pakistan for the year in review, no statistics can be reported.

Matters related to intellectual property regimes (ToR I.A.1.3)

920. Pakistan does not offer an intellectual property regime for which transparency requirements under the Action 5 Report (OECD, 2015[3]) were imposed.

Summary of recommendations on implementation of the transparency framework

Aspect of implementation of the transparency framework that should be improved	Recommendation for improvement
Pakistan is taking steps to put the necessary information gathering process in place.	Pakistan is recommended to ensure that it has put in place an effective information gathering process to identify all relevant past and future rulings and all potential exchange jurisdictions and to implement a review and supervision mechanism, as soon as possible. This recommendation remains unchanged since the prior year's peer review report.
Pakistan is taking steps to put a process in place to complete the templates on relevant rulings, to make them available to the Competent Authority for exchange of information, and to exchange them with relevant jurisdictions.	Pakistan is recommended to develop a process to complete the templates for all relevant rulings and to ensure that the exchanges of information on rulings occur in accordance with the form and timelines under the transparency framework going forward. This recommendation remains unchanged since the prior year's peer review report.

References

OECD (2021), *BEPS Action 5 on Harmful Tax Practices - Terms of Reference and Methodology for the Conduct of the Peer Reviews of the Action 5 Transparency Framework*, OECD Publishing, Paris, https://www.oecd.org/tax/beps/beps-action-5-harmful-tax-practices-peer-review-transparency-framework.pdf. [1]

OECD (2015), *Countering Harmful Tax Practices More Effectively, Taking into Account Transparency and Substance, Action 5 - 2015 Final Report*, OECD/G20 Base Erosion and Profit Shifting Project, OECD Publishing, Paris, https://doi.org/10.1787/9789264241190-en. [3]

OECD/Council of Europe (2011), *The Multilateral Convention on Mutual Administrative Assistance in Tax Matters: Amended by the 2010 Protocol*, OECD Publishing, Paris, https://doi.org/10.1787/9789264115606-en. [2]

Notes

[1] Export regime on IT.

[2] https://www.fbr.gov.pk/advance-ruling-issued/132245/157.

[3] Participating jurisdictions to the Convention are available here: www.oecd.org/tax/exchange-of-tax-information/convention-on-mutual-administrative-assistance-in-tax-matters.htm. Pakistan also has bilateral agreements with Austria, Azerbaijan, Bahrain, Bangladesh, Belarus, Belgium, Bosnia and Herzegovina, Brunei Darussalam, Bulgaria, Canada, China (People's Republic of), Czechia, Denmark, Egypt, Finland, France, Germany, Hong Kong (China), Hungary, Indonesia, Iran, Ireland, Italy, Japan, Jordan, Kazakhstan, Korea, Kuwait, Kyrgyzstan, Lebanon, Libya, Malaysia, Malta, Mauritius, Morocco, Nepal, Netherlands, Nigeria, Norway, Oman, Philippines, Poland, Portugal, Qatar, Romania, Saudi Arabia, Serbia, Singapore, South Africa, Spain, Sri Lanka, Sweden, Switzerland, Syria, Tajikistan, Thailand, Tunisia, Türkiye, Turkmenistan, Ukraine, United Arab Emirates, United Kingdom, United States, Uzbekistan, Viet Nam, and Yemen.

Peru

Peru has met all aspects of the terms of reference (OECD, 2021[1]) (ToR) for the calendar year 2022 (year in review), and no recommendations are made.

Peru can legally issue one type of rulings within the scope of the transparency framework.

In practice, Peru issued no rulings within the scope of the transparency framework.

As no exchanges were required to take place, no peer input was received in respect of the exchanges of information on rulings received from Peru.

Information gathering process (ToR I.A)

921. Peru can legally issue the following type of ruling within the scope of the transparency framework: cross-border unilateral APAs and any other cross-border unilateral tax rulings (such as an advance tax ruling) covering transfer pricing or the application of transfer pricing principles.[1]

922. For Peru, past rulings are any tax rulings within scope that are issued either: (i) on or after 1 January 2015 but before 1 September 2017; or (ii) on or after 1 January 2012 but before 1 January 2015, provided they were still in effect as at 1 January 2015. Future rulings are any tax rulings within scope that are issued on or after 1 September 2017.

923. In the prior years' peer review reports, it was determined that Peru's undertakings to identify past and future rulings and all potential exchange jurisdictions were sufficient to meet the minimum standard. In addition, it was determined that Peru's review and supervision mechanism was sufficient to meet the minimum standard. In prior year report, it was determined that officials from the Large National Taxpayer Unit manually verify all tax rulings issued to identify those that fall within the scope of the transparency framework and report this information to the relevant departments. For the purpose of formalising the process, Peru noted that a structured procedure will be established by mid-2024 to capture and verify relevant information appropriately. During the year in review, Peru continued its work on the development of this procedure. Peru's implementation remains unchanged, and therefore continues to meet the minimum standard.

924. Peru has met all of the ToR for the information gathering process and no recommendations are made.

Exchange of information (ToR II.B)

925. Peru has the necessary domestic legal basis to exchange information spontaneously. Peru notes that there are no legal or practical impediments that prevent the spontaneous exchange of information on rulings as contemplated in the Action 5 minimum standard.

926. Peru has international agreements permitting spontaneous exchange of information, including: (i) the *Multilateral Convention on Mutual Administrative Assistance in Tax Matters: Amended by the 2010 Protocol* (OECD/Council of Europe, 2011[2]) ("the Convention"), (ii) bilateral agreements in force with seven jurisdictions and (iii) tax information exchange agreements in force with two jurisdictions.[2]

927. During the year in review, no exchanges were required to take place and no data on the timeliness of exchanges is reported.

928. In the prior years' peer review reports, it was determined that Peru's process for the completion and exchange of templates were sufficient to meet the minimum standard. With respect to past rulings, no further action was required. Peru's implementation in this regard remains unchanged and therefore continues to meet the minimum standard.

929. Peru has the necessary legal basis for spontaneous exchange of information, a process for completing the templates in a timely way and has completed all exchanges. In the prior year report, it was noted that Peru will establish a structured procedure for the completion and exchange of templates for the purpose of formalising the process by mid-2024. During the year in review, Peru continued its work on the development of this procedure. Peru has met all of the ToR for the exchange of information process and no recommendations are made.

Statistics (ToR IV.D)

930. As no rulings were issued, no statistics can be reported.

Matters related to intellectual property regimes (ToR I.A.1.3)

931. Peru does not offer an intellectual property regime for which transparency requirements under the Action 5 Report (OECD, 2015[3]) were imposed.

Summary of recommendations on implementation of the transparency framework

Aspect of implementation of the transparency framework that should be improved	Recommendation for improvement
	No recommendations are made.

References

OECD (2021), *BEPS Action 5 on Harmful Tax Practices - Terms of Reference and Methodology for the Conduct of the Peer Reviews of the Action 5 Transparency Framework*, OECD Publishing, Paris, https://www.oecd.org/tax/beps/beps-action-5-harmful-tax-practices-peer-review-transparency-framework.pdf. [1]

OECD (2015), *Countering Harmful Tax Practices More Effectively, Taking into Account Transparency and Substance, Action 5 - 2015 Final Report*, OECD/G20 Base Erosion and Profit Shifting Project, OECD Publishing, Paris, https://doi.org/10.1787/9789264241190-en. [3]

OECD/Council of Europe (2011), *The Multilateral Convention on Mutual Administrative Assistance in Tax Matters: Amended by the 2010 Protocol*, OECD Publishing, Paris, https://doi.org/10.1787/9789264115606-en. [2]

Notes

[1] Rulings other than APAs are known in Peru as "particular consultations". Particular consultations are issued in accordance with article 95-A of the Tax Code and relate to the tax regime applicable to specific facts or situations addressed by a taxpayer with a legitimate interest. Particular consultations are specific rulings on which the particular taxpayer is entitled to rely. However, Peru clarified that particular consultations cannot be issued on any of the categories of rulings within the scope of the transparency framework except for issues covering transfer pricing or the application of transfer pricing principles that fall outside the scope of an APA. Therefore, particular consultations fall in the "any other cross-border unilateral tax rulings (such as an advance tax ruling) covering transfer pricing or the application of transfer pricing principles".

[2] Participating jurisdictions to the Convention are available here: www.oecd.org/tax/exchange-of-tax-information/convention-on-mutual-administrative-assistance-in-tax-matters.htm. Peru also has bilateral agreements with Brazil, Canada, Chile, Japan, Korea, Mexico and Portugal; and tax information exchange agreements in force with Ecuador and the United States.

Philippines

The Philippines has met all aspects of the terms of reference (OECD, 2021[1]) (ToR) for the calendar year 2022 (year in review), except for having in place a process to ensure the timely exchange of information on rulings in the form required by the transparency framework (ToR II.B). The Philippines receives one recommendation on this point for the year in review.

In the prior year report, as well as in the 2017-2020 peer reviews, the Philippines had received three recommendations. Philippines has addressed and resolved two recommendations regarding identifying all potential exchange jurisdictions for both past and future rulings (ToR I.A.2.1 and ToR I.A.2.2). The one other recommendation has not been addressed and remains in place.

The Philippines can legally issue one type of rulings within the scope of the transparency framework.

In practice, the Philippines issued rulings within the scope of the transparency framework as follows:

Type of ruling	Number of rulings
Past rulings	28[1]
Future rulings in the period 1 April 2017 – 31 December 2017	4
Future rulings in the calendar year 2018	30
Future rulings in the calendar year 2019	10
Future rulings in the calendar year 2020	15
Future rulings in the calendar year 2021	54
Future rulings in the year in review	45

As no exchanges took place, no peer input was received in respect of the exchanges of information on rulings received from the Philippines.

Information gathering process (ToR I.A)

932. The Philippines can legally issue the following type of rulings within the scope of the transparency framework: permanent establishment rulings

Past rulings (ToR I.A.1.1, I.A.1.2, I.A.2.1, I.A.2.2)

933. For the Philippines, past rulings are any tax rulings within scope that are issued either: (i) on or after 1 January 2015 but before 1 September 2017; or (ii) on or after 1 January 2012 but before 1 January 2015, provided they were still in effect as at 1 January 2015.

934. In the prior years' peer review reports, it was determined that the Philippines' undertakings to identify past rulings met the ToR. However, the Philippines was recommended to apply the "best efforts approach" to identify potential exchange jurisdictions, in particular for the ultimate parent company, as this was the only type of information on potential exchange jurisdictions that was not provided by the taxpayer upon application. During the year in review, the Philippines checked additional information such as transfer pricing documentation, internal files from the tax administration, and additional obtained data from the taxpayer, in order to identify potential exchange jurisdictions. The Philippines used the "best efforts approach" and therefore, the prior years' recommendation can be removed.

Future rulings (ToR I.A.1.1, I.A.1.2, I.A.2.1)

935. For the Philippines, future rulings are any tax rulings within scope that are issued on or after 1 September 2017.

936. In the prior years' peer review reports, it was determined that the Philippines' undertakings in respect of future rulings met the ToR, except for identifying all potential exchange jurisdictions (ToR I.A.2.1). Therefore, the Philippines was recommended to ensure that all potential exchange jurisdictions are identified swiftly for future rulings. During the year in review, the Philippines made changes to the ruling application form, and now requires for all rulings that the taxpayer provides information on the head office of the permanent establishment and information on the ultimate and immediate parent entities. Therefore, the prior years' recommendation can be removed.

Review and supervision (ToR I.A.3)

937. In the prior year's peer review report, it was determined that The Philippines's review and supervision mechanism was sufficient to meet the minimum standard. The Philippines's implementation in this regard remains unchanged, and therefore continues to meet the minimum standard.

Conclusion on section A

938. The Philippines has met all of the ToR for the information gathering process.

Exchange of information (ToR II.B)

Legal basis for spontaneous exchange of information (ToR II.B.1, II.B.2)

939. The Philippines has the necessary domestic legal basis to exchange information spontaneously. The Philippines notes that there are no legal or practical impediments that prevent the spontaneous exchange of information on rulings as contemplated in the Action 5 minimum standard.

940. The Philippines has bilateral agreements with 42 jurisdictions permitting spontaneous exchange of information. [2] The Philippines signed the *Multilateral Convention on Mutual Administrative Assistance in Tax Matters: Amended by the 2010 Protocol* (OECD/Council of Europe, 2011[2]) ("the Convention") in September 2014, but the Philippines has not yet ratified the Convention. The Philippines is therefore encouraged to continue its efforts to ratify the Convention and expand its international exchange of

information on rulings. It is noted, however, that jurisdictions are assessed on their compliance with the transparency framework in respect of the exchange of information network in effect for the year of the particular annual review.

Completion and exchange of templates (ToR II.B.3, II.B.4, II.B.5, II.B.6, II.B.7)

941. In the prior years' peer review reports, it was determined that the Philippines' did not have a process for the completion and exchange of templates. Therefore, the Philippines was recommended to continue its work to complete its processes for the completion and exchange of information as soon as possible.

942. During the year in review, the Philippines started to implement a process for completing the templates for the exchanges of information, which was adopted in 2023. During the year 2023, the Philippines made exchanges regarding five rulings. However, during the year of review, as the Philippines did not have the process for completion and exchange of templates in force yet, the recommendation remains and the Philippines' efforts will be taken on account on the next year's report.

943. For the year in review, as there is no process for the completion and exchange of templates and therefore no exchanges took place, no data on the timeliness of exchanges can be reported.

Conclusion on section B

944. The Philippines has the necessary legal basis for spontaneous exchange of information. The Philippines is recommended to continue its efforts to put in place a process to complete the templates for all relevant rulings and to ensure that the exchanges of information on rulings occur as soon as possible (ToR II.B).

Statistics (ToR IV.D)

945. As there was no information on rulings exchanged by Philippines for the year in review, no statistics can be reported.

Matters related to intellectual property regimes (ToR I.A.1.3)

946. The Philippines does not offer an intellectual property regime for which transparency requirements under the Action 5 Report (OECD, 2015[3]) were imposed.

Summary of recommendations on implementation of the transparency framework

Aspect of implementation of the transparency framework that should be improved	Recommendation for improvement
The Philippines does not yet have a process in place to ensure the timely exchange of information on rulings in the form required by the transparency framework. The Philippines has made efforts on this during the year 2023, which will be taken into account in next year's peer review report.	The Philippines is recommended to continue its efforts to put in place a process to complete the templates for all relevant rulings and to ensure that the exchanges of information on rulings occur as soon as possible. This recommendation remains unchanged since the 2017, 2018, 2019, 2020 and 2021 peer review reports.

References

OECD (2021), *BEPS Action 5 on Harmful Tax Practices - Terms of Reference and Methodology for the Conduct of the Peer Reviews of the Action 5 Transparency Framework*, OECD Publishing, Paris, https://www.oecd.org/tax/beps/beps-action-5-harmful-tax-practices-peer-review-transparency-framework.pdf. [1]

OECD (2015), *Countering Harmful Tax Practices More Effectively, Taking into Account Transparency and Substance, Action 5 - 2015 Final Report*, OECD/G20 Base Erosion and Profit Shifting Project, OECD Publishing, Paris, https://doi.org/10.1787/9789264241190-en. [3]

OECD/Council of Europe (2011), *The Multilateral Convention on Mutual Administrative Assistance in Tax Matters: Amended by the 2010 Protocol*, OECD Publishing, Paris, https://doi.org/10.1787/9789264115606-en. [2]

Notes

[1] In previous peer review reports, it was noted that there were 78 past rulings. However, the Philippines has done a second review of the issued past rulings. Based on the review, the Philippines identified that 50 out of the 78 rulings did not fall in the definition of a past ruling.

[2] Participating jurisdictions to the Convention are available here: www.oecd.org/tax/exchange-of-tax-information/convention-on-mutual-administrative-assistance-in-tax-matters.htm. Philippines also has bilateral agreements with Australia, Austria, Bangladesh, Belgium, Brazil, Canada, China (People's Republic of), Czechia, Denmark, Finland, France, Germany, Hungary, India, Indonesia, Israel, Italy, Japan, Korea, Kuwait, Malaysia, Mexico, Netherlands, New Zealand, Nigeria, Norway, Pakistan, Poland, Qatar, Romania, Russia, Singapore, Spain, Sri Lanka, Sweden, Switzerland, Thailand, Türkiye, United Arab Emirates, United Kingdom, United States and Viet Nam.

Poland

Poland has met all aspects of the terms of reference (OECD, 2021[1]) (ToR) for the calendar year 2022 (year in review), and no recommendations are made.

Poland can legally issue five types of rulings within the scope of the transparency framework.

In practice, Poland issued rulings within the scope of the transparency framework as follows:

Type of ruling	Number of rulings
Past rulings	84
Future rulings in the period 1 April 2016 – 31 December 2016	6
Future rulings in the calendar year 2017	20
Future rulings in the calendar year 2018	16
Future rulings in the calendar year 2019	100
Future rulings in the calendar year 2020	108
Future rulings in the calendar year 2021	170
Future rulings in the year in review	162

Peer input was received from seven jurisdictions in respect of the exchanges of information on rulings received from Poland. The input was generally positive, noting that overall information was complete, in a correct format and received in a timely manner. However, four peer inputs indicated that information included in the summary section of Annex C of the Action 5 report (OECD, 2015[3]) was not sufficient and did not provide details needed. These issues will be reassessed in next year's peer review.

Information gathering process (ToR I.A)

947. Poland can legally issue the following five types of rulings within the scope of the transparency framework: (i) preferential regimes; (ii) cross-border unilateral APAs and any other cross-border unilateral tax rulings (such as an advance tax ruling) covering transfer pricing or the application of transfer pricing principles; (iii) rulings providing for unilateral downward adjustments; (iv) permanent establishment rulings; and (v) related party conduit rulings.

948. For Poland, past rulings are any tax rulings within scope that are issued either: (i) on or after 1 January 2014 but before 1 April 2016; or (ii) on or after 1 January 2010 but before 1 January 2014, provided they were still in effect as at 1 January 2014.

949. In the prior years' peer review reports, it was determined that Poland's undertakings to identify past and future rulings and all potential exchange jurisdictions were sufficient to meet the minimum standard. In addition, it was determined that Poland's review and supervision mechanism was sufficient to meet the minimum standard. Poland's implementation remains unchanged, and therefore continues to meet the minimum standard.

950. Poland has met all of the ToR for the information gathering process and no recommendations are made.

Exchange of information (ToR II.B)

951. Poland has the necessary domestic legal basis to exchange information spontaneously. Poland notes that there are no legal or practical impediments that prevent the spontaneous exchange of information on rulings as contemplated in the Action 5 minimum standard.

952. Poland has international agreements permitting spontaneous exchange of information, including: (i) the *Multilateral Convention on Mutual Administrative Assistance in Tax Matters: Amended by the 2010 Protocol* (OECD/Council of Europe, 2011[2]) ("the Convention"), (ii) the Directive 2011/16/EU with all other European Union Member States and (iii) bilateral agreements in force with 86 jurisdictions.[1]

953. For the year in review, the timeliness of exchanges is as follows:

Future rulings within the scope of the transparency framework	Number of exchanges transmitted within three months of the information becoming available to the competent authority or immediately after legal impediments have been lifted	Delayed exchanges		
		Number of exchanges transmitted later than three months of the information on rulings becoming available to the competent authority	Reasons for the delays	Any other comments
	281	2	Extraordinary circumstances on exchanges of information with Ukraine.	N/A

Follow-up requests received for exchange of the ruling	Number	Average time to provide response	Number of requests not answered
	0	N/A	N/A

954. In the prior years' peer review reports, it was determined that Poland's process for the completion and exchange of templates were sufficient to meet the minimum standard. With respect to past rulings, no

further action was required. Poland's implementation in this regard remains unchanged and therefore continues to meet the minimum standard.

955. Poland has the necessary legal basis for spontaneous exchange of information, a process for completing the templates in a timely way and has completed all exchanges. Poland has met all of the ToR for the exchange of information process and no recommendations are made.

Statistics (ToR IV.D)

956. The statistics for the year in review are as follows:

Category of ruling	Number of exchanges	Jurisdictions exchanged with
Ruling related to a preferential regime	0	N/A
Cross-border unilateral APAs and any other cross-border unilateral tax rulings (such as an advance tax ruling) covering transfer pricing or the application of transfer pricing principles	6	China (People's Republic of), Japan, Korea, Switzerland, United States
Cross-border rulings providing for a unilateral downward adjustment to the taxpayer's taxable profits that is not directly reflected in the taxpayer's financial / commercial accounts	119	Argentina, Australia, Brazil, Canada, China (People's Republic of), Guernsey, India, Israel, Jersey, Korea, Mexico, Norway, Pakistan, Qatar, Russia, Serbia, Singapore, South Africa, Switzerland, Thailand, Türkiye, Ukraine, United Arab Emirates, United Kingdom, United States
Permanent establishment rulings	10	Canada, China (People's Republic of), Guernsey, Korea, Romania, United Arab Emirates, United Kingdom, United States
Related party conduit rulings	148	Australia, Brazil, Canada, China (People's Republic of), Egypt, Georgia, India, Israel, Japan, Korea, Mexico, Norway, Singapore, South Africa, Switzerland, Thailand, Türkiye, Tunisia, Ukraine, United Arab Emirates, United Kingdom, United States
IP regimes: total exchanges on taxpayers benefitting from the third category of IP assets, new entrants benefitting from grandfathered IP regimes; and taxpayers making use of the option to treat the nexus ratio as a rebuttable presumption	0	N/A
Total	283	

Matters related to intellectual property regimes (ToR I.A.1.3)

957. In the prior years' peer review reports, it was determined that Poland's information gathering and exchange of information processes for matters related to intellectual property regimes[2] were sufficient to meet the minimum standard. Poland's implementation in this regard remains unchanged and therefore continues to meet the minimum standard.

Summary of recommendations on implementation of the transparency framework

Aspect of implementation of the transparency framework that should be improved	Recommendation for improvement
	No recommendations are made.

References

OECD (2021), *BEPS Action 5 on Harmful Tax Practices - Terms of Reference and Methodology for the Conduct of the Peer Reviews of the Action 5 Transparency Framework*, OECD Publishing, Paris, https://www.oecd.org/tax/beps/beps-action-5-harmful-tax-practices-peer-review-transparency-framework.pdf. [1]

OECD (2015), *Countering Harmful Tax Practices More Effectively, Taking into Account Transparency and Substance, Action 5 - 2015 Final Report*, OECD/G20 Base Erosion and Profit Shifting Project, OECD Publishing, Paris, https://doi.org/10.1787/9789264241190-en. [3]

OECD/Council of Europe (2011), *The Multilateral Convention on Mutual Administrative Assistance in Tax Matters: Amended by the 2010 Protocol*, OECD Publishing, Paris, https://doi.org/10.1787/9789264115606-en. [2]

Notes

[1] Parties to the Convention are available here: www.oecd.org/tax/exchange-of-tax-information/convention-on-mutual-administrative-assistance-in-tax-matters.htm. Poland also has bilateral agreements with Albania, Armenia, Australia, Austria, Azerbaijan, Bangladesh, Belarus, Belgium, Bosnia and Herzegovina, Bulgaria, Canada, Chile, China (People's Republic of), Croatia, Cyprus, Czechia, Denmark, Egypt, Estonia, Ethiopia, Finland, France, Georgia, Germany, Greece, Guernsey, Hungary, Iceland, India, Indonesia, Iran, Ireland, Isle of Man, Israel, Italy, Japan, Jersey, Jordan, Kazakhstan, Korea, Kuwait, Kyrgyzstan, Latvia, Lebanon, Lithuania, Luxembourg, Malaysia, Malta, Mexico, Moldova, Mongolia, Montenegro, Morocco, Netherlands, New Zealand, North Macedonia, Norway, Pakistan, Philippines, Portugal, Qatar, Romania, Russia, Saudi Arabia, Serbia, Singapore, Slovak Republic, Slovenia, South Africa, Spain, Sri Lanka, Sweden, Switzerland, Syrian Arab Republic, Chinese Taipei, Tajikistan, Thailand, Tunisia, Türkiye, Ukraine, United Arab Emirates, United Kingdom, United States, Uzbekistan, Viet Nam and Zimbabwe.

[2] IP box.

Portugal

Portugal has met all aspects of the terms of reference (OECD, 2021[1]) (ToR) for the calendar year 2022 (year in review), and no recommendations are made.

Portugal can legally issue two types of rulings within the scope of the transparency framework.

In practice, Portugal issued rulings within the scope of the transparency framework as follows:

Type of ruling	Number of rulings
Past rulings	24
Future rulings in the period 1 April 2016 – 31 December 2016	2
Future rulings in the calendar year 2017	11
Future rulings in the calendar year 2018	11
Future rulings in the calendar year 2019	6
Future rulings in the calendar year 2020	6
Future rulings in the calendar year 2021	7
Future rulings in the year in review	13

No peer input was received in respect of the exchanges of information on rulings received from Portugal.

Information gathering process (ToR I.A)

958. Portugal can legally issue the following two types of rulings within the scope of the transparency framework: (i) cross-border unilateral APAs and any other cross-border unilateral tax rulings (such as an advance tax ruling) covering transfer pricing or the application of transfer pricing principles; and (ii) permanent establishment rulings.

959. For Portugal, past rulings are any tax rulings within scope that are issued either: (i) on or after 1 January 2014 but before 1 April 2016; or (ii) on or after 1 January 2010 but before 1 January 2014, provided they were still in effect as at 1 January 2014. Future rulings are any tax rulings within scope that are issued on or after 1 April 2016.

960. In the prior years' peer review reports, it was determined that Portugal's undertakings to identify past and future rulings and all potential exchange jurisdictions were sufficient to meet the minimum standard. In addition, it was determined that Portugal's review and supervision mechanism was sufficient to meet the minimum standard. Portugal's implementation remains unchanged, and therefore continues to meet the minimum standard.

961. Portugal has met all of the ToR for the information gathering process and no recommendations are made.

Exchange of information (ToR II.B)

962. Portugal has the necessary domestic legal basis to exchange information spontaneously. Portugal notes that there are no legal or practical impediments that prevent the spontaneous exchange of information on rulings as contemplated in the Action 5 minimum standard.

963. Portugal has international agreements permitting spontaneous exchange of information, including: (i) the *Multilateral Convention on Mutual Administrative Assistance in Tax Matters: Amended by the 2010 Protocol* (OECD/Council of Europe, 2011[2]) ("the Convention"), (ii) the Directive 2011/16/EU with all other European Union Member States and (iii) bilateral agreements in force with 79 jurisdictions.[1]

964. For the year in review, the timeliness of exchanges is as follows:

Future rulings within the scope of the transparency framework	Number of exchanges transmitted within three months of the information becoming available to the competent authority or immediately after legal impediments have been lifted	Delayed exchanges		
		Number of exchanges transmitted later than three months of the information on rulings becoming available to the competent authority	Reasons for the delays	Any other comments
	30	0	N/A	N/A

Follow-up requests received for exchange of the ruling	Number	Average time to provide response	Number of requests not answered
	0	N/A	N/A

965. In the prior years' peer review reports, it was determined that Portugal's process for the completion and exchange of templates were sufficient to meet the minimum standard. With respect to past rulings, no further action was required. Portugal's implementation in this regard remains unchanged and therefore continues to meet the minimum standard.

966. Portugal has the necessary legal basis for spontaneous exchange of information, a process for completing the templates in a timely way and has completed all exchanges. Portugal has met all of the ToR for the exchange of information process and no recommendations are made.

Statistics (ToR IV.D)

967. The statistics for the year in review are as follows:

Category of ruling	Number of exchanges	Jurisdictions exchanged with
Cross-border unilateral APAs and any other cross-border unilateral tax rulings (such as an advance tax ruling) covering transfer pricing or the application of transfer pricing principles	29	Belgian, Canada, China (People's Republic of), Cyprus, France, Germany, India, Luxembourg, Netherlands, Poland, Romania, Spain, Sweden, Switzerland, United Kingdom, United States
Permanent establishment rulings	1	*De minimis* rule applies
IP regimes: total exchanges on taxpayers benefitting from the third category of IP assets, new entrants benefitting from grandfathered IP regimes; and taxpayers making use of the option to treat the nexus ratio as a rebuttable presumption	0	N/A
Total	30	

Matters related to intellectual property regimes (ToR I.A.1.3)

968. In the prior years' peer review reports, it was determined that Portugal's information gathering and exchange of information processes for matters related to intellectual property regimes[2] were sufficient to meet the minimum standard. Portugal's implementation in this regard remains unchanged and therefore continues to meet the minimum standard.

Summary of recommendations on implementation of the transparency framework

Aspect of implementation of the transparency framework that should be improved	Recommendation for improvement
	No recommendations are made.

References

OECD (2021), *BEPS Action 5 on Harmful Tax Practices - Terms of Reference and Methodology for the Conduct of the Peer Reviews of the Action 5 Transparency Framework*, OECD Publishing, Paris, https://www.oecd.org/tax/beps/beps-action-5-harmful-tax-practices-peer-review-transparency-framework.pdf. [1]

OECD (2015), *Countering Harmful Tax Practices More Effectively, Taking into Account Transparency and Substance, Action 5 - 2015 Final Report*, OECD/G20 Base Erosion and Profit Shifting Project, OECD Publishing, Paris, https://doi.org/10.1787/9789264241190-en. [3]

OECD/Council of Europe (2011), *The Multilateral Convention on Mutual Administrative Assistance in Tax Matters: Amended by the 2010 Protocol*, OECD Publishing, Paris, https://doi.org/10.1787/9789264115606-en. [2]

Note

[1] Participating jurisdictions to the Convention are available here: www.oecd.org/tax/exchange-of-tax-information/convention-on-mutual-administrative-assistance-in-tax-matters.htm. Portugal also has bilateral agreements with Algeria, Andorra, Angola, Austria, Bahrain, Barbados, Belgium, Brazil, Bulgaria, Cabo Verde, Canada, Chile, China (People's Republic of), Colombia, Côte d'Ivoire, Croatia, Cuba, Cyprus, Czechia, Denmark, Estonia, Ethiopia, France, Georgia, Germany, Greece, Guinea-Bissau, Hong Kong (China), Hungary, Iceland, India, Indonesia, Ireland, Israel, Italy, Japan, Korea, Kuwait, Latvia, Lithuania, Luxembourg, Macau (China), Malta, Mexico, Moldova, Montenegro, Morocco, Mozambique, Netherlands, Norway, Oman, Pakistan, Panama, Peru, Poland, Qatar, Romania, Russia, San Marino, Sao Tome and Principe, Saudi Arabia, Senegal, Singapore, Slovak Republic, Slovenia, South Africa, Spain, Switzerland, Timor-Leste, Tunisia, Türkiye, Ukraine, United Arab Emirates, United Kingdom, United States, Uruguay, Venezuela and Viet Nam.

[2] Partial exemption for income from patents and other industrial property rights.

Qatar

Qatar has met all aspects of the terms of reference (OECD, 2021[1]) (ToR) for the calendar year 2022 (year in review).

Qatar can legally issue five types of rulings within the scope of the transparency framework.

In practice, Qatar issued rulings within the scope of the transparency framework as follows:

Type of ruling	Number of rulings
Past rulings	0
Future rulings in the period 1 April 2018 – 31 December 2018	0
Future rulings in the calendar year 2019	1
Future rulings in the calendar year 2020	1
Future rulings in the calendar year 2021	5
Future rulings in the year in review	4

Peer input was received from three jurisdictions in respect of the exchanges of information on rulings received from Qatar. The input the jurisdictions was positive, noting that overall information was complete, in a correct format and received in a timely manner.

Information gathering process (ToR I.A)

969. Qatar can legally issue the following five types of rulings within the scope of the transparency framework: (i) preferential regimes;[1] (ii) cross-border unilateral APAs and any other cross-border unilateral tax rulings (such as an advance tax ruling) covering transfer pricing or the application of transfer pricing principles; (iii) rulings providing for unilateral downward adjustments; (iv) permanent establishment rulings; and (v) related party conduit rulings.

970. For Qatar, past rulings are any tax rulings issued prior to 1 September 2018. Future rulings are any tax rulings within scope that are issued on or after 1 September 2018.

971. In the prior year's peer review report, it was determined that Qatar's undertakings to identify future rulings and all potential exchange jurisdictions were sufficient to meet the minimum standard. In addition, it was determined that Qatar's review and supervision mechanism was sufficient to meet the minimum standard. Qatar's implementation in this regard remains unchanged, and therefore continues to meet the minimum standard.

972. Qatar has met all of the ToR for the information gathering process and no recommendations are made.

Exchange of information (ToR II.B)

973. Qatar has the necessary domestic legal basis to exchange information spontaneously. Qatar notes that there are no legal or practical impediments that prevent the spontaneous exchange of information on rulings as contemplated in the Action 5 minimum standard.

974. Qatar has international agreements permitting spontaneous exchange of information, including: (i) the *Multilateral Convention on Mutual Administrative Assistance in Tax Matters: Amended by the 2010 Protocol* (OECD/Council of Europe, 2011[2]) ("the Convention") and (ii) bilateral agreements in force with 78 jurisdictions.[2]

975. For the year in review, the timeliness of exchanges is as follows:

Future rulings within the scope of the transparency framework	Number of exchanges transmitted within three months of the information becoming available to the competent authority or immediately after legal impediments have been lifted	Delayed exchanges		
		Number of exchanges transmitted later than three months of the information on rulings becoming available to the competent authority	Reasons for the delays	Any other comments
	25	0	N/A	N/A

Follow-up requests received for exchange of the ruling	Number	Average time to provide response	Number of requests not answered
	0		

976. In the prior years' peer review reports, it was determined that Qatar's process for the completion and exchange of templates were sufficient to meet the minimum standard. With respect to past rulings, no action was required. Qatar's implementation in this regard remains unchanged and therefore continues to meet the minimum standard.

977. Qatar has the necessary legal basis for spontaneous exchange of information, a process for completing the templates in a timely way and has completed all exchanges. Qatar has met all of the ToR for the exchange of information process and no recommendations are made.

Statistics (ToR IV.D)

978. The statistics for the year in review are as follows:

Category of ruling	Number of exchanges	Jurisdictions exchanged with
Ruling related to a preferential regime	*De minimis* rule applies	N/A
Cross-border unilateral APAs and any other cross-border unilateral tax rulings (such as an advance tax ruling) covering transfer pricing or the application of transfer pricing principles	*De minimis* rule applies	N/A
Cross-border rulings providing for a unilateral downward adjustment to the taxpayer's taxable profits that is not directly reflected in the taxpayer's financial / commercial accounts	0	N/A
Permanent establishment rulings	0	N/A
Related party conduit rulings	0	N/A
De minimis rule	25	
IP regimes: total exchanges on taxpayers benefitting from the third category of IP assets, new entrants benefitting from grandfathered IP regimes; and taxpayers making use of the option to treat the nexus ratio as a rebuttable presumption	0	N/A
Total	25	

Matters related to intellectual property regimes (ToR I.A.1.3)

979. In the prior year's peer review report, it was determined that Qatar's information gathering and exchange of information processes for matters related to intellectual property regimes[3] were sufficient to meet the minimum standard. Qatar's implementation in this regard remains unchanged and therefore continues to meet the minimum standard.

Summary of recommendations on implementation of the transparency framework

Aspect of implementation of the transparency framework that should be improved	Recommendation for improvement
	No recommendations are made.

References

OECD (2021), *BEPS Action 5 on Harmful Tax Practices - Terms of Reference and Methodology for the Conduct of the Peer Reviews of the Action 5 Transparency Framework*, OECD Publishing, Paris, https://www.oecd.org/tax/beps/beps-action-5-harmful-tax-practices-peer-review-transparency-framework.pdf. [1]

OECD (2015), *Countering Harmful Tax Practices More Effectively, Taking into Account Transparency and Substance, Action 5 - 2015 Final Report*, OECD/G20 Base Erosion and Profit Shifting Project, OECD Publishing, Paris, https://doi.org/10.1787/9789264241190-en. [3]

OECD/Council of Europe (2011), *The Multilateral Convention on Mutual Administrative Assistance in Tax Matters: Amended by the 2010 Protocol*, OECD Publishing, Paris, https://doi.org/10.1787/9789264115606-en. [2]

Notes

[1] Rulings issued in relation to certain exemptions and concessionary rate under the Qatar Financial Centre (QFC) Tax Regulations.

[2] Participating jurisdictions to the Convention are available here: www.oecd.org/tax/exchange-of-tax-information/convention-on-mutual-administrative-assistance-in-tax-matters.htm. Qatar also has bilateral agreements with Albania, Algeria, Argentina, Armenia, Austria, Azerbaijan, Barbados, Belarus, Bermuda, Bosnia and Herzegovina, Brunei Darussalam, Bulgaria, Chad, China (People's Republic of), Croatia, Cuba, Cyprus, Ecuador, France, Georgia, Greece, Guernsey, Hong Kong (China), Hungary, India, Indonesia, Iran, Ireland, Isle of Man, Italy, Japan, Jersey, Jordan, Kazakhstan, Kenya, Korea, Kyrgyzstan, Latvia, Lebanon, Luxembourg, Malaysia, Malta, Mauritius, Mexico, Monaco, Morocco, Nepal, Netherlands, North Macedonia, Norway, Pakistan, Panama, Philippines, Poland, Rwanda, Portugal, Romania, Russia, San Marino, Senegal, Serbia, Seychelles, Singapore, Slovenia, Somalia, South Africa, Spain, Sri Lanka, Sudan, Switzerland, Syria, Tunisia, Türkiye, Ukraine, United Kingdom, Venezuela, Viet Nam, Yemen.

[3] 1) Free zone at science & technology park and 2) Free zone areas.

Romania

Romania has met all aspects of the terms of reference (OECD, 2021[1]) (ToR) for the calendar year 2022 (year in review), and no recommendations are made.

Romania can legally issue two types of rulings within the scope of the transparency framework.

In practice, Romania issued rulings within the scope of the transparency framework as follows:

Type of ruling	Number of rulings
Past rulings	16
Future rulings in the period 1 April 2017 – 31 December 2017	5
Future rulings in the calendar year 2018	1
Future rulings in the calendar year 2019	4
Future rulings in the calendar year 2020	5
Future rulings in the calendar year 2021	7
Future rulings in the year in review	0

No peer input was received in respect of the exchanges of information on rulings received from Romania.

Information gathering process (ToR I.A)

980. Romania can legally issue the following two types of rulings within the scope of the transparency framework: (i) cross-border unilateral APAs and any other cross-border unilateral tax rulings (such as an advance tax ruling) covering transfer pricing or the application of transfer pricing principles and (ii) permanent establishment rulings.

981. For Romania, past rulings are any tax rulings within scope that are issued either: (i) on or after 1 January 2015 but before 1 April 2017; or (ii) on or after 1 January 2012 but before 1 January 2015, provided they were still in effect as at 1 January 2015. Future rulings are any tax rulings within scope that are issued on or after 1 April 2017.

982. In the prior years' peer review reports, it was determined that Romania's undertakings to identify past and future rulings and all potential exchange jurisdictions were sufficient to meet the minimum standard. In addition, it was determined that Romania's review and supervision mechanism was sufficient to meet the minimum standard. Romania's implementation remains unchanged, and therefore continues to meet the minimum standard.

983. Romania has met all of the ToR for the information gathering process and no recommendations are made.

Exchange of information (ToR II.B)

984. Romania has the necessary domestic legal basis to exchange information spontaneously. Romania notes that there are no legal or practical impediments that prevent the spontaneous exchange of information on rulings as contemplated in the Action 5 minimum standard.

985. Romania has international agreements permitting spontaneous exchange of information, including: (i) the *Multilateral Convention on Mutual Administrative Assistance in Tax Matters: Amended by the 2010 Protocol* (OECD/Council of Europe, 2011[2]) ("the Convention"), (ii) the Directive 2011/16/EU with all other European Union Member States and (iii) bilateral agreements in force with 88 jurisdictions.[1]

986. For the year in review, the timeliness of exchanges is as follows:

Future rulings within the scope of the transparency framework	Number of exchanges transmitted within three months of the information becoming available to the competent authority or immediately after legal impediments have been lifted	Delayed exchanges		
		Number of exchanges transmitted later than three months of the information on rulings becoming available to the competent authority	Reasons for the delays	Any other comments
	1	0	N/A	N/A

Follow-up requests received for exchange of the ruling	Number	Average time to provide response	Number of requests not answered
	0	N/A	N/A

987. In the prior year's peer review report, it was determined that Romania's process for the completion and exchange of templates were sufficient to meet the minimum standard. With respect to past rulings, no further action was required. Romania's implementation in this regard remains unchanged and therefore continues to meet the minimum standard.

988. Romania has the necessary legal basis for spontaneous exchange of information, a process for completing the templates in a timely way and has completed all exchanges. Romania has met all of the ToR for the exchange of information process and no recommendations are made.

Statistics (ToR IV.D)

989. The statistics for the year in review are as follows:

Category of ruling	Number of exchanges	Jurisdictions exchanged with
Cross-border unilateral APAs and any other cross-border unilateral tax rulings (such as an advance tax ruling) covering transfer pricing or the application of transfer pricing principles	0	N/A
Permanent establishment rulings	0	N/A
De minimis rule	1	N/A
Total	1	

Matters related to intellectual property regimes (ToR I.A.1.3)

990. Romania does not offer an intellectual property regime for which transparency requirements under the Action 5 Report (OECD, 2015[3]) were imposed.

Summary of recommendations on implementation of the transparency framework

Aspect of implementation of the transparency framework that should be improved	Recommendation for improvement
	No recommendations are made.

References

OECD (2021), *BEPS Action 5 on Harmful Tax Practices - Terms of Reference and Methodology for the Conduct of the Peer Reviews of the Action 5 Transparency Framework*, OECD Publishing, Paris, https://www.oecd.org/tax/beps/beps-action-5-harmful-tax-practices-peer-review-transparency-framework.pdf. [1]

OECD (2015), *Countering Harmful Tax Practices More Effectively, Taking into Account Transparency and Substance, Action 5 - 2015 Final Report*, OECD/G20 Base Erosion and Profit Shifting Project, OECD Publishing, Paris, https://doi.org/10.1787/9789264241190-en. [3]

OECD/Council of Europe (2011), *The Multilateral Convention on Mutual Administrative Assistance in Tax Matters: Amended by the 2010 Protocol*, OECD Publishing, Paris, https://doi.org/10.1787/9789264115606-en. [2]

Note

[1] Participating jurisdictions to the Convention are available here: www.oecd.org/tax/exchange-of-tax-information/convention-on-mutual-administrative-assistance-in-tax-matters.htm. Romania also has bilateral agreements with Albania, Algeria, Armenia, Australia, Austria, Azerbaijan, Bangladesh, Belarus, Belgium, Bosnia and Herzegovina, Bulgaria, Canada, China (People's Republic of), Croatia, Cyprus, Czechia, Democratic People's Republic of Korea, Denmark, Ecuador, Egypt, Estonia, Ethiopia, Finland, France, Georgia, Germany, Greece, Hong Kong (China), Hungary, Iceland, India, Indonesia, Iran, Ireland, Israel, Italy, Japan, Jordan, Kazakhstan, Korea, Kuwait, Latvia, Lebanon, Lithuania, Luxembourg, Malaysia, Malta, Mexico, Moldova, Montenegro, Morocco, Namibia, Netherlands, Nigeria, North Macedonia, Norway, Pakistan, Philippines, Poland, Portugal, Qatar, Russia, San Marino, Saudi Arabia, Serbia, Montenegro, Singapore, Slovenia, Slovak Republic, South Africa, Spain, Sri Lanka, Sudan, Sweden, Switzerland, Syrian Arab Republic, Tajikistan, Thailand, Tunisia, Türkiye, Turkmenistan, Ukraine, United Arab Emirates, United Kingdom, United States, Uruguay, Uzbekistan, Viet Nam and Zambia.

Saint Kitts and Nevis

Saint Kitts and Nevis has met all aspects of the terms of reference (OECD, 2021[1]) (ToR) for the calendar year 2022 (year in review), and no recommendations are made.

Saint Kitts and Nevis can legally issue five types of rulings within the scope of the transparency framework.

In practice, Saint Kitts and Nevis issued no rulings within the scope of the transparency framework.

As no exchanges were required to take place, no peer input was received in respect of the exchanges of information on rulings received from Saint Kitts and Nevis.

Information gathering process (ToR I.A)

991. Saint Kitts and Nevis can legally issue the following five types of rulings within the scope of the transparency framework: (i) preferential regimes;[1] (ii) cross-border unilateral APAs and any other cross-border unilateral tax rulings (such as an advance tax ruling) covering transfer pricing or the application of transfer pricing principles; (iii) rulings providing for unilateral downward adjustments; (iv) permanent establishment rulings; and (v) related party conduit rulings.

992. For Saint Kitts and Nevis, past rulings are any tax rulings within scope that are issued prior to 1 September 2018. However, there is no obligation for Saint Kitts and Nevis to conduct spontaneous exchange information on past rulings. Future rulings are any tax rulings within scope that are issued on or after 1 September 2018.

993. In the prior years' peer review reports, it was determined that Saint Kitts and Nevis' undertakings to identify rulings and all potential exchange jurisdictions were sufficient to meet the minimum standard. In addition, it was determined that Saint Kitts and Nevis' review and supervision mechanism was sufficient to meet the minimum standard. Saint Kitts and Nevis' implementation remains unchanged, and therefore continues to meet the minimum standard.

994. Saint Kitts and Nevis has met all of the ToR for the information gathering process and no recommendations are made.

Exchange of information (ToR II.B)

995. Saint Kitts and Nevis has the necessary domestic legal basis to exchange information spontaneously. Saint Kitts and Nevis notes that there are no legal or practical impediments that prevent the spontaneous exchange of information on rulings as contemplated in the Action 5 minimum standard.

996. Saint Kitts and Nevis has international agreements permitting spontaneous exchange of information, including: the *Multilateral Convention on Mutual Administrative Assistance in Tax Matters: Amended by the 2010 Protocol* (OECD/Council of Europe, 2011[2]) ("the Convention").[2]

997. During the year in review, no exchanges were required to take place and no data on the timeliness of exchanges is reported.

998. In the prior years' peer review reports, it was determined that Saint Kitts and Nevis' process for the completion and exchange of templates were sufficient to meet the minimum standard. Saint Kitts and Nevis' implementation in this regard remains unchanged and therefore continues to meet the minimum standard.

999. Saint Kitts and Nevis has the necessary legal basis for spontaneous exchange of information and a process for completing the templates in a timely way. Saint Kitts and Nevis has met all of the ToR for the exchange of information process and no recommendations are made.

Statistics (ToR IV.D)

1000. As no rulings were issued, no statistics can be reported.

Matters related to intellectual property regimes (ToR I.A.1.3)

1001. In the prior years' peer review reports, it was determined that Saint Kitts and Nevis' information gathering and exchange of information processes for matters related to intellectual property regimes[3] were sufficient to meet the minimum standard. Saint Kitts and Nevis' implementation in this regard remains unchanged and therefore continues to meet the minimum standard.

Summary of recommendations on implementation of the transparency framework

Aspect of implementation of the transparency framework that should be improved	Recommendation for improvement
	No recommendations are made.

References

OECD (2021), *BEPS Action 5 on Harmful Tax Practices - Terms of Reference and Methodology for the Conduct of the Peer Reviews of the Action 5 Transparency Framework*, OECD Publishing, Paris, https://www.oecd.org/tax/beps/beps-action-5-harmful-tax-practices-peer-review-transparency-framework.pdf. [1]

OECD (2015), *Countering Harmful Tax Practices More Effectively, Taking into Account Transparency and Substance, Action 5 - 2015 Final Report*, OECD/G20 Base Erosion and Profit Shifting Project, OECD Publishing, Paris, https://doi.org/10.1787/9789264241190-en. [3]

OECD/Council of Europe (2011), *The Multilateral Convention on Mutual Administrative Assistance in Tax Matters: Amended by the 2010 Protocol*, OECD Publishing, Paris, https://doi.org/10.1787/9789264115606-en. [2]

Notes

[1] 1) Nevis LLC, 2) Nevis business corporation, and 3) Companies act – exempt companies.

[2] Participating jurisdictions to the Convention are available here: www.oecd.org/tax/exchange-of-tax-information/convention-on-mutual-administrative-assistance-in-tax-matters.htm.

[3] International business company, International trust and International partnership regimes.

Saint Lucia

Saint Lucia has met all aspects of the terms of reference (OECD, 2021[1]) (ToR) for the calendar year 2022 (year in review), except for identifying all potential exchange jurisdictions for future rulings (ToR I.A.2.1). Saint Lucia receives one recommendation on this point for the year in review.

In the prior year report, as well as in the 2018-2020 peer reviews, Saint Lucia had received the same recommendation. As it has not been addressed, the recommendation remains in place

Saint Lucia can legally issue two types of rulings within the scope of the transparency framework.

In practice, Saint Lucia issued rulings within the scope of the transparency framework as follows:

As no exchanges were required to take place, no peer input was received in respect of the exchanges of information on rulings received from Saint Lucia.

Information gathering process (ToR I.A)

1002. Saint Lucia can legally issue the following two types of rulings within the scope of the transparency framework: (i) preferential regimes;[1] and (ii) permanent establishment rulings.

Past rulings (ToR I.A.1.1, I.A.1.2, I.A.2.1, I.A.2.2)

1003. For Saint Lucia, past rulings are any tax rulings issued prior to 1 September 2018. However, there is no obligation for Saint Lucia to conduct spontaneous exchange information on past rulings.

Future rulings (ToR I.A.1.1, I.A.1.2, I.A.2.1)

1004. For Saint Lucia, future rulings are any tax rulings within scope that are issued on or after 1 September 2018.

1005. In the prior year's peer review report, it was determined that Saint Lucia's undertakings to identify future rulings and all potential exchange jurisdictions have met all the ToR, except for the fact that taxpayers are not required to provide information on permanent establishments and ultimate parent companies, which means that not all information on potential exchange jurisdictions is collected. Therefore, Saint Lucia was recommended to ensure that all potential exchange jurisdictions are identified swiftly for all future rulings.

1006. During the year in review, no additional work was undertaken and therefore, the prior year recommendation remains.

Review and supervision (ToR I.A.3)

1007. In the prior year's peer review report, it was determined that Saint Lucia's review and supervision mechanism was sufficient to meet the minimum standard. Saint Lucia's implementation in this regard remains unchanged, and therefore continues to meet the minimum standard.

Conclusion on section A

1008. Saint Lucia has met all of the ToR for the information gathering process except for identifying all potential exchange jurisdictions for future rulings (ToR I.A.2.1). Saint Lucia is recommended to ensure that all potential exchange jurisdictions are identified swiftly for all future rulings.

Exchange of information (ToR II.B)

1009. Saint Lucia has the necessary domestic legal basis to exchange information spontaneously. Saint Lucia notes that there are no legal or practical impediments that prevent the spontaneous exchange of information on rulings as contemplated in the Action 5 minimum standard.

1010. Saint Lucia has international agreements permitting spontaneous exchange of information, including: (i) the *Multilateral Convention on Mutual Administrative Assistance in Tax Matters: Amended by the 2010 Protocol* (OECD/Council of Europe, 2011[2]) ("the Convention") and (ii) bilateral agreements in force with 16 jurisdictions.[2]

1011. During the year in review, no exchanges were required to take place and no data on the timeliness of exchanges is reported.

1012. In the prior years' peer review reports, it was determined that Saint Lucia's process for the completion and exchange of templates were sufficient to meet the minimum standard. Saint Lucia's implementation in this regard remains unchanged and therefore continues to meet the minimum standard.

1013. Saint Lucia has the necessary legal basis for spontaneous exchange of information, a process for completing the templates in a timely way and has completed all exchanges. Saint Lucia has met all of the ToR for the exchange of information process and no recommendations are made.

Statistics (ToR IV.D)

1014. As no rulings were issued, no statistics can be reported.

Matters related to intellectual property regimes (ToR I.A.1.3)

1015. Saint Lucia does not offer an intellectual property regime for which transparency requirements under the Action 5 Report (OECD, 2015[3]) were imposed.

Summary of recommendations on implementation of the transparency framework

Aspect of implementation of the transparency framework that should be improved	Recommendation for improvement
Saint Lucia does not require taxpayers to provide all necessary information to identify all potential exchange jurisdictions for future rulings.	Saint Lucia is recommended to ensure that all potential exchange jurisdictions are identified swiftly for all future rulings. This recommendation remains unchanged since the 2018, 2019, 2020 and 2021 peer review reports.

References

OECD (2021), *BEPS Action 5 on Harmful Tax Practices - Terms of Reference and Methodology for the Conduct of the Peer Reviews of the Action 5 Transparency Framework*, OECD Publishing, Paris, https://www.oecd.org/tax/beps/beps-action-5-harmful-tax-practices-peer-review-transparency-framework.pdf. [1]

OECD (2015), *Countering Harmful Tax Practices More Effectively, Taking into Account Transparency and Substance, Action 5 - 2015 Final Report*, OECD/G20 Base Erosion and Profit Shifting Project, OECD Publishing, Paris, https://doi.org/10.1787/9789264241190-en. [3]

OECD/Council of Europe (2011), *The Multilateral Convention on Mutual Administrative Assistance in Tax Matters: Amended by the 2010 Protocol*, OECD Publishing, Paris, https://doi.org/10.1787/9789264115606-en. [2]

Notes

[1] 1) International business company, 2) International trust and 3) International partnership regimes.

[2] Participating jurisdictions to the Convention are available here: www.oecd.org/tax/exchange-of-tax-information/convention-on-mutual-administrative-assistance-in-tax-matters.htm. Saint Lucia also has bilateral agreements with CARICOM jurisdictions and the United States.

Saint Vincent and the Grenadines

Saint Vincent and the Grenadines is taking steps to implement the aspects of the terms of reference (OECD, 2021[1]) (ToR) for the transparency framework and to commence administrative preparations to ensure that it establishes an information gathering process (ToR I.A) and that information on rulings will be identified and exchanged in a timely manner (ToR II.B). Saint Vincent and Grenadines receives two recommendations on these points for the year of review.

In the prior years' peer reviews, Saint Vincent and the Grenadines was not assessed for the transparency framework, as it could not issue any rulings. However, as Saint Vincent and the Grenadines now has implemented an administrative process to issue rulings, it is reviewed, and recommendations have been made as relevant.

Saint Vincent and the Grenadines can legally issue four types of rulings within the scope of the transparency framework.

In practice, Saint Vincent and the Grenadines issued no rulings within the scope of the transparency framework.

As no exchanges took place, no peer input was received in respect of the exchanges of information on rulings received from Saint Vincent and the Grenadines.

Information gathering process (ToR I.A)

1016. Saint Vincent and the Grenadines can legally issue the following four types of rulings within the scope of the transparency framework: (i) cross-border unilateral APAs and any other cross-border unilateral tax rulings (such as an advance tax ruling) covering transfer pricing or the application of transfer pricing principles; (ii) rulings providing for unilateral downward adjustments; (iii) permanent establishment rulings; and (iv) related party conduit rulings.

1017. Saint Vincent and the Grenadines' Tax Administration Act came into force in December 2020. As stated in the Act, the Comptroller of the Inland Revenue Department that has the authority to issue public rulings on tax related matters within the scope of the transparency framework. The Comptroller can adopt procedures and issue guidelines for improving the process of issuing rulings. However, to date, no rulings within the scope of the transparency framework have been issued by the Comptroller of the Inland Revenue Department.

Past rulings (ToR I.A.1.1, I.A.1.2, I.A.2.1, I.A.2.2)

1018. For Saint Vincent and the Grenadines, past rulings are any tax rulings within scope that are issued either (i) on or after 1 January 2015 but before 1 April 2017; and (ii) on or after 1 January 2012 but before 1 January 2015, provided they were still in effect as of 1 January 2015. As Saint Vincent and the Grenadines can only issue rulings as of 2020, there are no past rulings in scope and this section is not assessed.

Future rulings (ToR I.A.1.1, I.A.1.2, I.A.2.1)

1019. For Saint Vincent and the Grenadines, future rulings are any tax rulings within scope that are issued on or after 1 April 2017.

1020. The Tax Administration Act provides a provision that a taxpayer can apply for an advanced ruling. However, Saint Vincent and the Grenadines is currently establishing a process to identify future rulings and all potential exchange jurisdictions. Therefore, Saint Vincent and the Grenadines is recommended to continue its work to complete its information gathering process on future rulings as soon as possible.

Review and supervision (ToR I.A.3)

1021. As this is Saint Vincent and the Grenadines' first year of review, Saint Vincent and the Grenadines did not have a review and supervision mechanism in place in the prior years. During the year of review, Saint Vincent and the Grenadines created a process for the implementation of a review and supervision mechanism for ensuring implementation of the transparency framework. The Inland Revenue Department ensures that the declaration forms and their annexes capture the information accurately. Experienced staff within the Inland Revenue Department must review the relevant return in the first instance and after the review, the verification of the return is carried out by another experienced staff member. The process includes various monitoring and supervisory processes, including appropriate checklists and IT tools. As Saint Vincent and the Grenadines oversees the information collection and assessment process closely through different departments, Saint Vincent and the Grenadines has review and supervision mechanism in place.

1022. Saint Vincent and the Grenadines' review and supervision mechanism is sufficient to meet the minimum standard.

Conclusion on section A

1023. Saint Vincent and the Grenadines is recommended to ensure that it has put in place an effective information gathering process to identify all relevant future rulings and all potential exchange jurisdictions as soon as possible (ToR I.A).

Exchange of information (ToR II.B)

Legal basis for spontaneous exchange of information (ToR II.B.1, II.B.2)

1024. Saint Vincent and the Grenadines has the necessary domestic legal basis to exchange information spontaneously. Saint Vincent and the Grenadines notes that there are no legal or practical impediments that prevent the spontaneous exchange of information on rulings as contemplated in the Action 5 minimum standard.

1025. Saint Vincent and the Grenadines has international agreements permitting spontaneous exchange of information, including (i) the *Multilateral Convention on Mutual Administrative Assistance in Tax Matters: Amended by the 2010 Protocol* (OECD/Council of Europe, 2011[2]) ("the Convention") and (ii) bilateral agreements in force with 10 jurisdictions.[1]

Completion and exchange of templates (ToR II.B.3, II.B.4, II.B.5, II.B.6, II.B.7)

1026. Saint Vincent and the Grenadines does not yet have a process to complete the templates on all relevant rulings, to make them available to the Competent Authority for exchange of information, and to exchange them with relevant jurisdictions

1027. During the year in review, no exchanges were required to take place and no data on the timeliness of exchanges is reported.

Conclusion on section B

1028. Saint Vincent and the Grenadines is recommended to develop a process to complete the templates for all relevant rulings and to ensure that the exchanges of information on rulings occur in accordance with the form and timelines under the transparency framework going forward (ToR II.B).

Statistics (ToR IV.D)

1029. As there was no information on rulings exchanged by Saint Vincent and the Grenadines for the year in review, no statistics can be reported.

Matters related to intellectual property regimes (ToR I.A.1.3)

1030. Saint Vincent and the Grenadines does not offer an intellectual property regime for which transparency requirements under the Action 5 Report (OECD, 2015[3]) were imposed.

Summary of recommendations on implementation of the transparency framework

Aspect of implementation of the transparency framework that should be improved	Recommendation for improvement
Saint Vincent and the Grenadines does not yet have an effective information gathering process in place to identify all relevant future rulings and all potential exchange jurisdictions.	Saint Vincent and the Grenadines is recommended to continue its work on its information gathering process for identifying all past and future rulings within the scope of the transparency framework as soon as possible.
Saint Vincent and the Grenadines does not yet have a process to complete the templates on all relevant rulings, to make them available to the Competent Authority for exchange of information, and to exchange them with relevant jurisdictions	Saint Vincent and the Grenadines is recommended to develop a process to complete the templates for all relevant rulings and to ensure that the exchanges of information on rulings occur in accordance with the form and timelines under the transparency framework going forward.

References

OECD (2021), *BEPS Action 5 on Harmful Tax Practices - Terms of Reference and Methodology for the Conduct of the Peer Reviews of the Action 5 Transparency Framework*, OECD Publishing, Paris, https://www.oecd.org/tax/beps/beps-action-5-harmful-tax-practices-peer-review-transparency-framework.pdf. [1]

OECD (2015), *Countering Harmful Tax Practices More Effectively, Taking into Account Transparency and Substance, Action 5 - 2015 Final Report*, OECD/G20 Base Erosion and Profit Shifting Project, OECD Publishing, Paris, https://doi.org/10.1787/9789264241190-en. [3]

OECD/Council of Europe (2011), *The Multilateral Convention on Mutual Administrative Assistance in Tax Matters: Amended by the 2010 Protocol*, OECD Publishing, Paris, https://doi.org/10.1787/9789264115606-en. [2]

Note

[1] Participating jurisdictions to the Convention are available here: www.oecd.org/tax/exchange-of-tax-information/convention-on-mutual-administrative-assistance-in-tax-matters.htm. Saint Vincent and the Grenadines also has bilateral agreements with jurisdictions party to the CARICOM agreement.

Samoa

Samoa has met all aspects of the terms of reference (OECD, 2021[1]) (ToR) for the calendar year 2022 (year in review) that can be met in absence of rulings being issued in practice.

Samoa can legally issue five types of rulings within the scope of the transparency framework.

In practice, Samoa issued no rulings within the scope of the transparency framework.

As no exchanges were required to take place, no peer input was received in respect of the exchanges of information on rulings received from Samoa.

Information gathering process (ToR I.A)

1031. Samoa can legally issue the following five types of rulings within the scope of the transparency framework: (i) preferential regimes;[1] (ii) cross-border unilateral APAs and any other cross-border unilateral tax rulings (such as an advance tax ruling) covering transfer pricing or the application of transfer pricing principles; (iii) rulings providing for unilateral downward adjustments; (iv) permanent establishment rulings; and (v) related party conduit rulings.

1032. For Samoa, past rulings are any tax rulings issued prior to 1 September 2021. However, there is no obligation for Samoa to conduct spontaneous exchange information on past rulings. Future rulings are any tax rulings within scope that are issued on or after 1 September 2021.

1033. In the prior years' peer review reports, it was determined that Samoa's undertakings to identify past and future rulings and all potential exchange jurisdictions were sufficient to meet the minimum standard. In addition, it was determined that Samoa's review and supervision mechanism was sufficient to meet the minimum standard. Samoa's implementation remains unchanged, and therefore continues to meet the minimum standard.

1034. Samoa has met all of the ToR for the information gathering process and no recommendations are made.

Exchange of information (ToR II.B)

1035. Samoa has the necessary domestic legal basis to exchange information spontaneously. Samoa notes that there are no legal or practical impediments that prevent the spontaneous exchange of information on rulings as contemplated in the Action 5 minimum standard.

1036. Samoa has international agreements permitting spontaneous exchange of information, including: (i) the *Multilateral Convention on Mutual Administrative Assistance in Tax Matters: Amended by the 2010 Protocol* (OECD/Council of Europe, 2011[2]) ("the Convention") and (ii) bilateral agreement in force with one jurisdiction.[2]

1037. During the year in review, no exchanges were required to take place and no data on the timeliness of exchanges is reported.

1038. In the prior year's peer review report, it was determined that Samoa's process for the completion and exchange of templates were sufficient to meet the minimum standard. With respect to past rulings, no action was required. Samoa's implementation in this regard remains unchanged and therefore continues to meet the minimum standard.

1039. Samoa has the necessary legal basis for spontaneous exchange of information, a process for completing the templates in a timely way and has completed all exchanges. Samoa has met all of the ToR for the exchange of information process and no recommendations are made.

Statistics (ToR IV.D)

1040. As no rulings were issued, no statistics can be reported.

Matters related to intellectual property regimes (ToR I.A.1.3)

1041. Samoa does not offer an intellectual property regime for which transparency requirements under the Action 5 Report (OECD, 2015[3]) were imposed.

Summary of recommendations on implementation of the transparency framework

Aspect of implementation of the transparency framework that should be improved	Recommendation for improvement
	No recommendations are made.

References

OECD (2021), *BEPS Action 5 on Harmful Tax Practices - Terms of Reference and Methodology for the Conduct of the Peer Reviews of the Action 5 Transparency Framework*, OECD Publishing, Paris, https://www.oecd.org/tax/beps/beps-action-5-harmful-tax-practices-peer-review-transparency-framework.pdf. [1]

OECD (2015), *Countering Harmful Tax Practices More Effectively, Taking into Account Transparency and Substance, Action 5 - 2015 Final Report*, OECD/G20 Base Erosion and Profit Shifting Project, OECD Publishing, Paris, https://doi.org/10.1787/9789264241190-en. [3]

OECD/Council of Europe (2011), *The Multilateral Convention on Mutual Administrative Assistance in Tax Matters: Amended by the 2010 Protocol*, OECD Publishing, Paris, https://doi.org/10.1787/9789264115606-en. [2]

Notes

[1] Samoa grants several preferential regimes, possibly in scope of the Forum on Harmful Tax Practices (FHTP) work, that have not yet been reviewed by the FHTP, but for which rulings could be issued under the Action 5 transparency framework.

[2] Participating jurisdictions to the Convention are available here: www.oecd.org/tax/exchange-of-tax-information/convention-on-mutual-administrative-assistance-in-tax-matters.htm. Samoa also has a bilateral agreement with New Zealand.

San Marino

San Marino has met all aspects of the terms of reference (OECD, 2021[1]) (ToR) for the calendar year 2022 (year in review), and no recommendations are made.

San Marino can legally issue two types of rulings within the scope of the transparency framework.

In practice, San Marino issued rulings within the scope of the transparency framework as follows:

Type of ruling	Number of rulings
Past rulings	2
Future rulings in the period 1 April 2017 – 31 December 2017	0
Future rulings in the calendar year 2018	0
Future rulings in the calendar year 2019	0
Future rulings in the calendar year 2020	0
Future rulings in the calendar year 2021	0
Future rulings in the year in review	0

As no exchanges were required to take place, no peer input was received in respect of the exchanges of information on rulings received from San Marino.

Information gathering process (ToR I.A)

1042. San Marino can legally issue the following two types of rulings within the scope of the transparency framework: (i) preferential regimes[1] and (ii) permanent establishment rulings.

1043. For San Marino, past rulings are any tax rulings within scope that are issued either (i) on or after 1 January 2015 but before 1 April 2017; and (ii) on or after 1 January 2012 but before 1 January 2015, provided they were still in effect as at 1 January 2015. Future rulings are any tax rulings within scope that are issued on or after 1 April 2017.

1044. In the prior year's peer review report, it was determined that San Marino's undertakings to identify past and future rulings and all potential exchange jurisdictions were sufficient to meet the minimum standard. In addition, it was determined that San Marino's review and supervision mechanism was sufficient to meet the minimum standard. San Marino's implementation remains unchanged, and therefore continues to meet the minimum standard.

1045. San Marino has met all of the ToR for the information gathering process and no recommendations are made.

Exchange of information (ToR II.B)

1046. San Marino has the necessary domestic legal basis to exchange information spontaneously. San Marino notes that there are no legal or practical impediments that prevent the spontaneous exchange of information on rulings as contemplated in the Action 5 minimum standard.

1047. San Marino has international agreements permitting spontaneous exchange of information, including: (i) the *Multilateral Convention on Mutual Administrative Assistance in Tax Matters: Amended by the 2010 Protocol* (OECD/Council of Europe, 2011[2]) ("the Convention"), and (ii) bilateral agreements in force with 25 jurisdictions.[2]

1048. During the year in review, no exchanges were required to take place and no data on the timeliness of exchanges is reported.

1049. In the prior years' peer review reports, it was determined that San Marino's process for the completion and exchange of templates were sufficient to meet the minimum standard. With respect to past rulings, no further action was required. San Marino's implementation in this regard remains unchanged and therefore continues to meet the minimum standard.

1050. San Marino has the necessary legal basis for spontaneous exchange of information, a process for completing the templates in a timely way and has completed all exchanges. San Marino has met all of the ToR for the exchange of information process and no recommendations are made.

Statistics (ToR IV.D)

1051. As no rulings were issued, no statistics can be reported.

Matters related to intellectual property regimes (ToR I.A.1.3)

1052. In the prior years' peer review reports, it was determined that San Marino's information gathering and exchange of information processes for matters related to intellectual property regimes[3] were sufficient to meet the minimum standard. San Marino's implementation in this regard remains unchanged and therefore continues to meet the minimum standard.

1053. It is noted that San Marino's IP regimes are abolished as of 1 October 2022. As the regimes were "not harmful", the FHTP concluded that no specific grandfathering provisions apply. Therefore, as of 1 October 2022, San Marino has no more obligations under the transparency framework regarding its IP regimes.

Summary of recommendations on implementation of the transparency framework

Aspect of implementation of the transparency framework that should be improved	Recommendation for improvement
	No recommendations are made.

References

OECD (2021), *BEPS Action 5 on Harmful Tax Practices - Terms of Reference and Methodology for the Conduct of the Peer Reviews of the Action 5 Transparency Framework*, OECD Publishing, Paris, https://www.oecd.org/tax/beps/beps-action-5-harmful-tax-practices-peer-review-transparency-framework.pdf. [1]

OECD (2015), *Countering Harmful Tax Practices More Effectively, Taking into Account Transparency and Substance, Action 5 - 2015 Final Report*, OECD/G20 Base Erosion and Profit Shifting Project, OECD Publishing, Paris, https://doi.org/10.1787/9789264241190-en. [3]

OECD/Council of Europe (2011), *The Multilateral Convention on Mutual Administrative Assistance in Tax Matters: Amended by the 2010 Protocol*, OECD Publishing, Paris, https://doi.org/10.1787/9789264115606-en. [2]

Notes

[1] IP regime. In the prior year report, it was noted that San Marino could legally issue rulings with respect to the following preferential regimes: 1) New companies regime (New companies regime provided by art. 73, law no. 166/2013) and 2) IP regime. San Marino has since clarified that rulings can be issued only with respect to the IP regime.

[2] Participating jurisdictions to the Convention are available here: www.oecd.org/tax/exchange-of-tax-information/convention-on-mutual-administrative-assistance-in-tax-matters.htm. San Marino also has bilateral agreements with Andorra, Austria, Azerbaijan, Barbados, Belgium, Croatia, Cyprus, Czechia, Georgia, Greece, Hungary, Italy, Liechtenstein, Luxembourg, Malaysia, Malta, Portugal, Qatar, Romania, Saint Kitts and Nevis, Serbia, Seychelles, Singapore, United Arab Emirates and Viet Nam.

[3] 1) New companies regime (New companies regime provided by art. 73, law no. 166/2013) and 2) IP regime.

Senegal

Senegal has met all aspects of the terms of reference (OECD, 2021[1]) (ToR) for the calendar year 2022 (year in review) that can be met in absence of rulings being issued in practice.

Senegal can legally issue one type of ruling within the scope of the transparency framework.

In practice, Senegal issued no rulings within the scope of the transparency framework.

As no exchanges were required to take place, no peer input was received in respect of the exchanges of information on rulings received from Senegal.

Information gathering process (ToR I.A)

1054. Senegal can legally issue the following type of ruling within the scope of the transparency framework: cross-border unilateral APAs and any other cross-border unilateral tax rulings (such as an advance tax ruling) covering transfer pricing or the application of transfer pricing principles.

1055. For Senegal, past rulings are any tax rulings within scope that are issued either (i) on or after 1 January 2016 but before 1 April 2018; and (ii) on or after 1 January 2014 but before 1 January 2016, provided still in effect as at 1 January 2016. Future rulings are any tax rulings within scope that are issued on or after 1 April 2018.

1056. In the prior years' peer review reports, it was determined that there was no need to identify potential exchange jurisdictions as no past rulings were issued during the past rulings period. In addition, it was determined that Senegal's undertakings to identify future rulings and all potential exchange jurisdictions were sufficient to meet the minimum standard, and that Senegal's review and supervision mechanism was sufficient to meet the minimum standard. Senegal's implementation remains unchanged, and therefore continues to meet the minimum standard.

1057. Senegal has met all of the ToR for the information gathering process that can be met in absence of rulings being issued in practice and no recommendations are made.

Exchange of information (ToR II.B)

1058. Senegal has the necessary domestic legal basis to exchange information spontaneously. Senegal notes that there are no legal or practical impediments that prevent the spontaneous exchange of information on rulings as contemplated in the Action 5 minimum standard.

1059. Senegal has international agreements permitting spontaneous exchange of information, including: (i) the *Multilateral Convention on Mutual Administrative Assistance in Tax Matters: Amended by the 2010 Protocol* (OECD/Council of Europe, 2011[2]) ("the Convention") and (ii) bilateral agreements in force with 21 jurisdictions.[1]

1060. During the year in review, no exchanges were required to take place and no data on the timeliness of exchanges is reported.

1061. In the prior year's peer review report, it was determined that Senegal's process for the completion and exchange of templates were sufficient to meet the minimum standard. With respect to past rulings, no further action was required. Senegal's implementation in this regard remains unchanged and therefore continues to meet the minimum standard.

1062. Senegal has the necessary legal basis for spontaneous exchange of information, a process for completing the templates in a timely way and has completed all exchanges. Senegal has met all of the ToR for the exchange of information process and no recommendations are made.

Statistics (ToR IV.D)

1063. As no rulings were issued, no statistics can be reported.

Matters related to intellectual property regimes (ToR I.A.1.3)

1064. Senegal does not offer an intellectual property regime for which transparency requirements under the Action 5 Report (OECD, 2015[3]) were imposed.

Summary of recommendations on implementation of the transparency framework

Aspect of implementation of the transparency framework that should be improved	Recommendation for improvement
	No recommendations are made.

References

OECD (2021), *BEPS Action 5 on Harmful Tax Practices - Terms of Reference and Methodology for the Conduct of the Peer Reviews of the Action 5 Transparency Framework*, OECD Publishing, Paris, https://www.oecd.org/tax/beps/beps-action-5-harmful-tax-practices-peer-review-transparency-framework.pdf. [1]

OECD (2015), *Countering Harmful Tax Practices More Effectively, Taking into Account Transparency and Substance, Action 5 - 2015 Final Report*, OECD/G20 Base Erosion and Profit Shifting Project, OECD Publishing, Paris, https://doi.org/10.1787/9789264241190-en. [3]

OECD/Council of Europe (2011), *The Multilateral Convention on Mutual Administrative Assistance in Tax Matters: Amended by the 2010 Protocol*, OECD Publishing, Paris, https://doi.org/10.1787/9789264115606-en. [2]

Note

[1] Participating jurisdictions to the Convention are available here: www.oecd.org/tax/exchange-of-tax-information/convention-on-mutual-administrative-assistance-in-tax-matters.htm. Senegal also has bilateral agreements with West African Economic and Monetary Union jurisdictions, African and Malagasy Common Organisation jurisdictions and Belgium, Canada, France, Italy, Kuwait, Lebanon, Malaysia, Mauritania, Mauritius, Morocco, Norway, Portugal, Spain, Chinese Taipei, United Arab Emirates and United Kingdom.

Seychelles

Seychelles has met all aspects of the terms of reference (OECD, 2021[1]) (ToR) for the calendar year 2022 (year in review), and no recommendations are made.

Seychelles can legally issue five types of rulings within the scope of the transparency framework.

In practice, Seychelles issued no rulings within the scope of the transparency framework.

As no exchanges were required to take place, no peer input was received in respect of the exchanges of information on rulings received from Seychelles.

Information gathering process (ToR I.A)

1065. Seychelles can legally issue the following five types of rulings within the scope of the transparency framework: (i) preferential regimes; [1] (ii) cross-border unilateral APAs and any other cross-border unilateral tax rulings (such as an advance tax ruling) covering transfer pricing or the application of transfer pricing principles; (iii) rulings providing for unilateral downward adjustments; (iv) permanent establishment rulings; and (v) related party conduit rulings.

1066. For Seychelles, past rulings are any tax rulings within scope that are issued either: (i) on or after 1 January 2015 but before 1 April 2017; or (ii) on or after 1 January 2012 but before 1 January 2015, provided they were still in effect as at 1 January 2015. Future rulings are any tax rulings within scope that are issued on or after 1 April 2017.

1067. In the prior years' peer review reports, it was determined that Seychelles' undertakings to identify past and future rulings and all potential exchange jurisdictions were sufficient to meet the minimum standard. In addition, it was determined that Seychelles' review and supervision mechanism was sufficient to meet the minimum standard. Seychelles' implementation remains unchanged, and therefore continues to meet the minimum standard.

1068. Seychelles has met all of the ToR for the information gathering process and no recommendations are made.

Exchange of information (ToR II.B)

1069. Seychelles has the necessary domestic legal basis to exchange information spontaneously. Seychelles notes that there are no legal or practical impediments that prevent the spontaneous exchange of information on rulings as contemplated in the Action 5 minimum standard.

1070. Seychelles has international agreements permitting spontaneous exchange of information, including: (i) the *Multilateral Convention on Mutual Administrative Assistance in Tax Matters: Amended by the 2010 Protocol* (OECD/Council of Europe, 2011[2]) ("the Convention") and (ii) bilateral agreements in force with 39 jurisdictions.[2]

1071. During the year in review, no exchanges were required to take place and no data on the timeliness of exchanges is reported.

1072. In the prior years' peer review reports, it was determined that Seychelles' process for the completion and exchange of templates were sufficient to meet the minimum standard. With respect to past rulings, no action was required. Seychelles' implementation in this regard remains unchanged and therefore continues to meet the minimum standard.

1073. Seychelles has the necessary legal basis for spontaneous exchange of information and a process for completing the templates in a timely way. Seychelles has met all of the ToR for the exchange of information process and no recommendations are made.

Statistics (ToR IV.D)

1074. As no rulings were issued, no statistics can be reported.

Matters related to intellectual property regimes (ToR I.A.1.3)

1075. Seychelles does not offer an intellectual property regime for which transparency requirements under the Action 5 Report (OECD, 2015[3]) were imposed.

Summary of recommendations on implementation of the transparency framework

Aspect of implementation of the transparency framework that should be improved	Recommendation for improvement
	No recommendations are made.

References

OECD (2021), *BEPS Action 5 on Harmful Tax Practices - Terms of Reference and Methodology for the Conduct of the Peer Reviews of the Action 5 Transparency Framework*, OECD Publishing, Paris, https://www.oecd.org/tax/beps/beps-action-5-harmful-tax-practices-peer-review-transparency-framework.pdf. [1]

OECD (2015), *Countering Harmful Tax Practices More Effectively, Taking into Account Transparency and Substance, Action 5 - 2015 Final Report*, OECD/G20 Base Erosion and Profit Shifting Project, OECD Publishing, Paris, https://doi.org/10.1787/9789264241190-en. [3]

OECD/Council of Europe (2011), *The Multilateral Convention on Mutual Administrative Assistance in Tax Matters: Amended by the 2010 Protocol*, OECD Publishing, Paris, https://doi.org/10.1787/9789264115606-en. [2]

Notes

[1] 1) Fund administration business, and 2) Securities business under the securities act.

[2] Participating jurisdictions to the Convention are available here: www.oecd.org/tax/exchange-of-tax-information/convention-on-mutual-administrative-assistance-in-tax-matters.htm. Seychelles also has bilateral agreements with Bahrain, Barbados, Belgium, Bermuda, Botswana, China (People's Republic of), Cyprus, Denmark, Ethiopia, Faroe Islands, Finland, Greenland, Guernsey, Iceland, India, Indonesia, Isle of Man, Jersey, Kenya, Luxembourg, Malaysia, Mauritius, Monaco, Netherlands, Norway, Oman, Qatar, San Marino, Seychelles, Singapore, South Africa, Sri Lanka, Swaziland, Sweden, Switzerland, Thailand, United Arab Emirates, Viet Nam and Zambia.

Singapore

Singapore has met all aspects of the terms of reference (OECD, 2021[1]) (ToR) for the calendar year 2022 (year in review), and no recommendations are made.

Singapore can legally issue five types of rulings within the scope of the transparency framework.

In practice, Singapore issued rulings within the scope of the transparency framework as follows:

Type of ruling	Number of rulings
Past rulings	1008
Future rulings in the period 1 April 2017 – 31 December 2017	85
Future rulings in the calendar year 2018	222
Future rulings in the calendar year 2019	274
Future rulings in the calendar year 2020	211
Future rulings in the calendar year 2021	156
Future rulings in the year in review	188

Peer input was received from eight jurisdictions in respect of the exchanges of information on rulings received from Singapore. The input was generally positive, noting that overall information was complete, in a correct format and received in a timely manner.

Information gathering process (ToR I.A)

1076. Singapore can legally issue the following five types of rulings within the scope of the transparency framework: (i) preferential regimes;[1] (ii) cross-border unilateral APAs and any other cross-border unilateral tax rulings (such as an advance tax ruling) covering transfer pricing or the application of transfer pricing principles; (iii) rulings providing for unilateral downward adjustments; (iv) permanent establishment rulings; and (v) related party conduit rulings.

1077. For Singapore, past rulings are any tax rulings within scope that are issued either: (i) on or after 1 January 2015 but before 1 April 2017; or (ii) on or after 1 January 2012 but before 1 January 2015, provided they were still in effect as at 1 January 2015. Future rulings are any tax rulings within scope that are issued on or after 1 April 2017.

1078. In the prior years' peer review reports, it was determined that Singapore's undertakings to identify past and future rulings and all potential exchange jurisdictions were sufficient to meet the minimum standard. In addition, it was determined that Singapore's review and supervision mechanism was sufficient to meet the minimum standard. Singapore's implementation remains unchanged, and therefore continues to meet the minimum standard.

1079. Singapore has met all of the ToR for the information gathering process and no recommendations are made.

Exchange of information (ToR II.B)

1080. Singapore has the necessary domestic legal basis to exchange information spontaneously. Singapore notes that there are no legal or practical impediments that prevent the spontaneous exchange of information on rulings as contemplated in the Action 5 minimum standard.

1081. Singapore has international agreements permitting spontaneous exchange of information, including: (i) the *Multilateral Convention on Mutual Administrative Assistance in Tax Matters: Amended by the 2010 Protocol* (OECD/Council of Europe, 2011[2]) ("the Convention") and (ii) bilateral agreements in force with 86 jurisdictions.[2]

1082. For the year in review, the timeliness of exchanges is as follows:

Future rulings within the scope of the transparency framework	Number of exchanges transmitted within three months of the information becoming available to the competent authority or immediately after legal impediments have been lifted	Delayed exchanges		
		Number of exchanges transmitted later than three months of the information on rulings becoming available to the competent authority	Reasons for the delays	Any other comments
	696	9	See below	N/A

Follow-up requests received for exchange of the ruling	Number	Average time to provide response	Number of requests not answered
	1	132[3]	0

1083. Singapore notes that of the nine delayed exchanges, six were inadvertently missed out for exchange as the rulings were submitted to the Inland Revenue Authority of Singapore (IRAS) at a different timing outside the regular submission cycle. One exchange was not processed by the system due to special character used and had to be reuploaded and processed for exchange. Furthermore, two other exchanges were in fact not late, but an incorrect earlier date was inadvertently stated in the SEOI template.

Singapore notes further that the nine delayed exchanges have since been completed and that it has streamlined its procedures for off-cycle submissions and put in place safeguards to ensure all information is accurate and formatted correctly before exchange to minimise delayed exchanges. Considering the small number of exchanges that were delayed, and the fact that Singapore has taken appropriate steps to deal with the issues, no recommendation is made at this stage.

1084. In the prior years' peer review reports, it was determined that Singapore's process for the completion and exchange of templates were sufficient to meet the minimum standard. With respect to past rulings, no further action was required. Singapore's implementation in this regard remains unchanged and therefore continues to meet the minimum standard.

1085. Singapore has the necessary legal basis for spontaneous exchange of information, a process for completing the templates in a timely way and has completed all exchanges. Singapore has met all of the ToR for the exchange of information process and no recommendations are made.

Statistics (ToR IV.D)

1086. The statistics for the year in review are as follows:

Category of ruling	Number of exchanges	Jurisdictions exchanged with
Ruling/ letters of awards related to a preferential regime	698	Argentina, Australia, Austria, Barbados, Belgium, Brazil, Canada, Chile, China (People's Republic of), Colombia, Costa Rica, Czechia, Denmark, Estonia, Finland, France, Germany, Hong Kong (China), Hungary, India, Indonesia, Ireland, Isle of Man, Israel, Italy, Japan, Jersey, Korea, Luxembourg, Malaysia, Malta, Mauritius, Mexico, Netherlands, New Zealand, Norway, Pakistan, Panama, Poland, Portugal, Russian Federation, Saudi Arabia, Slovak Republic, South Arica, Spain, Sweden, Switzerland, Türkiye, United Kingdom, United States, Uruguay
Cross-border unilateral APAs and any other cross-border unilateral tax rulings (such as an advance tax ruling) covering transfer pricing or the application of transfer pricing principles	6	Australia, Ireland, United Kingdom, United States
Cross-border rulings providing for a unilateral downward adjustment to the taxpayer's taxable profits that is not directly reflected in the taxpayer's financial / commercial accounts	0	N/A
Permanent establishment rulings	1	*De minimis* rule applies
Related party conduit rulings	0	N/A
IP regimes: total exchanges on taxpayers benefitting from the third category of IP assets, new entrants benefitting from grandfathered IP regimes; and taxpayers making use of the option to treat the nexus ratio as a rebuttable presumption	0	N/A
Total	705	

Matters related to intellectual property regimes (ToR I.A.1.3)

1087. In the prior years' peer review reports, it was determined that Singapore's information gathering and exchange of information processes for matters related to intellectual property regimes[4] were sufficient to meet the minimum standard. Singapore's implementation in this regard remains unchanged and therefore continues to meet the minimum standard.

Summary of recommendations on implementation of the transparency framework

Aspect of implementation of the transparency framework that should be improved	Recommendation for improvement
	No recommendations are made.

References

OECD (2021), *BEPS Action 5 on Harmful Tax Practices - Terms of Reference and Methodology for the Conduct of the Peer Reviews of the Action 5 Transparency Framework*, OECD Publishing, Paris, https://www.oecd.org/tax/beps/beps-action-5-harmful-tax-practices-peer-review-transparency-framework.pdf. [1]

OECD (2015), *Countering Harmful Tax Practices More Effectively, Taking into Account Transparency and Substance, Action 5 - 2015 Final Report*, OECD/G20 Base Erosion and Profit Shifting Project, OECD Publishing, Paris, https://doi.org/10.1787/9789264241190-en. [3]

OECD/Council of Europe (2011), *The Multilateral Convention on Mutual Administrative Assistance in Tax Matters: Amended by the 2010 Protocol*, OECD Publishing, Paris, https://doi.org/10.1787/9789264115606-en. [2]

Notes

[1] 1) Development and expansion incentive - services, 2) Pioneer service company, 3) Aircraft leasing scheme, 4) Finance and treasury centre, 5) Insurance business development, 6) Financial sector incentive, 7) Global trader programme.

[2] Participating jurisdictions to the Convention are available here: www.oecd.org/tax/exchange-of-tax-information/convention-on-mutual-administrative-assistance-in-tax-matters.htm. Singapore also has bilateral agreements with Albania, Australia, Bahrain, Bangladesh, Barbados, Belarus, Belgium, Brazil, Brunei Darussalam, Bulgaria, Cambodia, Canada, China (People's Republic of), Cyprus, Czechia, Denmark, Ecuador, Egypt, Estonia, Ethiopia, Fiji, Finland, France, Georgia, Germany, Ghana, Greece, Guernsey, Hungary, India, Indonesia, Ireland, Isle of Man, Israel, Italy, Japan, Jersey, Kazakhstan, Korea, Kuwait, Lao People's Democratic Republic, Latvia, Libya, Lithuania, Luxembourg, Malaysia, Malta, Mauritius, Mexico, Mongolia, Morocco, Myanmar, Netherlands, New Zealand, Nigeria, Norway, Oman, Pakistan, Papua New Guinea, Philippines, Poland, Portugal, Qatar, Romania, Russia, Rwanda, San Marino, Saudi Arabia, Seychelles, Slovak Republic, Slovenia, South Africa, Spain, Sri Lanka, Sweden, Thailand, Tunisia, Türkiye, Turkmenistan, Ukraine, United Arab Emirates, United Kingdom, United States, Uruguay, Uzbekistan and Viet Nam.

[3] Singapore notes that the requesting jurisdiction was updated on the status of the request within 90 days of the receipt of the follow-up request.

[4] 1) Pioneer service company and 2) Development and expansion incentive – services.

Sint Maarten

Sint Maarten has met all aspects of the terms of reference (OECD, 2021[1]) (ToR) for the calendar year 2022 (year in review).

Sint Maarten can legally issue five types of rulings within the scope of the transparency framework.

In practice, Sint Maarten issued no rulings within the scope of the transparency framework.

As no exchanges were required to take place, no peer input was received in respect of the exchanges of information on rulings received from Sint Maarten.

Information gathering process (ToR I.A)

1088. Sint Maarten can legally issue the following five types of rulings within the scope of the transparency framework: (i) preferential regimes;[1] (ii) cross-border unilateral APAs and any other cross-border unilateral tax rulings (such as an advance tax ruling) covering transfer pricing or the application of transfer pricing principles; (iii) rulings providing for unilateral downward adjustments; (iv) permanent establishment rulings; and (v) related party conduit rulings.

1089. For Sint Maarten, past rulings are any tax rulings within scope that are issued either: (i) on or after 1 January 2015 but before 1 September 2017; or (ii) on or after 1 January 2012 but before 1 January 2015, provided they were still in effect as at 1 January 2015. Future rulings are any tax rulings within scope that are issued on or after 1 September 2017.

1090. In the prior year's peer review report, it was determined that Sint Maarten's undertakings to identify past and future rulings and all potential exchange jurisdictions were sufficient to meet the minimum standard. In addition, it was determined that Sint Maarten's review and supervision mechanism was sufficient to meet the minimum standard. Sint Maarten's implementation remains unchanged, and therefore continues to meet the minimum standard.

1091. Sint Maarten has met all of the ToR for the information gathering process and no recommendations are made.

Exchange of information (ToR II.B)

1092. Sint Maarten has the necessary domestic legal basis to exchange information spontaneously. Sint Maarten notes that there are no legal or practical impediments that prevent the spontaneous exchange of information on rulings as contemplated in the Action 5 minimum standard.

1093. Sint Maarten has international agreements permitting spontaneous exchange of information, including being a jurisdiction participating in (i) the *Multilateral Convention on Mutual Administrative Assistance in Tax Matters: Amended by the 2010 Protocol* (OECD/Council of Europe, 2011[2]) ("the Convention") and (ii) bilateral agreements in force with three jurisdictions.[2]

1094. During the year in review, no exchanges were required to take place and no data on the timeliness of exchanges is reported.

1095. In the prior years' peer review reports, it was determined that Sint Maarten's process for the completion and exchange of templates were sufficient to meet the minimum standard. With respect to past rulings, no further action was required. Sint Maarten's implementation in this regard remains unchanged and therefore continues to meet the minimum standard.

1096. Sint Maarten has the necessary legal basis for spontaneous exchange of information, a process for completing the templates in a timely way and has completed all exchanges. Sint Maarten has met all of the ToR for the exchange of information process and no recommendations are made.

Statistics (ToR IV.D)

1097. As no rulings were issued, no statistics can be reported.

Matters related to intellectual property regimes (ToR I.A.1.3)

1098. Sint Maarten does not offer an intellectual property regime for which transparency requirements under the Action 5 Report (OECD, 2015[3]) were imposed.

Summary of recommendations on implementation of the transparency framework

Aspect of implementation of the transparency framework that should be improved	Recommendation for improvement
	No recommendations are made.

References

OECD (2021), *BEPS Action 5 on Harmful Tax Practices - Terms of Reference and Methodology for the Conduct of the Peer Reviews of the Action 5 Transparency Framework*, OECD Publishing, Paris, https://www.oecd.org/tax/beps/beps-action-5-harmful-tax-practices-peer-review-transparency-framework.pdf. [1]

OECD (2015), *Countering Harmful Tax Practices More Effectively, Taking into Account Transparency and Substance, Action 5 - 2015 Final Report*, OECD/G20 Base Erosion and Profit Shifting Project, OECD Publishing, Paris, https://doi.org/10.1787/9789264241190-en. [3]

OECD/Council of Europe (2011), *The Multilateral Convention on Mutual Administrative Assistance in Tax Matters: Amended by the 2010 Protocol*, OECD Publishing, Paris, https://doi.org/10.1787/9789264115606-en. [2]

Notes

[1] Tax exempt company.

[2] Participating jurisdictions to the Convention are available here: www.oecd.org/tax/exchange-of-tax-information/convention-on-mutual-administrative-assistance-in-tax-matters.htm. Sint Maarten also has bilateral agreements with the Netherlands, Norway and the United States.

Slovak Republic

The Slovak Republic has met all aspects of the terms of reference (OECD, 2021[1]) (ToR) for the calendar year 2022 (year in review), and no recommendations are made.

The Slovak Republic can legally issue two types of rulings within the scope of the transparency framework.

In practice, the Slovak Republic issued rulings within the scope of the transparency framework as follows:

Type of ruling	Number of rulings
Past rulings	1
Future rulings in the period 1 April 2016 – 31 December 2016	2
Future rulings in the calendar year 2017	5
Future rulings in the calendar year 2018	3
Future rulings in the calendar year 2019	3
Future rulings in the calendar year 2020	3
Future rulings in the calendar year 2021	4
Future rulings in the year in review	2

No peer input was received in respect of the exchanges of information on rulings received from the Slovak Republic.

Information gathering process (ToR I.A)

1099. The Slovak Republic can legally issue the following two types of rulings within the scope of the transparency framework: (i) cross-border unilateral APAs and any other cross-border unilateral tax rulings (such as an advance tax ruling) covering transfer pricing or the application of transfer pricing principles and (ii) permanent establishment rulings.

1100. For the Slovak Republic, past rulings are any tax rulings within scope that are issued either: (i) on or after 1 January 2014 but before 1 April 2016; or (ii) on or after 1 January 2010 but before 1 January 2014, provided they were still in effect as at 1 January 2014. Future rulings are any tax rulings within scope that are issued on or after 1 April 2016.

1101. In the prior years' peer review reports, it was determined that the Slovak Republic's undertakings to identify past and future rulings and all potential exchange jurisdictions were sufficient to meet the minimum standard. In addition, it was determined that the Slovak Republic's review and supervision mechanism was sufficient to meet the minimum standard. The Slovak Republic's implementation remains unchanged, and therefore continues to meet the minimum standard.

1102. The Slovak Republic has met all of the ToR for the information gathering process and no recommendations are made.

Exchange of information (ToR II.B)

1103. The Slovak Republic has the necessary domestic legal basis to exchange information spontaneously. The Slovak Republic notes that there are no legal or practical impediments that prevent the spontaneous exchange of information on rulings as contemplated in the Action 5 minimum standard.

1104. The Slovak Republic has international agreements permitting spontaneous exchange of information, including: (i) the *Multilateral Convention on Mutual Administrative Assistance in Tax Matters: Amended by the 2010 Protocol* (OECD/Council of Europe, 2011[2]) ("the Convention"), (ii) the Directive 2011/16/EU with all other European Union Member States and (iii) bilateral agreements in force with 70 jurisdictions.[1]

1105. For the year in review, the timeliness of exchanges is as follows:

Future rulings within the scope of the transparency framework	Number of exchanges transmitted within three months of the information becoming available to the competent authority or immediately after legal impediments have been lifted	Delayed exchanges		
		Number of exchanges transmitted later than three months of the information on rulings becoming available to the competent authority	Reasons for the delays	Any other comments
	3	1	Inadvertently delayed	See below

Follow-up requests received for exchange of the ruling	Number	Average time to provide response	Number of requests not answered
	0	N/A	N/A

1106. Similarly to the prior year's peer review report, the Slovak Republic notes that the delay occurred due to a human error and the delayed exchange is the same as last year. The ruling was issued in the first half of 2021 and exchanged in 2022. As soon as the delay was noted, communication regarding the necessity to comply with the exchange deadlines has taken place between the Head of the AEOI Unit and the Director of the Tax Office for Selected Entities. The Slovak Republic has updated internal procedures. Therefore, no recommendations are made.

1107. In the prior years' peer review reports, it was determined that the Slovak Republic's process for the completion and exchange of templates were sufficient to meet the minimum standard. With respect to past rulings, no further action was required. The Slovak Republic's implementation in this regard remains unchanged and therefore continues to meet the minimum standard.

1108. The Slovak Republic has the necessary legal basis for spontaneous exchange of information, a process for completing the templates in a timely way and has completed all exchanges. The Slovak Republic has met all of the ToR for the exchange of information process and no recommendations are made.

Statistics (ToR IV.D)

1109. The statistics for the year in review are as follows:

Category of ruling	Number of exchanges	Jurisdictions exchanged with
Cross-border unilateral APAs and any other cross-border unilateral tax rulings (such as an advance tax ruling) covering transfer pricing or the application of transfer pricing principles	*De minimis* rule applies	N/A
Permanent establishment rulings	0	N/A
De minimis rule	4	N/A
IP regimes: total exchanges on taxpayers benefitting from the third category of IP assets, new entrants benefitting from grandfathered IP regimes; and taxpayers making use of the option to treat the nexus ratio as a rebuttable presumption	0	N/A
Total	4	

Matters related to intellectual property regimes (ToR I.A.1.3)

1110. In the prior years' peer review reports, it was determined that the Slovak Republic's information gathering and exchange of information processes for matters related to intellectual property regimes[2] were sufficient to meet the minimum standard. The Slovak Republic's implementation in this regard remains unchanged and therefore continues to meet the minimum standard.

Summary of recommendations on implementation of the transparency framework

Aspect of implementation of the transparency framework that should be improved	Recommendation for improvement
	No recommendations are made.

References

OECD (2021), *BEPS Action 5 on Harmful Tax Practices - Terms of Reference and Methodology for the Conduct of the Peer Reviews of the Action 5 Transparency Framework*, OECD Publishing, Paris, https://www.oecd.org/tax/beps/beps-action-5-harmful-tax-practices-peer-review-transparency-framework.pdf. [1]

OECD (2015), *Countering Harmful Tax Practices More Effectively, Taking into Account Transparency and Substance, Action 5 - 2015 Final Report*, OECD/G20 Base Erosion and Profit Shifting Project, OECD Publishing, Paris, https://doi.org/10.1787/9789264241190-en. [3]

OECD/Council of Europe (2011), *The Multilateral Convention on Mutual Administrative Assistance in Tax Matters: Amended by the 2010 Protocol*, OECD Publishing, Paris, https://doi.org/10.1787/9789264115606-en. [2]

Notes

[1] Participating jurisdictions to the Convention are available here: www.oecd.org/tax/exchange-of-tax-information/convention-on-mutual-administrative-assistance-in-tax-matters.htm. The Slovak Republic also has bilateral agreements with Armenia, Australia, Austria, Belarus, Belgium, Bosnia and Herzegovina, Brazil, Bulgaria, Canada, China (People's Republic of), Croatia, Cyprus, Czechia, Denmark, Estonia, Ethiopia, Finland, France, Georgia, Germany, Greece, Hungary, Iceland, India, Indonesia, Iran, Ireland, Israel, Italy, Japan, Kazakhstan, Korea, Kuwait, Latvia, Libya, Lithuania, Luxembourg, Malaysia, Malta, Mexico, Moldova, Montenegro, Netherlands, Nigeria, North Macedonia, Norway, Oman, Poland, Portugal, Romania, Russia, Serbia, Singapore, Slovenia, South Africa, Spain, Sri Lanka, Sweden, Switzerland, Syrian Arab Republic, Chinese Taipei, Tunisia, Türkiye, Turkmenistan, Ukraine, United Arab Emirates, United Kingdom, United States, Uzbekistan and Viet Nam.

[2] Patent box.

Slovenia

Slovenia has met all aspects of the terms of reference (OECD, 2021[1]) (ToR) for the calendar year 2022 (year in review), and no recommendations are made.

Slovenia can legally issue three types of rulings within the scope of the transparency framework.

In practice, Slovenia issued rulings within the scope of the transparency framework as follows:

Type of ruling	Number of rulings
Past rulings	8
Future rulings in the period 1 April 2016 – 31 December 2016	0
Future rulings in the calendar year 2017	1
Future rulings in the calendar year 2018	1
Future rulings in the calendar year 2019	2
Future rulings in the calendar year 2020	0
Future rulings in the calendar year 2021	0
Future rulings in the year in review	1

No peer input was received in respect of the exchanges of information on rulings received from Slovenia.

Information gathering process (ToR I.A)

1111. Slovenia can legally issue the following three types of rulings within the scope of the transparency framework: (i) cross-border unilateral APAs and any other cross-border unilateral tax rulings (such as an advance tax ruling) covering transfer pricing or the application of transfer pricing principles; (ii) permanent establishment rulings; and (iii) related party conduit rulings.

1112. For Slovenia, past rulings are any tax rulings within scope that are issued either: (i) on or after 1 January 2014 but before 1 April 2016; or (ii) on or after 1 January 2010 but before 1 January 2014, provided they were still in effect as at 1 January 2014. Future rulings are any tax rulings within scope that are issued on or after 1 April 2016.

1113. In the prior years' peer review reports, it was determined that Slovenia's undertakings to identify past and future rulings and all potential exchange jurisdictions were sufficient to meet the minimum standard. In addition, it was determined that Slovenia's review and supervision mechanism was sufficient to meet the minimum standard. Slovenia's implementation remains unchanged, and therefore continues to meet the minimum standard.

1114. Slovenia has met all of the ToR for the information gathering process and no recommendations are made.

Exchange of information (ToR II.B)

1115. Slovenia has the necessary domestic legal basis to exchange information spontaneously. Slovenia notes that there are no legal or practical impediments that prevent the spontaneous exchange of information on rulings as contemplated in the Action 5 minimum standard.

1116. Slovenia has international agreements permitting spontaneous exchange of information, including: (i) the *Multilateral Convention on Mutual Administrative Assistance in Tax Matters: Amended by the 2010 Protocol* (OECD/Council of Europe, 2011[2]) ("the Convention"), (ii) the Directive 2011/16/EU with all other European Union Member States and (iii) bilateral agreements in force with 60 jurisdictions.[1]

1117. For the year in review, the timeliness of exchanges is as follows:

Future rulings within the scope of the transparency framework	Number of exchanges transmitted within three months of the information becoming available to the competent authority or immediately after legal impediments have been lifted	Delayed exchanges		
		Number of exchanges transmitted later than three months of the information on rulings becoming available to the competent authority	Reasons for the delays	Any other comments
	1	0	N/A	N/A

Follow-up requests received for exchange of the ruling	Number	Average time to provide response	Number of requests not answered
	0	N/A	0

1118. In the prior years' peer review reports, it was determined that Slovenia's process for the completion and exchange of templates were sufficient to meet the minimum standard. With respect to past rulings, no further action was required. Slovenia's implementation in this regard remains unchanged and therefore continues to meet the minimum standard.

1119. Slovenia has the necessary legal basis for spontaneous exchange of information, a process for completing the templates in a timely way and has completed all exchanges. Slovenia has met all of the ToR for the exchange of information process and no recommendations are made.

Statistics (ToR IV.D)

1120. The statistics for the year in review are as follows:

Category of ruling	Number of exchanges	Jurisdictions exchanged with
Cross-border unilateral APAs and any other cross-border unilateral tax rulings (such as an advance tax ruling) covering transfer pricing or the application of transfer pricing principles	0	N/A
Permanent establishment rulings	0	N/A
Related party conduit rulings	0	N/A
De minimis rule	1	N/A
Total	1	

Matters related to intellectual property regimes (ToR I.A.1.3)

1121. Slovenia does not offer an intellectual property regime for which transparency requirements under the Action 5 Report (OECD, 2015[3]) were imposed.

Summary of recommendations on implementation of the transparency framework

Aspect of implementation of the transparency framework that should be improved	Recommendation for improvement
	No recommendations are made.

References

OECD (2021), *BEPS Action 5 on Harmful Tax Practices - Terms of Reference and Methodology for the Conduct of the Peer Reviews of the Action 5 Transparency Framework*, OECD Publishing, Paris, https://www.oecd.org/tax/beps/beps-action-5-harmful-tax-practices-peer-review-transparency-framework.pdf. [1]

OECD (2015), *Countering Harmful Tax Practices More Effectively, Taking into Account Transparency and Substance, Action 5 - 2015 Final Report*, OECD/G20 Base Erosion and Profit Shifting Project, OECD Publishing, Paris, https://doi.org/10.1787/9789264241190-en. [3]

OECD/Council of Europe (2011), *The Multilateral Convention on Mutual Administrative Assistance in Tax Matters: Amended by the 2010 Protocol*, OECD Publishing, Paris, https://doi.org/10.1787/9789264115606-en. [2]

Note

1 Participating jurisdictions to the Convention are available here: www.oecd.org/tax/exchange-of-tax-information/convention-on-mutual-administrative-assistance-in-tax-matters.htm. Slovenia also has bilateral agreements with Albania, Armenia, Austria, Azerbaijan, Belgium, Belarus, Bosnia and Herzegovina, Bulgaria, Canada, China (People's Republic of), Croatia, Cyprus, Czechia, Denmark, Estonia, Finland, France, Georgia, Germany, Greece, Hungary, Iceland, India, Iran, Ireland, Isle Of Man, Israel, Italy, Japan, Kazakhstan, Korea, Kosovo, Kuwait, Latvia, Lithuania, Luxembourg, Malta, Moldova, Netherlands, North Macedonia, Norway, Poland, Portugal, Qatar, Romania, Russia, Serbia, Montenegro, Singapore, Slovak Republic, Spain, Sweden, Switzerland, Thailand, Türkiye, Ukraine, United Arab Emirates, United Kingdom, United States and Uzbekistan.

South Africa

South Africa has met all aspects of the terms of reference (OECD, 2021[1]) (ToR) for the calendar year 2022 (year in review), and no recommendations are made.

South Africa can legally issue one type of ruling within the scope of the transparency framework.

In practice, South Africa issued rulings within the scope of the transparency framework as follows:

Type of ruling	Number of rulings
Past rulings	1
Future rulings in the period 1 April 2016 – 31 December 2016	0
Future rulings in the calendar year 2017	0
Future rulings in the calendar year 2018	0
Future rulings in the calendar year 2019	0
Future rulings in the calendar year 2020	0
Future rulings in the calendar year 2021	0
Future rulings in the year in review	0

As no exchanges were required to take place, no peer input was received in respect of the exchanges of information on rulings received from South Africa.

Information gathering process (ToR I.A)

1122. South Africa can legally issue the following type of ruling within the scope of the transparency framework: preferential regimes.[1]

1123. For South Africa, past rulings are any tax rulings within scope that are issued either: (i) on or after 1 January 2014 but before 1 April 2016; or (ii) on or after 1 January 2010 but before 1 January 2014, provided they were still in effect as at 1 January 2014. Future rulings are any tax rulings within scope that are issued on or after 1 April 2016.

1124. In the prior years' peer review reports, it was determined that South Africa's undertakings to identify past and future rulings and all potential exchange jurisdictions were sufficient to meet the minimum standard. In addition, it was determined that South Africa's review and supervision mechanism was sufficient to meet the minimum standard. South Africa's implementation remains unchanged, and therefore continues to meet the minimum standard.

1125. South Africa's has met all of the ToR for the information gathering process and no recommendations are made.

Exchange of information (ToR II.B)

1126. South Africa has the necessary domestic legal basis to exchange information spontaneously. South Africa notes that there are no legal or practical impediments that prevent the spontaneous exchange of information on rulings as contemplated in the Action 5 minimum standard.

1127. South Africa has international agreements permitting spontaneous exchange of information, including: (i) the *Multilateral Convention on Mutual Administrative Assistance in Tax Matters: Amended by the 2010 Protocol* (OECD/Council of Europe, 2011[2]) ("the Convention") and (ii) bilateral agreements in force with 69 jurisdictions.[2]

1128. During the year in review, no exchanges were required to take place and no data on the timeliness of exchanges is reported.

1129. In the prior years' peer review reports, it was determined that South Africa's process for the completion and exchange of templates were sufficient to meet the minimum standard. With respect to past rulings, no further action was required. South Africa's implementation in this regard remains unchanged and therefore continues to meet the minimum standard.

1130. South Africa has the necessary legal basis for spontaneous exchange of information, a process for completing the templates in a timely way and has completed all exchanges. South Africa has met all of the ToR for the exchange of information process and no recommendations are made.

Statistics (ToR IV.D)

1131. As no rulings were issued, no statistics can be reported.

Matters related to intellectual property regimes (ToR I.A.1.3)

1132. South Africa does not offer an intellectual property regime for which transparency requirements under the Action 5 Report (OECD, 2015[3]) were imposed.

Summary of recommendations on implementation of the transparency framework

Aspect of implementation of the transparency framework that should be improved	Recommendation for improvement
	No recommendations are made.

References

OECD (2021), *BEPS Action 5 on Harmful Tax Practices - Terms of Reference and Methodology for the Conduct of the Peer Reviews of the Action 5 Transparency Framework*, OECD Publishing, Paris, https://www.oecd.org/tax/beps/beps-action-5-harmful-tax-practices-peer-review-transparency-framework.pdf. [1]

OECD (2015), *Countering Harmful Tax Practices More Effectively, Taking into Account Transparency and Substance, Action 5 - 2015 Final Report*, OECD/G20 Base Erosion and Profit Shifting Project, OECD Publishing, Paris, https://doi.org/10.1787/9789264241190-en. [3]

OECD/Council of Europe (2011), *The Multilateral Convention on Mutual Administrative Assistance in Tax Matters: Amended by the 2010 Protocol*, OECD Publishing, Paris, https://doi.org/10.1787/9789264115606-en. [2]

Notes

[1] 1) Shipping regime, and 2) Headquarters regime.

[2] Participating jurisdictions to the Convention are available here: www.oecd.org/tax/exchange-of-tax-information/convention-on-mutual-administrative-assistance-in-tax-matters.htm. South Africa also has bilateral agreements with Algeria, Australia, Austria, Belarus, Belgium, Botswana, Brazil, Bulgaria, Cameroon, Canada, Chile, China (People's Republic of), Croatia, Cyprus, Czechia, Democratic Republic of the Congo, Denmark, Egypt, Ethiopia, Finland, France, Ghana, Greece, Hong Kong (China), Hungary, India, Indonesia, Iran, Ireland, Italy, Japan, Kenya, Korea, Lesotho, Luxembourg, Malaysia, Malta, Mauritius, Mexico, Mozambique, Namibia, Netherlands, New Zealand, Nigeria, Norway, Oman, Pakistan, Poland, Portugal, Qatar, Rwanda, Samoa, Saudi Arabia, Seychelles, Singapore, Slovak Republic, Spain, Eswatini, Sweden, Tanzania, Türkiye, Turks and Caicos Islands, Uganda, Ukraine, United Arab Emirates, United Kingdom, United States, Uruguay, Zimbabwe.

Spain

Spain has met all aspects of the terms of reference (OECD, 2021[1]) (ToR) for the calendar year 2022 (year in review), and no recommendations are made.

Spain can legally issue three types of rulings within the scope of the transparency framework.

In practice, Spain issued rulings within the scope of the transparency framework as follows:

Type of ruling	Number of rulings
Past rulings	146
Future rulings in the period 1 April 2016 – 31 December 2016	28
Future rulings in the calendar year 2017	46
Future rulings in the calendar year 2018	22
Future rulings in the calendar year 2019	19
Future rulings in the calendar year 2020	43
Future rulings in the calendar year 2021	21
Future rulings in the year in review	24

Peer input was received from two jurisdictions in respect of the exchanges of information on rulings received from Spain. The input was positive, noting that information was complete, in a correct format and received in a timely manner.

Information gathering process (ToR I.A)

1133. Spain can legally issue the following three types of rulings within the scope of the transparency framework: (i) preferential regimes;[1] (ii) cross-border unilateral APAs and any other cross-border unilateral tax rulings (such as an advance tax ruling) covering transfer pricing or the application of transfer pricing principles; and (iii) permanent establishment rulings.

1134. For Spain, past rulings are any tax rulings within scope that are issued either: (i) on or after 1 January 2014 but before 1 April 2016; or (ii) on or after 1 January 2010 but before 1 January 2014, provided they were still in effect as at 1 January 2014. Future rulings are any tax rulings within scope that are issued on or after 1 April 2016.

1135. In the prior years' peer review reports, it was determined that Spain's undertakings to identify past and future rulings and all potential exchange jurisdictions were sufficient to meet the minimum standard. In addition, it was determined that Spain's review and supervision mechanism was sufficient to meet the minimum standard. Spain's implementation remains unchanged, and therefore continues to meet the minimum standard.

1136. Spain has met all of the ToR for the information gathering process and no recommendations are made.

Exchange of information (ToR II.B)

1137. Spain has the necessary domestic legal basis to exchange information spontaneously. Spain notes that there are no legal or practical impediments that prevent the spontaneous exchange of information on rulings as contemplated in the Action 5 minimum standard.

1138. Spain has international agreements permitting spontaneous exchange of information, including: (i) the *Multilateral Convention on Mutual Administrative Assistance in Tax Matters: Amended by the 2010 Protocol* (OECD/Council of Europe, 2011[2]) ("the Convention"), (ii) the Directive 2011/16/EU with all other European Union Member States and (iii) bilateral agreements in force with 93 jurisdictions.[2]

1139. For the year in review, the timeliness of exchanges is as follows:

Future rulings within the scope of the transparency framework	Number of exchanges transmitted within three months of the information becoming available to the competent authority or immediately after legal impediments have been lifted	Delayed exchanges		
		Number of exchanges transmitted later than three months of the information on rulings becoming available to the competent authority	Reasons for the delays	Any other comments
	40	0	N/A	N/A

Follow-up requests received for exchange of the ruling	Number	Average time to provide response	Number of requests not answered
	1	2 months	0

1140. In the prior years' peer review reports, it was determined that Spain's process for the completion and exchange of templates were sufficient to meet the minimum standard. With respect to past rulings, no further action was required. Spain's implementation in this regard remains unchanged and therefore continues to meet the minimum standard.

Statistics (ToR IV.D)

1141. The statistics for the year in review are as follows:

Category of ruling	Number of exchanges	Jurisdictions exchanged with
Ruling related to a preferential regime	0	N/A
Cross-border unilateral APAs and any other cross-border unilateral tax rulings (such as an advance tax ruling) covering transfer pricing or the application of transfer pricing principles	37	Argentina, Belgium, Chile, Colombia, Croatia, Finland, France, Italy, Korea, Malaysia, Mexico, Poland, Portugal, Romania, Saudi Arabia, Singapore, Slovak Republic, Türkiye, United Kingdom
Permanent establishment rulings	3	*De minimis* rule applies
IP regimes: total exchanges on taxpayers benefitting from the third category of IP assets, new entrants benefitting from grandfathered IP regimes; and taxpayers making use of the option to treat the nexus ratio as a rebuttable presumption	0	N/A
Total	40	

Matters related to intellectual property regimes (ToR I.A.1.3)

1142. In the prior year peer review report, it was determined that Spain's information gathering and exchange of information processes for matters related to intellectual property regimes[3] were sufficient to meet the minimum standard. Spain's implementation in this regard remains unchanged and therefore continues to meet the minimum standard.

Summary of recommendations on implementation of the transparency framework

Aspect of implementation of the transparency framework that should be improved	Recommendation for improvement
	No recommendations are made.

References

OECD (2021), *BEPS Action 5 on Harmful Tax Practices - Terms of Reference and Methodology for the Conduct of the Peer Reviews of the Action 5 Transparency Framework*, OECD Publishing, Paris, https://www.oecd.org/tax/beps/beps-action-5-harmful-tax-practices-peer-review-transparency-framework.pdf. [1]

OECD (2015), *Countering Harmful Tax Practices More Effectively, Taking into Account Transparency and Substance, Action 5 - 2015 Final Report*, OECD/G20 Base Erosion and Profit Shifting Project, OECD Publishing, Paris, https://doi.org/10.1787/9789264241190-en. [3]

OECD/Council of Europe (2011), *The Multilateral Convention on Mutual Administrative Assistance in Tax Matters: Amended by the 2010 Protocol*, OECD Publishing, Paris, https://doi.org/10.1787/9789264115606-en. [2]

Notes

[1] 1) Partial exemption for income from certain intangible assets and 2) Shipping regime.

[2] Parties to the Convention are available here: www.oecd.org/tax/exchange-of-tax-information/convention-on-mutual-administrative-assistance-in-tax-matters.htm. Spain also has bilateral agreements with: Albania, Algeria, Andorra, Argentina, Armenia, Australia, Austria, Azerbaijan, Barbados, Belarus, Belgium, Bolivia, Bosnia and Herzegovina, Brazil, Bulgaria, Cabo Verde, Canada, Chile, China (People's Republic of), Colombia, Costa Rica, Croatia, Cuba, Cyprus, Czechia, Dominican Republic, Ecuador, Egypt, El Salvador, Estonia, Finland, France, Georgia, Germany, Greece, Hong Kong (China), Hungary, Iceland, India, Indonesia, Iran, Ireland, Israel, Italy, Jamaica, Japan, Kazakhstan, Korea, Kuwait, Latvia, Lithuania, Luxembourg, Malaysia, Malta, Mexico, Moldova, Morocco, Netherlands, New Zealand, Nigeria, North Macedonia, Norway, Oman, Pakistan, Panama, Philippines, Poland, Portugal, Qatar, Romania, Russia, Saudi Arabia, Senegal, Serbia, Singapore, Slovak Republic, Slovenia, South Africa, Sweden, Switzerland, Tajikistan, Thailand, Trinidad and Tobago, Tunisia, Türkiye, Ukraine, United Arab Emirates, United Kingdom, United States, Uruguay, Uzbekistan, Venezuela and Viet Nam.

[3] Partial exemptions for income from certain intangible assets for: 1) Federal regime, 2) Basque country and 3) Navarra.

Sri Lanka

Sri Lanka has met all aspects of the terms of reference (OECD, 2021[1]) (ToR) for the calendar year 2022 (year in review), and no recommendations are made.

Sri Lanka can legally issue three types of rulings within the scope of the transparency framework.

In practice, Sri Lanka issued no rulings within the scope of the transparency framework.

As no exchanges were required to take place, no peer input was received in respect of the exchanges of information on rulings received from Sri Lanka.

Information gathering process (ToR I.A)

1143. Sri Lanka can legally issue the following three types of rulings within the scope of the transparency framework: (i) rulings providing for unilateral downward adjustments; (ii) permanent establishment rulings; and (iii) related party conduit rulings.[1]

1144. For Sri Lanka, past rulings are any tax rulings within scope that are issued either (i) on or after 1 January 2015 but before 1 April 2017; and (ii) on or after 1 January 2012 but before 1 January 2015, provided they were still in effect as at 1 January 2015.

1145. Future rulings are any tax rulings within scope that are issued on or after 1 April 2017.

1146. In the prior year's peer review report, it was determined that Sri Lanka's undertakings to identify past and future rulings and all potential exchange jurisdictions were sufficient to meet the minimum standard. In addition, it was determined that Sri Lanka's review and supervision mechanism was sufficient to meet the minimum standard. Sri Lanka's implementation remains unchanged, and therefore continues to meet the minimum standard.

1147. Sri Lanka has met all of the ToR for the information gathering process and no recommendations are made.

Exchange of information (ToR II.B)

1148. Sri Lanka has the necessary domestic legal basis to exchange information spontaneously. Sri Lanka notes that there are no legal or practical impediments that prevent the spontaneous exchange of information on rulings as contemplated in the Action 5 minimum standard.

1149. Sri Lanka has international agreements permitting spontaneous exchange of information, including: (i) the *Multilateral Convention on Mutual Administrative Assistance in Tax Matters: Amended by the 2010 Protocol* (OECD/Council of Europe, 2011[2]) ("the Convention") and (ii) bilateral agreements in force with 42 jurisdictions.[2]

1150. During the year in review, no exchanges were required to take place and no data on the timeliness of exchanges is reported.

1151. In the prior year's peer review report, it was determined that Sri Lanka's process for the completion and exchange of templates were sufficient to meet the minimum standard. Sri Lanka's implementation in this regard remains unchanged and therefore continues to meet the minimum standard.

1152. Sri Lanka has the necessary legal basis for spontaneous exchange of information, a process for completing the templates in a timely way and has completed all exchanges. Sri Lanka has met all of the ToR for the exchange of information process and no recommendations are made.

Statistics (ToR IV.D)

1153. As no rulings were issued, no statistics can be reported.

Matters related to intellectual property regimes (ToR I.A.1.3)

1154. Sri Lanka does not offer an intellectual property regime for which transparency requirements under the Action 5 Report (OECD, 2015[3]) were imposed.

Summary of recommendations on implementation of the transparency framework

Aspect of implementation of the transparency framework that should be improved	Recommendation for improvement
	No recommendations are made.

References

OECD (2021), *BEPS Action 5 on Harmful Tax Practices - Terms of Reference and Methodology for the Conduct of the Peer Reviews of the Action 5 Transparency Framework*, OECD Publishing, Paris, https://www.oecd.org/tax/beps/beps-action-5-harmful-tax-practices-peer-review-transparency-framework.pdf. [1]

OECD (2015), *Countering Harmful Tax Practices More Effectively, Taking into Account Transparency and Substance, Action 5 - 2015 Final Report*, OECD/G20 Base Erosion and Profit Shifting Project, OECD Publishing, Paris, https://doi.org/10.1787/9789264241190-en. [3]

OECD/Council of Europe (2011), *The Multilateral Convention on Mutual Administrative Assistance in Tax Matters: Amended by the 2010 Protocol*, OECD Publishing, Paris, https://doi.org/10.1787/9789264115606-en. [2]

Notes

1 Sri Lanka is planning to put in place a legal framework for issuing APAs in the near future.

2 Participating jurisdictions to the Convention are available here: www.oecd.org/tax/exchange-of-tax-information/convention-on-mutual-administrative-assistance-in-tax-matters.htm. Sri Lanka also has bilateral agreements with Australia, Bangladesh, Bahrain, Belarus, Belgium, Canada, China (People's Republic of), Czechia, Denmark, Finland, France, Germany, India, Indonesia, Iran, Italy, Japan, Korea, Kuwait, Luxembourg, Malaysia, Mauritius, Nepal, Netherlands, Norway, Oman, Pakistan, Palestinian Authority, Philippines, Poland, Qatar, Romania, Russia, Seychelles, Singapore, Sweden, Switzerland, Thailand, United Arab Emirates, United Kingdom, United States, and Viet Nam.

Sweden

Sweden has met all aspects of the terms of reference (OECD, 2021[1]) (ToR) for the calendar year 2022 (year in review), and no recommendations are made.

Sweden can legally issue three types of rulings within the scope of the transparency framework.

In practice, Sweden issued rulings within the scope of the transparency framework as follows:

Type of ruling	Number of rulings
Past rulings	28
Future rulings in the period 1 April 2016 – 31 December 2016	5
Future rulings in the calendar year 2017	3
Future rulings in the calendar year 2018	6
Future rulings in the calendar year 2019	1
Future rulings in the calendar year 2020	1
Future rulings in the calendar year 2021	3
Future rulings in the year in review	6

No peer input was received in respect of the exchanges of information on rulings received from Sweden.

Information gathering process (ToR I.A)

1155. Sweden can legally issue the following three types of rulings within the scope of the transparency framework: (i) preferential regimes;[1] (ii) permanent establishment rulings; and (iii) related party conduit rulings.

1156. For Sweden, past rulings are any tax rulings within scope that are issued either: (i) on or after 1 January 2014 but before 1 April 2016; or (ii) on or after 1 January 2010 but before 1 January 2014, provided they were still in effect as at 1 January 2014. Future rulings are any tax rulings within scope that are issued on or after 1 April 2016.

1157. In the prior year's peer review report, it was determined that Sweden's undertakings to identify past and future rulings and all potential exchange jurisdictions were sufficient to meet the minimum standard. In addition, it was determined that Sweden's review and supervision mechanism was sufficient to meet the minimum standard. Sweden's implementation remains unchanged, and therefore continues to meet the minimum standard.

1158. Sweden has met all of the ToR for the information gathering process and no recommendations are made.

Exchange of information (ToR II.B)

1159. Sweden has the necessary domestic legal basis to exchange information spontaneously. Sweden notes that there are no legal or practical impediments that prevent the spontaneous exchange of information on rulings as contemplated in the Action 5 minimum standard.

1160. Sweden has international agreements permitting spontaneous exchange of information, including: (i) the *Multilateral Convention on Mutual Administrative Assistance in Tax Matters: Amended by the 2010 Protocol* (OECD/Council of Europe, 2011[2]) ("the Convention"), (ii) the Directive 2011/16/EU with all other European Union Member States and (iii) the Nordic Convention on Assistance in Tax Matters, and (iv) bilateral agreements in force with 68 jurisdictions.[2]

1161. For the year in review, the timeliness of exchanges is as follows:

Future rulings within the scope of the transparency framework	Number of exchanges transmitted within three months of the information becoming available to the competent authority or immediately after legal impediments have been lifted	Delayed exchanges		
		Number of exchanges transmitted later than three months of the information on rulings becoming available to the competent authority	Reasons for the delays	Any other comments
	6	0	N/A	N/A

Follow-up requests received for exchange of the ruling	Number	Average time to provide response	Number of requests not answered
	0	N/A	N/A

1162. In the prior years' peer review reports, it was determined that Sweden's process for the completion and exchange of templates were sufficient to meet the minimum standard. With respect to past rulings, no further action was required from Sweden. Sweden's implementation in this regard remains unchanged and therefore continues to meet the minimum standard.

1163. Sweden has the necessary legal basis for spontaneous exchange of information, a process for completing the templates in a timely way and has completed all exchanges. Sweden has met all of the ToR for the exchange of information process and no recommendations are made.

Statistics (ToR IV.D)

1164. The statistics for the year in review are as follows:

Category of ruling	Number of exchanges	Jurisdictions exchanged with
Ruling related to a preferential regime	3	*De minimis* rule applies
Permanent establishment rulings	3	*De minimis* rule applies
Related party conduit rulings	0	N/A
Total	6	

Matters related to intellectual property regimes (ToR I.A.1.3)

1165. Sweden does not offer an intellectual property regime for which transparency requirements under the Action 5 Report (OECD, 2015[3]) were imposed.

Summary of recommendations on implementation of the transparency framework

Aspect of implementation of the transparency framework that should be improved	Recommendation for improvement
	No recommendations are made.

References

OECD (2021), *BEPS Action 5 on Harmful Tax Practices - Terms of Reference and Methodology for the Conduct of the Peer Reviews of the Action 5 Transparency Framework*, OECD Publishing, Paris, https://www.oecd.org/tax/beps/beps-action-5-harmful-tax-practices-peer-review-transparency-framework.pdf. [1]

OECD (2015), *Countering Harmful Tax Practices More Effectively, Taking into Account Transparency and Substance, Action 5 - 2015 Final Report*, OECD/G20 Base Erosion and Profit Shifting Project, OECD Publishing, Paris, https://doi.org/10.1787/9789264241190-en. [3]

OECD/Council of Europe (2011), *The Multilateral Convention on Mutual Administrative Assistance in Tax Matters: Amended by the 2010 Protocol*, OECD Publishing, Paris, https://doi.org/10.1787/9789264115606-en. [2]

Notes

[1] Tonnage tax regime.

[2] Participating jurisdictions to the Convention are available here: www.oecd.org/tax/exchange-of-tax-information/convention-on-mutual-administrative-assistance-in-tax-matters.htm. Sweden also has bilateral agreements with Albania, Argentina, Armenia, Australia, Austria, Barbados, Belarus, Belgium, Bosnia and Herzegovina, Botswana, Brazil, Bulgaria, Canada, Chile, China (People's Republic of), Croatia, Czechia, Egypt, Estonia, France, Georgia, Germany, Hungary, India, Indonesia, Ireland, Israel, Italy, Jamaica, Japan, Kazakhstan, Kenya, Korea, Latvia, Lithuania, Luxembourg, Malaysia, Malta, Mauritius, Mexico, Montenegro, Namibia, Netherlands, New Zealand, Nigeria, North Macedonia, Pakistan, Poland, Romania, Russia, Saudi Arabia, Serbia, Singapore, Slovak Republic, Slovenia, South Africa, Spain, Sri Lanka, Switzerland, Thailand, Trinidad and Tobago, Tunisia, Türkiye, Ukraine, United Kingdom, United States, Viet Nam and Zambia.

Switzerland

Switzerland has met all aspects of the terms of reference (OECD, 2021[1]) (ToR) for the calendar year 2022 (year in review), except for the timely exchange of information on past and future rulings (ToR II.B.6). Switzerland receives one recommendation on this point for the year in review.

In the prior year report, Switzerland had received the same recommendation. Efforts have been made during the year in review to address the recommendation, but as the issue has not yet been fully resolved, the recommendation remains in place.

Switzerland can legally issue four types of rulings within the scope of the transparency framework.

In practice, Switzerland issued rulings within the scope of the transparency framework as follows:

Type of ruling	Number of rulings
Past rulings	883[1]
Future rulings in the calendar year 2017	300
Future rulings in the calendar year 2018	228
Future rulings in the calendar year 2019	293
Future rulings in the calendar year 2020	214
Future rulings in the calendar year 2021	234
Future rulings in the year in review	282

Peer input was received from five jurisdictions in respect of the exchanges of information on rulings received from Switzerland. The input was generally positive, noting that overall information was complete and in a correct format. However, one peer indicated that exchanges on rulings were not timely.

Information gathering process (ToR I.A)

1166. Switzerland can legally issue the following four types of rulings within the scope of the transparency framework: (i) preferential regimes;[2] (ii) cross-border unilateral APAs and any other cross-border unilateral tax rulings (such as an advance tax ruling) covering transfer pricing or the application of transfer pricing principles; (iii) permanent establishment rulings; and (iv) related party conduit rulings.

1167. For Switzerland, past rulings are any tax rulings within scope that are issued on or after 1 January 2010 until 31 December 2016, provided they were still in effect as at 1 January 2018. For Switzerland, future rulings are any tax rulings within scope that are issued on or after 1 January 2017, provided they are still in effect on or after 1 January 2018.

1168. In the prior year's peer review reports, it was determined that Switzerland's undertakings to identify past and future rulings and all potential exchange jurisdictions were sufficient to meet the minimum standard. In addition, it was determined that Switzerland's review and supervision mechanism was sufficient to meet the minimum standard. Switzerland's implementation remains unchanged, and therefore continues to meet the minimum standard.

1169. Switzerland has met all of the ToR for the information gathering process and no recommendations are made.

Exchange of information (ToR II.B)

Legal basis for spontaneous exchange of information (ToR II.B.1, II.B.2)

1170. Switzerland has the necessary domestic legal basis to exchange information spontaneously. Switzerland notes that there are no legal or practical impediments that prevent the spontaneous exchange of information on rulings as contemplated in the Action 5 minimum standard.

1171. Switzerland's international agreement permitting spontaneous exchange of information is the *Multilateral Convention on Mutual Administrative Assistance in Tax Matters: Amended by the 2010 Protocol* (OECD/Council of Europe, 2011[2]) ("the Convention").[3] The necessary domestic and international legal framework for spontaneous exchange of information entered into force on 1 January 2017, allowing for exchanges from 1 January 2018.

Completion and exchange of templates (ToR II.B.3, II.B.4, II.B.5, II.B.6, II.B.7)

1172. In the prior years' peer review reports, it was determined that Switzerland's process for the completion and exchange of templates met all the ToR, except for timely exchange of information on past and future rulings (ToR II.B.6).

1173. For the year in review, the timeliness of exchanges is as follows:

Past rulings within the scope of the transparency framework	Number of exchanges transmitted by 31 December 2022	Delayed exchanges		
		Number of exchanges not transmitted by 31 December 2022	Reasons for the delays	Any other comments
	1[4]	0	N/A	N/A
Future rulings within the scope of the transparency framework	Number of exchanges transmitted within three months of the information becoming available to the competent authority or immediately after legal impediments have been lifted	Delayed exchanges		
		Number of exchanges transmitted later than three months of the information on rulings becoming available to the competent authority	Reasons for the delays	Any other comments

	361	32	N/A	N/A
Total	362	32		

Follow-up requests received for exchange of the ruling	Number	Average time to provide response	Number of requests not answered
	0		

1174. Similar to the prior year's report, Switzerland encountered delays with the exchange of information on one past ruling and future rulings due to legal impediments and modernisation of the SEOI platform. Switzerland notes that it has further improved its IT system (CTS implementation), including an automatic periodical approval of rulings on the SEOI platform. Despite Switzerland's efforts, there were still delays during the year in review. Therefore, the recommendation remains in place and the situation will be further reviewed during next year's peer review.

1175. Switzerland still encountered delays regarding the exchange of information on past and future rulings. Therefore, the recommendation to continue to ensure that all information on past and future rulings is exchanged as soon as possible (ToR II.B.6) remains in place.

Conclusion on section B

1176. Switzerland has met all of the ToR for the exchange of information process except for the timely exchange of information on past and future rulings (ToR II.B.6). Switzerland is recommended to continue to ensure that all information on past and future rulings is exchanged as soon as possible.

Statistics (ToR IV.D)

1177. The statistics for the year in review are as follows:

Category of ruling	Number of exchanges	Jurisdictions exchanged with
Ruling related to a preferential regime	6	*De minimis* rule applies
Cross-border unilateral APAs and any other cross-border unilateral tax rulings (such as an advance tax ruling) covering transfer pricing or the application of transfer pricing principles	257	Antigua and Barbuda, Australia, Austria, Barbados, Belgium, Brazil, Canada, China (People's Republic of), Curaçao, Cyprus, Denmark, Germany, Greece, Estonia, France, Guernsey, Hong Kong (China), India, Ireland, Israel, Italy, Jersey, Japan, Korea, Liechtenstein, Luxembourg, Malta, Mexico, Netherlands, New Zealand, Nigeria, Norway, Panama, Poland, Russia, San Marino, Singapore, Spain, South Africa, Sweden, United Kingdom
Permanent establishment rulings	48	Barbados, Brazil, Canada, Colombia, Denmark, Germany, Finland, Hong Kong (China), Hungary, Italy, Liechtenstein, Luxembourg, Mauritius, Netherlands, Spain, United Kingdom
Related party conduit rulings	0	
Total	311	

Matters related to intellectual property regimes (ToR I.A.1.3)

1178. In the prior years' peer review report, it was determined that Switzerland's information gathering and exchange of information processes for matters related to intellectual property regimes[5] were sufficient to meet the minimum standard. Switzerland's implementation in this regard remains unchanged and therefore continues to meet the minimum standard.

Summary of recommendations on implementation of the transparency framework

Aspect of implementation of the transparency framework that should be improved	Recommendation for improvement
Switzerland experienced delays in the exchange of information on past and future rulings.	Switzerland is recommended to continue to ensure that all information on past and future rulings is exchanged as soon as possible. This recommendation remains unchanged since the 2019, 2020 and 2021 peer review reports.

References

OECD (2021), *BEPS Action 5 on Harmful Tax Practices - Terms of Reference and Methodology for the Conduct of the Peer Reviews of the Action 5 Transparency Framework*, OECD Publishing, Paris, https://www.oecd.org/tax/beps/beps-action-5-harmful-tax-practices-peer-review-transparency-framework.pdf. [1]

OECD (2015), *Countering Harmful Tax Practices More Effectively, Taking into Account Transparency and Substance, Action 5 - 2015 Final Report*, OECD/G20 Base Erosion and Profit Shifting Project, OECD Publishing, Paris, https://doi.org/10.1787/9789264241190-en. [3]

OECD/Council of Europe (2011), *The Multilateral Convention on Mutual Administrative Assistance in Tax Matters: Amended by the 2010 Protocol*, OECD Publishing, Paris, https://doi.org/10.1787/9789264115606-en. [2]

Notes

[1] Out of these 883 rulings, 225 fall in two or more categories.

[2] Patent box.

[3] Participating jurisdictions to the Convention are available here: www.oecd.org/tax/exchange-of-tax-information/convention-on-mutual-administrative-assistance-in-tax-matters.htm.

[4] Switzerland had one exchange of a past ruling that was issued in 2015 and only identified in 2021 because of various changes of personnel in one of the cantons. Switzerland notes that this was an exceptional case.

[5] Patent box.

Thailand

Thailand has met all aspects of the terms of reference (OECD, 2021[1]) (ToR) for the calendar year 2022 (year in review), except for the timely exchange of information on future rulings (ToR II.B.6). Thailand receives one recommendation on this point for the year in review.

In the prior year report, Thailand had received one recommendation, related to having a domestic legal framework allowing spontaneous exchange of information on rulings. Thailand has resolved this issue, and the recommendation is removed. However, as Thailand experienced delays in the exchange of information on future rulings, a new recommendation has been made as relevant.

Thailand can legally issue one type of rulings within the scope of the transparency framework.

In practice, Thailand issued rulings within the scope of the transparency framework as follows:

Type of ruling	Number of rulings
Past rulings	182
Future rulings in the period 1 April 2018 – 31 December 2018	36
Future rulings in the calendar year 2019	157
Future rulings in the calendar year 2020	23
Future rulings in the calendar year 2021	21
Future rulings in the year in review	74

Peer input was received from two jurisdictions in respect of the exchanges of information on rulings received from Thailand. The input was generally positive, noting that overall information was complete, in a correct format and almost all received in a timely manner. However, one peer input indicated that exchanges on rulings were not timely.

Information gathering process (ToR I.A)

1179. Thailand can legally issue the following type of ruling within the scope of the transparency framework: preferential regimes.[1]

1180. For Thailand, past rulings are any tax rulings within scope that are issued either: (i) on or after 1 January 2016 but before 1 April 2018; or (ii) on or after 1 January 2014 but before 1 January 2016, provided they were still in effect as at 1 January 2016.

1181. In the prior years' peer review reports, it was determined that Thailand's undertakings to identify past rulings and all potential exchange jurisdictions were sufficient to meet the minimum standard. Thailand's undertakings in this regard remain unchanged, and therefore continue to meet the minimum standard.

1182. Thailand has met all of the ToR for the information gathering process and no recommendations are made.

Exchange of information (ToR II.B)

Legal basis for spontaneous exchange of information (ToR II.B.1, II.B.2)

1183. In the prior years' peer review reports, it was determined that Thailand did not have the necessary domestic legal basis to exchange information spontaneously. Thailand received a recommendation for this.

1184. During the year in review, Thailand made an amendment to Section 10 of the Revenue Code, which is a new legal provision allowing spontaneous exchanges of information. The amendment entered into effect on 25 January 2022, and Thailand has commenced the relevant exchanges regarding the Action 5 transparency framework as of that date. As the legal impediments have been lifted in 2022 and Thailand now has a domestic legal framework which allows spontaneous exchange of information on rulings, the prior years' recommendation is removed.

1185. Thailand has international agreements permitting spontaneous exchange of information, including: (i) the *Multilateral Convention on Mutual Administrative Assistance in Tax Matters: Amended by the 2010 Protocol* (OECD/Council of Europe, 2011[2]) ("the Convention") and (ii) bilateral agreements in force with 61 jurisdictions.[2] Thailand signed the Convention on 3 June 2020 and deposited its instrument of ratification on 22 December 2021. The Convention entered into force on 1 April 2022 and will have effect for administrative assistance related to taxable periods beginning on or after 1 January 2023.

Completion and exchange of templates (ToR II.B.3, II.B.4, II.B.5, II.B.6, II.B.7)

1186. For the year in review, the timeliness of exchanges is as follows:

Past rulings within the scope of the transparency framework	Number of exchanges transmitted by 31 December 2022	Delayed exchanges		
		Number of exchanges not transmitted by 31 December 2022	Reasons for the delays	Any other comments
	746	0	N/A	N/A
Future rulings within the scope of the transparency framework	Number of exchanges transmitted within three months of the information becoming available to the competent authority or immediately after legal impediments have been lifted	Delayed exchanges		
		Number of exchanges transmitted later than three months of the information on rulings becoming available to the competent authority	Reasons for the delays	Any other comments

	345	913	See below.	N/A
Total	1 091	913		

Follow-up requests received for exchange of the ruling	Number	Average time to provide response	Number of requests not answered
	0	N/A	N/A

1187. As Thailand has the necessary domestic legal basis to exchange information on rulings as of 2022, it has now commenced exchanges. Out of the 2,004 exchanges to be transmitted from previous years, 1,091 exchanges were processed in 2022, including all information on past rulings. Thailand notes that the remaining exchanges related to future rulings will be completed by the second quarter of 2023. Therefore, Thailand is recommended to ensure that the remaining exchanges of information on future rulings occur as soon as possible.

Conclusion on section B

1188. Thailand has the necessary domestic legal basis for spontaneous exchange of information and has a process for completing the templates in a timely way. In the prior year's peer review report, Thailand received a recommendation to finalise the amendments to put the domestic legal basis in place to commence exchanges. Thailand has completed this during the year of review. Thailand has met all of the ToR for the exchange of information process, except the timely exchange on future rulings. Thailand is still in the process of completing exchanges and is expecting to finalise this in 2023. Therefore, Thailand receives one recommendation to exchange the information on the remaining rulings on this point for the year in review.

Statistics (ToR IV.D)

1189. The statistics for the year in review are as follows:

Category of ruling	Number of exchanges	Jurisdictions exchanged with
Ruling related to a preferential regime	1 091	Australia, Bangladesh, Belgium, Bulgaria, Cambodia, Canada, Chile, China (People's Republic of), Cyprus, Czechia, Denmark, Finland, France, Germany, Hong Kong (China), Hungary, India, Indonesia, Ireland, Israel, Italy, Japan, Korea, Lao People's Democratic Republic, Luxembourg, Malaysia, Mauritius, Myanmar, Netherlands, New Zealand, Norway, Oman, Pakistan, Philippines, Poland, Romania, Russia, Seychelles, Singapore, South Africa, Spain, Sri Lanka, Sweden, Switzerland, Chinese Taipei, Türkiye, United Arab Emirates, United Kingdom, United States, Viet Nam

Matters related to intellectual property regimes (ToR I.A.1.3)

1190. In the prior years' peer review reports, it was determined that Thailand offers an intellectual property regime[3] for which no transparency requirements under the Action 5 Report (OECD, 2015[3]) were imposed.

Summary of recommendations on implementation of the transparency framework

Aspect of implementation of the transparency framework that should be improved	Recommendation for improvement
Thailand implemented a legal provision which has taken effect in 2022 and now has the necessary legal framework to exchange information on rulings spontaneously. Thailand has commenced exchanges of information on past and future rulings. However, Thailand still experienced delays on exchanges of information on future rulings during the year in review.	Thailand is recommended to exchange information on the remaining future rulings as soon as possible.

References

OECD (2021), *BEPS Action 5 on Harmful Tax Practices - Terms of Reference and Methodology for the Conduct of the Peer Reviews of the Action 5 Transparency Framework*, OECD Publishing, Paris, https://www.oecd.org/tax/beps/beps-action-5-harmful-tax-practices-peer-review-transparency-framework.pdf. [1]

OECD (2015), *Countering Harmful Tax Practices More Effectively, Taking into Account Transparency and Substance, Action 5 - 2015 Final Report*, OECD/G20 Base Erosion and Profit Shifting Project, OECD Publishing, Paris, https://doi.org/10.1787/9789264241190-en. [3]

OECD/Council of Europe (2011), *The Multilateral Convention on Mutual Administrative Assistance in Tax Matters: Amended by the 2010 Protocol*, OECD Publishing, Paris, https://doi.org/10.1787/9789264115606-en. [2]

Notes

[1] International business centre.

[2] Participating jurisdictions to the Convention are available here: www.oecd.org/tax/exchange-of-tax-information/convention-on-mutual-administrative-assistance-in-tax-matters.htm. Thailand also has bilateral agreements with Armenia, Australia, Austria, Bahrain, Bangladesh, Belarus, Belgium, Bulgaria, Cambodia, Canada, Chile, China (People's Republic of), Cyprus, Czechia, Denmark, Estonia, Finland, France, Germany, Hong Kong (China), Hungary, India, Indonesia, Ireland, Israel, Italy, Japan, Korea, Kuwait, Lao People's Democratic Republic, Luxembourg, Malaysia, Mauritius, Myanmar, Nepal, Netherlands, New Zealand, Norway, Oman, Pakistan, Philippines, Poland, Romania, Russia, Seychelles, Singapore, Slovenia, South Africa, Spain, Sri Lanka, Sweden, Switzerland, Chinese Taipei, Tajikistan, Türkiye, Ukraine, United Arab Emirates, United Kingdom, United States, Uzbekistan and Viet Nam.

[3] International business centre.

Türkiye

Türkiye has met all aspects of the terms of reference (OECD, 2021[1]) (ToR) for the calendar year 2022 (year in review), and no recommendations are made.

Türkiye can legally issue one type of rulings within the scope of the transparency framework.

In practice, Türkiye issued rulings within the scope of the transparency framework as follows:

Type of ruling	Number of rulings
Past rulings	3
Future rulings in the period 1 April 2016 – 31 December 2016	0
Future rulings in the calendar year 2017	8
Future rulings in the calendar year 2018	0
Future rulings in the calendar year 2019	0
Future rulings in the calendar year 2020	0
Future rulings in the calendar year 2021	4
Future rulings in the year in review	2

No peer input was received in respect of the exchanges of information on rulings received from Türkiye.

Information gathering process (ToR I.A)

1191. Türkiye can legally issue the following type of ruling within the scope of the transparency framework: cross-border unilateral APAs and any other cross-border unilateral tax rulings (such as an advance tax ruling) covering transfer pricing or the application of transfer pricing principles.

1192. For Türkiye, past rulings are any tax rulings within scope that are issued either: (i) on or after 1 January 2014 but before 1 April 2016; or (ii) on or after 1 January 2010 but before 1 January 2014, provided they were still in effect as at 1 January 2014. Future rulings are any tax rulings within scope that are issued on or after 1 April 2016.

1193. In the prior years' peer review reports, it was determined that Türkiye's undertakings to identify past and future rulings and all potential exchange jurisdictions were sufficient to meet the minimum standard. In addition, it was determined that Türkiye's review and supervision mechanism was sufficient to meet the minimum standard. Türkiye's implementation remains unchanged, and therefore continues to meet the minimum standard.

1194. Türkiye has met all of the ToR for the information gathering process and no recommendations are made.

Exchange of information (ToR II.B)

1195. Türkiye has the necessary domestic legal basis to exchange information spontaneously. Türkiye notes that there are no legal or practical impediments that prevent the spontaneous exchange of information on rulings as contemplated in the Action 5 minimum standard.

1196. Türkiye has international agreements permitting spontaneous exchange of information, including: (i) the *Multilateral Convention on Mutual Administrative Assistance in Tax Matters: Amended by the 2010 Protocol* (OECD/Council of Europe, 2011[2]) ("the Convention") and (ii) bilateral agreements in force with 80 jurisdictions.[1]

1197. For the year in review, the timeliness of exchanges is as follows:

Future rulings within the scope of the transparency framework	Number of exchanges transmitted within three months of the information becoming available to the competent authority or immediately after legal impediments have been lifted	Delayed exchanges		
		Number of exchanges transmitted later than three months of the information on rulings becoming available to the competent authority	Reasons for the delays	Any other comments
	2	0	N/A	N/A

Follow-up requests received for exchange of the ruling	Number	Average time to provide response	Number of requests not answered
	0	N/A	N/A

1198. In the prior years' peer review reports, it was determined that Türkiye's process for the completion and exchange of templates were sufficient to meet the minimum standard. With respect to past rulings, no further action was required. Türkiye's implementation in this regard remains unchanged and therefore continues to meet the minimum standard.

1199. Türkiye has the necessary legal basis for spontaneous exchange of information, a process for completing the templates in a timely way and has completed all exchanges. Türkiye has met all of the ToR for the exchange of information process and no recommendations are made.

Statistics (ToR IV.D)

1200. The statistics for the year in review are as follows:

Category of ruling	Number of exchanges	Jurisdictions exchanged with
Cross-border unilateral APAs and any other cross-border unilateral tax rulings (such as an advance tax ruling) covering transfer pricing or the application of transfer pricing principles	*De minimis* rule applies	N/A
De minimis rule	2	
IP regimes: total exchanges on taxpayers benefitting from the third category of IP assets, new entrants benefitting from grandfathered IP regimes; and taxpayers making use of the option to treat the nexus ratio as a rebuttable presumption	3[2]	*De minimis* rule applies
Total	5	

Matters related to intellectual property regimes (ToR I.A.1.3)

1201. In the prior year's peer review report, it was determined that Türkiye's information gathering and exchange of information processes for matters related to intellectual property regimes were sufficient to meet the minimum standard. Türkiye's implementation in this regard remains unchanged and therefore continues to meet the minimum standard.

Summary of recommendations on implementation of the transparency framework

Aspect of implementation of the transparency framework that should be improved	Recommendation for improvement
	No recommendations are made.

References

OECD (2021), *BEPS Action 5 on Harmful Tax Practices - Terms of Reference and Methodology for the Conduct of the Peer Reviews of the Action 5 Transparency Framework*, OECD Publishing, Paris, https://www.oecd.org/tax/beps/beps-action-5-harmful-tax-practices-peer-review-transparency-framework.pdf. [1]

OECD (2015), *Countering Harmful Tax Practices More Effectively, Taking into Account Transparency and Substance, Action 5 - 2015 Final Report*, OECD/G20 Base Erosion and Profit Shifting Project, OECD Publishing, Paris, https://doi.org/10.1787/9789264241190-en. [3]

OECD/Council of Europe (2011), *The Multilateral Convention on Mutual Administrative Assistance in Tax Matters: Amended by the 2010 Protocol*, OECD Publishing, Paris, https://doi.org/10.1787/9789264115606-en. [2]

Notes

[1] Participating jurisdictions to the Convention are available here: www.oecd.org/tax/exchange-of-tax-information/convention-on-mutual-administrative-assistance-in-tax-matters.htm. Türkiye also has bilateral agreements with Albania, Algeria, Australia, Austria, Azerbaijan, Bahrain, Bangladesh, Belarus, Belgium, Bosnia and Herzegovina, Brazil, Bulgaria, Canada, Chad, China (People's Republic of), Croatia, Czechia, Denmark, Egypt, Estonia, Ethiopia, Finland, France, Gambia, Georgia, Germany, Greece, Hungary, India, Indonesia, Iran, Ireland, Israel, Italy, Japan, Jordan, Kazakhstan, Korea, Kosovo, Kuwait, Kyrgyzstan, Latvia, Lebanon, Lithuania, Luxembourg, Malaysia, Malta, Mexico, Moldova, Mongolia, Montenegro, Morocco, Netherlands, New Zealand, North Macedonia, Norway, Oman, Pakistan, Philippines, Poland, Portugal, Qatar, Romania, Rwanda, Russian Federation, Saudi Arabia, Serbia, Singapore, Slovak Republic, Slovenia, South Africa, Spain, Sudan, Sweden, Switzerland, Syrian Arab Republic, Tajikistan, Thailand, Tunisia, Turkish Republic of Northern Cyprus, Turkmenistan, Ukraine, United Arab Emirates, United Kingdom, United States, Uzbekistan, Venezuela, Viet Nam and Yemen.

[2] Exchanges that are made related to IP regimes are not counted as issued rulings, therefore, there is a difference between the number of exchanges and the number of issued rulings.

Ukraine

Ukraine has met all aspects of the terms of reference (OECD, 2021[1]) (ToR) for the calendar year 2022 (year in review), and no recommendations are made.

Ukraine can legally issue one type of ruling within the scope of the transparency framework.

In practice, Ukraine issued no rulings within the scope of the transparency framework.

As no exchanges were required to take place, no peer input was received in respect of the exchanges of information on rulings received from Ukraine.

Information gathering process (ToR I.A)

1202. Ukraine can legally issue the following type of ruling within the scope of the transparency framework: cross-border unilateral APAs and any other cross-border unilateral tax rulings (such as an advance tax ruling) covering transfer pricing or the application of transfer pricing principles.

1203. For Ukraine, past rulings are any tax rulings within scope that are issued either: (i) on or after 1 January 2016, but before 1 April 2018; and (ii) on or after 1 January 2014, but before 1 January 2016, provided still in effect as at 1 January 2016. Future rulings are any tax rulings within scope that are issued on or after 1 April 2018.

1204. In the prior years' peer review reports, it was determined that Ukraine's undertakings to identify past and future rulings and all potential exchange jurisdictions were sufficient to meet the minimum standard. In addition, it was determined that Ukraine's review and supervision mechanism was sufficient to meet the minimum standard. Ukraine's implementation remains unchanged, and therefore continues to meet the minimum standard.

1205. Ukraine has met all of the ToR for the information gathering process and no recommendations are made.

Exchange of information (ToR II.B)

1206. Ukraine has the necessary domestic legal basis to exchange information spontaneously. Ukraine notes that there are no legal or practical impediments that prevent the spontaneous exchange of information on rulings as contemplated in the Action 5 minimum standard.

1207. Ukraine has international agreements permitting spontaneous exchange of information, including: (i) the *Multilateral Convention on Mutual Administrative Assistance in Tax Matters: Amended by the 2010 Protocol* (OECD/Council of Europe, 2011[2]) ("the Convention") and (ii) bilateral agreements in force with 75 jurisdictions.[1]

1208. During the year in review, no exchanges were required to take place and no data on the timeliness of exchanges is reported.

1209. In the prior years' peer review reports, it was determined that Ukraine's process for the completion and exchange of templates were sufficient to meet the minimum standard. With respect to past rulings, no action was required. Ukraine's implementation in this regard remains unchanged and therefore continues to meet the minimum standard.

1210. Ukraine has the necessary legal basis for spontaneous exchange of information and a process for completion of templates and exchange of information on rulings. Ukraine has met all of the ToR for the exchange of information process and no recommendations are made.

Statistics (ToR IV.D)

1211. As no rulings were issued, no statistics can be reported.

Matters related to intellectual property regimes (ToR I.A.1.3)

1212. Ukraine does not offer an intellectual property regime for which transparency requirements under the Action 5 Report (OECD, 2015[3]) were imposed.

Summary of recommendations on implementation of the transparency framework

Aspect of implementation of the transparency framework that should be improved	Recommendation for improvement
	No recommendations are made.

References

OECD (2021), *BEPS Action 5 on Harmful Tax Practices - Terms of Reference and Methodology for the Conduct of the Peer Reviews of the Action 5 Transparency Framework*, OECD Publishing, Paris, https://www.oecd.org/tax/beps/beps-action-5-harmful-tax-practices-peer-review-transparency-framework.pdf. [1]

OECD (2015), *Countering Harmful Tax Practices More Effectively, Taking into Account Transparency and Substance, Action 5 - 2015 Final Report*, OECD/G20 Base Erosion and Profit Shifting Project, OECD Publishing, Paris, https://doi.org/10.1787/9789264241190-en. [3]

OECD/Council of Europe (2011), *The Multilateral Convention on Mutual Administrative Assistance in Tax Matters: Amended by the 2010 Protocol*, OECD Publishing, Paris, https://doi.org/10.1787/9789264115606-en. [2]

Note

[1] Participating jurisdictions to the Convention are available here: www.oecd.org/tax/exchange-of-tax-information/convention-on-mutual-administrative-assistance-in-tax-matters.htm. Ukraine also has bilateral agreements with Algeria, Armenia, Austria, Azerbaijan, Belarus, Belgium, Brazil, Bulgaria, Canada, China (People's Republic of), Croatia, Cyprus, Czechia, Denmark, Egypt, Estonia, Finland, France, Georgia, Germany, Greece, Hungary, Iceland, India, Indonesia, Iran, Ireland, Israel, Italy, Japan, Jordan, Kazakhstan, Korea, Kuwait, Kyrgyzstan, Latvia, Lebanon, Libya, Lithuania, Luxembourg, Malaysia, Malta, Mexico, Moldova, Mongolia, Montenegro, Morocco, Netherlands, North Macedonia, Norway, Pakistan, Poland, Portugal, Qatar, Romania, Russia, Saudi Arabia, Serbia, Singapore, Slovak Republic, Slovenia, South Africa, Spain, Sweden, Switzerland, Syrian Arab Republic, Tajikistan, Thailand, Türkiye, Turkmenistan, United Arab Emirates, United Kingdom, United States, Uzbekistan and Viet Nam.

United Kingdom

The United Kingdom has met all aspects of the terms of reference (OECD, 2021[1]) (ToR) for the calendar year 2022 (year in review), and no recommendations are made.

The United Kingdom can legally issue three types of rulings within the scope of the transparency framework.

In practice, the United Kingdom issued rulings within the scope of the transparency framework as follows:

Type of ruling	Number of rulings
Past rulings	599
Future rulings in the period 1 April 2016 – 31 December 2016	71
Future rulings in the calendar year 2017	16
Future rulings in the calendar year 2018	20
Future rulings in the calendar year 2019	14
Future rulings in the calendar year 2020	13
Future rulings in the calendar year 2021	13
Future rulings in the year in review	12

Peer input was received from two jurisdictions in respect of the exchanges of information on rulings received from the United Kingdom. The input was positive, noting that information was complete, in a correct format and received in a timely manner.

Information gathering process (ToR I.A)

1213. The United Kingdom can legally issue the following three types of rulings within the scope of the transparency framework: (i) preferential regimes;[1] (ii) cross-border unilateral APAs and any other cross-border unilateral tax rulings (such as an advance tax ruling) covering transfer pricing or the application of transfer pricing principles; and (iii) permanent establishment rulings.

1214. For the United Kingdom, past rulings are any tax rulings within scope that are issued either: (i) on or after 1 January 2014 but before 1 April 2016; or (ii) on or after 1 January 2010 but before 1 January 2014, provided they were still in effect as at 1 January 2014. Future rulings are any tax rulings within scope that are issued on or after 1 April 2016

1215. In the prior years' peer review reports, it was determined that the United Kingdom's undertakings to identify past and future rulings and all potential exchange jurisdictions were sufficient to meet the minimum standard. In addition, it was determined that The United Kingdom's review and supervision mechanism was sufficient to meet the minimum standard. The United Kingdom's implementation remains unchanged, and therefore continues to meet the minimum standard.

1216. The United Kingdom has met all of the ToR for the information gathering process and no recommendations are made.

Exchange of information (ToR II.B)

1217. The United Kingdom has the necessary domestic legal basis to exchange information spontaneously. The United Kingdom notes that there are no legal or practical impediments that prevent the spontaneous exchange of information on rulings as contemplated in the Action 5 minimum standard.

1218. The United Kingdom has international agreements permitting spontaneous exchange of information, including: (i) the *Multilateral Convention on Mutual Administrative Assistance in Tax Matters: Amended by the 2010 Protocol* (OECD/Council of Europe, 2011[2]) ("the Convention") and (ii) bilateral agreements in force with 155 jurisdictions.[2]

1219. For the year in review, the timeliness of exchanges is as follows:

Future rulings within the scope of the transparency framework	Number of exchanges transmitted within three months of the information becoming available to the competent authority or immediately after legal impediments have been lifted	Delayed exchanges		
		Number of exchanges transmitted later than three months of the information on rulings becoming available to the competent authority	Reasons for the delays	Any other comments
	13	0	N/A	N/A

Follow-up requests received for exchange of the ruling	Number	Average time to provide response	Number of requests not answered
	0	N/A	N/A

1220. In the prior years' peer review reports, it was determined that the United Kingdom's process for the completion and exchange of templates were sufficient to meet the minimum standard. With respect to past rulings, no further action was required. The United Kingdom's implementation in this regard remains unchanged and therefore continues to meet the minimum standard.

1221. The United Kingdom has the necessary legal basis for spontaneous exchange of information, a process for completing the templates in a timely way and has completed all exchanges. The United Kingdom has met all of the ToR for the exchange of information process and no recommendations are made.

Statistics (ToR IV.D)

1222. The statistics for the year in review are as follows:

Category of ruling	Number of exchanges	Jurisdictions exchanged with
Ruling related to a preferential regime	0	N/A
Cross-border unilateral APAs and any other cross-border unilateral tax rulings (such as an advance tax ruling) covering transfer pricing or the application of transfer pricing principles	0	N/A
Permanent establishment rulings	13	Australia, Germany, Ireland, Israel, Norway, Sweden, Switzerland, United States
IP regimes: total exchanges on taxpayers benefitting from the third category of IP assets, new entrants benefitting from grandfathered IP regimes; and taxpayers making use of the option to treat the nexus ratio as a rebuttable presumption	0	N/A
Total	13	

Matters related to intellectual property regimes (ToR I.A.1.3)

1223. In the prior years' peer review reports, it was determined that The United Kingdom's information gathering and exchange of information processes for matters related to intellectual property regimes[3] were sufficient to meet the minimum standard. The United Kingdom's implementation in this regard remains unchanged and therefore continues to meet the minimum standard.

Summary of recommendations on implementation of the transparency framework

Aspect of implementation of the transparency framework that should be improved	Recommendation for improvement
	No recommendations are made.

References

OECD (2021), *BEPS Action 5 on Harmful Tax Practices - Terms of Reference and Methodology for the Conduct of the Peer Reviews of the Action 5 Transparency Framework*, OECD Publishing, Paris, https://www.oecd.org/tax/beps/beps-action-5-harmful-tax-practices-peer-review-transparency-framework.pdf. [1]

OECD (2015), *Countering Harmful Tax Practices More Effectively, Taking into Account Transparency and Substance, Action 5 - 2015 Final Report*, OECD/G20 Base Erosion and Profit Shifting Project, OECD Publishing, Paris, https://doi.org/10.1787/9789264241190-en. [3]

OECD/Council of Europe (2011), *The Multilateral Convention on Mutual Administrative Assistance in Tax Matters: Amended by the 2010 Protocol*, OECD Publishing, Paris, https://doi.org/10.1787/9789264115606-en. [2]

Notes

[1] 1) Patent box and 2) Shipping regime.

[2] Participating jurisdictions to the Convention are available here: www.oecd.org/tax/exchange-of-tax-information/convention-on-mutual-administrative-assistance-in-tax-matters.htm. The United Kingdom also has bilateral agreements with Albania, Algeria, Anguilla, Antigua and Barbuda, Argentina, Armenia, Aruba, Australia, Austria, Azerbaijan, Bahamas, Bahrain, Bangladesh, Barbados, Belarus, Belgium, Belize, Bermuda, Bolivia, Bosnia and Herzegovina, Botswana, Brazil, British Virgin Islands, Brunei, Bulgaria, Cameroon, Canada, Cayman Islands, Chile, China (People's Republic of), Colombia, Côte d'Ivoire, Croatia, Curaçao, Cyprus, Czechia, Denmark, Dominica, Egypt, Estonia, Ethiopia, Falkland Islands, Faroe Islands, Fiji, Finland, France, Gambia, Georgia, Germany, Ghana, Gibraltar, Greece, Grenada, Guernsey, Guyana, Hong Kong (China), Hungary, Iceland, India, Indonesia, Iran, Ireland, Isle of Man, Israel, Italy, Jamaica, Japan, Jersey, Jordan, Kazakhstan, Kenya, Kiribati, Korea, Kosovo, Kuwait, Kyrgyzstan, Latvia, Lebanon, Lesotho, Liberia, Libya, Liechtenstein, Lithuania, Luxembourg, Macao (China), Macedonia, Malawi, Malaysia, Malta, Marshall Islands, Mauritius, Mexico, Moldova, Monaco, Mongolia, Montenegro, Montserrat, Morocco, Myanmar, Namibia, Netherlands, New Zealand, Nigeria, Norway, North Macedonia, Norway, Oman, Pakistan, Panama, Papua New Guinea, Philippines, Poland, Portugal, Qatar, Romania, Russia, Saint Lucia, Saint Kitts and Nevis, Saint Vincent and the Grenadines, San Marino, Saudi Arabia, Senegal, Serbia, Sierra Leone, Singapore, Sint Maarten, Slovak Republic, Slovenia, Solomon Islands, South Africa, Spain, Sri Lanka, Sudan, Eswatini, Switzerland, Chinese Taipei, Tajikistan, Thailand, Trinidad and Tobago, Tunisia, Türkiye, Turkmenistan, Turks and Caicos Islands, Tuvalu, Uganda, Ukraine, United Arab Emirates, United States, Uruguay, Uzbekistan, Venezuela, Viet Nam, Zaire, Zambia and Zimbabwe.

[3] Patent box.

United States

The United States has met all aspects of the terms of reference (OECD, 2021[1]) (ToR) for the calendar year 2022 (year in review), and no recommendations are made.

The United States can legally issue three types of rulings within the scope of the transparency framework.

In practice, the United States issued rulings within the scope of the transparency framework as follows:

Type of ruling	Number of rulings
Past rulings	114
Future rulings in the period 1 April 2016 – 31 December 2016	21
Future rulings in the calendar year 2017	31
Future rulings in the calendar year 2018	27
Future rulings in the calendar year 2019	30
Future rulings in the calendar year 2020	18
Future rulings in the calendar year 2021	26
Future rulings in the year in review	10

Peer input was received from four jurisdictions in respect of the exchanges of information on rulings received from the United States. The input was positive, noting that information was complete, in a correct format and received in a timely manner.

Information gathering process (ToR I.A)

1224. The United States can legally issue three types of rulings within the scope of the transparency framework: (i) cross-border unilateral APAs and any other cross-border unilateral tax rulings (such as an advance tax ruling) covering transfer pricing or the application of transfer pricing principles; (ii) permanent establishment rulings; and (iii) related party conduit rulings.

1225. For the United States, past rulings are any tax rulings within scope that are issued either: (i) on or after 1 January 2014 but before 1 April 2016; or (ii) on or after 1 January 2010 but before 1 January 2014, provided they were still in effect as at 1 January 2014. Future rulings are any tax rulings within scope that are issued on or after 1 April 2016.

1226. In the prior years' peer review reports, it was determined that the United States' undertakings to identify past and future rulings and all potential exchange jurisdictions were sufficient to meet the minimum standard. In addition, it was determined that the United States' review and supervision mechanism was sufficient to meet the minimum standard. The United States' implementation remains unchanged, and therefore continues to meet the minimum standard.

1227. The United States has met all of the ToR for the information gathering process and no recommendations are made.

Exchange of information (ToR II.B)

1228. The United States has the necessary domestic legal basis to exchange information spontaneously. The United States notes that there are no legal or practical impediments that prevent the spontaneous exchange of information on rulings as contemplated in the Action 5 minimum standard.

1229. The United States has international agreements permitting spontaneous exchange of information, including: (i) the *Multilateral Convention on Mutual Administrative Assistance in Tax Matters: Amended by the 2010 Protocol* (OECD/Council of Europe, 2011[2]) ("the Convention") and (ii) bilateral agreements in force with 54 jurisdictions.[1]

1230. For the year in review, the timeliness of exchanges is as follows:

Future rulings within the scope of the transparency framework	Number of exchanges transmitted within three months of the information becoming available to the competent authority or immediately after legal impediments have been lifted	Delayed exchanges		
		Number of exchanges transmitted later than three months of the information on rulings becoming available to the competent authority	Reasons for the delays	Any other comments
	24	0	N/A	N/A

Follow-up requests received for exchange of the ruling	Number	Average time to provide response	Number of requests not answered
	0	N/A	N/A

1231. In the prior years' peer review reports, it was determined that the United States' process for the completion and exchange of templates were sufficient to meet the minimum standard. With respect to past rulings, no further action was required. The United States' implementation in this regard remains unchanged and therefore continues to meet the minimum standard.

1232. The United States has the necessary legal basis for spontaneous exchange of information, a process for completing the templates in a timely way and has completed all exchanges. The United States has met all of the ToR for the exchange of information process and no recommendations are made.

Statistics (ToR IV.D)

1233. The statistics for the year in review are as follows:

Category of ruling	Number of exchanges	Jurisdictions exchanged with
Cross-border unilateral APAs and any other cross-border unilateral tax rulings (such as an advance tax ruling) covering transfer pricing or the application of transfer pricing principles	24	Australia, Chile, China (People's Republic of), Colombia, Costa Rica, Curaçao, Honduras, Hungary, Ireland, Japan, Korea, Luxembourg, Mexico, Netherlands, Peru, Russia, Singapore, Slovak Republic
Permanent establishment rulings	0	N/A
Related party conduit rulings	0	N/A
Total	24	

Matters related to intellectual property regimes (ToR I.A.1.3)

1234. The United States does not offer an intellectual property regime for which transparency requirements under the Action 5 Report (OECD, 2015[3]) were imposed.

Summary of recommendations on implementation of the transparency framework

Aspect of implementation of the transparency framework that should be improved	Recommendation for improvement
	No recommendations are made.

References

OECD (2021), *BEPS Action 5 on Harmful Tax Practices - Terms of Reference and Methodology for the Conduct of the Peer Reviews of the Action 5 Transparency Framework*, OECD Publishing, Paris, https://www.oecd.org/tax/beps/beps-action-5-harmful-tax-practices-peer-review-transparency-framework.pdf. [1]

OECD (2015), *Countering Harmful Tax Practices More Effectively, Taking into Account Transparency and Substance, Action 5 - 2015 Final Report*, OECD/G20 Base Erosion and Profit Shifting Project, OECD Publishing, Paris, https://doi.org/10.1787/9789264241190-en. [3]

OECD/Council of Europe (2011), *The Multilateral Convention on Mutual Administrative Assistance in Tax Matters: Amended by the 2010 Protocol*, OECD Publishing, Paris, https://doi.org/10.1787/9789264115606-en. [2]

Note

[1] Participating jurisdictions to the Convention are available here: www.oecd.org/tax/exchange-of-tax-information/convention-on-mutual-administrative-assistance-in-tax-matters.htm. The United States also has bilateral agreements with Australia, Austria, Bangladesh, Barbados, Belgium, Bulgaria, Canada, China (People's Republic of), Costa Rica, Czechia, Denmark, Egypt, Estonia, Finland, France, Germany, Greece, Hungary, Iceland, India, Indonesia, Ireland, Israel, Italy, Jamaica, Japan, Kazakhstan, Latvia, Lithuania, Luxembourg, Malta, Mexico, Netherlands, New Zealand, Norway, Pakistan, Poland, Portugal, Romania, Russia, Slovak Republic, Slovenia, South Africa, Spain, Sri Lanka, Sweden, Switzerland, Thailand, Trinidad and Tobago, Tunisia, Türkiye, Ukraine, United Kingdom and Venezuela.

Uruguay

Uruguay has met all aspects of the terms of reference (OECD, 2021[1]) (ToR) for the calendar year 2022 (year in review), and no recommendations are made.

Uruguay can legally issue one type of rulings within the scope of the transparency framework.

In practice, Uruguay issued rulings within the scope of the transparency framework as follows:

Type of ruling	Number of rulings
Past rulings	1
Future rulings in the period 1 April 2018 – 31 December 2018	0
Future rulings in the calendar year 2019	0
Future rulings in the calendar year 2020	0
Future rulings in the calendar year 2021	0
Future rulings in the year in review	0

As no exchanges were required to take place, no peer input was received in respect of the exchanges of information on rulings received from Uruguay.

Information gathering process (ToR I.A)

1235. Uruguay can legally issue the following type of ruling within the scope of the transparency framework: cross-border unilateral APAs and any other cross-border unilateral tax rulings (such as an advance tax ruling) covering transfer pricing or the application of transfer pricing principles

1236. For Uruguay, past rulings are any tax rulings within scope that are issued either: (i) on or after 1 January 2016 but before 1 April 2018; or (ii) on or after 1 January 2014 but before 1 January 2016, provided they were still in effect as at 1 January 2016. Future rulings are any tax rulings within scope that are issued on or after 1 April 2018.

1237. In the prior years' peer review reports, it was determined that Uruguay's undertakings to identify past and future rulings and all potential exchange jurisdictions were sufficient to meet the minimum standard. In addition, it was determined that Uruguay's review and supervision mechanism was sufficient to meet the minimum standard. Uruguay's implementation remains unchanged, and therefore continues to meet the minimum standard.

1238. Uruguay has met all of the ToR for the information gathering process and no recommendations are made.

Exchange of information (ToR II.B)

1239. Uruguay has the necessary domestic legal basis to exchange information spontaneously. Uruguay notes that there are no legal or practical impediments that prevent the spontaneous exchange of information on rulings as contemplated in the Action 5 minimum standard.

1240. Uruguay has international agreements permitting spontaneous exchange of information, including: (i) the *Multilateral Convention on Mutual Administrative Assistance in Tax Matters: Amended by the 2010 Protocol* (OECD/Council of Europe, 2011[2]) ("the Convention") and (ii) bilateral agreements in force with 22 jurisdictions.[1]

1241. During the year in review, no exchanges were required to take place and no data on the timeliness of exchanges is reported.

1242. In the prior years' peer review reports, it was determined that Uruguay's process for the completion and exchange of templates were sufficient to meet the minimum standard. With respect to past rulings, no further action was required. Uruguay's implementation in this regard remains unchanged and therefore continues to meet the minimum standard.

1243. Uruguay has the necessary legal basis for spontaneous exchange of information, a process for completing the templates in a timely way and has completed all exchanges. Uruguay has met all of the ToR for the exchange of information process and no recommendations are made.

Statistics (ToR IV.D)

1244. As no rulings were issued, no statistics can be reported.

Matters related to intellectual property regimes (ToR I.A.1.3)

1245. In the prior year's peer review report, it was determined that Uruguay's information gathering and exchange of information processes for matters related to intellectual property regimes[2] were sufficient to meet the minimum standard. Uruguay's implementation in this regard remains unchanged and therefore continues to meet the minimum standard.

Summary of recommendations on implementation of the transparency framework

Aspect of implementation of the transparency framework that should be improved	Recommendation for improvement
	No recommendations are made.

References

OECD (2021), *BEPS Action 5 on Harmful Tax Practices - Terms of Reference and Methodology for the Conduct of the Peer Reviews of the Action 5 Transparency Framework*, OECD Publishing, Paris, https://www.oecd.org/tax/beps/beps-action-5-harmful-tax-practices-peer-review-transparency-framework.pdf. [1]

OECD (2015), *Countering Harmful Tax Practices More Effectively, Taking into Account Transparency and Substance, Action 5 - 2015 Final Report*, OECD/G20 Base Erosion and Profit Shifting Project, OECD Publishing, Paris, https://doi.org/10.1787/9789264241190-en. [3]

OECD/Council of Europe (2011), *The Multilateral Convention on Mutual Administrative Assistance in Tax Matters: Amended by the 2010 Protocol*, OECD Publishing, Paris, https://doi.org/10.1787/9789264115606-en. [2]

Notes

[1] Participating jurisdictions to the Convention are available here: www.oecd.org/tax/exchange-of-tax-information/convention-on-mutual-administrative-assistance-in-tax-matters.htm. Uruguay also has bilateral agreements with Belgium, Chile, Ecuador, Finland, Germany, India, Italy, Japan, Korea, Liechtenstein, Luxembourg, Malta, Mexico, Paraguay, Portugal, Romania, Singapore, Spain, Switzerland, United Arab Emirates, United Kingdom and Viet Nam.

[2] (i) Benefits under law 16.906 for biotechnology, (ii) Benefits under lit S art. 52 for biotechnology and for software and (iii) Free zones regimes.

Viet Nam

Viet Nam has met all aspects of the terms of reference (OECD, 2021[1]) (ToR) for the calendar year 2022 (year in review), except for having in place a process for completion of templates and exchange of information on rulings (ToR II.B). Viet Nam receives one recommendation on this point for the year in review.

In the prior year report, as well as in the 2017-2020 peer reviews, Viet Nam had received the same recommendation. As it has not been addressed, the recommendation remains in place.

Viet Nam can legally issue one type of ruling within the scope of the transparency framework.

In practice, Viet Nam issued no rulings within the scope of the transparency framework.

As no exchanges took place, no peer input was received in respect of the exchanges of information on rulings received from Viet Nam.

Information gathering process (ToR I.A)

1246. Viet Nam can legally issue the following type of rulings within the scope of the transparency framework: cross-border unilateral APAs and any other cross-border unilateral tax rulings (such as an advance tax ruling) covering transfer pricing or the application of transfer pricing principles.

1247. For Viet Nam, past rulings are any tax rulings within scope that are issued either: (i) on or after 1 January 2015 but before 1 September 2017; or (ii) on or after 1 January 2012 but before 1 January 2015, provided they were still in effect as at 1 January 2015. Future rulings are any tax rulings within scope that are issued on or after 1 September 2017.

1248. In the prior years' peer review reports, it was determined that Viet Nam's undertakings to identify past and future rulings and all potential exchange jurisdictions were sufficient to meet the minimum standard. In addition, it was determined that Viet Nam's review and supervision mechanism was sufficient to meet the minimum standard. Viet Nam's implementation remains unchanged, and therefore continues to meet the minimum standard.

1249. Viet Nam has met all of the ToR for the information gathering process and no recommendations are made.

Exchange of information (ToR II.B)

Legal basis for spontaneous exchange of information (ToR II.B.1, II.B.2)

1250. Viet Nam has the necessary domestic legal basis to exchange information spontaneously. Viet Nam notes that there are no legal or practical impediments that prevent the spontaneous exchange of information on rulings as contemplated in the Action 5 minimum standard.

1251. Viet Nam has international agreements permitting spontaneous exchange of information, including bilateral agreements in force with 76 jurisdictions.[1] Viet Nam signed the *Multilateral Convention on Mutual Administrative Assistance in Tax Matters: Amended by the 2010 Protocol* (OECD/Council of Europe, 2011[2]) ("the Convention") on 23 March 2023 and deposited its instrument of ratification on 31 August 2023. The Convention entered into force on 1 December 2023 and will have effect for administrative assistance related to taxable periods beginning on or after 1 January 2024. It is noted, however, that jurisdictions are assessed on their compliance with the transparency framework in respect of the exchange of information network in effect for the year of the particular annual review.

Completion and exchange of templates (ToR II.B.3, II.B.4, II.B.5, II.B.6, II.B.7)

1252. In the prior years' peer review reports, it was determined that Viet Nam's process for the completion and exchange of templates met all the ToR, except for the completion and exchange of templates (ToR II.B). Therefore, Viet Nam was recommended to continue to put in place a process to complete the templates for all relevant rulings and to ensure the timely exchange of information on rulings in the form required by the transparency framework.

1253. Viet Nam is continuing its work on the development of a process to complete the templates on relevant rulings, to make them available to the Competent Authority for exchange of information, and to exchange them with relevant jurisdictions. However, it this work has not been completed during the year in review, and therefore, the prior year recommendation remains.

1254. During the year in review, no exchanges were required to take place and no data on the timeliness of exchanges is reported.

Conclusion on section B

1255. Viet Nam has the necessary legal basis for spontaneous exchange of information. Viet Nam is still developing a process for completion of templates and exchange of information on rulings (ToR II.B). Viet Nam is recommended to develop a process to complete the templates on relevant rulings and to ensure that the exchanges of information on rulings occur in accordance with the form and timelines under the transparency framework.

Statistics (ToR IV.D)

1256. As no rulings were issued, no statistics can be reported.

Matters related to intellectual property regimes (ToR I.A.1.3)

1257. Viet Nam does not offer an intellectual property regime for which transparency requirements under the Action 5 Report (OECD, 2015[3]) were imposed.

Summary of recommendations on implementation of the transparency framework

Aspect of implementation of the transparency framework that should be improved	Recommendation for improvement
Viet Nam is still developing a process for completion of templates and exchange of information on rulings.	Viet Nam is recommended to develop a process to complete the templates on relevant rulings and to ensure that the exchanges of information on rulings occur in accordance with the form and timelines under the transparency framework. This recommendation remains unchanged since the 2017, 2018, 2019, 2020 and 2021 peer review reports.

References

OECD (2021), *BEPS Action 5 on Harmful Tax Practices - Terms of Reference and Methodology for the Conduct of the Peer Reviews of the Action 5 Transparency Framework*, OECD Publishing, Paris, https://www.oecd.org/tax/beps/beps-action-5-harmful-tax-practices-peer-review-transparency-framework.pdf. [1]

OECD (2015), *Countering Harmful Tax Practices More Effectively, Taking into Account Transparency and Substance, Action 5 - 2015 Final Report*, OECD/G20 Base Erosion and Profit Shifting Project, OECD Publishing, Paris, https://doi.org/10.1787/9789264241190-en. [3]

OECD/Council of Europe (2011), *The Multilateral Convention on Mutual Administrative Assistance in Tax Matters: Amended by the 2010 Protocol*, OECD Publishing, Paris, https://doi.org/10.1787/9789264115606-en. [2]

Notes

[1] Viet Nam has bilateral agreements with Australia, Austria, Azerbaijan, Bangladesh, Belarus, Belgium, Brunei Darussalam, Bulgaria, Cambodia, Canada, China (People's Republic of), Croatia, Cuba, Czechia, Democratic People's Republic of Korea, Denmark, Estonia, Finland, France, Germany, Hong Kong (China), Hungary, Iceland, India, Indonesia, Iran, Ireland, Israel, Italy, Japan, Kazakhstan, Korea, Kuwait, Lao People's Democratic Republic, Latvia, Luxembourg, Macau (China), Malaysia, Malta, Mongolia, Morocco, Mozambique, Myanmar, Netherlands, New Zealand, Norway, Oman, Pakistan, Palestinian Authority, Panama, Philippines, Poland, Portugal, Qatar, Romania, Russia, San Marino, Saudi Arabia, Serbia, Seychelles, Singapore, Slovak Republic, Spain, Sri Lanka, Sweden, Switzerland, Chinese Taipei, Thailand, Tunisia, Türkiye, Ukraine, United Arab Emirates, United Kingdom, Uruguay, Uzbekistan and Venezuela.